Direct3D Rendering Cookbook

50 practical recipes to guide you through the advanced rendering techniques in Direct3D to help bring your 3D graphics project to life

Justin Stenning

[PACKT]
PUBLISHING

BIRMINGHAM - MUMBAI

Direct3D Rendering Cookbook

First published: January 2014

Production Reference: 1130114

Published by Packt Publishing Ltd.
Livery Place
35 Livery Street
Birmingham B3 2PB, UK.

ISBN 978-1-84969-710-1

www.packtpub.com

Cover Image by Justin Stenning (justin.stenning@gmail.com)

Credits

Author
Justin Stenning

Reviewers
Julian Amann
Stephan Hodes
Brian Klamik
Todd J. Seiler
Chuck Walbourn
Vinjn Zhang

Acquisition Editor
James Jones

Lead Technical Editor
Priya Singh

Technical Editors
Iram Malik
Shali Sasidharan
Anand Singh

Copy Editors
Roshni Banerjee
Gladson Monteiro
Adithi Shetty

Project Coordinator
Wendell Palmer

Proofreaders
Amy Johnson
Lindsey Thomas
Mario Cecere

Indexers
Hemangini Bari
Monica Ajmera Mehta
Rekha Nair

Graphics
Ronak Dhruv
Abhinash Sahu

Production Coordinator
Nitesh Thakur

Cover Work
Nitesh Thakur

About the Author

Justin Stenning, a software enthusiast since DOS was king, has been working as a software engineer since he was 20. He has been the technical lead on a range of projects, from enterprise content management and software integrations to mobile apps, mapping, and biosecurity management systems. Justin has been involved in a number of open source projects, including capturing images from fullscreen Direct3D games and displaying in-game overlays, and enjoys giving a portion of his spare time to the open source community. Justin completed his Bachelor of Information Technology at Central Queensland University, Rockhampton. When not coding or gaming, he thinks about coding or gaming, or rides his motorbike. Justin lives with his awesome wife, and his cheeky and quirky children in Central Victoria, Australia.

To Lee, thanks for keeping things running smoothly using your special skill of getting stuff done and of course for your awesomeness. To the kids, yes, I will now be able to play more Minecraft and Terraria with you.

I would like to thank Michael for taking a punt on me all those years ago and mentoring me in the art of coding.

I would also like to thank the SharpDX open source project for producing a great interface to Direct3D from the managed code, and Blendswap.com and its contributors for providing such a great service to the Blender community.

Thank you to the reviewers who provided great feedback and suggestions throughout.

Lastly, a big thank you to James, Priya, Wendell, and all the folks at Packt Publishing who have made this book possible.

About the Reviewers

Julian Amann started working with DirectX 13 years ago, as a teenager. He received his master's degree in Computer Science from the Technische Universität München (Germany) in 2011. He has worked as a research assistant at the Chair of Computer Graphics at Bauhaus-Universität Weimar, where he did his research on image quality algorithms and has also been involved in teaching computer graphics. Currently, Julian works at the **Chair of Computational Modeling and Simulation** (**CMS**) at the Technische Universität München. He is writing his PhD thesis about product data models for infrastructure projects in the field of Civil Engineering. In his spare time, Julian enjoys programming computer-graphics-related applications and blogging at `vertexwahn.de`.

Stephan Hodes has been working as a software engineer in the games industry for 15 years while GPUs made the transition from fixed function pipeline to a programmable shader hardware. During this time, he worked on a number of games released for PC as well as Xbox 360 and PS3.

Since he joined AMD as a Developer Relations Engineer in 2011, he has been working with a number of European developers on optimizing their technology to take full advantage of the processing power that the latest GPU hardware provides. He is currently living with his wife and son in Berlin, Germany.

Brian Klamik has worked as a software design engineer at Microsoft Corporation for 15 years. Nearly all of this time was spent evolving the Direct3D API in Windows by working together with the graphics hardware partners and industry's leading application developers. He enjoys educating developers about using Direct3D optimally, as well as enjoying the results of their labor.

Todd J. Seiler works in the CAD/CAM dental industry as a Graphics Software Engineer at E4D Technologies in Dallas, TX. He has worked as a Software Development Engineer in Test on Games for Windows LIVE at Microsoft, and he has also worked in the mobile game development industry. He has a B.S. in Computer Graphics and Interactive Media from the University of Dubuque in Dubuque, IA with a minor in Computer Information Systems. He also has a B.S. in Real-time Interactive Simulations from DigiPen Institute of Technology in Redmond, WA, with minors in Mathematics and Physics.

In his spare time, he plays video games, studies Catholic apologetics and theology, writes books and articles, and toys with new technology when he can. He periodically blogs about random things at http://www.toddseiler.com.

Chuck Walbourn, a software design engineer at Microsoft Corporation, has been working on games for the Windows platform since the early days of DirectX and Windows 95. He entered the gaming industry by starting his own development house during the mid-90s in Austin. He shipped several Windows titles for Interactive Magic and Electronic Arts, and he developed the content tools pipeline for Microsoft Game Studios Xbox titled as Voodoo Vince. Chuck worked for many years in the game developer relations groups at Microsoft, presenting at GDC, Gamefest, X-Fest, and other events. He was the lead developer on the DirectX SDK (June 2010) release. He currently works in the Xbox platform group at Microsoft, where he supports game developers working on the Microsoft platforms through the *Games for Windows and the DirectX SDK* blog, the *DirectX Tool Kit* and *DirectXTex* libraries on CodePlex, and other projects. Chuck holds a bachelor's degree and a master's degree in Computer Science from the University of Texas, Austin.

Vinjn Zhang is an enthusiastic software engineer. His interest in programming includes game development, graphics shader writing, human-computer interaction, and computer vision. He has translated two technical books into Chinese, one for the processing language and other for OpenCV.

Vinjn Zhang has worked for several game production companies, including Ubisoft and 2K Games. He currently works as a GPU architect in NVIDIA, where he gets the chance to see the secrets of GPU. Besides his daily work, he is an active GitHub user who turns projects into open source; even his blog is an open source available at `http://vinjn.github.io/`.

www.PacktPub.com

Support files, eBooks, discount offers and more

You might want to visit www.PacktPub.com for support files and downloads related to your book.

Did you know that Packt offers eBook versions of every book published, with PDF and ePub files available? You can upgrade to the eBook version at www.PacktPub.com and as a print book customer, you are entitled to a discount on the eBook copy. Get in touch with us at service@packtpub.com for more details.

At www.PacktPub.com, you can also read a collection of free technical articles, sign up for a range of free newsletters and receive exclusive discounts and offers on Packt books and eBooks.

PACKT™

http://PacktLib.PacktPub.com

Do you need instant solutions to your IT questions? PacktLib is Packt's online digital book library. Here, you can access, read and search across Packt's entire library of books.

Why Subscribe?

▸ Fully searchable across every book published by Packt

▸ Copy and paste, print and bookmark content

▸ On demand and accessible via web browser

Free Access for Packt account holders

If you have an account with Packt at www.PacktPub.com, you can use this to access PacktLib today and view nine entirely free books. Simply use your login credentials for immediate access.

Table of Contents

Preface

The latest 3D graphics cards bring us amazing visuals in the latest games, from Indie to AAA titles. This is made possible on Microsoft platforms including PC, Xbox consoles, and mobile devices thanks to Direct3D—a component of the DirectX API dedicated to exposing 3D graphics hardware to programmers. Microsoft DirectX is the graphics technology powering today's hottest games on Microsoft platforms. DirectX 11 features hardware tessellation for rich geometric detail, compute shaders for custom graphics effects, and improved multithreading for better hardware utilization. With it comes a number of fundamental game changing improvements to the way in which we render 3D graphics.

The last decade has also seen the rise of **General-Purpose computation on Graphics Processing Units** (**GPGPU**), exposing the massively parallel computing power of **Graphics Processing Units** (**GPUs**) to programmers for scientific or technical computing. Some uses include implementing **Artificial Intelligence** (**AI**), advanced postprocessing and physics within games, powering complex scientific modeling, or contributing to large scale distributed computing projects.

Direct3D and related DirectX graphics APIs continue to be an important part of the Microsoft technology stack. Remaining an integral part of their graphics strategy on all platforms, the library advances in leaps and bounds with each new release, opening further opportunities for developers to exploit. With the release of the third generation Xbox console—the Xbox One—and the latest games embracing the recent DirectX 11 changes in 11.1 and 11.2, we will continue to see Direct3D be a leading 3D graphics API.

Direct3D Rendering Cookbook is a practical, example-driven, technical cookbook with numerous Direct3D 11.1 and 11.2 rendering techniques supported by illustrations, example images, strong sample code, and concise explanations.

What this book covers

Chapter 1, Getting Started with Direct3D, reviews the components of Direct3D and the graphics pipeline, explores the latest features in DirectX 11.1 and 11.2, and looks at how to build and debug Direct3D applications with C# and SharpDX.

Chapter 2, Rendering with Direct3D, introduces a simple rendering framework, teaches how to render primitive shapes, and compiles HLSL shaders and use textures.

Chapter 3, Rendering Meshes, explores rendering more complex objects and demonstrates how to use the Visual Studio graphics content pipeline to compile and render 3D assets.

Chapter 4, Animating Meshes with Vertex Skinning, teaches how to implement vertex skinning for the animation of 3D models.

Chapter 5, Applying Hardware Tessellation, covers tessellating primitive shapes, parametric surfaces, mesh subdivision/refinement, and techniques for optimizing tessellation performance.

Chapter 6, Adding Surface Detail with Normal and Displacement Mapping, teaches how to combine tessellation with normal and displacement mapping to increase surface detail. Displacement decals are explored and then optimized for performance with displacement adaptive tessellation.

Chapter 7, Performing Image Processing Techniques, describes how to use compute shaders to implement a number of image-processing techniques often used within postprocessing.

Chapter 8, Incorporating Physics and Simulations, explores implementing physics, simulating ocean waves, and rendering particles.

Chapter 9, Rendering on Multiple Threads and Deferred Contexts, benchmarks multithreaded rendering and explores the impact of multithreading on two common environment-mapping techniques.

Chapter 10, Implementing Deferred Rendering, provides insight into the techniques necessary to implement deferred rendering solutions.

Chapter 11, Integrating Direct3D with XAML and Windows 8.1, covers how to implement Direct3D Windows Store apps and optionally integrate with XAML based UIs and effects. Loading and compiling resources within Windows 8.1 is also explored.

Appendix, Further Reading, includes all the references and papers that can be referred for gathering more details and information related to the topics covered in the book.

What you need for this book

To complete the recipes in this book, it is necessary that you have a graphics card that supports a minimum of DirectX 11.1.

It is recommended that you have the following software:

- Windows 8.1
- Microsoft Visual Studio 2013 Express (or higher edition)
- Microsoft .NET Framework 4.5
- Windows Software Development Kit (SDK) for Windows 8.1
- SharpDX 2.5.1 or higher—http://sharpdx.org/news/

Other resources and libraries are indicated in individual recipes.

For those running Windows 7 or Windows 8, you will require a minimum of the following software. Please note that although some portions of Chapter 11, *Integrating Direct3D with XAML and Windows 8.1*, can be adapted to Windows 8, you will not be able to complete the final chapter in its entirety as it is specific to Windows 8.1.

- Microsoft Visual Studio 2012 or 2013 Express (or higher edition)
- Microsoft .NET Framework 4.5
- Windows 8 or Windows 7 with Platform Update for SP1*
- Windows Software development Kit (SDK) for Windows 8
- SharpDX 2.5.1 or higher—http://sharpdx.org/news/

Other resources and libraries as indicated in individual recipes.

> *Chapter 11, Integrating Direct3D with XAML and Windows 8.1,* is not compatible with Windows 7, and the *Rendering to a XAML SwapChainPanel* recipe requires a minimum of Windows 8.1.

Who this book is for

Direct3D Rendering Cookbook is for C# .NET developers who want to learn the advanced rendering techniques made possible with DirectX 11.1 and 11.2. It is expected that the reader has at least a cursory knowledge of graphics programming, and although some knowledge of Direct3D 10+ is helpful, it is not necessary. An understanding of vector and matrix algebra is recommended.

Conventions

In this book, you will find a number of styles of text that distinguish between different kinds of information. Here are some examples of these styles, and an explanation of their meaning.

Code words in text are shown as follows: A command list is represented by the `ID3D11CommandList` interface in unmanaged C++ and the `Direct3D11.CommandList` class in managed C# with SharpDX.

A block of code is set as follows:

```
SharpDX.Direct3D.FeatureLevel.Level_11_1,
SharpDX.Direct3D.FeatureLevel.Level_11_0,
SharpDX.Direct3D.FeatureLevel.Level_10_1,
SharpDX.Direct3D.FeatureLevel.Level_10_0,
```

When we wish to draw your attention to a particular part of a code block, the relevant lines or items are set in bold:

```
// Create the device and swapchain
Device.CreateWithSwapChain(
    SharpDX.Direct3D.DriverType.Hardware,
    DeviceCreationFlags.None,
```

New terms and **important words** are shown in bold. Words that you see on the screen, in menus or dialog boxes for example, appear in the text like this: "These are accessible by navigating to the **DEBUG**/**Graphics** menu".

> Warnings or important notes appear in a box like this.

> Tips and tricks appear like this.

Reader feedback

Feedback from our readers is always welcome. Let us know what you think about this book—what you liked or may have disliked. Reader feedback is important for us to develop titles that you really get the most out of.

To send us general feedback, simply send an e-mail to feedback@packtpub.com, and mention the book title via the subject of your message.

If there is a topic that you have expertise in and you are interested in either writing or contributing to a book, see our author guide on www.packtpub.com/authors.

Customer support

Now that you are the proud owner of a Packt book, we have a number of things to help you to get the most from your purchase.

Downloading the example code

You can download the example code files for all Packt books you have purchased from your account at http://www.packtpub.com. If you purchased this book elsewhere, you can visit http://www.packtpub.com/support and register to have the files e-mailed directly to you.

Downloading the color images of this book

We also provide you a PDF file that has color images of the screenshots/diagrams used in this book. The color images will help you better understand the changes in the output. You can download this file from: https://www.packtpub.com/sites/default/files/downloads/7101OT_ColoredImages.pdf

Errata

Although we have taken every care to ensure the accuracy of our content, mistakes do happen. If you find a mistake in one of our books—maybe a mistake in the text or the code—we would be grateful if you would report this to us. By doing so, you can save other readers from frustration and help us improve subsequent versions of this book. If you find any errata, please report them by visiting http://www.packtpub.com/submit-errata, selecting your book, clicking on the **errata submission form** link, and entering the details of your errata. Once your errata are verified, your submission will be accepted and the errata will be uploaded on our website, or added to any list of existing errata, under the Errata section of that title. Any existing errata can be viewed by selecting your title from http://www.packtpub.com/support.

Piracy

Piracy of copyright material on the Internet is an ongoing problem across all media. At Packt, we take the protection of our copyright and licenses very seriously. If you come across any illegal copies of our works, in any form, on the Internet, please provide us with the location address or website name immediately so that we can pursue a remedy.

Please contact us at copyright@packtpub.com with a link to the suspected pirated material.

We appreciate your help in protecting our authors, and our ability to bring you valuable content.

Questions

You can contact us at questions@packtpub.com if you are having a problem with any aspect of the book, and we will do our best to address it.

1
Getting Started with Direct3D

In this chapter, we will cover the following topics:

- ▶ Components of Direct3D
- ▶ Stages of the programmable pipeline
- ▶ Introducing Direct3D 11.1 and 11.2
- ▶ Building a Direct3D 11 application with C# and SharpDX
- ▶ Initializing a Direct3D 11.1/11.2 device and swap chain
- ▶ Debugging your Direct3D application

Introduction

Direct3D is the component of the DirectX API dedicated to exposing 3D graphics hardware to programmers on Microsoft platforms including PC, console, and mobile devices. It is a native API allowing you to create not only 3D graphics for games, scientific and general applications, but also to utilize the underlying hardware for **General-purpose computing on graphics processing units** (**GPGPU**).

Programming with Direct3D can be a daunting task, and although the differences between the unmanaged C++ API and the managed .NET SharpDX API (from now on referred to as the unmanaged and managed APIs respectively) are subtle, we will briefly highlight some of these while also gaining an understanding of the graphics pipeline.

We will then learn how to get started with programming for Direct3D using C# and SharpDX along with some useful debugging techniques.

Components of Direct3D

Direct3D is a part of the larger DirectX API comprised of many components that sits between applications and the graphics hardware drivers. Everything in Direct3D begins with the device and you create resources and interact with the graphics pipeline through various **Component Object Model** (**COM**) interfaces from there.

Device

The main role of the device is to enumerate the capabilities of the display adapter(s) and to create resources. Applications will typically only have a single device instantiated and must have at least one device to use the features of Direct3D.

Unlike previous versions of Direct3D, in Direct3D 11 the device is thread-safe. This means that resources can be created from any thread.

The device is accessed through the following interfaces/classes:

> ▸ Managed: `Direct3D11.Device` (Direct3D 11), `Direct3D11.Device1` (Direct3D 11.1), and `Direct3D11.Device2` (Direct3D 11.2)
>
> ▸ Unmanaged: `ID3D11Device`, `ID3D11Device1`, and `ID3D11Device2`

> Each subsequent version of the COM interface descends from the previous version; therefore, if you start with a Direct3D 11 device instance and query the interface for the Direct3D 11.2 implementation, you will still have access to the Direct3D 11 methods with the resulting device reference.

One important difference between the unmanaged and managed version of the APIs used throughout this book is that when creating resources on a device with the managed API, the appropriate class constructor is used with the first parameter passed in being a device instance, whereas the unmanaged API uses a `Create` method on the device interface.

For example, creating a new blend state would look like the following for the managed C# API:

```
var blendState = new BlendState(device, desc);
```

And like this for the unmanaged C++ API:

```
ID3D11BlendState* blendState;
HRESULT r = device->CreateBlendState(&desc, &blendState);
```

Further, a number of the managed classes use overloaded constructors and methods that only support valid parameter combinations, relying less on a programmer's deep understanding of the Direct3D API.

With Direct3D 11, Microsoft introduced Direct3D feature levels to manage the differences between video cards. The feature levels define a matrix of Direct3D features that are mandatory or optional for hardware devices to implement in order to meet the requirements for a specific feature level. The minimum feature level required for an application can be specified when creating a device instance, and the maximum feature level supported by the hardware device is available on the `Device.FeatureLevel` property. More information on feature levels and the features available at each level can be found at `http://msdn.microsoft.com/en-us/library/windows/desktop/ff476876(v=vs.85).aspx`.

Device context

The device context encapsulates all rendering functions. These include setting the pipeline state and generating rendering commands with resources created on the device.

Two types of device context exist in Direct3D 11, the immediate context and deferred context. These implement immediate rendering and deferred rendering respectively.

The interfaces/classes for both context types are:

- Managed: `Direct3D11.DeviceContext`, `Direct3D11.DeviceContext1`, and `Direct3D11.DeviceContext2`
- Unmanaged: `ID3D11DeviceContext`, `ID3D11DeviceContext1`, and `ID3D11DeviceContext2`

Immediate context

The immediate context provides access to data on the GPU and the ability to execute/playback command lists immediately against the device. Each device has a single immediate context and only one thread may access the context at the same time; however, multiple threads can interact with the immediate context provided appropriate thread synchronization is in place.

All commands to the underlying device eventually must pass through the immediate context if they are to be executed.

The immediate context is available on the device through the following methods/properties:

- ▶ Managed: `Device.ImmediateContext`, `Device1.ImmediateContext1`, and `Device2.ImmediateContext2`
- ▶ Unmanaged: `ID3D11Device::GetImmediateContext`, `ID3D11Device1::GetImmediateContext1`, and `ID3D11Device2::GetImmediateContext2`

Deferred context

The same rendering methods are available on a deferred context as for an immediate context; however, the commands are added to a queue called a command list for later execution upon the immediate context.

Using deferred contexts results in some additional overhead, and only begins to see benefits when parallelizing CPU-intensive tasks. For example, rendering the same simple scene for the six sides of a cubic environment map will not immediately see any performance benefits, and in fact will increase the time it takes to render a frame as compared to using the immediate context directly. However, render the same scene again with enough CPU load and it is possible to see some improvements over rendering directly on the immediate context. The usage of deferred contexts is no substitute for a well written engine and needs to be carefully evaluated to be correctly taken advantage of.

Multiple deferred context instances can be created and accessed from multiple threads; however, each may only be accessed by one thread at a time. For example, with the deferred contexts A and B, we can access both at the exact same time from threads 1 and 2 provided that thread 1 is only accessing deferred context A and thread 2 is only accessing deferred context B (or vice versa). Any sharing of contexts between threads requires thread synchronization.

The resulting command lists are not executed against the device until they are played back by an immediate context.

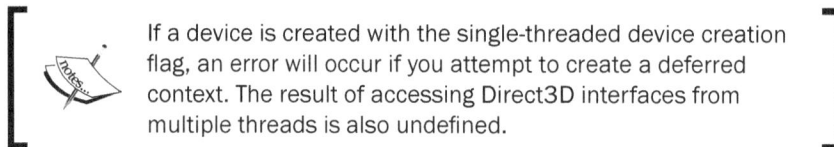

> If a device is created with the single-threaded device creation flag, an error will occur if you attempt to create a deferred context. The result of accessing Direct3D interfaces from multiple threads is also undefined.

A deferred context is created with:

- ▶ Managed: `new DeviceContext(device)`
- ▶ Unmanaged: `ID3D11Device::CreateDeferredContext`

Command lists

A command list stores a queue of Direct3D API commands for deferred execution or merging into another deferred context. They facilitate the efficient playback of a number of API commands queued from a device context.

A command list is represented by the `ID3D11CommandList` interface in unmanaged C++ and the `Direct3D11.CommandList` class in managed C# with SharpDX. They are created using:

- ▸ Managed: `DeviceContext.FinishCommandList`
- ▸ Unmanaged: `ID3D11DeviceContext::FinishCommandList`

Command lists are played back on the immediate context using:

- ▸ Managed: `DeviceContext.ExecuteCommandList`
- ▸ Unmanaged: `ID3D11DeviceContext::ExecuteCommandList`

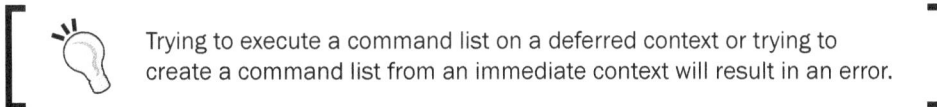

> Trying to execute a command list on a deferred context or trying to create a command list from an immediate context will result in an error.

Swap chains

A swap chain facilitates the creation of one or more back buffers. These buffers are used to store rendered data before being presented to an output display device. The swap chain takes care of the low-level presentation of this data and with Direct3D 11.1, supports stereoscopic 3D display behavior (left and right eye for 3D glasses/displays).

If the output of rendering is to be sent to an output connected to the current adapter, a swap chain is required.

Swap chains are part of the **DirectX Graphics Infrastructure** (**DXGI**) API, which is responsible for enumerating graphics adapters, display modes, defining buffer formats, sharing resources between processes, and finally (via the swap chain) presenting rendered frames to a window or output device for display.

A swap chain is represented by the following types:

- ▸ Managed: `SharpDX.DXGI.SwapChain` and `SharpDX.DXGI.SwapChain1`
- ▸ Unmanaged: `IDXGISwapChain` and `IDXGISwapChain1`

States

A number of state types exist to control the behavior of some fixed function stages of the pipeline and how samplers behave for shaders.

All shaders can accept several sampler states. The output merger can accept both, a blend state and depth-stencil state, and the rasterizer accepts a rasterizer state. The types used are shown in the following table.

Managed type (SharpDX.Direct3D11)	Unmanaged type
BlendState	ID3D11BlendState
BlendState1	ID3D11BlendState1
DepthStencilState	ID3D11DepthStencilState
RasterizerState	ID3D11RasterizerState
RasterizerState1	ID3D11RasterizerState1
SamplerState	ID3D11SamplerState

Resources

A resource is any buffer or texture that is used as an input and/or output from the Direct3D pipeline. A resource is consumed by creating one or more views to the resource and then binding them to stages of the pipeline.

Textures

A texture resource is a collection of elements known as texture pixels or **texels**—which represent the smallest unit of a texture that can be read or written to by the pipeline. A texel is generally comprised of between one and four components depending on which format is being used for the texture; for example, a format of `Format.R32G32B32_Float` is used to store three 32-bit floating point numbers in each texel whereas a format of `Format.R8G8_UInt` represents two 8-bit unsigned integers per texel. There is a special case when dealing with compressed formats (`Format.BC`) where the smallest unit consists of a block of 4 x 4 texels.

A texture resource can be created in a number of different formats as defined by the DXGI format enumeration (`SharpDX.DXGI.Format` and `DXGI_FORMAT` for managed/unmanaged, respectively). The format can be either applied at the time of creation, or specified when it is bound by a resource view to the pipeline.

Hardware device drivers may support different combinations of formats for different purposes, although there is a list of mandatory formats that the hardware must support depending on the version of Direct3D. The device's `CheckFormatSupport` method can be used to determine what resource type and usage a particular format supports on the current hardware.

Textures do not just store image data. They are used for information, such as height-maps, displacement-maps, or for any data structure that needs to be read or written within a shader that can benefit from the speed benefits of hardware support for textures and texture sampling.

Types of texture resources include:

- 1D Textures and 1D Texture Arrays
- 2D Textures and 2D Texture Arrays
- 3D Textures (or volume textures)
- Unordered access textures
- Read/Write textures

The following table maps the managed to unmanaged types for the different textures.

Managed type (SharpDX.Direct3D11)	Unmanaged type
Texture1D	ID3D11Texture1D
Texture2D	ID3D11Texture2D
Texture3D	ID3D11Texture3D

Arrays of 1D and 2D textures are configured with the subresource data associated with the description of the texture passed into the appropriate constructor. A common use for texture arrays is supporting **Multiple Render Targets** (**MRT**).

Resource views

Before a resource can be used within a stage of the pipeline it must first have a view. This view describes to the pipeline stages what format to expect the resource in and what region of the resource to access. The same resource can be bound to multiple stages of the pipeline using the same view, or by creating multiple resource views.

It is important to note that although a resource can be bound to multiple stages of the pipeline, there may be restrictions on whether the same resource can be bound for input and output at the same time. As an example, a **Render Target View** (**RTV**) and **Shader Resource View** (**SRV**) for the same resource both cannot be bound to the pipeline at the same time. When a conflict arises the read-only resource view will be automatically unbound from the pipeline, and if the debug layer is enabled, a warning message will be output to the debug output.

Using resources created with a typeless format, allows the same underlying resource to be represented by multiple resource views, where the compatible resolved format is defined by the view. For example, using a resource with both a **Depth Stencil View** (**DSV**) and SRV requires that the underlying resource be created with a format like `Format.R32G8X24_Typeless`. The SRV then specifies a format of `Format.R32_Float_X8X24_Typeless`, and finally the DSV is created with a format of `Format.D32_Float_S8X24_UInt`.

Some types of buffers can be provided to certain stages of the pipeline without a resource view, generally when the structure and format of the buffer is defined in some other way, for example, using state objects or structures within shader files.

Types of resource views include:

- Depth Stencil View (DSV),
- Render Target View (RTV),
- Shader Resource View (SRV)
- Unordered Access View (UAV)
- Video decoder output view
- Video processor input view
- Video processor output view

The following table shows the managed and unmanaged types for the different resource views.

Managed type (SharpDX.Direct3D11)	Unmanaged type
DepthStencilView	ID3D11DepthStencilView
RenderTargetView	ID3D11RenderTargetView
ShaderResourceView	ID3D11ShaderResourceView
UnorderedAccessView	ID3D11UnorderedAccessView
VideoDecoderOutputView	ID3D11VideoDecoderOutputView
VideoProcessorInputView	ID3D11VideoProcessorInputView
VideoProcessorOutputView	ID3D11VideoProcessorOutputView

Buffers

A buffer resource is used to provide structured and unstructured data to stages of in the graphics pipeline.

Types of buffer resources include:

- Vertex buffer
- Index buffer
- Constant buffer
- Unordered access buffers
  - Byte address buffer
  - Structured buffer
  - Read/Write buffers
  - Append/Consume structured buffers

All buffers are represented by the `SharpDX.Direct3D11.Buffer` class (`ID3D11Buffer` for the unmanaged API). The usage is defined by how and where it is bound to the pipeline. The following table shows the binding flags for different buffers:

Buffer type	Managed BindFlags flags	Unmanaged D3D11_BIND_FLAG flags
Vertex buffer	`VertexBuffer`	`D3D11_BIND_VERTEX_BUFFER`
Index buffer	`IndexBuffer`	`D3D11_BIND_INDEX_BUFFER`
Constant buffer	`ConstantBuffer`	`D3D11_BIND_CONSTANT_BUFFER`
Unordered access buffers	`UnorderedAccess`	`D3D11_BIND_UNORDERED_ACCESS`

Unordered access buffers are further categorized into the following types using an additional option/miscellaneous flag within the buffer description as shown in the following table:

Buffer type	Managed ResourceOptionFlags flags	Unmanaged D3D11_RESOURCE_ MISC_FLAG flags
Byte address buffer	`BufferAllowRawViews`	`D3D11_RESOURCE_MISC_BUFFER_ ALLOW_RAW_VIEWS`
Structured buffer	`BufferStructured`	`D3D11_RESOURCE_MISC_BUFFER_ STRUCTURED`
Read/Write buffers	Either use Byte address buffer / Structured buffer and then use `RWBuffer` or `RWStructuredBuffer<MyStruct>` instead of `Buffer` and `StructuredBuffer<MyStruct>` in HLSL.	
Append/Consume buffers	A structured buffer and then use `AppendStructuredBuffer` or `ConsumeStructuredBuffer` in HLSL. Use `UnorderedAccessViewBufferFlags.Append` when creating the UAV.	

Shaders and High Level Shader Language

The graphics pipeline is made up of fixed function and programmable stages. The programmable stages are referred to as shaders, and are programmed using small **High Level Shader Language** (**HLSL**) programs. The HLSL is implemented with a series of shader models, each building upon the previous version. Each shader model version supports a set of shader profiles, which represent the target pipeline stage to compile a shader. Direct3D 11 introduces **Shader Model 5** (**SM5**), a superset of **Shader Model 4** (**SM4**).

An example shader profile is `ps_5_0`, which indicates a shader program is for use in the pixel shader stage and requires SM5.

Stages of the programmable pipeline

All Direct3D operations take place via one of the two pipelines, known as pipelines for the fact that information flows in one direction from one stage to the next. For all drawing operations, the graphics pipeline is used (also known as drawing pipeline or rendering pipeline). To run compute shaders, the dispatch pipeline is used (aka DirectCompute pipeline or compute shader pipeline).

Although these two pipelines are conceptually separate. They cannot be active at the same time. Context switching between the two pipelines also incurs additional overhead so each pipeline should be used in blocks—for example, run any compute shaders to prepare data, perform all rendering, and finally post processing.

Methods related to stages of the pipeline are found on the device context. For the managed API, each stage is grouped into a property named after the pipeline stage. For example, for the vertex shader stage, `deviceContext.VertexShader.SetShaderResources`, whereas the unmanaged API groups the methods by a stage acronym directly on the device context, for example, `deviceContext->VSSetShaderResources`, where `VS` represents the vertex shader stage.

The graphics pipeline

The graphics pipeline is comprised of nine distinct stages that are generally used to create 2D raster representations of 3D scenes, that is, take our 3D model and turn it into what we see on the display. Four of these stages are fixed function and the remaining five programmable stages are called shaders (the following diagram shows the programmable stages as a circle). The output of each stage is taken as input into the next along with bound resources or in the case of the last stage, **Output Merger** (**OM**), the output is sent to one or more render targets. Not all of the stages are mandatory and keeping the number of stages involved to a minimum will generally result in faster rendering.

Optional tessellation support is provided by the three tessellation stages (two programmable and one fixed function): the hull shader, tessellator, and domain shader. The tessellation stages require a Direct3D feature level of 11.0 or later.

As of Direct3D 11.1, each programmable stage is able to read/write to an **Unordered Access View** (**UAV**). A UAV is a view of a buffer or texture resource that has been created with the `BindFlags.UnorderedAccess` flag (`D3D11_BIND_UNORDERED_ACCESS` from the `D3D11_BIND_FLAG` enumeration).

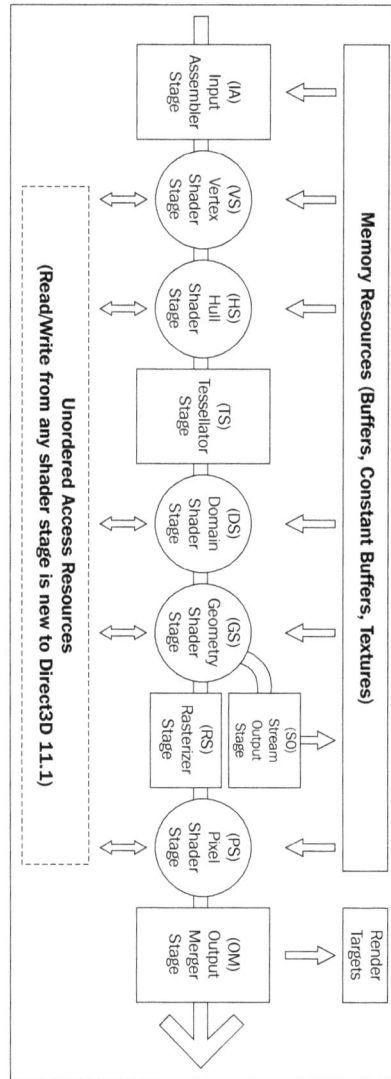

Direct3D Graphics Pipeline

Input Assembler (IA) stage

The IA stage reads primitive data (points, lines, and/or triangles) from buffers and assembles them into primitives for use in subsequent stages.

Usually one or more vertex buffers, and optionally an index buffer, are provided as input. An input layout tells the input assembler what structure to expect the vertex buffer in.

The vertex buffer itself is also optional, where a vertex shader only has a vertex ID as input (using the `SV_VertexID` shader system value input semantic) and then can either generate the vertex data procedurally or retrieve it from a resource using the vertex ID as an index. In this instance, the input assembler is not provided with an input layout or vertex buffer, and simply receives the number of vertices that will be drawn. For more information, see `http://msdn.microsoft.com/en-us/library/windows/desktop/bb232912(v=vs.85).aspx`.

Device context commands that act upon the input assembler directly are found on the `DeviceContext.InputAssembler` property, for example, `DeviceContext.InputAssembler.SetVertexBuffers`, or for unmanaged begin with IA, for example, `ID3D11DeviceContext::IASetVertexBuffers`.

Vertex Shader (VS) stage

The vertex shader allows per-vertex operations to be performed upon the vertices provided by the input assembler. Operations include manipulating per-vertex properties such as position, color, texture coordinate, and a vertex's normal.

A vertex can be comprised of up to sixteen 32-bit vectors (up to four components each). A minimal vertex usually consists of position, color, and the normal vector. In order to support larger sets of data or as an alternative to using a vertex buffer, the vertex shader can also retrieve data from a texture or UAV.

A vertex shader is required; even if no transform is needed, a shader must be provided that simply returns vertices without modifications.

Device context commands that are used to control the vertex shader stage are grouped within the `DeviceContext.VertexShader` property or for unmanaged begin with VS, for example, `DeviceContext.VertexShader.SetShaderResources` and `ID3D11DeviceContext::VSSetShaderResources`, respectively.

Hull Shader (HS) stage

The hull shader is the first stage of the three optional stages that together support hardware accelerated tessellation. The hull shader outputs control points and patches constant data that controls the fixed function tessellator stage. The shader also performs culling by excluding patches that do not require tessellation (by applying a tessellation factor of zero).

Unlike other shaders, the hull shader consists of two HLSL functions: the patch constant function, and hull shader function.

This shader stage requires that the IA stage has one of the patch list topologies set as its active primitive topology (for example, `SharpDX.Direct3D.PrimitiveTopology.PatchListWith3ControlPoints` for managed and `D3D11_PRIMITIVE_TOPOLOGY_3_CONTROL_POINT_PATCHLIST` for unmanaged).

Device context commands that control the hull shader stage are grouped within the `DeviceContext.HullShader` property or for unmanaged device begin with HS.

Tessellator stage

The tessellator stage is the second stage of the optional tessellation stages. This fixed function stage subdivides a quad, triangle, or line into smaller objects. The tessellation factor and type of division is controlled by the output of the hull shader stage.

Unlike all other fixed function stages the tessellator stage does not include any direct method of controlling its state. All required information is provided within the output of the hull shader stage and implied through the choice of primitive topology and configuration of the hull and domain shaders.

Domain Shader (DS) stage

The domain shader is the third and final stage of the optional tessellation stages. This programmable stage calculates the final vertex position of a subdivided point generated during tessellation.

The types of operations that take place within this shader stage are often fairly similar to a vertex shader when not using the tessellation stages.

Device context commands that control the domain shader stage are grouped by the `DeviceContext.DomainShader` property, or for unmanaged begin with DS.

Geometry Shader (GS) stage

The optional geometry shader stage runs shader code that takes an entire primitive or primitive with adjacency as input. The shader is able to generate new vertices on output (triangle strip, line strip, or point list).

> The geometry shader stage is unique in that its output can go to the rasterizer stage and/or be sent to a vertex buffer via the stream output stage (SO).

It is critical for performance that the amount of data sent into and out of the geometry shader is kept to a minimum. The geometry shader stage has the potential to slow down the rendering performance quite significantly.

Uses of the geometry shader might include rendering multiple faces of environment maps in a single pass (refer to *Chapter 9*, *Rendering on Multiple Threads and Deferred Contexts*), and point sprites/billboarding (commonly used in particle systems). Prior to Direct3D 11, the geometry shader could be used to implement tessellation.

Device context commands that control the geometry shader stages are grouped in the `GeometryShader` property, or for unmanaged begin with GS.

Stream Output (SO) stage

The stream output stage is an optional fixed function stage that is used to output geometry from the geometry shader into vertex buffers for re-use or further processing in another pass through the pipeline.

There are only two commands on the device context that control the stream output stage found on the `StreamOutput` property of the device content: `GetTargets` and `SetTargets` (unmanaged `SOGetTargets` and `SOSetTargets`).

Rasterizer stage (RS)

The rasterizer stage is a fixed function stage that converts the vector graphics (points, lines, and triangles) into raster graphics (pixels). This stage performs view frustum clipping, back-face culling, early depth/stencil tests, perspective divide (to convert our vertices from clip-space coordinates to normalized device coordinates), and maps vertices to the viewport. If a pixel shader is specified, this will be called by the rasterizer for each pixel, with the result of interpolating per-vertex values across each primitive passed as the pixel shader input.

There are additional interpolation modifiers that can be applied to the pixel shader input structure that tell the rasterizer stage the method of interpolation that should be used for each property (for more information see Interpolation Modifiers introduced in Shader Model 4 on MSDN at `http://msdn.microsoft.com/en-us/library/windows/desktop/bb509668(v=vs.85).aspx#Remarks`).

When using multisampling, the rasterizer stage can provide an additional coverage mask to the pixel shader that indicates which samples are covered by the pixel. This is provided within the `SV_Coverage` system-value input semantic. If the pixel shader specifies the `SV_SampleIndex` input semantic, instead of being called once per pixel by the rasterizer, it will be called once per sample per pixel (that is, a 4xMSAA render target would result in four calls to the pixel shader for each pixel).

Device context commands that control the rasterizer stage state are grouped in the `Rasterizer` property of the device context or for unmanaged begin with RS.

Pixel Shader (PS) stage

The final programmable stage is the pixel shader. This stage executes a shader program that performs per-pixel operations to determine the final color of each pixel. Operations that take place here include per-pixel lighting and post processing.

Device context commands that control the pixel shader stage are grouped by the `PixelShader` property or begin with PS for the unmanaged API.

Output Merger (OM) stage

The final stage of the graphics pipeline is the output merger stage. This fixed function stage generates the final rendered pixel color. You can bind a depth-stencil state to control z-buffering, and bind a blend state to control blending of pixel shader output with the render target.

Device context commands that control the state of the output merger stage are grouped by the `OutputMerger` property or for unmanaged begin with OM.

The dispatch pipeline

The dispatch pipeline is where compute shaders are executed. There is only one stage in this pipeline, the compute shader stage. The dispatch pipeline and graphics pipeline cannot run at the same time and there is an additional context change cost when switching between the two, therefore calls to the dispatch pipeline should be grouped together where possible.

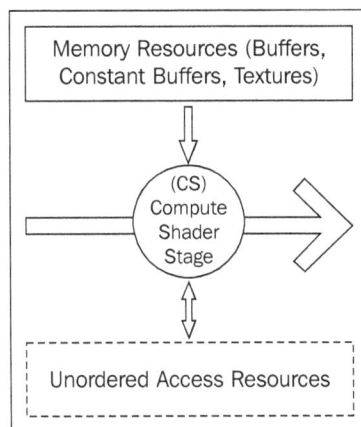

Direct3D Dispatch/DirectCompute Pipeline

Compute Shader (CS) stage

The compute shader (also known as DirectCompute) is an optional programmable stage that executes a shader program upon multiple threads, optionally passing in a dispatch thread identifier (SV_DispatchThreadID) and up to three thread group identifier values as input (SV_GroupIndex, SV_GroupID, and SV_GroupThreadID). This shader supports a whole range of uses including post processing, physics simulation, AI, and GPGPU tasks.

Compute shader support is mandatory for hardware devices from feature level 11_0 onwards, and optionally available on hardware for feature levels 10_0 and 10_1.

The thread identifier is generally used as an index into a resource to perform an operation. The same shader program is run upon many thousands of threads at the same time, usually with each reading and/or writing to an element of a UAV resource.

Device context commands that control the compute shader stage are grouped in the ComputeShader property or begin with CS in the unmanaged API.

After the compute shader is prepared, it is executed by calling the Dispatch command on the device context, passing in the number of thread groups to use.

Introducing Direct3D 11.1 and 11.2

With the release of Windows 8 came a minor release of Direct3D, Version 11.1 and the DXGI API, Version 1.2. A number of features that do not require **Windows Display Driver Model** (**WDDM**) 1.2 were later made available for Windows 7 and Windows Server 2008 R2 with the Platform Update for Windows 7 SP1 and Windows Server 2008 R2 SP1.

Now with the release of Windows 8.1 in October 2013 and the arrival of the Xbox One not long after, Microsoft has provided another minor release of Direct3D, Version 11.2 and DXGI Version 1.3. These further updates are not available on previous versions of Windows 7 or Windows 8.

Direct3D 11.1 and DXGI 1.2 features

Direct3D 11.1 introduces a number of enhancements and additional features, including:

- **Unordered Access Views** (**UAVs**) can now be used in any shader stage, not just the pixel and compute shaders
- A larger number of UAVs can be used when you bind resources to the output merger stage
- Support for reducing memory bandwidth and power consumption (HLSL minimum precision and swap chain dirty regions and scroll present parameters)

- ▸ Shader tracing and compiler enhancements

- ▸ Direct3D device sharing

- ▸ Create larger constant buffers than a shader can access (by binding a subset of a constant buffer)

- ▸ Support logical operations in a render target with new blend state options

- ▸ Create SRV/RTV and UAVs to video resources so that Direct3D shaders can process video resources

- ▸ Ability to use Direct3D in Session 0 processes (from background services)

- ▸ Extended resource sharing for shared Texture2D resources

DXGI 1.2 enhancements include:

- ▸ A new flip-model swap chain

- ▸ Support for stereoscopic 3D displays

- ▸ Restricting output to a specific display

- ▸ Support for dirty rectangles and scrolled areas that can reduce memory bandwidth and power consumption

- ▸ Events for notification of application occlusion status (that is, knowing when rendering is not necessary)

- ▸ A new desktop duplication API that replaces the previous mirror drivers

- ▸ Improved event-based synchronization to share resources

- ▸ Additional debugging APIs

Direct3D 11.2 and DXGI 1.3 features

Direct3D 11.2 is a smaller incremental update by comparison and includes the following enhancements:

- ▸ HLSL compilation within Windows Store apps under Windows 8.1. This feature was missing from Windows 8 Windows Store apps and now allows applications to compile shaders at runtime for Windows Store apps.

- ▸ HLSL shader linking, adding support for precompiled HLSL functions that can be packaged into libraries and linked into shaders at runtime.

- ▸ Support for tiled resources, large resources that use small amounts of physical memory—suitable for large terrains.

- ▸ Ability to annotate graphics commands, sending strings and an integer value to **Event Tracing for Windows** (**ETW**).

DXGI 1.3 enhancements include:

▸ Overlapping swap chains and scaling, for example, presenting a swap chain that is rendered at a lower resolution, then up-scaling and overlapping with a UI swap chain at the displays native resolution.

▸ Trim device command, allowing memory to be released temporarily. Suitable for when an application is being suspended and to reduce the chances that it will be terminated to reclaim resources for other apps.

▸ Ability to set the source size of the back buffer allowing the swap chain to be resized (smaller) without recreating the swap chain resources.

▸ Ability to implement more flexible and lower frame latencies by specifying the maximum frame latency (number of frames that can be queued at one time) and retrieving a wait handle to use with WaitForSingleObjectEx before commencing the next frame's drawing commands.

Building a Direct3D 11 application with C# and SharpDX

In this recipe we will prepare a blank project that contains the appropriate SharpDX references and a minimal rendering loop. The project will initialize necessary Direct3D objects and then provide a basic rendering loop that sets the color of the rendering surface to `Color.LightBlue`.

Getting ready

Make sure you have Visual Studio 2012 Express for Windows Desktop or Professional and higher installed. Download the SharpDX binary package and have it at hand.

To simplify the recipes in this book, lets put all our projects in a single solution:

1. Create a new Blank Solution in Visual Studio by navigating to **File** | **New** | **Project...** (*Ctrl + Shift + N*), search for and select **Blank Solution** by typing that in the search box at the top right of the **New Project** form (*Ctrl + E*).

2. Enter a solution name and location and click on **Ok**.

> The recipes in this book will assume that the solution has been named D3DRendering.sln and that it is located in C:\Projects\D3DRendering.

3. You should now have a new Blank Solution at `C:\Projects\D3DRendering\`
   `D3DRendering.sln`.

4. Extract the contents of the SharpDX package into `C:\Projects\D3DRendering\`
   `External`. The `C:\Projects\D3DRendering\External\Bin` folder should
   now exist among others.

How to do it...

With the solution open, let's create a new project:

1. Add a new Windows Form Application project to the solution with .NET
   Framework 4.5 selected.

2. We will name the project `Ch01_01EmptyProject`.

3. Add the SharpDX references to the project by selecting the project in the solution
   explorer and then navigate to **PROJECT | Add Reference** from the main menu.
   Now click on the **Browse** option on the left and click on the **Browse...** button in
   Reference Manager.

4. For a Direct3D 11.1 project compatible with Windows 7, Windows 8, and Windows
   8.1, navigate to `C:\Projects\D3DRendering\External\Bin\DirectX11_1-`
   `net40` and select **SharpDX.dll, SharpDX.DXGI.dll**, and **SharpDX.Direct3D11.dll**.

5. For a Direct3D 11.2 project compatible only with Windows 8.1, navigate to `C:\`
   `Projects\D3DRendering\External\Bin\DirectX11_2-net40` and add the
   same references located there.

> SharpDX.dll, SharpDX.DXGI.dll, and SharpDX.Direct3D11.dll are the minimum
> references required to create Direct3D 11 applications with SharpDX.

6. Click on **Ok** in **Reference Manager** to accept the changes.

7. Add the following `using` directives to `Program.cs`:

```
using SharpDX;
using SharpDX.Windows;
using SharpDX.DXGI;
using SharpDX.Direct3D11;
// Resolve name conflicts by explicitly stating the class to use:
using Device = SharpDX.Direct3D11.Device;
```

8. In the same source file, replace the `Main()` function with the following code to initialize our Direct3D device and swap chain.

```
[STAThread]
static void Main()
{
    #region Direct3D Initialization
    // Create the window to render to
    Form1 form = new Form1();
    form.Text = "D3DRendering - EmptyProject";
    form.Width = 640;
    form.Height = 480;

    // Declare the device and swapChain vars
    Device device;
    SwapChain swapChain;

    // Create the device and swapchain
    Device.CreateWithSwapChain(
        SharpDX.Direct3D.DriverType.Hardware,
        DeviceCreationFlags.None,
        new [] {
            SharpDX.Direct3D.FeatureLevel.Level_11_1,
            SharpDX.Direct3D.FeatureLevel.Level_11_0,
            SharpDX.Direct3D.FeatureLevel.Level_10_1,
            SharpDX.Direct3D.FeatureLevel.Level_10_0,
        },
        new SwapChainDescription()
        {
            ModeDescription =
                new ModeDescription(
                    form.ClientSize.Width,
                    form.ClientSize.Height,
                    new Rational(60, 1),
                    Format.R8G8B8A8_UNorm
                ),
            SampleDescription = new SampleDescription(1,0),
            Usage = SharpDX.DXGI.Usage.BackBuffer | Usage.
RenderTargetOutput,
            BufferCount = 1,
            Flags = SwapChainFlags.None,
            IsWindowed = true,
```

```
                OutputHandle = form.Handle,
                SwapEffect = SwapEffect.Discard,
            },
            out device, out swapChain
        );

// Create references for backBuffer and renderTargetView
    var backBuffer = Texture2D.FromSwapChain<Texture2D>(swapChain,
0);
    var renderTargetView = new RenderTargetView(device,
backBuffer);

    #endregion

...
}
```

9. Within the same `Main()` function, we now create a simple render loop using a SharpDX utility class `SharpDX.Windows.RenderLoop` that clears the render target with a light blue color.

```
#region Render loop
// Create and run the render loop
RenderLoop.Run(form, () =>
{
    // Clear the render target with light blue
    device.ImmediateContext.ClearRenderTargetView(
      renderTargetView,
      Color.LightBlue);
    // Execute rendering commands here...

    // Present the frame
    swapChain.Present(0, PresentFlags.None);
});
#endregion
```

10. And finally, after the render loop we have our code to clean up the Direct3D COM references.

```
#region Direct3D Cleanup
// Release the device and any other resources created
renderTargetView.Dispose();
backBuffer.Dispose();
device.Dispose();
swapChain.Dispose();
#endregion
```

11. Start debugging the project (*F5*). If all is well, the application will run and show a window like the following screenshot. Nothing very exciting yet but we now have a working device and swap chain.

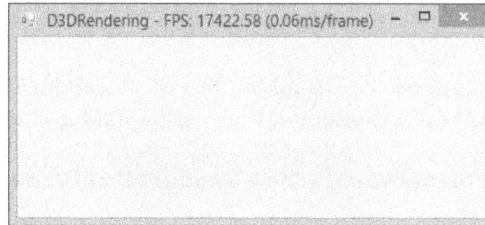

Output from the empty project

How it works...

We've created a standard Windows Forms Application to simplify the example so that the project can be built on Windows 7, Windows 8, and Windows 8.1.

Adding the `SharpDX.dll` reference to your project provides access to all the common enumerations and structures that have been generated in SharpDX from the Direct3D SDK header files, along with a number of base classes and helpers such as a matrix implementation and the `RenderLoop` we have used. Adding the `SharpDX.DXGI.dll` reference provides access to the DXGI API (where we get our `SwapChain` from), and finally `SharpDX.Direct3D11.dll` provides us with access to the Direct3D 11 types.

The `using` directives added are fairly self-explanatory except perhaps the `SharpDX.Windows` namespace. This contains the implementation for `RenderLoop` and also a `System.Windows.Form` descendant that provides some helpful events for Direct3D applications (for example, when to pause/resume rendering).

When adding the `using` directives, there are sometimes conflicts in type names between namespaces. In this instance there is a definition for the `Device` class in the namespaces `SharpDX.DXGI` and `SharpDX.Direct3D11`. Rather than having to always use fully qualified type names, we can instead explicitly state which type should be used with a device using an alias directive as we have done with:

```
using Device = SharpDX.Direct3D11.Device;
```

Our Direct3D recipes will typically be split into three stages:

> **Initialization**: This is where we will create the Direct3D device and resources

> **Render loop**: This is where we will execute our rendering commands and logic

> **Finalization**: This is where we will cleanup and free any resources

The previous code listing has each of the key lines of code highlighted so that you can easily follow along.

Initialization

First is the creation of a window so that we have a valid handle to provide while creating the `SwapChain` object. We then declare the `device` and `swapChain` variables that will store the output of our call to the static method `Device.CreateDeviceAndSwapChain`.

The creation of the device and swap chain takes place next. This is the first highlighted line in the code listing.

Here we are telling the API to create a Direct3D 11 device using the hardware driver, with no specific flags (the native enumeration for `DeviceCreationFlags` is `D3D11_CREATE_DEVICE_FLAG`) and to use the feature levels available between 11.1 and 10.0. Because we have not used the `Device.CreateDeviceAndSwapChain` override that accepts a `SharpDX.DXGI.Adapter` object instance, the device will be constructed using the first adapter found.

This is a common theme with the SharpDX constructors and method overrides, often implementing default behavior or excluding invalid combinations of parameters to simplify their usage, while still providing the option of more detailed control that is necessary with such a complex API.

`SwapChainDescription` (natively `DXGI_SWAP_CHAIN_DESC`) is describing a back buffer that is the same size as the window with a fullscreen refresh rate of 60 Hz. We have specified a format of `SharpDX.DXGI.Format.R8G8B8A8_UNorm`, meaning each pixel will be made up of 32-bits consisting of four 8-bit unsigned normalized values (for example, values between 0.0-1.0 represent the range 0-255) representing Red, Green, Blue, and Alpha respectively. `UNorm` refers to the fact that each of the values stored are normalized to 8-bit values between 0.0 and 1.0, for example, a red component stored in an unsigned byte of 255 is 1 and 127 becomes 0.5. A texture format ending in `_UInt` on the other hand is storing unsigned integer values, and `_Float` is using floating point values. Formats ending in `_SRgb` store gamma-corrected values, the hardware will linearize these values when reading and convert back to the sRGB format when writing out pixels.

The back buffer can only be created using a limited number of the available resource formats. The feature level also impacts the formats that can be used. Supported back buffer formats for feature level >= 11.0 are:

`SharpDX.DXGI.Format.R8G8B8A8_UNorm`

`SharpDX.DXGI.Format.R8G8B8A8_UNorm_SRgb`

`SharpDX.DXGI.Format.B8G8R8A8_UNorm`

`SharpDX.DXGI.Format.B8G8R8A8_UNorm_SRgb`

`SharpDX.DXGI.Format.R16G16B16A16_Float`

`SharpDX.DXGI.Format.R10G10B10A2_UNorm`

`SharpDX.DXGI.Format.R10G10B10_Xr_Bias_A2_UNorm`

We do not want to implement any multisampling of pixels at this time, so we have provided the default sampler mode for no anti-aliasing, that is, one sample and a quality of zero: `new SampleDescription(1, 0)`.

The buffer usage flag is set to indicate that the buffer will be used as a back buffer and as a render-target output resource. The bitwise OR operator can be applied to all flags in Direct3D.

The number of back buffers for the swap chain is set to one and there are no flags that we need to add to modify the swap chain behavior.

With `IsWindowed = true`, we have indicated that the output will be windowed to begin with and we have passed the handle of the form we created earlier for the output window.

The swap effect used is `SwapEffect.Discard`, which will result in the back buffer contents being discarded after each `swapChain.Present`.

> Windows Store apps must use a swap effect of `SwapEffect.FlipSequential`, which in turn limits the valid resource formats for the back buffer to one of the following:
>
> `SharpDX.DXGI.Format.R8G8B8A8_UNorm`
>
> `SharpDX.DXGI.Format.B8G8R8A8_UNorm`
>
> `SharpDX.DXGI.Format.R16G16B16A16_Float`

With the device and swap chain initialized, we now retrieve a reference to the back buffer so that we can create `RenderTargetView`. You can see here that we are not creating any new objects. We are simply querying the existing objects for a reference to the applicable Direct3D interfaces. We do still have to dispose of these correctly as the underlying COM reference counters will have been incremented.

Render loop

The next highlighted piece of code is the `SharpDX.Windows.RenderLoop.Run` helper function. This takes our form and `delegate` or `Action` as input, with `delegate` executed within a loop. The loop takes care of all application messages, and will listen for any application close events and exit the loop automatically, for example, if the form is closed. The render loop blocks the thread so that any code located after the call to `RenderLoop.Run` will not be executed until the loop has exited.

Now we execute our first rendering command which is to clear `renderTargetView` with a light blue color. This line is retrieving the immediate device context from the device and then executing the `ClearRenderTargetView` command. As this is not a deferred context the command is executed immediately.

Finally we tell the swap chain to present the back buffer (our `renderTargetView` that we just set to light blue) to the front buffer.

Finalization

The finalization stage is quite straight forward. After the `RenderLoop` exits, we clean up any resources that we have created and dispose of the device and swap chain.

All SharpDX classes that represent Direct3D objects implement the `IDisposable` interface and should be disposed off to release unmanaged resources.

There's more...

To make the example a little more interesting, try using a **Linear interpolation** (**LERP**) of the color that is being passed to the `ClearRenderTargetView` command. For example, the following code will interpolate the color between light and dark blue over 2 seconds:

```
var lerpColor = SharpDX.Color.Lerp(SharpDX.Color.LightBlue,
                    SharpDX.Color.DarkBlue,
                    (float)(totalSeconds / 2.0 % 1.0));
device.ImmediateContext.ClearRenderTargetView(
    renderTargetView,
    lerpColor);
```

You will have noticed that there are a number of other SharpDX assemblies available within the SharpDX binaries directory.

The `SharpDX.Direct2D1.dll` assembly provides you with the Direct2D API. `SharpDX.D3DCompiler.dll` provides runtime shader compilation, which we will be using to compile our shaders in later chapters. `SharpDX.XAudio2.dll` exposes the XAudio2 API for mixing voices and `SharpDX.RawInput.dll` provides access to the raw data sent from user input devices, such as the keyboard, mouse, and gamepads or joysticks. The Microsoft Media Foundation, for dealing with audio/video playback, is wrapped by the `SharpDX.MediaFoundation.dll` assembly.

Finally, the `SharpDX.Toolkit.dll` assemblies provide a high-level game API for Direct3D 11 much like XNA 4.0 does for Direct3D 9. These assemblies hide away a lot of the low-level Direct3D interaction and provide a number of compilation tools and convenience functions to streamline including shaders and other game content in your project. The framework is worth taking a look at for high-level operations, but as we will tend to be working with the low-level API, it is generally not suitable for our purposes here.

The SharpDX package provides binaries for various platforms. We have used the DirectX 11.1 .NET 4.0 or the DirectX 11.2 .NET 4.0 build here and will use the WinRT build in *Chapter 11, Integrating Direct3D with XAML and Windows 8.1*. SharpDX also provides assemblies and classes for Direct3D 11, Direct3D 10, and Direct3D 9.

See also

> ▶ We will see how to gain access to the Direct3D 11.1/11.2 device and swap chain in the next recipe, *Initializing a Direct3D 11.1/11.2 device and swap chain*.

> ▶ In *Chapter 2, Rendering with Direct3D*, we will cover more detail about rendering, and focus on resource creation, the rendering loop, and simple shaders.

> ▶ *Chapter 11, Integrating Direct3D with XAML and Windows 8.1*, shows how to build a Windows Store app for Windows 8.1.

> ▶ The **Microsoft Developer Network** (**MSDN**) provides a great deal of useful information. The Direct3D launch page can be found at `http://msdn.microsoft.com/en-us/library/windows/desktop/hh309466(v=vs.85).aspx`.

Initializing a Direct3D 11.1/11.2 device and swap chain

We now know how to create our device and swap chain, however, we do not yet have access to some of the features available in Direct3D 11.1 or 11.2 as we are only creating Direct3D 11 references.

In this recipe we will modify the previous example so that we are instead creating `SharpDX.Direct3D11.Device1` and `SharpDX.DXGI.SwapChain1` (natively these are `ID3D11Device1` and `IDXGISwapChain1`, respectively) to access Direct3D 11.1 features, and `SharpDX.Direct3D11.Device2`, and `SharpDX.DXGI.SwapChain2` (natively these are `ID3D11Device2` and `IDXGISwapChain2`, respectively) to access the features of Direct3D 11.2.

`Device1` allows, among others, the creation of blend states that utilize logical operations and access to `DeviceContext1` to access larger constant buffers in shaders than would normally be possible.

`SharpDX.DXGI.SwapChain1` includes support for stereoscopic 3D display and supports WinRT and Windows Phone 8 development.

> The Direct3D 11.2 API is only available on Windows 8.1.

Getting ready

First we will create a new Windows Form Application project named `Ch01_02Direct3D11_1` in our `D3DRendering.sln` solution.

Now add the SharpDX references as outlined in the previous recipe, choosing the appropriate version – Building a Direct3D 11 application with C# and SharpDX.

Set the new project as the startup project by right-clicking on the project in the solution explorer and click on **Set as StartUp Project**.

> For Windows 7/Windows Server 2008 R2 users, this recipe requires that you have installed the platform update for Windows 7 Service Pack 1/Windows Server 2008 R2 SP1.
>
> It is not possible to use the Direct3D 11.2 API with Windows 7, as this version is available to Windows 8.1 only.

How to do it...

We'll begin by creating the Direct3D 11 device as done in the previous recipe and then query the object for an implementation of the Direct3D 11.1 `Device1` COM interface.

1. Open `Program.cs` and add the `using` directives from the previous recipe along with one additional alias:

   ```
   using SharpDX;
   using SharpDX.Windows;
   using SharpDX.DXGI;
   using SharpDX.Direct3D11;
   // Resolve name conflicts by explicitly stating the class to use:
   using Device = SharpDX.Direct3D11.Device;
   using Device1 = SharpDX.Direct3D11.Device1;
   ```

2. Now copy the contents of the `Main()` method from the previous recipe.

3. Build the project (*F6*) just to be sure everything is setup correctly before continuing.

4. Within the `Main()` method, replace the existing device initialization with the following code:

```
// Create the device and swapchain
Device1 device;
SwapChain1 swapChain;

// First create a regular D3D11 device
using (var device11 = new Device(
        SharpDX.Direct3D.DriverType.Hardware,
        DeviceCreationFlags.None,
        new [] {
            SharpDX.Direct3D.FeatureLevel.Level_11_1,
            SharpDX.Direct3D.FeatureLevel.Level_11_0,
        }))
{
  // Query device for the Device1 interface (ID3D11Device1)
  device = device11.QueryInterfaceOrNull<Device1>();
  if (device == null)
      throw new NotSupportedException(
          "SharpDX.Direct3D11.Device1 is not supported");
}
```

> We are explicitly excluding feature levels below 11_0 as we will be using SM5 and other Direct3D 11 features.
>
> Retrieving the Direct3D 11.2 interfaces is performed in the exact same way except with `SharpDX.Direct3D11.Device2`.

5. With the device created, we now need to initialize our swap chain as shown in the following code:

```
// Rather than create a new DXGI Factory we reuse the
// one that has been used internally to create the device
using (var dxgi = device.QueryInterface<SharpDX.DXGI.Device2>())
using (var adapter = dxgi.Adapter)
using (var factory = adapter.GetParent<Factory2>())
{
    var desc1 = new SwapChainDescription1()
    {
        Width = form.ClientSize.Width,
        Height = form.ClientSize.Height,
```

```
        Format = Format.R8G8B8A8_UNorm,
        Stereo = false,
        SampleDescription = new SampleDescription(1, 0),
        Usage = Usage.BackBuffer | Usage.RenderTargetOutput,
        BufferCount = 1,
        Scaling = Scaling.Stretch,
        SwapEffect = SwapEffect.Discard,
    };


    swapChain = new SwapChain1(factory,
        device,
        form.Handle,
        ref desc1,
        new SwapChainFullScreenDescription()
        {
            RefreshRate = new Rational(60, 1),
            Scaling = DisplayModeScaling.Centered,
            Windowed = true
        },
        // Restrict output to specific Output (monitor)
        null);
}
```

> To retrieve the Direct3D 11.2 swap chain, create the swap chain as done here and then use a call to `swapChain.QueryInterfaceO rNull<SwapChain2>();`

6. Finally we will change the `swapChain.Present` call from within the render loop of the previous recipe to:

```
// Present the frame
swapChain.Present(0, PresentFlags.None, new
    PresentParameters());
```

7. Run the project (*F5*). The result should be identical to the previous recipe.

How it works...

Our first change to the previous code is the addition of a new directive using an alias directive for `SharpDX.Direct3D11.Device1`. We keep the `SharpDX.Direct3D11.Device` alias because we first create a regular device and then query it for the 11.1 implementation.

Within the `Direct3D Initialization` region and after the window is created, we have changed the declaration of the `device` and `swapChain` variables to be of type `Device1` and `SwapChain1`. We then create `Device` with the same parameters as before except using a constructor rather than the previous `Device.CreateWithSwapChain` method. This is done within a `using` statement so that the reference to the first device is automatically disposed. Within the using block we query the device for a reference to the `Device1` class. If the implementation of `Device1` was unavailable in the Direct3D API, the return value from `device11.QueryInterfaceOrNull<Device1>` would be `null` while using the regular `QueryInterface<T>` method would result in a `SharpDX.SharpDXException` being thrown.

> All SharpDX classes that wrap a native COM object support a number of variations of the `QueryInterface` method to query the underlying `IUnknown` interface.

To create the swap chain, we need to first get a reference to a `SharpDX.DXGI.Factory2` instance. Rather than creating a new factory, we will use the one that was initialized internally to create our device. All device instances also implement the interface for `SharpDX.DXGI.Device`, which gives us access to the `Adapter` property. As this is provided by the DXGI API we can work our way back from the device to a `SharpDX.DXGI.Factory2` instance via the `GetParent` method.

The equivalent unmanaged example of this section would look something like:

```
// pd3dDevice creation omitted
IDXGIDevice2* pDXGIDevice;
hr = pd3dDevice->QueryInterface(__uuidof(IDXGIDevice2),
    &pDXGIDevice);
IDXGIAdapter* pDXGIAdapter;
hr = pDXGIDevice->GetParent(__uuidof(IDXGIAdapter),
    &pDXGIAdapter);
IDXGIFactory2* pDXGIFactory;
pDXGIAdapter->GetParent(__uuidof(IDXGIFactory2), &pDXGIFactory);
```

Describing the swap chain for Direct3D 11.1 is slightly different as it separates the description into two structures. The first structure, `SwapChainDescription1`, describes the buffer size, format, size, usage, and so on like the original but introduces a `Stereo` and `Scaling` option and excludes the fullscreen properties. The second structure, `SwapChainFullScreenDescription`, describes the fullscreen behavior of the swap chain also with a `Scaling` option.

As this is a desktop application, we use the `SwapChain1` constructor that accepts the window handle to create a swap chain for it. We also pass in the swap chain description structures.

> For Windows Store apps, we would instead use the appropriate constructor that accepts a `Windows.UI.Core.CoreWindow` instance. In the case of `Windows.UI.Xaml.Controls.SwapChainPanel`, no window object is provided and the created swap chain is assigned to the native panel. Details on this are provided in *Chapter 11, Integrating Direct3D with XAML and Windows 8.1*.

The last parameter of the factory's swap chain creation method allows the application to restrict the display of information to a particular display device. In this case we are not restricting the output, so we are passing `null`.

Finally we present the back buffer using the recommended `Present` method override for DXGI 1.2 (`IDXGISwapChain1.Present1`). The additional `PresentParameters` parameter allows an application to optimize presentation by specifying scrolling and dirty rectangles, which reduces memory bandwidth and power consumption. In this case we just pass through an empty instance.

There's more...

There are a number of different ways to initialize your Direct3D device and swap chain. For example, if you are enumerating the available adapters and allowing a user to select, which shall be used by the device constructor instead of defaulting to the first, you will already have created a DXGI factory object and the previous code would look a little different.

The output restriction configuration of the swap chain is an interesting concept and easy to demonstrate if you have more than one screen. With the previous example in place:

1. Change `null` in the last parameter passed to the `new SwapChain1(...)` constructor to `adapter.Outputs[0]`.

2. Change the swap chain present line to:

```
swapChain.Present(0, PresentFlags.RestrictToOutput, new
PresentParameters());
```

If you then drag the window so that it sits between your two displays, the result will look something like the following screenshot. Any portion that sits outside of the designated output will not be rendered and appear black.

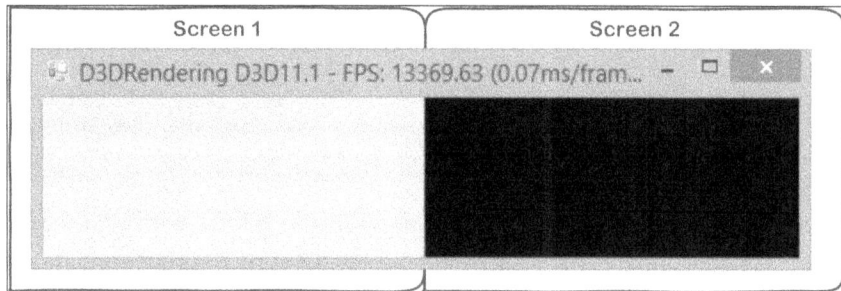

Result of restricting output to the first screen

See also

▸ `IDXGIFactory2` documentation on MSDN can be found at http://msdn.microsoft.com/en-us/library/windows/desktop/hh404556(v=vs.85).aspx.

▸ Refer *Chapter 11, Integrating Direct3D with XAML and Windows 8.1,* for more details on creating a device and swap chain for Direct3D 11.2 on Windows 8.1 and Windows Store apps.

Debugging your Direct3D application

Debugging the Direct3D pipeline can be a difficult task at times. There are so many elements that are impacting upon the result that pinpointing the cause of an issue can take some work and ingenuity.

This recipe will show you how to get your project ready for debugging, set up object tracking, and show you how to start the Visual Studio 2012 Graphics Debugger in managed applications.

First it is worth taking a look at a number of areas of Direct3D that require different techniques for debugging:

▸ **Debugging Direct3D errors**: Direct3D errors such as the parameter being incorrect or invalid can be diagnosed with the help of enabling the Direct3D debug layer by passing the `DeviceCreationFlags.Debug` flag during device creation. When the debug layer is enabled, the Direct3D API will send additional details to the debug output window about any errors that occur. There are four classes of messages, the first two `CORRUPTION` and `ERROR` are problems that require addressing, while `WARNING` and `INFO` messages may or may not require programmer intervention.

▸ **Tracking resources**: Direct3D resource leaks are another area that can take some tracking down, especially in complicated scenes. SharpDX allows you to enable object tracking that you can query at any time to retrieve a list of Direct3D objects that have not been released along with their creation stack trace. On application exit, a complete list of any unreleased objects is printed to the debug output. Enabling the debug layer and the object tracking takes a toll on performance and should only be enabled as needed rather than always enabled during development.

▸ **Debugging a pixel**: Finally there is per-pixel output and shader debugging. Traditionally the DirectX SDK PIX tool has been used for recording Direct3D API calls, now with the Windows 8 SDK and Visual Studio 2012 you can use the Graphics Debugger. When active, this debugger allows you to capture frames that can then be analyzed. You can determine what has impacted an individual pixel, including support for stepping through shaders.

Getting ready

Before we can debug our Direct3D application, we need to prepare the project settings with the following steps:

1. Create a new Windows Form Application named `Ch01_03Debugging` in our `D3DRendering.sln` solution. Set this new project as the startup project.

2. To support the Visual Studio 2012 Graphics Debugger and to allow native debug messages from Direct3D to appear in the debugger output window, we must first enable native code debugging for the project. To do this, right-click on the project in the solution explorer and click on **Properties**, now click on the **Debug** settings and check **Enable native code debugging**.

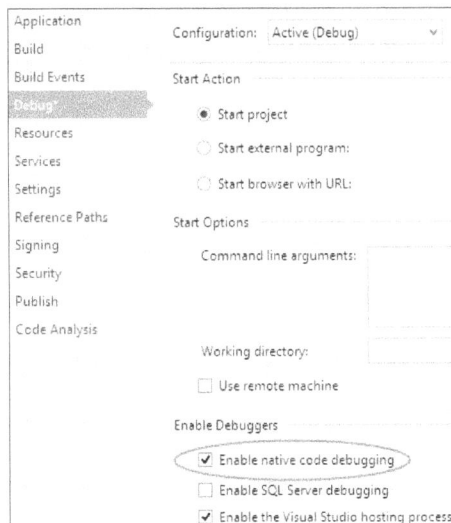

Enabling native code debugging

> Mixed mode debugging for x64 is only supported starting with .NET Framework 4.

How to do it...

First we will be adding some debug information to our code and then use the Visual Studio Graphics Debugger to capture a frame. We'll then continue to enable the Direct3D 11 debug layer and SharpDX object tracking.

Starting the Visual Studio Graphics Debugger:

1. Implement all the steps from the first recipe, *Building a Direct3D 11 application with C# and SharpDX*.

2. Build the project (*F6*) to be sure everything is working correctly.

3. Just before the render loop region, we will add the following:

```
// Setup object debug names
device.DebugName = "The Device";
swapChain.DebugName = "The SwapChain";
backBuffer.DebugName = "The Backbuffer";
renderTargetView.DebugName = "The RenderTargetView";
```

4. Let's now run the Visual Studio 2012 graphics debugger by navigating to **DEBUG | Graphics | Start diagnostics** (*Alt+F5*).

> If the option is unavailable or does not do anything, be sure to check that you have enabled native debugging and that the selected .NET Framework version is 4.0 or later. The project must also be using a debug configuration not release.

5. We can ignore the warning that says that there are no native symbols in the symbol file. This is because we are trying to debug a managed application. Click on **Yes** to continue.

6. If all is well, we should see some statistics in the top left of our application as shown in the following screenshot:

Graphics debugger text overlay in top left

7. Press the *Prt Scr* key and you should now have a frame captured in Visual Studio. Select the frame, and then click anywhere within the preview of the frame. This will now select a single pixel in **Graphics Pixel History** as shown in the following screenshot:

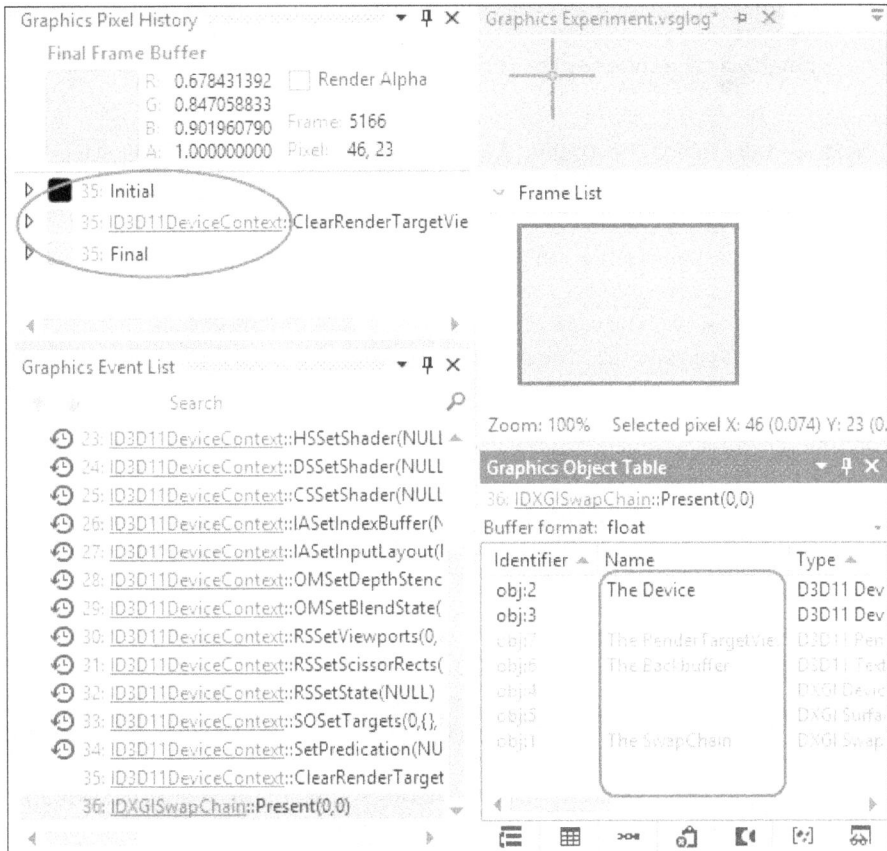

The graphics debugger windows with the pixel history and object table highlighted

8. Stop the debugger.

Enabling the debug layer and object tracking:

Now that we are able to run the debugger, let's turn on the Direct3D debug layer and enable object tracking with the following steps:

1. Continuing from where we were, add the following to `Program.cs` at the start of the `Main()` function:

```
// Enable object tracking
SharpDX.Configuration.EnableObjectTracking = true;
```

2. Within the `Direct3D Initialization` region, change the `CreateWithSwapChain` call to pass in the debug flag:

```
Device.CreateWithSwapChain(
    SharpDX.Direct3D.DriverType.Hardware,
    // Enable Device debug layer
    DeviceCreationFlags.Debug,
    new SwapChainDescription()
    {
```

3. Next, we will replace the existing `swapChain.Present` with the following:

```
// Output the current active Direct3D objects
System.Diagnostics.Debug.Write(
  SharpDX.Diagnostics.ObjectTracker.ReportActiveObjects());

// This is a deliberate invalid call to Present
swapChain.Present(0, PresentFlags.RestrictToOutput);
```

4. Debug the project (*F5*) and there should be an exception thrown. The debug output should contain something like this for the `ReportActiveObjects` call:

```
[0]: Active COM Object: [0x11BFB00] Class: [SharpDX.DXGI.
SwapChain] Time [05/17/2013 16:32:33] Stack:
      c:\Projects\D3DRendering\Ch01_03Debugging\Program.cs(60,13)
: Void Main()

[1]: Active COM Object: [0x11A9C1C] Class: [SharpDX.Direct3D11.
Device] Time [05/17/2013 16:32:33] Stack:
      c:\Projects\D3DRendering\Ch01_03Debugging\Program.cs(60,13)
: Void Main()

[2]: Active COM Object: [0x11ABE48] Class: [SharpDX.Direct3D11.
DeviceContext] Time [05/17/2013 16:32:33] Stack:
      c:\Projects\D3DRendering\Ch01_03Debugging\Program.cs(60,13)
: Void Main()

[3]: Active COM Object: [0x11C0034] Class: [SharpDX.Direct3D11.
Texture2D] Time [05/17/2013 16:32:33] Stack:
      c:\Projects\D3DRendering\Ch01_03Debugging\Program.cs(85,13)
: Void Main()

[4]: Active COM Object: [0x11E0A74] Class: [SharpDX.Direct3D11.
RenderTargetView] Time [05/17/2013 16:32:33] Stack:
      c:\Projects\D3DRendering\Ch01_03Debugging\Program.cs(86,13)
: Void Main()
```

```
Count per Type:
Device : 1
DeviceContext : 1
RenderTargetView : 1
SwapChain : 1
Texture2D : 1
```

5. The incorrect call to `Present` should have resulted in the following being written to the debug output:

```
DXGI ERROR: IDXGISwapChain::Present: Present is being called
with DXGI_PRESENT_RESTRICT_TO_OUTPUT, which is only valid if
the SwapChain was created with a valid pRestrictToOutput. [
MISCELLANEOUS ERROR #120: ]
```

How it works...

We begin with the code from the first recipe that was rendering a pleasant light blue background for our window.

The debug names that we have added are arbitrary values for you to use to distinguish between different objects of the same type. You may have noticed that these appeared within the **Graphics Object Table** when a frame has been captured (marked with a red square in the previous screenshot). This will help when you are trying to debug with lots of objects of the same type. From here, it is possible to inspect each object by double clicking, to view the contents of textures and buffers, or the properties of a device or swap chain.

Once we have captured the frame and selected a pixel, the **Graphics Pixel History** window (circled in red in the previous screenshot) shows the initial color, the color after the call to `ClearRenderTarget` and the final color of the selected pixel. If there were other operations that took place on the pixel (including shaders), this is where we would be able to delve deeper.

The second part of this recipe introduces Direct3D error debugging and object tracking.

First we enabled object tracking on the first line of `Main()` to demonstrate how SharpDX will keep track of objects for us.

We create the device as before, but pass through `DeviceCreationFlags.Debug` instead of `DeviceCreationFlags.None`. This enables the Direct3D debug layer for this device and we will receive additional messages for any errors after this point.

Next we generate a report of all active Direct3D COM objects. This is the same report that is generated if we were to forget to dispose of any resources before application exit. The report includes the stack trace, and double clicking on the line in the stack trace will take you to the appropriate line in the source code editor.

Finally we have introduced a deliberate error in the call to `Present`. The message quite clearly indicates that there is a problem with our use of the `PresentFlags.RestrictToOutput` flag. Either our initialization of the swap chain is incorrect or the call to `Present needs changing`. In this case we have not configured the swap chain with an output to be restricted to.

There's more...

The graphics debugger has a number of useful debug windows that you can access while you have the recorded graphics experiment open. These are accessible by navigating to the **DEBUG**/**Graphics** menu and include **Events List** (shown on the bottom left of the earlier screenshot) and **Pipeline Stages** in addition to the ones we have already discussed.

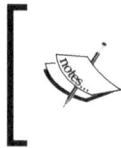

> Because the graphics debugger has been initially designed for unmanaged code, the **Graphics Event Call Stack** window does not resolve the managed source code line numbers correctly. This may change with a future update to Visual Studio.

The `SharpDX.Diagnostics.ObjectTracker` static class has a number of additional methods that are useful at runtime, such as finding an object reference by its native `IntPtr` or perhaps iterating the list to check the number of active `DeviceContext` objects.

It is also possible to debug the HLSL shader code by stepping through the logic based on the selected pixel.

See also

NVIDIA, AMD, and Intel all provide development tools specific to their hardware that can assist with debugging and can be found on the respective websites as follows:

  ▸ NVIDIA Nsight Visual Studio Edition at `https://developer.nvidia.com/nvidia-nsight-visual-studio-edition`

  ▸ AMD GPU PerfStudio at `http://developer.amd.com/tools-and-sdks/graphics-development/gpu-perfstudio-2/`

  ▸ Intel® GPA at `http://software.intel.com/en-us/vcsource/tools/intel-gpa`

2

Rendering with Direct3D

In this chapter, we will cover the following topics:

- ▶ Using the sample rendering framework
- ▶ Creating device-dependent resources
- ▶ Creating size-dependent resources
- ▶ Creating a Direct3D renderer class
- ▶ Rendering primitives
- ▶ Applying multisample anti-aliasing
- ▶ Implementing texture sampling

Introduction

Code for rendering complex scenes can soon become quite difficult to organize. To improve this, we will build a simple rendering framework. This framework will take care of the low-level device and swap chain management, assist with device resource lifecycle management, and allow the application to focus on the elements of the scene instead.

All 3D objects ultimately consist of one or more vertices that together form one of these core primitive shapes: **points**, **lines**, or **triangles**. As we discussed in the previous chapter, vertices can include information such as position, color or texture coordinate, and a normal vector. In this chapter we will learn how to define these structures in shaders and the **Input Assembler** (**IA**) fixed pipeline stage.

A vital component to any 3D scene is setting up the camera and projection. We will learn how to initialize each of these and where vertices are transformed from the local object or model space into the **World/View/Projection** (**WVP**) space (also known as **clip space**).

Using the sample rendering framework

To work with complex scenes more easily, we are going to explore a set of classes that will serve as our simple rendering framework throughout the book. This framework will take care of initializing our Direct3D device, swap chain and render targets, and provide appropriate methods and events for implementing the Direct3D resource lifecycle management in our example applications.

The three key elements of this framework include the following:

▶ **Device manager**: This is a class that manages the lifecycle of our Direct3D device and device context.

▶ **Direct3D application**: This is a set of classes that manage our swap chain and render targets, along with other common-size dependent resources, such as the depth/stencil buffer and viewport setup. We descend from one of these to create our Direct3D application/render loop.

▶ **Renderer**: This is a small class that we use to implement a renderer for a single element/area of a scene. We create instances of these within our Direct3D application class.

> The framework is based on elements of the SharpDX Windows 8 sample code and the C++ DirectX Windows Store app template. Changes have been made to simplify the code and to make it suitable for desktop applications.

Getting ready

The sample rendering framework can be found with the downloadable companion content for this book. After downloading this content, we can prepare a project for use with the framework as follows:

1. From the downloadable companion content for this book, retrieve the `Common.csproj` C# class library project and source files.

2. Copy and add `Common.csproj` to our solution (for example, `D3DRendering.sln`).

3. Add a new **Windows Form Application** project to the solution in order to create your Direct3D application.

> For Windows Store apps, use the `Common.WinRT.csproj` class library instead. *Chapter 11, Integrating Direct3D with XAML and Windows 8.1*, provides an overview of working with this library.

How to do it...

Here, we will walk through the steps necessary to work with the sample rendering framework.

1. Add a reference to `Common.csproj` within your Direct3D application project.

2. In addition to the SharpDX **References** we added to our project in the *Building a Direct3D 11 application with C# and SharpDX* recipe in *Chapter 1, Getting Started with Direct3D*, we will now also include `.\External\bin\SharpDX.Direct2D1.dll` for supporting 2D text rendering. References to `System.Drawing` and `System.Windows.Forms` are also required for desktop applications.

3. Create a new class file that will house a descendent of the `D3DApplicationDesktop` class. Let's call this new class `D3DApp`. The following code snippet shows the class declaration and the required `using` directives:

```
using System;
...
using System.Windows.Forms;

// SharpDX namespaces
using SharpDX;
using SharpDX.DXGI;
using SharpDX.Direct3D11;

using Common;

// Resolve class name conflicts by explicitly stating
// which class they refer to:
using Buffer = SharpDX.Direct3D11.Buffer;
...
public class D3DApp : D3DApplicationDesktop
{
    public PrimitivesApp(System.Windows.Forms.Form window)
        : base(window)
    { }
    ...
}
```

4. Apart from the constructor shown previously, our `D3DApp` class must also implement the `public void Run()` method for the abstract `D3DApplicationDesktop` class. This will typically contain the main application message loop and rendering loop like the following code snippet:

```
public override void Run()
{
```

```
    While(running)
    {
        ... Process messages
        ... Render frame
        Present();
    }
}
```

5. For desktop applications, SharpDX provides a helper class `SharpDX.Windows.RenderLoop` that implements the rendering loop and processes any window messages for us. The following code demonstrates its use within a `D3DApplicationDesktop.Run` implementation:

```
public override void Run()
{
    SharpDX.Windows.RenderLoop.Run(Window, () => {
        ... Render frame
        Present();
    });
}
```

6. To take advantage of the lifecycle management built into the `Common.DeviceManager` class and the `Common.D3DApplicationBase` abstract base class, we can optionally override the following methods in our `D3DApp` implementation:

```
// Override / extend the default SwapChainDescription1
protected override SwapChainDescription1
CreateSwapChainDescription()
{ ... }

// Event-handler for DeviceManager.OnInitialize
protected override void CreateDeviceDependentResources(DeviceManag
er deviceManager)
{ ... }

// Event-handler for D3DApplicationBase.OnSizeChanged
protected override void CreateSizeDependentResources(D3DApplicatio
nBase app)
{ ... }
```

7. We are now able to create an instance of `D3DApp`, initialize the Direct3D device and resources, and then start the application loop. To ensure all resources are correctly released, we can use a `using` code block. The following code snippet shows how this might be done:

```
using (var app = new D3DApp(form))
{
    // Only render frames at the maximum rate the
```

```
    // display device can handle.
    app.VSync = true;

    // Initialize the framework (creates D3D device etc)
    // and any device dependent resources are also created.
    app.Initialize();

    // Run the application message/rendering loop.
    app.Run();
}
```

How it works...

The Common project includes a simple framework that consists of three main areas: the device manager, the Direct3D application classes, and the renderer classes with a number of classes inheriting the latter two. The following class diagram shows the relevant methods and properties of the device manager and Direct3D base application classes. The methods that we have overridden and their respective events are highlighted along with the Direct3D device and context properties on the device manager.

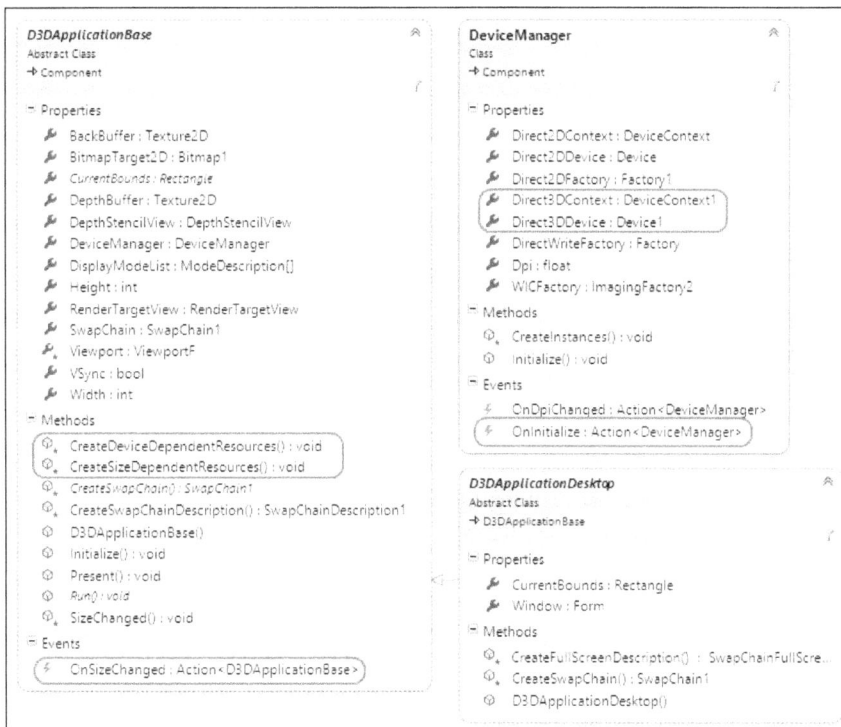

Common project's class diagram showing the device manager and Direct3D application base

The device manager (the `DeviceManager` class) takes care of creating our Direct3D device and context within its `Initialize` function. In addition, the device manager provides an event to notify any listeners whenever the device manager is initialized/reinitialized—the event that our `CreateDeviceDependentResources` function is tied to. This facilitates the recreation of resources when a device is lost/recreated. This is necessary as resources that have been created with a specific device must now be recreated with the new device.

The `D3DApplicationBase` base class provides appropriate methods that can be overridden to participate within the rendering process and Direct3D resource management. The `D3DApplicationDesktop` class descends from this base class and provides the ability to initialize a swap chain from a Windows Desktop window handle. We then implement the abstract base `Run()` method in order to provide a render and message loop.

By overriding the `D3DApplicationBase.CreateSwapChainDescription` method, we are able to control the creation of the swap chain and render target. For example, if we wanted to implement **multisample antialiasing** (**MSAA**), we would override this method and update the description accordingly.

We override the `D3DApplicationBase.CreateDeviceDependentResources` method to create any Direct3D resources that depend on the Direct3D device instance. This is an event-handler that is attached to the device manager that is triggered whenever the Direct3D device is created/recreated.

In addition, we create any resources that depend upon the swap chain/render target size within an overridden `D3DApplicationBase.CreateSizeDependentResources` function. This is an event-handler that is attached to any appropriate window size change events.

Many of our `Common` project classes descend from the `SharpDX.Component` class. This utility class includes methods for managing the `IDisposable` objects. As a majority of our code interacts with Direct3D, a native COM-based API, it is important that we are correctly disposing of these objects to prevent memory/resource leaks. The `SharpDX.Component.ToDispose<T>(T obj)` method allows us to create an instance of `IDisposable` objects without having to explicitly dispose of the instance; instead, any objects registered within the `ToDispose` method will be automatically released upon disposal of our `SharpDX.Component` instance.

By declaring the `D3DApp` instance within a `using` block, as long as our `D3DApp` class passes all created Direct3D resources into the `ToDispose` method, they will be correctly released. The counterpart to this is the `SharpDX.Component.RemoveAndDispose<T>(ref T obj)` function, where we can manually release resources at the beginning of the implementation of our `CreateDeviceDependentResources` or `CreateSizeDependentResources` methods. The following code snippet shows how to reinitialize a resource. Note that there is no need to check for `null`:

```
RemoveAndDispose(ref myDirect3DResource);
...
myDirect3DResource = ToDispose(new ...);
```

See also

▸ The following recipes *Creating the device-dependent resources*, *Creating the size-dependent resources*, and *Creating a Direct3D renderer class* explore the sample rendering framework further, before we implement a full example within *Rendering primitives*

▸ *Chapter 11, Integrating Direct3D with XAML and Windows 8.1* includes the changes to the rendering framework that are necessary to work with the Windows Store apps

Creating device-dependent resources

In this recipe, we will see how the included sample framework deals with the initialization of device-dependent Direct3D resources and how our custom classes can make use of this throughout this book.

Getting ready

We continue from where we left off in the *Using the sample rendering framework* recipe.

How to do it...

We will review the base class's implementation of the `CreateDeviceDependentResources` function, and then look at how to implement overrides within the descending classes.

1. The following protected virtual `D3DApplicationBase.CreateDeviceDependentResources` implementation is assigned as an event-handler to the `DeviceManager.OnInitialize` event.

```
protected virtual void CreateDeviceDependentResources(DeviceManag
er deviceManager)
{
    if (_swapChain != null)
    {
        // Release the swap chain
        RemoveAndDispose(ref _swapChain);
        // Force reinitialize size dependent resources
        SizeChanged(true);
    }
}
```

2. Within your class descending from `D3DApplicationBase`
    (or `D3DApplicationDesktop` and so on), be sure to call the base
    implementation, and then initialize the resources as required. The following
    code snippet shows how initializing a Direct3D shader resource might look like.

```
public class D3DApp: Common.D3DApplicationDesktop
{
  Texture2D myShaderResource;

protected override  void
  CreateDeviceDependentResources(
    DeviceManager deviceManager)
  {
    // Call base implementation
    base.CreateDeviceDependentResources(deviceManager);
    // Release existing resources
    RemoveAndDispose(ref myShaderResource);

    // Retrieve device reference
    var device = deviceManager.Direct3DDevice;

    // Create a shader resource view
    myShaderResource = ToDispose(
        ShaderResourceView.FromFile(device, "Texture.png"));
    ...
  }
  ...
```

How it works...

By handling the device manager's `OnInitialize` event our Direct3D applications
descendent class is able to create its Direct3D device resources when the device is
ready, or whenever the device instance is recreated.

The `D3DApplicationBase` base class provides the minimal code necessary to
ensure that any existing swap chain is released and then recreated by triggering the
`D3DApplicationBase.OnSizeChanged` event. Unless completely overriding the
base implementation, it is important that our overrides call this base implementation.

After calling the base implementation, our own code needs to release any resources that
may have been created previously by using the `SharpDX.Component.RemoveAndDispose`
method. Then we retrieve the currently active Direct3D device from the device manager and
continue to create any necessary resources.

With this approach it is important to ensure that any resources that wrap a native COM object are passed to `ToDispose`, so that they are correctly registered to be released when our class instance is disposed.

> SharpDX classes that wrap COM objects all descend from `SharpDX.ComObject`. This class provides access to the native pointer and also a number of helpful variations on the native `IUnknown` interface's `QueryInterface` method.

Creating size-dependent resources

In this recipe, we will look at how the included sample framework deals with the initialization of size-dependent Direct3D resources within the base Direct3D application class. We review the base class's implementation, and then implement an override for a descending class.

We also review two important graphics pipeline preparation steps that are dependent upon the render target size: creating the viewport for the **Rasterizer Stage** (**RS**) and creating a depth/stencil buffer and view for the **Output Merger** (**OM**) stage.

Getting ready

We continue on from where we left off in the *Using the sample rendering framework* recipe.

How to do it...

The application base class `D3DApplicationBase` initializes the swap chain buffers and render targets within the `CreateSizeDependentResources` method, which is an event-handler attached to the `D3DApplicationBase.OnSizeChanged` event. This method has been implemented as follows:

1. The base implementation is a protected virtual method that allows the descending classes to extend the default behavior.

   ```
   protected virtual void CreateSizeDependentResources(D3DApplication
   Base app)
   { ... }
   ```

> Unless completely overriding the base class's implementation, it is important to always call `base.CreateSizeDependentResources(this)` within your overridden implementation.

2. After retrieving the device and device context from the device manager, the first action should be ensuring that any previous references to buffers have been released.

```
// Retrieve references to device and context
var device = DeviceManager.Direct3DDevice;
var context = DeviceManager.Direct3DContext;

// Before swapchain can resize, buffers must be released
RemoveAndDispose(ref _backBuffer);
RemoveAndDispose(ref _renderTargetView);
RemoveAndDispose(ref _depthStencilView);
RemoveAndDispose(ref _depthBuffer);
RemoveAndDispose(ref _bitmapTarget);
```

3. If we are resizing an existing swap chain, then we will resize it using the `ResizeBuffers` method.

```
// If the swap chain already exists, resize it.
if (_swapChain != null)
{
    _swapChain.ResizeBuffers(
        _swapChain.Description1.BufferCount,
        Width, Height,
        SharpDX.DXGI.Format.B8G8R8A8_UNorm,
        SharpDX.DXGI.SwapChainFlags.None);
}
// Otherwise, create a new one.
else
{
    ... create swap chain
}
```

4. If the swap chain has not already been initialized (or the device was reset), we need to create a new swap chain. This is done almost exactly as described in the *Initializing a Direct3D 11.1/11.2 device and swap chain* recipe in *Chapter 1, Getting Started with Direct3D*.

```
// SwapChain description
var desc = CreateSwapChainDescription();

// Rather than create a new DXGI Factory we reuse the one
// that has been used internally to create the device.
```

```
// Retrieve the underlying DXGI Device from the D3D Device.
// Access the adapter used for that device and then create
// the swap chain
using (var dxgiDevice2 = device.QueryInterface<SharpDX.DXGI.
Device2>())
using (var dxgiAdapter = dxgiDevice2.Adapter)
using (var dxgiFactory2 = dxgiAdapter.GetParent<SharpDX.DXGI.
Factory2>())
using (var output = dxgiAdapter.Outputs.First())
{
    // The CreateSwapChain method allows us to override the
    // method of swap chain creation.
    _swapChain = ToDispose(CreateSwapChain(dxgiFactory2, device,
    desc));

    // Retrieve the list of supported display modes
    DisplayModeList = output.GetDisplayModeList(desc.Format,
    DisplayModeEnumerationFlags.Scaling
}
```

5. With the swap chain resized or initialized, we retrieve the back buffer and create a **render target view** (**RTV**) for it.

```
// Obtain the backbuffer for this window
BackBuffer = ToDispose(
    Texture2D.FromSwapChain<Texture2D>(_swapChain, 0));
// Create an RTV for the rendertarget.
RenderTargetView = ToDispose(new RenderTargetView(device,
    BackBuffer));
```

6. Next, we create the viewport. This is used by the rasterizer stage to map vertices from 3D clip space to 2D render target positions. We assign the viewport to the rasterizer stage using the SetViewport method.

```
// Create a viewport descriptor of the render size.
var viewport = new SharpDX.ViewportF(
    (float)RenderTargetBounds.X,
    (float)RenderTargetBounds.Y,
    (float)RenderTargetBounds.Width,
    (float)RenderTargetBounds.Height,
    0.0f,  // min depth
    1.0f); // max depth

// Set the current viewport for the rasterizer stage.
context.Rasterizer.SetViewport(viewport);
```

> It is not necessary for the viewport to be of the same size as the render target, as vertices will be scaled to fit the viewport dimensions. If the view port is smaller than the target, then the output will only render to a subregion of the render target and appears zoomed-out. If the view port is larger than the target, then a portion of the output render will not be visible and the visible region will appear zoomed-in.

7. Next, we create the depth buffer and a **depth stencil view** (**DSV**). After creating the DSV, we set the DSV and RTV as the render targets of the OM.

```
// Create a descriptor for the depth/stencil buffer.
// Allocate a 2-D texture as the depth/stencil buffer.
// Create a DSV to use on bind.
this.DepthBuffer = ToDispose(new Texture2D(device, new
Texture2DDescription()
{
    Format = SharpDX.DXGI.Format.D24_UNorm_S8_UInt,
    ArraySize = 1,
    MipLevels = 1,
    Width = (int)RenderTargetSize.Width,
    Height = (int)RenderTargetSize.Height,
    SampleDescription = SwapChain.Description.SampleDescription,
    BindFlags = BindFlags.DepthStencil,
}));
this.DepthStencilView = ToDispose(new DepthStencilView(
    device,
    DepthBuffer,
    new DepthStencilViewDescription()
    {
        Dimension =
(SwapChain.Description.SampleDescription.Count > 1 ||
SwapChain.Description.SampleDescription.Quality > 0)
? DepthStencilViewDimension.Texture2DMultisampled :
DepthStencilViewDimension.Texture2D
    }));

// Set the OutputMerger targets
context.OutputMerger.SetTargets(DepthStencilView,
RenderTargetView);
```

> Using a 16-bit depth buffer can result in undesirable artifacts known as **z-fighting** or **flimmering**. A 24- or 32-bit buffer performs much better. However, it isn't possible to completely eliminate artifacts without the use of additional algorithms. Moving the near z-plane as far from the camera as possible can help against depth fighting artefacts. It is then possible to use the 16-bit depth buffer more effectively.

8. Lastly, an example of the `CreateSizeDependentResources` method within a descending class to override the RS viewport might look something like the following code snippet:

```
protected override void CreateSizeDependentResources(
  D3DApplicationBase app)
{
    // Call base implementation
    base.CreateSizeDependentResources(app);

    // Retrieve device immediate context
    var context = this.DeviceManager.Direct3DContext;

    // Create a viewport descriptor of the render size.
    this.Viewport = new SharpDX.ViewportF(
        (float)RenderTargetBounds.X + 100,
        (float)RenderTargetBounds.Y + 100,
        (float)RenderTargetBounds.Width - 200,
        (float)RenderTargetBounds.Height - 200,
        0.0f,   // min depth
        1.0f);  // max depth

    // Set the current viewport for the rasterizer.
    context.Rasterizer.SetViewport(Viewport);
}
```

How it works...

Before trying to create/resize a swap chain, we first make sure that any existing views that access swap chain resources are released. This is necessary to allow the call to `SwapChain.ResizeBuffers` to work, and it is a good practice when reinitializing to ensure resources are released in a timely manner.

When creating a new swap chain instance, the swap chain description is retrieved by a call to the protected virtual function `CreateSwapChainDescription`, and the actual creation of the swap chain is moved into the protected abstract function `CreateSwapChain`. This allows the descending classes to override the default swap chain behavior. Then, it creates the swap chain from an `Hwnd` handle for the desktop applications or with the `Windows.UI.Core.CoreWindow` or `SwapChainPanel` object for the Windows Store apps.

The DSV allows the OM to determine which **fragments** (all the information necessary to create a single pixel) will become actual pixels in the render target. The depth buffer (also known as the **Z-buffer**) is represented by a `Texture2D` instance. It stores one or two components, the depth and, optionally, the stencil. We use the 64-bit `D32_Float_S8X24_UInt` format that provides 32 bits for the depth and 8 bits for the stencil, while the remaining 24-bits are unused. The `BindFlags` instance indicates that this texture will be bound as a DSV.

All render targets (including the depth buffer) bound to the OM must be of the same size and dimension; therefore when creating the depth buffer, it is important to use the same `SampleDescription` structure that was used to create the back buffer (that is, the one returned from `CreateSwapChainDescription`). If multisampling is enabled then we must use `DepthStencilViewDimension.Texture2DMultisampled` as the `Dimension` value in the `DepthStencilViewDescription` structure; otherwise, we pass `DepthStencilViewDimension.Texture2D`.

Finally, our descendent class's overridden method shows how to call the base implementation to prepare the swap chain, default render target, and depth/stencil buffer. Then it changes the viewport settings to render to the center of the render target with a 200 x 200 pixel reduction in size.

There's more...

The way the depth buffer works is better explained with a simple example. Imagine that a scene to be rendered includes a wall, and a cube is located behind this wall (from the viewer's perspective). If the wall is drawn first, then when the OM is determining whether the fragments for the cube should be rendered to pixels, it will check the depth buffer. If it sees that the depth of the wall is closer, then the cube fragments will not be drawn. If the cube was drawn first and then the wall, the pixels for the cube in the render target will be discarded. Then the fragments of the wall will be rendered as pixels in their place.

The stencil is used as a mask on a per-pixel basis, determining whether or not a pixel should be rendered. This can be used for rendering techniques such as dissolves, decaling (for example, scratches on a wall), outlining, silhouettes, shadows, fades, swipes, and composites (for example, a rear view mirror in a driving simulation), or within deferred rendering techniques for determining where lighting should be applied.

See also

▶ *Chapter 3, Rendering Meshes*, provides further information about the depth buffer

Creating a Direct3D renderer class

In this recipe, we will look at the final component of our sample rendering framework, the **renderer**. These are classes that implement specific rendering logic, such as drawing a mesh or utility classes that wish to participate within the Direct3D resource lifecycle management of the rendering framework.

Getting ready

We continue on from where we left off in the *Using the sample rendering framework* recipe.

How to do it...

We will first look at the steps necessary to create a `Common.RendererBase` descendent and then how this class would be created, initialized, and finally execute its Direct3D draw commands.

1. Creating a renderer class within the sample framework requires the following minimal code:

```
public class MyRenderer : Common.RendererBase
{
    // Create device dependent resources
    protected override void CreateDeviceDependentResources()
    { ... }

    // Create size dependent resources
    protected override void CreateSizeDependentResources()
    { ... }

    // Perform rendering commands
    protected override void DoRender()
    { ... }
}
```

2. Within a class that is ultimately descending from `D3DApplicationBase`, you would create and initialize an instance of this renderer class as follows:

```
var myRenderer = ToDispose(new MyRenderer());
myRenderer.Initialize(this);
```

3. Finally, within a render loop, we can tell the renderer instance to perform its draw commands as shown in the following line of code:

```
myRenderer.Render();
```

How it works...

The `Common.RendererBase` abstract class is similar to the `D3DApplicationBase` class. It follows the same approach for managing the lifecycle of Direct3D resources by using the `SharpDX.Component` class and the `CreateDeviceDependentResources` and `CreateSizeDependentResources` methods. In addition, a public `Render` method is available for executing the renderer's Direct3D commands.

The following class diagram shows the available methods and properties:

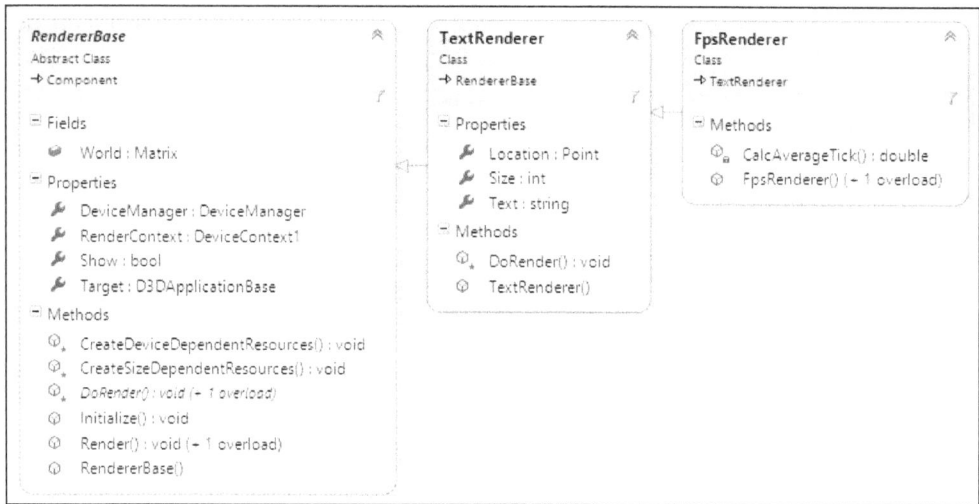

Sample rendering framework renderer class diagram

Implementations of the `RendererBase` class included in the rendering framework sample code includes the `TextRenderer` and the `FpsRenderer` classes. The text renderer uses the Direct2D device and context to render text of the specified font, size, and color at the desired screen location. The FPS renderer descends from the text renderer and displays the current frame rate and frame time (100 frames simple moving average).

See also

▶ The recipes in *Chapter 9*, *Rendering on Multiple Threads and Deferred Contexts*, demonstrate how to control the current device context for a renderer instance

Rendering primitives

Now that we have our rendering framework ready, we can finally work on the more interesting stuff—actually rendering something!

All rendered objects, at their simplest form, are made up of one or more primitives: points, lines, or triangles which are made up of one or more vertices. In this recipe, we will render the following primitives:

- A set of colored arrows representing the x, y, and z axes (red, green, and blue) using lines
- A triangle using a triangle
- A quad (made up of two triangles)

We will also implement our WVP matrix and see how multisampling affects the rendered image. The final result is shown in the following figure:

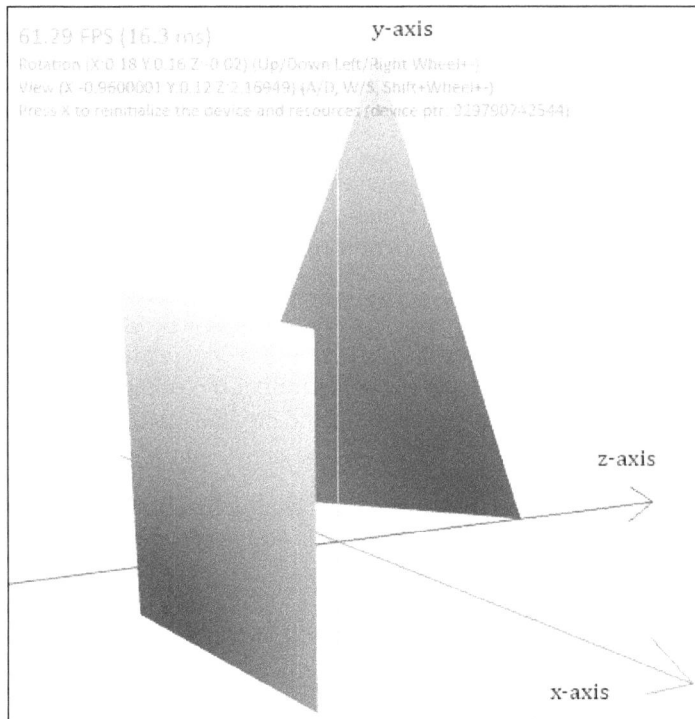

Rendering primitives final output

Getting ready

We'll start by creating a new Windows Form Application project named `Ch02_01RenderingPrimitives` in the `D3DRendering.sln` solution:

1. Add the `SharpDX.dll`, `SharpDX.DXGI.dll` and `SharpDX.Direct3D11.dll` references like we did in the previous recipes.

2. Next, we will add a reference to `.\External\bin\SharpDX.D3DCompiler.dll` for dealing with our shader code.

3. An important step before we get started is to ensure that we are copying the Direct3D `d3dcompiler_46.dll` DLL to the build directory, as this will let us compile our shaders at runtime. To do this, open the project properties, select **Build Events**, and add the following code to the **Post-build event** command line:

   ```
   copy "$(SolutionDir)\External\Bin\Redist\D3D\x86\d3d*.dll"
   "$(TargetDir)"
   ```

   > If you are not entirely familiar with .NET 4.5 yet, the behavior of **AnyCPU** has changed. Now there is an additional option **Prefer 32-bit**. For all new .NET 4.5 projects, this is selected by default—this is why we are using the 32-bit version of d3dcompiler_46.dll.

4. Make sure that you have the `Common` rendering framework project (that we used in the *Using the sample rendering framework* recipe earlier in this chapter) added to your `D3DRendering.sln` solution, and add a reference to it to our new project.

How to do it...

For this recipe, we will first create a HLSL shader to render our primitive shapes. We will create a `D3DApp` class that compiles our shaders and creates instances of our line, triangle, and quad renderers.

1. The first thing we will do is create our HLSL shader file. Do this by adding a new **Text File** to the project and call it `Simple.hlsl`. Add the following code to the shader file:

   ```
   // Constant buffer to be updated by application per frame
   cbuffer PerObject : register(b0)
   {
       // WorldViewProjection matrix
       float4x4 WorldViewProj;
   };
   ```

```
// Vertex Shader input structure with position and color
struct VertexShaderInput
{
    float4 Position : SV_Position;
    float4 Color : COLOR;
};
// Vertex Shader output structure consisting of the
// transformed position and original color
// This is also the pixel shader input
struct VertexShaderOutput
{
    float4 Position : SV_Position;
    float4 Color : COLOR;
};
// Vertex shader main function
VertexShaderOutput VSMain(VertexShaderInput input)
{
    VertexShaderOutput output = (VertexShaderOutput)0;

    // Transform the position from object space to homogeneous
    // projection space
    output.Position = mul(input.Position, WorldViewProj);
    // Pass through the color of the vertex
    output.Color = input.Color;

    return output;
}
// A simple Pixel Shader that simply passes through the
// interpolated color
float4 PSMain(VertexShaderOutput input) : SV_Target
{
    return input.Color;
}
```

> By default, Visual Studio will create the file using the UTF-8 with signature encoding. The Direct3D 11 shader compiler requires ANSI encoding. To do this in Visual Studio, navigate to **FILE | Save Simple. hlsl As...** from the menu and select the **Western European (Windows) - Codepage 1252** encoding.
>
> Select **Yes** when you are asked if you want to overwrite the file.

2. Select the shader file in the **Solution Explorer** and select **Copy if newer** for the **Copy to Output Directory** setting within the **Properties** window.

3. In our project, let's add a new class called D3DApp, which is descending from D3DApplicationDesktop (note the additional using directives):

```
using SharpDX;
using SharpDX.Windows;
using SharpDX.DXGI;
using SharpDX.Direct3D11;
using SharpDX.D3DCompiler;

using Common;
using Buffer = SharpDX.Direct3D11.Buffer;
public class D3DApp: D3DApplicationDesktop
{
    public PrimitivesApp(System.Windows.Forms.Form window)
        : base(window)
    { }
    ...
}
```

4. We will include the following private member fields:

```
// The vertex shader
ShaderBytecode vertexShaderBytecode;
VertexShader vertexShader;

// The pixel shader
ShaderBytecode pixelShaderBytecode;
PixelShader pixelShader;

// The vertex layout for the IA
InputLayout vertexLayout;

// A buffer that will be used to update the constant buffer
// used by the vertex shader. This contains our
// worldViewProjection matrix
Buffer worldViewProjectionBuffer;

// Our depth stencil state
DepthStencilState depthStencilState;
```

5. Next, we will implement our `CreateDeviceDependentResources` method override as described in the *Creating the device dependent resources* recipe. Within this method, we will begin by calling the base implementation, releasing existing references, and retrieving our Direct3D device and immediate context:

```
base.CreateDeviceDependentResources(deviceManager);
// Release all resources
RemoveAndDispose(ref vertexShader);
RemoveAndDispose(ref vertexShaderBytecode);
RemoveAndDispose(ref pixelShader);
RemoveAndDispose(ref pixelShaderBytecode);
RemoveAndDispose(ref vertexLayout);
RemoveAndDispose(ref worldViewProjectionBuffer);
RemoveAndDispose(ref depthStencilState);

// Get a reference to the Device1 instance and context
var device = deviceManager.Direct3DDevice;
var context = deviceManager.Direct3DContext;
```

6. Next, we will compile our HLSL source code into a vertex and pixel shader. We will enabling the debug flag if we are using the **Debug** build configuration:

```
ShaderFlags shaderFlags = ShaderFlags.None;
#if DEBUG
shaderFlags = ShaderFlags.Debug;
#endif

// Compile and create the vertex shader
vertexShaderBytecode = ToDispose(ShaderBytecode.
CompileFromFile("Simple.hlsl", "VSMain", "vs_5_0", shaderFlags));
vertexShader = ToDispose(new VertexShader(device,
vertexShaderBytecode));

// Compile and create the pixel shader
pixelShaderBytecode = ToDispose(ShaderBytecode.
CompileFromFile("Simple.hlsl", "PSMain", "ps_5_0", shaderFlags));
pixelShader = ToDispose(new PixelShader(device,
pixelShaderBytecode));
```

7. Next, initialize a vertex layout to match the structure defined in our HLSL vertex shader.

```
// Layout from VertexShader input signature
vertexLayout = ToDispose(new InputLayout(device,
    vertexShaderBytecode.GetPart(
```

```
                ShaderBytecodePart.InputSignatureBlob),
    new[]{
    // input semantic SV_Position=vertex coord in object space
    new InputElement("SV_Position",0,Format.R32G32B32A32_Float, 0, 0),
    // input semantic COLOR = vertex color
    new InputElement("COLOR", 0, Format.R32G32B32A32_Float, 16, 0)
    }));
```

8. Now, we will create a new `Buffer` used to populate the WVP matrix constant buffer defined within our HLSL code.

```
// Create the buffer that will store our WVP matrix
worldViewProjectionBuffer = ToDispose(new SharpDX.Direct3D11.
Buffer(device, Utilities.SizeOf<Matrix>(), ResourceUsage.
  Default, BindFlags.ConstantBuffer, CpuAccessFlags.None,
    ResourceOptionFlags.None, 0));
```

9. Create the depth stencil state to control how the OM stage will handle depth:

```
// Configure the OM to discard pixels that are
// further than the current pixel in the depth buffer.
depthStencilState = ToDispose(new DepthStencilState(device,
new DepthStencilStateDescription()
{
    IsDepthEnabled = true, // enable depth?
    DepthComparison = Comparison.Less,
    DepthWriteMask = SharpDX.Direct3D11.DepthWriteMask.All,
    IsStencilEnabled = false,// enable stencil?
    StencilReadMask = 0xff, // 0xff (no mask)
    StencilWriteMask = 0xff,// 0xff (no mask)
    // Configure FrontFace depth/stencil operations
    FrontFace = new DepthStencilOperationDescription()
    {
        Comparison = Comparison.Always,
        PassOperation = StencilOperation.Keep,
        FailOperation = StencilOperation.Keep,
        DepthFailOperation = StencilOperation.Increment
    },
    // Configure BackFace depth/stencil operations
    BackFace = new DepthStencilOperationDescription()
    {
        Comparison = Comparison.Always,
        PassOperation = StencilOperation.Keep,
        FailOperation = StencilOperation.Keep,
        DepthFailOperation = StencilOperation.Decrement
    },
}));
```

10. Lastly, we need to assign our input layout, constant buffer, vertex and pixel shaders, and the depth stencil state to the appropriate graphics pipeline stages.

```
// Tell the IA what the vertices will look like
context.InputAssembler.InputLayout = vertexLayout;

// Bind constant buffer to vertex shader stage
context.VertexShader.SetConstantBuffer(0,
worldViewProjectionBuffer);

// Set the vertex shader to run
context.VertexShader.Set(vertexShader);

// Set the pixel shader to run
context.PixelShader.Set(pixelShader);

// Set our depth stencil state
context.OutputMerger.DepthStencilState = depthStencilState;
```

Now that the resources have been initialized, we can implement the `D3DApplicationBase.Run` method as described in the *Using the sample rendering framework* recipe. Here, we will host our rendering loop, initialize the renderers, and call their Render methods.

11. First we will initialize the instances of our renderers (the implementation of these classes will follow shortly):

```
// Create and initialize the axis lines renderer
var axisLines = ToDispose(new AxisLinesRenderer());
axisLines.Initialize(this);
// Create and initialize the triangle renderer
var triangle = ToDispose(new TriangleRenderer());
triangle.Initialize(this);
// Create and initialize the quad renderer
var quad = ToDispose(new QuadRenderer());
quad.Initialize(this);
```

12. Next, we will prepare our world, view, and projection matrices. These matrices are multiplied and the result is used to update the WVP constant buffer within the render loop to perform vertex transformations within the vertex shader.

```
// Initialize the world matrix
var worldMatrix = Matrix.Identity;

// Set camera position slightly to the right (x), above (y)
// and behind (-z)
```

```
var cameraPosition = new Vector3(1, 1, -2);
var cameraTarget = Vector3.Zero; // Looking at origin 0,0,0
var cameraUp = Vector3.UnitY; // Y+ is Up

// Create view matrix from our camera pos, target and up
var viewMatrix = Matrix.LookAtLH(cameraPosition, cameraTarget,
cameraUp);

// Create the projection matrix
// Field of View 60degrees = Pi/3 radians
// Aspect ratio (based on window size), Near clip, Far clip
var projectionMatrix = Matrix.PerspectiveFovLH((float)Math.PI /
3f, Width / (float)Height, 0.5f, 100f);

// Maintain the correct aspect ratio on resize
Window.Resize += (s, e) => {
  projectionMatrix = Matrix.PerspectiveFovLH( (float)Math.PI / 3f,
Width / (float)Height, 0.5f, 100f);
};
```

> Note that we are using a **left-handed coordinate system** for this recipe.

13. We can now implement our render loop. This is done the same way as in the previous chapter, that is, by a call to `RenderLoop.Run(Window, () => { ... });`. After retrieving our device context, we first clear the depth stencil view and clear the render target.

```
// Clear depth stencil view
context.ClearDepthStencilView(DepthStencilView,
DepthStencilClearFlags.Depth|DepthStencilClearFlags.
Stencil,1.0f,0);
// Clear render target view
context.ClearRenderTargetView(RenderTargetView, Color.White);
```

14. Next, we will multiply the view and projection matrices, and then create our WVP matrix. Then this matrix is assigned to our constant buffer resource.

```
// Create viewProjection matrix
var viewProjection = Matrix.Multiply(viewMatrix,
projectionMatrix);

// Create WorldViewProjection Matrix
```

```
var worldViewProjection = worldMatrix * viewProjection;
// HLSL defaults to "column-major" order matrices so
// transpose first (SharpDX uses row-major matrices).
worldViewProjection.Transpose();
// Write the worldViewProjection to the constant buffer
context.UpdateSubresource(ref worldViewProjection,
worldViewProjectionBuffer);
```

15. We can now call each of our renderer's `Render` method and present the final result.

```
// Render the primitives
axisLines.Render();
triangle.Render();
quad.Render();

// Render FPS
fps.Render();
// Render instructions + position changes
textRenderer.Render();

// Present the frame
Present();
```

16. This completes our `D3DApp` class. Open `Program.cs`, and replace the `Main()` method with the following code so that we are now utilizing our `D3DApp` class:

```
static void Main()
{
#if DEBUG
    // Enable object tracking
    SharpDX.Configuration.EnableObjectTracking = true;
#endif
    // Create the form to render to
    var form = new Form1();
    form.Text = "D3DRendering - Primitives";
    form.ClientSize = new System.Drawing.Size(1024, 768);
    form.Show();
    // Create and initialize the new D3D application
    // Then run the application.
    using (D3DApp app = new D3DApp(form))
    {
        // Only render frames at the maximum rate the
        // display device can handle.
        app.VSync = true;
```

```
          // Initialize (create Direct3D device etc)
          app.Initialize();

          // Run the application
          app.Run();
      }
  }
```

17. Let's first add stubs for the renderer classes so that we can test whether our project is compiling correctly. We will add these with names according to the following files: `AxisLinesRenderer.cs`, `TriangleRenderer.cs`, and `QuadRenderer.cs`. Go ahead and create these empty classes now and descend them from `Common.RendererBase` as demonstrated in the *Creating a Direct3D renderer class* recipe.

18. At this point we should be able to compile and run (*F5*) the project. A blank form will appear with the frames per second displayed in the top-left corner.

19. We will first complete the **axis-lines renderer** class of the renderers . Begin by opening the `AxisLinesRenderer.cs` file and adding the following private member fields:

```
// The vertex buffer for axis lines
Buffer axisLinesVertices;

// The binding structure of the axis lines vertex buffer
VertexBufferBinding axisLinesBinding;
```

20. Now we will add the following resource initialization code to the `CreateDeviceDependentResources` method. This consists of first ensuring that the resources have been released via `RemoveAndDispose` and then creating a local reference to the device.

```
// Ensure that if already set the device resources
// are correctly disposed of before recreating
RemoveAndDispose(ref axisLinesVertices);

// Retrieve our SharpDX.Direct3D11.Device1 instance
var device = this.DeviceManager.Direct3DDevice;
```

21. Next, we create our vertex buffer and binding for use in the IA stage:

```
// Create xyz-axis arrows
// X is Red, Y is Green, Z is Blue
// The arrows point along the + for each axis
axisLinesVertices = ToDispose(Buffer.Create(device, BindFlags.
VertexBuffer, new[]
{
```

```
/*  Vertex Position      Vertex Color */
new Vector4(-1f,0f,0f,1f),(Vector4)Color.Red, // - x-axis
new Vector4(1f,0f,0f,1f), (Vector4)Color.Red,  // + x-axis
new Vector4(0.9f,-0.05f,0f,1f),(Vector4)Color.Red,//head start
new Vector4(1f,0f,0f,1f), (Vector4)Color.Red,
new Vector4(0.9f,0.05f,0f,1f), (Vector4)Color.Red,
new Vector4(1f,0f,0f,1f), (Vector4)Color.Red,  // head end

new Vector4(0f,-1f,0f,1f), (Vector4)Color.Lime, // - y-axis
new Vector4(0f,1f,0f,1f), (Vector4)Color.Lime,  // + y-axis
new Vector4(-0.05f,0.9f,0f,1f),(Vector4)Color.Lime,//head start
new Vector4(0f,1f,0f,1f), (Vector4)Color.Lime,
new Vector4(0.05f,0.9f,0f,1f), (Vector4)Color.Lime,
new Vector4(0f,1f,0f,1f), (Vector4)Color.Lime,  // head end

new Vector4(0f,0f,-1f,1f), (Vector4)Color.Blue, // - z-axis
new Vector4(0f,0f,1f,1f), (Vector4)Color.Blue,  // + z-axis
new Vector4(0f,-0.05f,0.9f,1f),(Vector4)Color.Blue,//head start
new Vector4(0f,0f,1f,1f), (Vector4)Color.Blue,
new Vector4(0f,0.05f,0.9f,1f), (Vector4)Color.Blue,
new Vector4(0f,0f,1f,1f), (Vector4)Color.Blue,  // head end
}));
axisLinesBinding = new VertexBufferBinding(axisLinesVertices,
Utilities.SizeOf<Vector4>() * 2, 0);
```

22. The axis lines drawing logic is made up of the following code which belongs to DoRender. This sets the topology to be used, passes the vertex buffer to the IA stage, and requests the pipeline to draw the 18 vertices we just defined.

```
// Get the context reference
var context = this.DeviceManager.Direct3DContext;

// Render the Axis lines
// Tell the IA we are using lines
context.InputAssembler.PrimitiveTopology = SharpDX.Direct3D.
PrimitiveTopology.LineList;
// Pass in the line vertices
context.InputAssembler.SetVertexBuffers(0, axisLinesBinding);
// Draw the 18 vertices or our xyz-axis arrows
context.Draw(18, 0);
```

23. Next, we will implement the **triangle renderer**. Open the `TriangleRenderer` class and add the following private member fields:

```
// The triangle vertex buffer
Buffer triangleVertices;

// The vertex buffer binding structure for the triangle
VertexBufferBinding triangleBinding;
```

24. We will initialize the device-dependent resources with this code. As with the axis lines renderer, here we also need to create a vertex buffer and binding.

```
RemoveAndDispose(ref triangleVertices);

// Retrieve our SharpDX.Direct3D11.Device1 instance
var device = this.DeviceManager.Direct3DDevice;

// Create a triangle
triangleVertices = ToDispose(Buffer.Create(device, BindFlags.
VertexBuffer, new[] {
/*  Vertex Position
        Vertex Color */
    new Vector4(0.0f, 0.0f, 0.5f, 1.0f),
        new Vector4(0.0f, 0.0f, 1.0f, 1.0f), // Base-right
    new Vector4(-0.5f, 0.0f, 0.0f, 1.0f),
        new Vector4(1.0f, 0.0f, 0.0f, 1.0f), // Base-left
    new Vector4(-0.25f, 1f, 0.25f, 1.0f),
        new Vector4(0.0f, 1.0f, 0.0f, 1.0f), // Apex
}));
triangleBinding = new VertexBufferBinding(triangleVertices,
Utilities.SizeOf<Vector4>() * 2, 0);
```

25. And finally, render our triangle with the following code that is placed in `DoRender()`. This time, we use a different topology and only need to draw three vertices.

```
// Get the context reference
var context = this.DeviceManager.Direct3DContext;

// Render the triangle
// Tell the IA we are now using triangles
context.InputAssembler.PrimitiveTopology = SharpDX.Direct3D.
PrimitiveTopology.TriangleList;
// Pass in the triangle vertices
context.InputAssembler.SetVertexBuffers(0, triangleBinding);
// Draw the 3 vertices of our triangle
context.Draw(3, 0);
```

26. Lastly, we will implement our **quad renderer**. Open the `QuadRenderer` class, and add the following private member fields:

```
// The quad vertex buffer
Buffer quadVertices;
// The quad index buffer
Buffer quadIndices;
// The vertex buffer binding for the quad
VertexBufferBinding quadBinding;
```

27. Initialize the device-dependent resources with the following code. We are initializing our vertex buffer and binding in the same way as the axis lines and triangle renderer. In addition, we are creating an index buffer to re-use the existing vertices.

```
RemoveAndDispose(ref quadVertices);
RemoveAndDispose(ref quadIndices);

// Retrieve our SharpDX.Direct3D11.Device1 instance
var device = this.DeviceManager.Direct3DDevice;

// Create a quad (two triangles)
quadVertices = ToDispose(Buffer.Create(device, BindFlags.
VertexBuffer, new[] {
/*   Vertex Position
        Vertex Color */
    new Vector4(0.25f, 0.5f, -0.5f, 1.0f),
        new Vector4(0.0f, 1.0f, 0.0f, 1.0f), // Top-left
    new Vector4(0.75f, 0.5f, -0.5f, 1.0f),
        new Vector4(1.0f, 1.0f, 0.0f, 1.0f), // Top-right
    new Vector4(0.75f, 0.0f, -0.5f, 1.0f),
        new Vector4(1.0f, 0.0f, 0.0f, 1.0f), // Base-right
    new Vector4(0.25f, 0.0f, -0.5f, 1.0f),
        new Vector4(0.0f, 0.0f, 1.0f, 1.0f), // Base-left
}));
quadBinding = new VertexBufferBinding(quadVertices, Utilities.
SizeOf<Vector4>() * 2, 0);

// v0      v1
// |-----|
// | \ A |
// | B \ |
// |-----|
// v3      v2
quadIndices = ToDispose(Buffer.Create(device, BindFlags.
IndexBuffer, new ushort[] {
    0, 1, 2, // A
    2, 3, 0  // B
}));
```

28. We will now render the quad using the following code placed in the `DoRender` override. We will use the same topology as the triangle renderer; however, this time we also need to set the index buffer and use them when drawing the vertices:

```
var context = this.DeviceManager.Direct3DContext;
// Tell the IA we are using a triangle list
context.InputAssembler.PrimitiveTopology = SharpDX.Direct3D.
PrimitiveTopology.TriangleList;
// Set the index buffer
context.InputAssembler.SetIndexBuffer(quadIndices, Format.R16_
UInt, 0);
// Pass in the quad vertices (note: only 4 vertices)
context.InputAssembler.SetVertexBuffers(0, quadBinding);
// Draw the 6 vertices that make up the two triangles in the quad
// using the vertex indices
context.DrawIndexed(6, 0, 0);
// Note: we have called DrawIndexed to use the index buffer
```

29. Compile and run the project and you will now see a result similar to the figure shown at the beginning of this recipe.

> To add the key down and mouse wheel handlers for rotating the objects, copy the code from the sample code that can be downloaded for this book from Packt's website. With this code in place, the scene can be rotated around the x, y, and z axes using the arrow keys and mouse wheel. The camera is moved with the *W*, *A*, *S*, and *D* keys and *Shift* + mouse wheel. Pressing *X* will reinitialize the device—this is useful for testing the initialization code.

How it works...

We have started by creating our HLSL shader code. This consists of one constant buffer that stores the WVP matrix, two structures that store the input/output of the vertex shader and also the input for the pixel shader, and our two shader methods for the vertex shader and pixel shader.

```
cbuffer PerObject : register(b0) {
    // WorldViewProjection matrix
    float4x4 WorldViewProj;
};
```

The preceding constant buffer declaration is named `PerObject` and will be loaded using the first constant buffer register, that is, `b0` (also known as slot 0). The buffer consists of a single 4 x 4 affine transform matrix, which is our precalculated WVP matrix. The name itself is of no consequence. It is the register number/slot number and name of the properties within that are important.

> For performance reasons, it is best to group properties with a similar update frequency into the same constant buffer, for example, those updated per frame and those updated per object.

The vertex shader structures hold the position and color component. When initializing the IA stage, we will see how the `VertexShaderInput` structure and the input layout match up. Ultimately, these structures define our vertex layout.

There are two shader entry points: `VSMain` represents the vertex shader and `PSMain` is the pixel shader. The vertex shader will transform vertices from local object space into a **homogeneous projection space** based on the world, view, and projection (by applying the WVP matrix). The return value is the result of this along with the color, and it is the same structure that is passed into the pixel shader. This shader will run for each vertex.

The pixel shader is provided with an **interpolated** `VertexShaderOutput` structure by the rasterizer state—this pixel shader is doing nothing but returning the unchanged color component.

Next, we implemented our Direct3D application class. This houses the rendering loop, and it initializes the Direct3D pipeline and our individual renderers. We descend from `D3DApplicationDesktop`, which simply creates the `SwapChain1` instance based on a `System.Windows.Form`, as demonstrated in *Chapter 1, Getting Started with Direct3D*. We provided a compatible constructor that passes the form through to the base class.

Resource Initialization

The `CreateDeviceDependentResources` implementation that is provided creates our device-dependent resources and initializes the IA and OM stages of the rendering pipeline.

First, we created our shader programs by compiling them. For example, we compile our vertex shader by using `ShaderBytecode.CompileFromFile("Simple.hlsl", "VSMain", "vs_5_0", shaderFlags)`. This compiles `Simple.hlsl` by using the `vs_5_0` shader profile and uses `VSMain` as the entry point. If we have compiled for **Debug**, we are telling the shader to include the debug information via the `shaderFlags` enumeration value. This allows us to step through the shaders when using the graphics debugging tools in Visual Studio.

After the shaders are compiled, we prepare the **input layout** for the IA. This is used to tell the IA in which memory layout the vertices can be expected when copying them to the `VertexShaderInput` structure in our shader file.

```
new InputLayout(..., new[] {
 new InputElement("SV_Position",0,Format.R32G32B32A32_Float, 0, 0),
 new InputElement("COLOR", 0, Format.R32G32B32A32_Float, 16, 0)
});
```

The previous layout tells the input assembler that the COLOR component will be located after the 16 bytes of the SV_Position component. In the preceding code, we can see that the name and format of the input layout matches the type and input semantics (the name) used in the Simple.hlsl shader.

```
struct VertexShaderInput
{
    float4 Position : SV_Position;
    float4 Color : COLOR;
};
```

Next, we will create our constant buffer to store the WVP matrix. A second buffer for updating the per-frame information, such as light position, direction, and color, is another common resource.

```
new SharpDX.Direct3D11.Buffer(device, Utilities.SizeOf<Matrix>(),
ResourceUsage.Default, BindFlags.ConstantBuffer, CpuAccessFlags.None,
ResourceOptionFlags.None, 0)
```

Here we created a buffer that is the size of a single Matrix structure. This buffer that is available for read/write on the GPU (ResourceUsage.Default) is a constant buffer, and it will not be accessible directly from the CPU. There are no additional options set, and as it is only representing a single object there is no structure byte stride.

Next, we will create our DepthStencilState class which is used to control how the OM stage will behave when determining whether to keep or discard a fragment based on depth (recall that we created our depth buffer in D3DApplicationBase). The state object created here enables depth testing, disables the stencil, and will choose pixels that are closer to the camera over pixels that are further away. There is little need to change this state, other than to enable the stencil.

```
context.InputAssembler.InputLayout = vertexLayout;
context.VertexShader.SetConstantBuffer(0, worldViewProjectionBuffer);
context.VertexShader.Set(vertexShader);
context.PixelShader.Set(pixelShader);
context.OutputMerger.DepthStencilState = depthStencilState;
```

Finally, we assign the input layout to the IA, add the constant buffer to the vertex shader stage, set the vertex shader and pixel shader programs, and set the OM depth stencil state.

> Note that when setting the constant buffer, we have used slot 0. This correlates with `register(b0)` in the shader code.

Render loop

The code within our `D3DApp.Run()` method first initializes our renderers, then sets up our initial camera position, sets up our view and projection matrices, and finally starts our rendering loop.

We have initialized a world matrix using an identity matrix which effectively means that we are not translating, rotating, or scaling any of the objects in this scene.

In Direct3D, the traditional coordinate system is left-handed, with the camera view looking down the Z+ axis with X+ to the right, and Y+ as up. The view matrix is created with the camera position and where it is looking at and which direction is up. Here, we are placing the camera slightly up, to the right, and behind the origin to give us a better view of the scene.

```
var cameraPosition = new Vector3(1, 1, -2);
var cameraTarget = Vector3.Zero; // Looking at the origin 0,0,0
var cameraUp = Vector3.UnitY; // Y+ is Up
var viewMatrix = Matrix.LookAtLH(cameraPosition, cameraTarget,
cameraUp);
```

> Although we have used a left-handed coordinate system in this recipe, we will move to using a right-handed coordinate system in all subsequent chapters.

The projection matrix is created using the desired field-of-view angle, aspect ratio, and the near and far Z-planes. This matrix gives us our perspective.

```
// FoV 60degrees = Pi/3 radians
var projectionMatrix = Matrix.PerspectiveFovLH((float)Math.PI / 3f,
Width / (float)Height, 0.5f, 100f);
```

Combining the view and projection matrices, we get the **view frustum**—a region of space that defines what is visible through the camera. The process of excluding objects that do not lie within this space is called **frustum culling**. This region is roughly the shape of a pyramid on its side, with its top cut off as shown in the following figure. In this figure, everything between the Z-planes 1 (our 0.5f near plane) and 2 (our 100f far plane), and within the bounds of the pyramid, will appear on the screen.

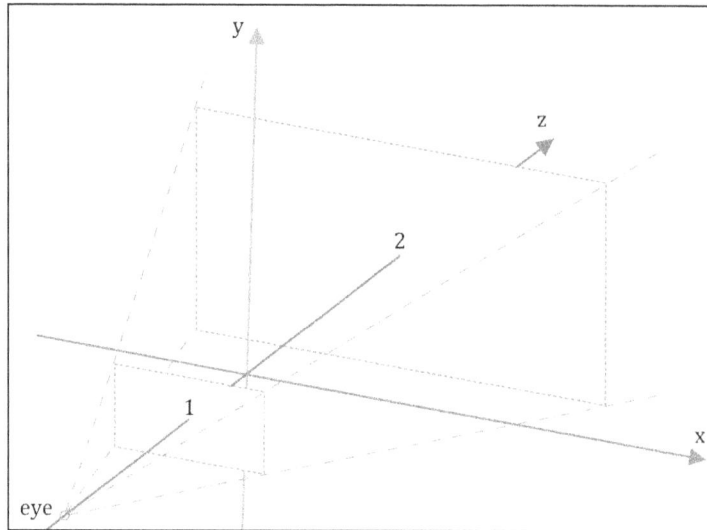

A view frustum for a view from the left-hand side

Other than our rendering commands, the render loop does two additional operations to the render loops of *Chapter 1, Getting Started with Direct3D*. We first cleared the depth/stencil view, which resets our depth buffer. This is important to do or we will have depth bleeding between frames.

Then after creating the WVP matrix, we updated the WVP matrix constant buffer with a call to `DeviceContext.UpdateSubresource`. HLSL, by default, expects the matrix to be in column-major order. Therefore, we must first transpose our SharpDX row major WVP matrix (write the rows of the matrix as the columns).

Renderers

The IA input layout that we defined requires that the vertices are two 4-component floats making up 32 bytes. The first 16 bytes represent the object-space position, and the second 16 bytes represent the vertex color.

When creating the **vertex buffer**, any structure can be used to represent the vertex as long as its memory layout matches the input layout. We have used an array of `Vector4` instances in this example; however, this could, just as easily, have been a new structure with two `Vector4` members or an array of floats. In this code, every second `Vector4` represents the color of the vertex (RGBA).

> Coordinates of the vertices in the vertex buffer are in the **object space** or **model space**, and they are usually created around the origin point.

The axis lines in the `AxisLinesRenderer` class are made up of 18 vertices to draw the lines and arrow shapes for the axes. We create the buffer like any other `Buffer` object but with a binding of `BindFlags.VertexBuffer`. Then, we create a `VertexBufferBinding`, passing the size of a single element as the stride and `0` as the offset.

```
buffer=Buffer.Create(device, BindFlags.VertexBuffer, new[] {...});
binding = new VertexBufferBinding(buffer, Utilities.SizeOf<Vector4>()
* 2, 0);
```

Before issuing the draw command for the axis lines, first we must tell the IA that the vertex buffer represents a list of lines by setting the `context.InputAssembler.PrimitiveTopology` to `PrimitiveTopology.LineList`. Then, we set the vertex buffers of the IA, and issue the `DeviceContext` draw command for 18 vertices—starting at the first vertex with a call to `context.Draw(18, 0)`.

> The axis-lines could be added to any scene during development to assist with the orientation.

The `TriangleRenderer` class is made in exactly the same way except that we need three vertices to render an object, and when drawing, we must set `PrimitiveTopology` to `PrimitiveTopology.TriangleList`. The `context.Draw` command passes three vertices.

The Input Assembler will automatically ignore malformed primitives, that is, lines require a start and end point. If an odd number of vertices was provided in the vertex buffer, the last vertex will be discarded. This applies to all vertex buffers.

The `QuadRenderer` class does not represent a quad primitive type (there is no such primitive). Instead, we create two triangles for the halves of the quad. This is done exactly the same as the triangle example, but, with two triangles. All complex shapes are made up of multiple triangles in a similar fashion.

Rather than creating duplicate vertices for the two points where the triangles align along their hypotenuse, we will use an index buffer. This allows us to reduce the number of vertices sent to the IA by reusing the same vertices by index—if we used an index buffer for the axis lines, we would have used 12 vertices instead of 18. Although this isn't entirely necessary for our examples, larger meshes will quickly see a reduction in the memory bandwidth used.

```
// v0      v1
// |-----|
// | \ A |
// | B \ |
// |-----|
// v3      v2
quadIndices = ToDispose(Buffer.Create(device, BindFlags.IndexBuffer,
new ushort[] {
    0, 1, 2, // A
    2, 3, 0  // B
}));
```

Here, we have four vertices in the vertex buffer. To build triangle *A*, we will use the indexes 0, 1, and 2; and to build triangle *B*, we will use the indexes 2, 3, and 0.

By default, a clockwise vertex direction will define the front face of a primitive (for example, from our camera position) drawing a triangle from top-left to right to bottom-right and then back to top-left will mean that the back face is away from the camera. Rotating the scene by 180 degrees using the arrow keys will show that the shape no longer renders because of **back-face culling**. Try reversing the vertex direction to see what happens. We can override the default direction by assigning a `RasterizerState` object to the `context.Rasterizer.State` property, where the `RasterizerStateDescription.IsFrontCounterClockwise` property can be set to `true` or `false`, as appropriate.

When we draw the triangle list for the quad, we must set an index buffer and a vertex buffer. Indices can be defined using 16 or 32 bits. In this example, we have used an unsigned short (16-bit). So we must use a format of `Format.R16_Uint` when setting the index buffer.

To let the pipeline know that we are using the index buffer, we must call the `DrawIndexed` method rather than `Draw`. Notice that although we only defined four vertices, we have asked it to draw six (the number of indices).

```
context.DrawIndexed(6, 0, 0);
```

There's more...

You may have noticed that the actual pixel colors have been interpolated between the vertices, that is, if vertex (*A*) of a line is red (1, 0, 0, 1) and vertex (*B*) is green (0, 1, 0, 1), all the pixels in between have been linearly interpolated between those two values by the rasterizer stage (remember that the rasterizer stage is immediately before the pixel shader). Half-way along the line, the value of the pixel will be `0.5`, `0.5`, `0`, and `1`. This applies to all the per-vertex attributes except the vertex position.

It is possible to control the interpolation method for individual vertex `struct` fields within HLSL by prefixing with one of the following interpolation modifiers:

- `linear`: This is the default mode of interpolation if no modifier is provided.

- `centroid`: This method may improve antialiasing if a pixel is partially covered, and it must be combined with `linear` or `noperspective`.

- `nointerpolation`: This method tells the rasterizer to perform no interpolation, instead using the value of the closest vertex. This is the only valid option for the `int/uint` types in a vertex.

- `noperspective`: This method causes the rasterizer to not perform perspective correction during interpolation.

- `sample`: This method interpolates per sample location rather than per pixel center (which is generally used in conjunction with antialiasing to change the behavior). It may be useful to combine this with the `SV_SampleIndex` pixel shader input semantic.

An example of this in HLSL is as follows:

```
struct VertexShaderOutput { ...
    nointerpolation float4 Color: COLOR; }
```

There are a number of additional primitive types that we didn't use. These include: `PointList`, `LineListWithAdjacency`, `LineStrip`, `TriangleListWithAdjacency`, `TriangleStrip`, and `PatchListWith1ControlPoints` through to `PatchListWith32ControlPoints`. The patch list topologies are used with the tessellation stages.

See also

▸ We will be rendering more complex objects in the recipes *Rendering a cube and sphere* and *Loading a static mesh from a file* in *Chapter 3, Rendering Meshes*

▸ We will cover how to use the patch topologies in the recipe *Tessellation of primitives* in *Chapter 5, Applying Hardware Tessellation*

▸ We use a triangle-strip in *Chapter 10, Implementing Deferred Rendering*, for implementing a screen-aligned quad renderer

Applying multisample anti-aliasing

In this recipe, we will enable **multisample antialiasing** (**MSAA**) to smoothen lines and edges.

Getting ready

We can apply this recipe to any of our recipes that are implemented with a class that descends from D3DApplicationBase. Otherwise, this can be easily adapted to work with the creation of any swap chain.

How to do it...

We can smooth the lines in our example by enabling multisampling:

1. To do this, simply override the D3DApplicationBase.
   CreateSwapChainDescription() method in our class as follows:

   ```
   protected override SwapChainDescription1
   CreateSwapChainDescription()
   {
       var description = base.CreateSwapChainDescription();
       description.SampleDescription.Count = 4;
       description.SampleDescription.Quality = 0;
       return description;
   }
   ```

2. Compile and run the project (*F5*), and you will now have antialiased edges.

How it works...

The following screenshot compares the difference between having antialiasing off and on—notice the jaggies along the bottom of the triangle are not there in the right-hand side image.

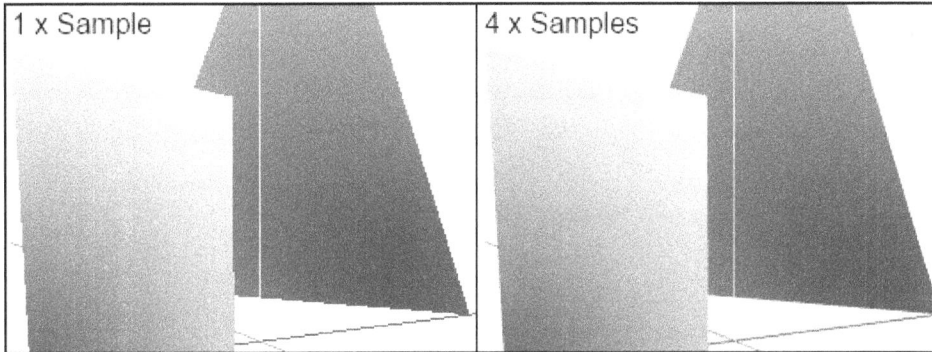

No antialiasing on the left and 4x multisampling on the right

It is important to note that all depth/stencil and render targets must use the same `SampleDescription` structure.

See also

▸ The *Incorporating multisample antialiasing* recipe in *Chapter 10, Implementing Deferred Rendering*, that covers some additional advanced topics for using MSAA textures where multisampling would otherwise be unavailable.

Implementing texture sampling

In this recipe we are going to take the quad and triangle renderers from the previous example and apply some texture using a **shader resource view** (**SRV**), a sampler state object, and changes to the shader program.

The final output from the example will look something like the following figure:

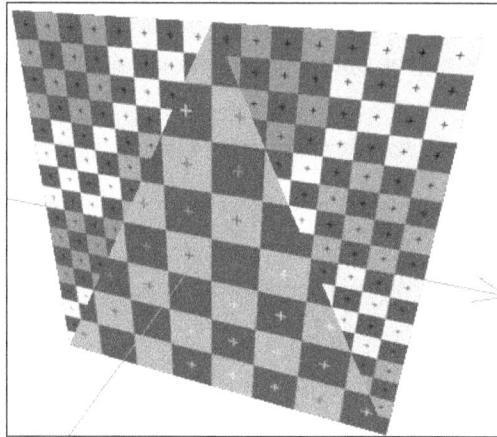

Textured triangle and quad

Getting ready

For this recipe, we will continue from where we left of in the *Rendering primitives* recipe.

There are two texture files included with the sample code that you will also need. Alternatively, you may use any BMP, JPG, PNG, or even DDS formats. For reference, the two textures used in this project are shown in the following figure:

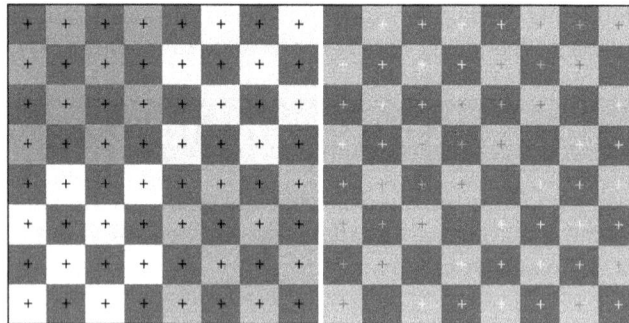

The two 256x256 textures used in this recipe

How to do it...

For this recipe, we will first change the HLSL shader code to accept the SRV and sampler state. Then, we will update our renderers to use texture coordinates, load the textures, and bind the SRVs to the appropriate stages of the pipeline. To do so, follow the given steps:

1. Add the two texture files, `Texture.png` and `Texture2.png`, to the project. Then, select **Copy if newer** as the **Copy to Output** value in the **Properties** window.

2. Add the following global variables to `Simple.hlsl`:

   ```
   // Globals for texture sampling
   Texture2D ShaderTexture : register(t0);
   SamplerState Sampler : register(s0);
   ```

3. Modify `Simple.hlsl` so that the vertex structures look like the following code snippet:

   ```
   struct VertexShaderInput {
       float4 Position : SV_Position;
       float2 TextureUV : TEXCOORD0;
   };
   struct VertexShaderOutput {
       float4 Position : SV_Position;
       float2 TextureUV : TEXCOORD0;
   };
   ```

4. Change the `VSMain` HLSL function so that it passes through a `TextureUV` property rather than `Color`.

   ```
   output.TextureUV = input.TextureUV;
   ```

5. Replace the content of the `PSMain` function so that it samples the texture as shown in the following code:

   ```
   // Sample the pixel color using the sampler and texture
   // using the input texture coordinate
   return ShaderTexture.Sample(Sampler, input.TextureUV);
   ```

6. Within our Direct3D application class (D3DApp), change the vertex layout initialization to include the texture coordinate:

```
vertexLayout = ToDispose(new InputLayout(device,
    ShaderSignature.GetInputSignature(vertexShaderBytecode),
new[] {
// input semantic SV_Position=vertex coord in object space
new InputElement("SV_Position",0,Format.R32G32B32A32_Float, 0, 0),
// input semantic TEXTCOORD = vertex texture coordinate
new InputElement("TEXCOORD", 0, Format.R32G32_Float, 16, 0)
}));
```

7. In each of the renderers, add the following private member fields:

```
// Shader texture resource
ShaderResourceView textureView;
// Control sampling behavior with this state
SamplerState samplerState;
```

8. And then, initialize member fields within the CreateDeviceDependentResources method, changing Texture.png to Texture2.png in the TriangleRenderer class.

```
// Load texture
textureView = ToDispose(
ShaderResourceView.FromFile(device, "Texture.png"));

// Create our sampler state
samplerState = ToDispose(
new SamplerState(device, new SamplerStateDescription() {
    AddressU = TextureAddressMode.Wrap,
    AddressV = TextureAddressMode.Wrap,
    AddressW = TextureAddressMode.Wrap,
    Filter = Filter.MinMagMipLinear,
}));
```

9. Within the DoRender method of each primitive renderer, add the following code:

```
// Set the shader resource
context.PixelShader.SetShaderResource(0, textureView);
// Set the sampler state
context.PixelShader.SetSampler(0, samplerState);
```

10. In `AxisLinesRenderer.cs`, change the vertex buffer creation so that each of the `Vector4` vertex positions are only an array of floats. Then, replace the color with a texture coordinate as shown here:

```
axisLinesVertices = ToDispose(Buffer.Create(device,
  BindFlags.VertexBuffer, new[] {
/* Vertex Position        Texture UV */
                          // ~45x10
-1f, 0f, 0f, 1f,          0.1757f, 0.039f,// - x-axis
1f, 0f, 0f, 1f,           0.1757f, 0.039f,// + x-axis
// SNIP...                // ~135x35
0f, -1f, 0f, 1f,          0.5273f, 0.136f,// - y-axis
// SNIP...                // ~220x250
0f, 0f, -1f, 1f,          0.859f, 0.976f, // - z-axis
// SNIP...
}));
axisLinesBinding = new VertexBufferBinding(axisLinesVertices,
  Utilities.SizeOf<float>() * 6, 0);
```

11. Within `TriangleRenderer.cs`, change the vertex buffer creation to use the following vertices (be sure to also update the `VertexBufferBinding` method).

```
/*  Vertex Position              Vertex UV */
0.75f, -0.75f, -0.001f, 1.0f,    1.0f, 1.0f, // Base-right
-0.75f, -0.75f, -0.001f, 1.0f,   0.0f, 1.0f, // Base-left
0.0f, 0.75f, -0.001f, 1.0f,      0.5f, 0.0f, // Apex
```

12. Within `QuadRenderer.cs`, change the vertex buffer creation as follows:

```
/*  Vertex Position         texture UV */
-0.75f, 0.75f, 0f, 1.0f,    0.0f, 0.0f, // Top-left
0.75f, 0.75f, 0f, 1.0f,     2.0f, 0.0f, // Top-right
0.75f, -0.75f, 0f, 1.0f,    2.0f, 2.0f, // Base-right
-0.75f, -0.75f, 0f, 1.0f,   0.0f, 2.0f, // Base-left
```

13. Compile and run (*F5*) your project. You should see the figure shown at the beginning of this recipe.

> If it looks like you are missing vertices or the primitives are drawing incorrectly, you may have specified the incorrect size when creating the vertex buffer binding. Make sure that it reads `Utilities.SizeOf<float>() * 6` noting that we are using `float` (not `Vector4`) and there are six of them per vertex.

How it works...

First, we will update our HLSL to include two global variables for storing the SRV and the sampler state we created in our renderers. Next, we will update our shader to accept a texture **UV coordinate** as input rather than a color (`float2 TextureUV : TEXCOORD0;`).

> Texels, in a 2D texture, are addressed using the x and y axes. However, as these names are already used in 3D space, we refer to them as UV coordinates instead. UV coordinates are normalized, where the upper left corner is 0(U),0(V) and the bottom right corner is 1(U),1(V). Therefore, the UV coordinate for the pixel located at 100, 150 within a 200 x 200 texture would be 0.5(U), 0.75(V) (that is, 100/200, 150/200). There is also a third component, W (z axis) that can be used to address 3D textures or volume textures and cube maps. Therefore, the full term is therefore a **UVW coordinate**, however, we generally use a 2D texture and drop the W.

The vertex shader now passes through an unchanged UV coordinate. The pixel shader then determines the color by sampling from the `ShaderTexture` global variable provided by the SRV by using the sampler state and interpolated vertex UV coordinate.

Since we changed the structure of the vertex, we must also update the input layout for the IA so that it is now expecting four floats for the vertex position and two floats for the UV.

In each of the renderers, we are loading a SRV directly from the texture file using `ShaderResourceView.FromFile`. Internally this creates a `Texture2D` resource and returns a SRV so that it can be bound to the pipeline.

> `ShaderResourceView.FromFile` is unavailable for the Windows Store apps, *Chapter 11*, *Integrating Direct3D with XAML and Windows 8.1*, covers how to replace this method in the recipe *Loading and compiling resources asynchronously*.

The `SamplerState` global variable that we create controls how the sampling in the pixel shader determines the correct coordinate and which filter method to use. The `AddressU/V/W` properties of the description control how to handle values outside of the 0.0 - 1.0 UVW range. For example, whereas `TextureAddressMode.Wrap` repeats the texture, using `TextureAddressMode.Clamp` will make anything outside the range appear smeared (clamping to zero or one)—try clamping the quad renderer to see this effect.

The `Filter` property of the sampler state description controls which texels will be used and how they are combined to generate the final pixel. Here, we have used `Filter.MinMagMipLinear`, which provides a better quality result than the default `Filter.MinMagMipPoint` value. The sampler will now use linear interpolation when minifying, when magnifying, and for mid-level sampling. Zooming in and out will show the effect of the filtering method used. Try changing the triangle or quad back to the default and see the contrast in quality. Also, try doing this with other filter values.

To make the SRV and sampler state available to the pixel shader, we have bound them with a call to `PixelShader.SetShaderResource` and `PixelShader.SetSampler` within `DoRender` of each renderer. We have specified slot 0 for both of these functions which correlate to `register(t0)` and `register(s0)` within the shader for the texture and sampler state respectively.

Next, we have defined our new vertex buffers. These buffers are now represented by an array of six floats for each vertex. The axis lines are sampling single texels for each line that approximates the original colors used (red/green/blue). The triangle is sampling within the bounds of the texture (between zero and one) to select the entire width of the texture at the base and the top-center of the texture at the apex. The quad is addressing twice the width and height of the texture (between zero and two) that combined with the `TextureAddressMode.Wrap` value that is repeating the texture four times within the surface.

> To address z-fighting/flimmering, the triangle has been brought forward by a tiny amount. To see the effects of these depth artifacts, try setting the z coordinate value back to zero.

See also

- See *Chapter 3, Rendering Meshes*, and *Chapter 4, Animating Meshes with Vertex Skinning*, for more examples of texture sampling and a discussion on UV unwrapping
- The recipe *Loading and compiling resources asynchronously* in *Chapter 11, Integrating Direct3D with XAML and Windows 8.1*, demonstrates how to load images into an SRV for Windows Store apps

3
Rendering Meshes

In this chapter, we will cover the following topics:

- ▸ Rendering a cube and sphere
- ▸ Preparing the vertex and constant buffers for materials and lighting
- ▸ Adding material and lighting
- ▸ Using a right-handed coordinate system
- ▸ Loading a static mesh from a file

Introduction

A mesh is technically just a vertex and index buffer that represents a 3D object, and if we look at what we have already covered, we can easily understand this. However, these objects nearly always require a number of additional properties, such as material (surface and lighting properties), textures, submeshes, bones, and animations. This is what Microsoft has done in the past with their `ID3DX10Mesh` interface; however, this is not available for Direct3D 11 (along with a number of other utility classes), and it is now recommended that you roll your own.

> There are other open source projects that provide the replacement functionality, part of which is used in the SharpDX Toolkit and part of which we will be using here. Most notable is the DirectX Tool Kit that is available at `https://directxtk.codeplex.com/`.

For our purpose, a mesh is the combination of submeshes, materials, object extent, bones, animations, and references to common assets such as textures and shaders. We will begin by working with these elements separately and then pulling them together within a mesh renderer.

With the addition of the graphics tools in Visual Studio 2012 and 2013, we now have the ability to compile shaders as part of our build, view, and edit image assets more efficiently and edit popular 3D model formats (OBJ, COLLADA, and Autodesk FBX) all within Visual Studio. There is also a new Shader Designer that allows us to design pixel shaders using **Visual Shader Graphs** that can be exported as HLSL source or as shader bytecode.

During this chapter, we will learn how to incorporate these tools with our C# Direct3D development, and learn how to load a static mesh from a Visual Studio **compiled mesh object** (**CMO**) file that has been compiled from one of the supported 3D model formats.

Rendering a cube and sphere

In this recipe, we will be rendering a simple cube and generating and rendering a sphere and a quad. We will explore the transformation of each of the objects within the 3D world space.

To prepare ourselves for materials and lighting, we will include a **normal vector** in our vertex structure. The normal vector is a vector that indicates what direction is perpendicular to a tangent on the surface of the object. For each fragment in the pixel shader, we can use the normal vector to determine the angles between the viewer, light source, and surface. This value is necessary so that we can calculate the impact of lighting.

Getting ready

For rendering our cube and sphere, we will first prepare ourselves by following the ensuing steps:

1. Begin by adding a new Direct3D project to our solution.

2. Prepare the new project for rendering as per the *Rendering primitives* recipe in *Chapter 2, Rendering with Direct3D*, remembering to add the necessary references and to add the build event to copy `D3DCompile*.DLL` to the output directory.

3. We will utilize the `GeometricPrimitives.cs` source file for generating our sphere. For this recipe, this file can be found in this book's code bundle, `Ch03_01CubeAndSphere`, provided on Packt's website.

How to do it...

First we will update the vertex layout to support a normal vector.

1. The **input layout** defined in `D3DApp.CreateDeviceDependentResources` needs to be changed to include the normal vector; change the format of the position to remove the fourth component (A32), and redefine the color to use a 4-component, 32-bit **unsigned normalized integer** (8 bits per component).

    ```
    vertexLayout = ToDispose(new InputLayout(device,
    ```

```
ShaderSignature.GetInputSignature(vertexShaderBytecode),
new[]
{
new InputElement("SV_Position",0,Format.R32G32B32_Float,0,0),
new InputElement("NORMAL", 0, Format.R32G32B32_Float, 12, 0),
new InputElement("COLOR", 0, Format.R8G8B8A8_UNorm, 24, 0),
}));
```

A float (`Format.*_Float`) and signed/unsigned normalized integer (`Format.*_SNorm`/`Format.*_UNorm`) format will resolve to a vector of floating-point values within the shader, whereas a signed/unsigned integer (`Format.*_SInt`/`Format.*_UInt`) will resolve to a vector of integers.

The vertex position (`SV_Position`) is a special case that will always resolve to a `float4` variable within the shader, even if only three floats are specified. The fourth float component (`Position.w`) will be automatically set to `1.0`. The legacy vertex `Position` semantic is still supported and is what the Visual Studio `.DGSL` file uses when producing shader code.

2. Rather than using an array of floats for our vertices, we will create `struct` for the vertex structure. This makes it easier to update the vertex structure and provides us with more flexibility. Add a new class file to the project and call it `Vertex.cs`. Add the following code to this file:

```
using System.Runtime.InteropServices;
using SharpDX;

[StructLayout(LayoutKind.Sequential, Pack = 1)]
public struct Vertex
{
    public Vector3 Position;
    public Vector3 Normal;
    public Color Color;

    // Constructor taking position, normal and color
    public Vertex(Vector3 position, Vector3 normal, Color color)
    {
        Position = position;
        Normal = normal;
        Color = color;
    }
    // Snip: additional constructors here
}
```

3. For convenience, we will create a couple of constructors. The first of these takes position and color as the input and uses the normalized vertex position as the normal vector—this works well for geometric meshes that are built around the origin (`Vector3.Zero`). The second one takes only a position and defaults the color using `Color.White`.

```
public Vertex(Vector3 position, Color color)
    : this(position, Vector3.Normalize(position), color)
{ }
public Vertex(Vector3 position)
    : this(position, Color.White)
{ }
...
```

We can now create our updated renderers.

4. The quad will represent a flat platform with the normal vectors pointing straight up the y axis. Open the `QuadRenderer.cs` file and make the following changes:

    ❑   Replace the vertices in `CreateDeviceDependentResources` and don't forget to set the size of the vertex binding to the size of our `Vertex` structure.

```
var color = Color.LightGray;
quadVertices = ToDispose(Buffer.Create(device, BindFlags.
VertexBuffer, new Vertex[] {
    /*  Position: float x 3, Normal: Vector3, Color */
    new Vertex(-0.5f, 0f, -0.5f, Vector3.UnitY, Color),
    new Vertex(-0.5f, 0f, 0.5f, Vector3.UnitY, color),
    new Vertex(0.5f, 0f, 0.5f, Vector3.UnitY, color),
    new Vertex(0.5f, 0f, -0.5f, Vector3.UnitY, color),
}));
quadBinding = new VertexBufferBinding(quadVertices, Utilities.
SizeOf<Vertex>(), 0);
```

The creation of the index buffer and the rendering commands do not change.

At this point, you should be able to compile and run the project (*F5*) to see the updated light gray quad.

> Although the shader used at this point does not support our `Normal` input semantic, the `SV_Position` and `COLOR` input semantics will be matched. The IA will simply ignore the `Normal` component of our input layout.

5. Next, we will create our cube renderer. Create a new renderer class, `CubeRenderer`. Add the appropriate SharpDX using directives and descend from `Common.RendererBase`.

6. Override `CreateDeviceDependentResources` and create the vertex buffer. Remember to create private member fields as appropriate and also to remove and dispose the buffers.

```
vertexBuffer = ToDispose(Buffer.Create(device, BindFlags.
VertexBuffer, new Vertex[] {
        /*  Vertex Position      Color */
new Vertex(-0.5f, 0.5f, -0.5f, Color.Gray), // 0-Top-left
new Vertex(0.5f, 0.5f, -0.5f,  Color.Gray), // 1-Top-right
new Vertex(0.5f, -0.5f, -0.5f, Color.Gray), // 2-Base-right
new Vertex(-0.5f, -0.5f, -0.5f,Color.Gray), // 3-Base-left

new Vertex(-0.5f, 0.5f, 0.5f,  Color.Gray), // 4-Topleft
new Vertex(0.5f, 0.5f, 0.5f,   Color.Gray), // 5-Top-right
new Vertex(0.5f, -0.5f, 0.5f,  Color.Gray), // 6-Base-right
new Vertex(-0.5f, -0.5f, 0.5f, Color.Gray), // 7-Base-left
}));
vertexBinding = new VertexBufferBinding(vertexBuffer, Utilities.
SizeOf<Vertex>(), 0);
```

> Note that the normal vector will be generated from the normalized position in our vertex constructor, for example, *-0.5, 0.5, -0.5 becomes -0.57735, 0.57735, -0.57735.*

7. After creating the vertex buffer, we need to create the index buffer and define all our triangles (front in this context is the –z axis, right is +x axis, and so on).

```
// Front      Right      Top       Back       Left       Bottom
// v0     v1 v1     v5 v1     v0 v5     v4 v4     v0 v3     v2
// |-----|    |-----|    |-----|    |-----|    |-----|    |-----|
// | \ A |    | \ A |    | \ A |    | \ A |    | \ A |    | \ A |
// | B \ |    | B \ |    | B \ |    | B \ |    | B \ |    | B \ |
// |-----|    |-----|    |-----|    |-----|    |-----|    |-----|
// v3     v2 v2     v6 v5     v4 v6     v7 v7     v3 v7     v6
indexBuffer = ToDispose(Buffer.Create(device, BindFlags.
IndexBuffer, new ushort[] {
    0, 1, 2, // Front A
    0, 2, 3, // Front B
    1, 5, 6, // Right A
    1, 6, 2, // Right B
    1, 0, 4, // Top A
```

```
        1, 4, 5, // Top B
        5, 4, 7, // Back A
        5, 7, 6, // Back B
        4, 0, 3, // Left A
        4, 3, 7, // Left B
        3, 2, 6, // Bottom A
        3, 6, 7, // Bottom B
}));
```

8. Finally, we implement `DoRender` in exactly the same way as for the `QuadRenderer` class, except here we're using `36` for the `DrawIndexed` method call to draw our vertices and use the `vertexBinding` and `indexBuffer` member fields.

9. Back in `D3DApp.cs`, we can now create and initialize our `CubeRenderer` instance and call it's `Render` method within the render loop (the same location where the quad is created and then rendered).

```
// Create and initialize cube
var cube = ToDispose(new CubeRenderer());
cube.Initialize(this);
...
// Render cube
cube.Render();
```

Now let's create our sphere renderer.

10. First, copy the `GeometricPrimitives.cs` source file from the downloaded code to your project—be sure to change the namespace as appropriate. This contains the `GeometricPrimitives` static class with a `GenerateSphere` method that will generate the vertices and indices for our sphere with the provided radius. This is based on a port of the DirectX Tool Kit C++ code.

11. Create a new renderer class: `SphereRenderer.cs`. Add the appropriate SharpDX using directives and descend from the `Common.RendererBase` abstract class.

12. Override the `CreateDeviceDependentResources` method and create the vertex and index buffer using the following code. Create the private member fields as appropriate and also remember to call `RemoveAndDispose` to release the buffers first.

```
Vertex[] vertices;
int[] indices;
// Generate vertices and indices
GeometricPrimitives.GenerateSphere(out vertices, out indices,
Color.Gray);

// Create vertex buffer
```

```
vertexBuffer = ToDispose(Buffer.Create(device, BindFlags.
VertexBuffer, vertices));
// Create vertex binding
vertexBinding = new VertexBufferBinding(vertexBuffer, Utilities.
SizeOf<Vertex>(), 0);

// Create index buffer
indexBuffer = ToDispose(Buffer.Create(device, BindFlags.
IndexBuffer, indices));
totalVertexCount = indices.Length;
```

13. The `DoRender` method is similar to the cube rendering code, except that we pass `totalVertexCount` into `DrawIndexed`.

14. Finally, back in `D3DApp`, create an instance of the sphere renderer and call its `Render` method as per the cube.

    Running the project at this point will show just the cube. This is because the quad and sphere are hidden inside the cube. To rectify this, we will create a matrix in `D3DApp.Run` for each of our 3D objects to translate them from the local model space to world space.

15. Where we initialize the renderers, add the following matrix definitions:

```
// Scale to 5x and translate the quad on Y axis by -0.5
quad.World = Matrix.Scaling(5f);
quad.World.TranslationVector = new Vector3(0, -0.5f, 0);
// Move the cube along the X axis by -1
cube.World = Matrix.Translation(-1, 0, 0);
// Move the sphere along the Z axis by 1.1f
sphere.World = Matrix.Translation(0, 0, 1.1f)
```

16. We need to change the `worldViewProjection` calculation immediately before the `quad.Render()` call with the following code:

```
var worldViewProjection = quad.World * worldMatrix *
viewProjection;
```

17. Immediately before the `cube.Render()` call, we add the following code:

```
worldViewProjection = cube.World*worldMatrix*viewProjection;
worldViewProjection.Transpose();
context.UpdateSubresource(ref worldViewProjection,
worldViewProjectionBuffer);
```

18. And finally, before the `sphere.Render()` call, we add the same code as for the cube with the exception of using `sphere.World` in this case.

Now the quad, cube, and sphere will be visible with the quad being 5 times larger than normal.

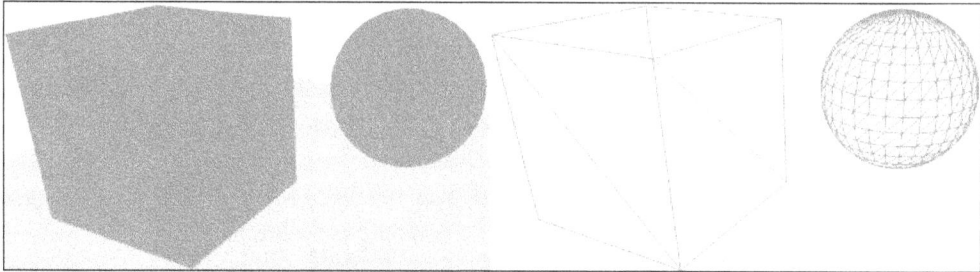

Scene after applying individual world translations – solid and wireframe

How it works...

The rendering of the cube and sphere is working in the same way as when we were rendering primitives in the previous chapter. By combining a number of triangles together, we have created our 3D mesh. However, we are now using a structure for the vertices.

By using a vertex structure, we now have more flexibility with what information can be included with the vertex rather than relying on an array of floats. It is important that we mark the structure using `LayoutKind.Sequential` and ensure that the data is packed correctly so that it exactly matches the input layout definition.

> By aligning the vertex buffer to 32 bytes, you may be able to slightly improve the performance. In the example presented here, we would need to add another 32-bit element (that is, 4 bytes) such as `Format.R8G8B8A8_UNorm` as padding to both the input layout and the C# vertex structure.

We are now using a world matrix for each individual 3D object. As we already know, rather than changing the vertices in each mesh and recreating the vertex buffers, we use local object coordinates in the vertex buffer and then transform these in the vertex shader using the WVP matrix. This means that we need to keep track of a world matrix for each individual object or the hierarchy of objects so that we can continue to draw them in the correct position/rotation/scale.

> Try changing the scale of the sphere with the following code, and set the rasterizer state to wireframe (`F-key` in the sample code) to see the impact upon the mesh:
> ```
> sphere.World.ScaleVector = new Vector3(1, 0.5f, 1);
> ```

You may have noticed that although we updated the input layout in our C# code, we have not yet changed the HLSL shader code to reflect this. When the input layout is being created, it will match the layout to the vertex shader's input signature. If any semantics are missing in the input signature, they will simply be ignored. This does not work in the other direction. Any semantics defined in the vertex shader's input signature must also be defined in our input layout; otherwise, we will receive a **The parameter is incorrect** error message.

There's more...

As we already know, data within constant buffers should be grouped by its update frequency. As the `View/Projection` matrix is only updated once per frame, an improvement upon our implementation would be to store the `View/Projection` matrix within the `PerFrame` constant buffer. The `World` matrix would remain within the `PerObject` constant buffer and then the calculation of the final `World/View/Projection` matrix would be performed within the vertex shader (for example, `float4x4 wvp = mul(World, ViewProjection);`). This would reduce the amount of data being sent to the constant buffer per object.

Preparing the vertex and constant buffers for materials and lighting

In this recipe, we will update the vertex and pixel shader structures and our constant buffers to provide additional information that our vertex shader and pixel shader need to be able to perform material and lighting operations.

After extending our per object constant buffer to support the transformation of the normal vector and position into world space, we will also add a per frame constant buffer that will contain our camera position and light configuration. How to create C# structures that reflect the HLSL constant buffers is also covered.

Our vertex shader input structure will be changed to accept the normal vector and UV coordinates from the previous recipe, and then update the pixel shader input structure to receive the normal vector transformed to world space in addition to the world space position and the UV coordinates.

As our shaders are becoming more complex, we will split them into multiple files; to support this, we will use the HLSL `#include` directive. We will implement a simple shader that outputs the depth to the red channel to demonstrate how to re-use this code.

Getting ready

We'll continue from where we left off the last recipe, *Rendering a cube and sphere*.

We will use the static class `Common.HLSLCompiler` from the sample rendering framework that wraps the Direct3D HLSL compiler and supports the use of an HLSL include handler.

How to do it...

We will reimplement our shaders, adding support for the normal vector in the vertex buffer and extend our constant buffers. We will then split our shader code across multiple files; this will make it easier to create pixel shaders for different shading techniques.

1. First right-click on the project in the Solution Explorer and select **New Folder** in **Add** and name it `Shaders`. Now create four new text files in this folder named `Common.hlsl`, `VS.hlsl`, `SimplePS.hlsl`, and `DepthPS.hlsl`. Remember to change the text encoding to **ANSI** and to select **Copy if newer** as described in *Chapter 2, Rendering with Direct3D*.

2. With `Common.hlsl` opened, we will add our new vertex shader structure, adding the new property `TextureUV`.

```
struct VertexShaderInput
{
    float4 Position : SV_Position;// Position
    float3 Normal : NORMAL;        // Normal - for lighting
    float4 Color : COLOR0;         // Vertex color
    float2 TextureUV: TEXCOORD;   // Texture UV coordinate
};
```

3. Also add the new pixel shader input structure along with a new property for the UV coordinate:

```
struct PixelShaderInput
{
    float4 Position : SV_Position;
    // Interpolation of vertex * material diffuse
    float4 Diffuse : COLOR;
    // Interpolation of vertex UV texture coordinate
    float2 TextureUV: TEXCOORD;

    // We need the World Position and normal for lighting
    float3 WorldNormal : NORMAL;
    float3 WorldPosition : WORLDPOS;
};
```

4. We will extend upon our previous per object constant buffer, adding the `World` and `WorldInverseTranspose` matrices.

```
// Constant buffer to be updated by application per object
cbuffer PerObject : register(b0)
{
    // WorldViewProjection matrix
    float4x4 WorldViewProjection;

    // We need the world matrix so that we can
    // calculate the lighting in world space
    float4x4 World;

    // Inverse transpose of world, used for
    // bringing normals into world space, especially
    // necessary where non-uniform scaling has been applied
    float4x4 WorldInverseTranspose;
};
```

5. And finally, we will add a new per frame constant buffer. This will be updated to include additional per frame information, such as lighting; however, for now this will contain the camera position only. Note that this uses the constant buffer slot `b1`.

```
cbuffer PerFrame: register (b1)
{
    float3 CameraPosition;
};
```

6. We will now code our new vertex shader in `VS.hlsl`. To reference the `Common.hlsl` class, add the HLSL include directive.

```
#include "Common.hlsl"
```

7. Then insert our new `VSMain` implementation.

```
PixelShaderInput VSMain(VertexShaderInput vertex)
{
    PixelShaderInput result = (PixelShaderInput)0;
    // Apply WVP matrix transformation
    result.Position = mul(vertex.Position,
        WorldViewProjection);
    result.Diffuse = vertex.Color;
    result.TextureUV = vertex.TextureUV;

    // transform normal to world space
```

```
result.WorldNormal = mul(vertex.Normal,
    (float3x3)WorldInverseTranspose);
// transform input position to world
result.WorldPosition = mul(vertex.Position, World).xyz;
return result;
}
```

> As we are now making use of the `World` matrix, it makes more sense to split the `WorldViewProjection` matrix and place the `ViewProjection` part into the `PerFrame` constant buffer, saving on bandwidth. We would then calculate the value of `result.WorldPosition` first and then multiply this by the `ViewProjection` matrix to calculate the final `result.Position` matrix.
>
> For simplicity, our recipes will continue to keep the matrices grouped together.

8. Next, we add our simple pixel shader, as derived earlier, in `SimplePS.hlsl` with the following code:

```
#include "Common.hlsl"
// A simple Pixel Shader that simply passes through the
// interpolated color
float4 PSMain(PixelShaderInput pixel) : SV_Target
{
    return pixel.Diffuse;
}
```

9. To demonstrate the reuse of existing structures, we will implement a second pixel shader for visualizing the depth information in `DepthPS.hlsl`.

```
#include "Common.hlsl"
float4 PSMain(PixelShaderInput pixel) : SV_Target {
// Take the (Z / W) and use as color, this gives the depth.
// Items close to the near clip-plane will be darker than
// those near the far clip-plane. Note depth is non-linear
    float4 output = float4(pixel.Position.z, 0, 0, 1);
    return output;
}
```

> Play with different values for the near clip plane in the projection matrix in `D3DApp` to see how this impacts the depth buffer.

We now need to define the new C# structures in our application in order to update the constant buffers.

10. Update the `Vertex` structure in `Vertex.cs` to include the UV coordinate, and update the constructor(s) appropriately.

```
public struct Vertex {
...
public Color Color;
public Vector2 UV;
```

11. After updating the `Vertex` structure, we must also change our vertex input layout to include the UV coordinate. The following code snippet shows the necessary changes:

```
...
// "COLOR"
new InputElement("COLOR", 0, Format.R8G8B8A8_UNorm, 24, 0),
// "UV"
new InputElement("TEXCOORD", 0, Format.R32G32_Float,28, 0),
```

12. Create a new class file, `ConstantBuffers.cs`.

13. Add the following code using directives and make the class public and static. We will add each of the structures within the class.

```
using System.Runtime.InteropServices;
using SharpDX;
public static class ConstantBuffers
{
    // structures defined here
}
```

14. We will start by defining the `PerObject` structure as follows:

```
[StructLayout(LayoutKind.Sequential)]
public struct PerObject
{
    public Matrix WorldViewProjection;
    // World matrix to calculate lighting in world space
    public Matrix World;
    // Inverse transpose of World (for normals)
    public Matrix WorldInverseTranspose;
    // Transpose the matrices so that they are in column
    // major order for HLSL
    internal void Transpose()
    {
        this.World.Transpose();
        this.WorldInverseTranspose.Transpose();
        this.WorldViewProjection.Transpose();
    }
}
```

15. Next we will define our `PerFrame` structure; the structures must be of 16 bytes that are aligned and evenly divisible by 16, thus the extra `_padding0` property.

```
[StructLayout(LayoutKind.Sequential, Pack = 1)]
public struct PerFrame
{
    public SharpDX.Vector3 CameraPosition;
    float _padding0;
}
```

16. Within our `D3DApp` class, we must change the initialization of the shaders in `CreateDeviceDependentResources`; we must also update our code to use the constant buffer structures we just defined.

17. Before we can compile our shaders at runtime that use include directives, we must provide an implementation of the `ID3DInclude` interface to the HLSL compiler. Within the sample rendering framework, this is implemented within the class, `Common.HLSLFileIncludeHandler`. A static helper class `Common.HLSLCompiler` wraps this logic for us.

18. Let's now compile the new shaders using the `Common.HLSLCompiler.CompileFromFile` method; we also need to add a new private member field for the depth pixel shader. The following code snippet shows how to compile the depth shader using the `Common.HLSLCompiler` class:

```
// Compile and create the depth pixel shader
using (var bytecode = HLSLCompiler.CompileFromFile(
        @"Shaders\DepthPS.hlsl", "PSMain", "vs_5_0"))
  depthShader = ToDispose(
      new VertexShader(device, bytecode));
...
```

> The graphics debugger (*Alt + F5*) can be used to step through the vertex and pixel shaders using the HLSL debugger in Visual Studio 2013 (any edition) or non-express versions of Visual Studio 2012.

19. Lastly, we must create the new `Buffer` instances. Within `CreateDeviceDependentResources`, initialize the new buffers. This is done exactly as before, except here we pass the size of the appropriate structure.

```
perObjectBuffer = ToDispose(new
  SharpDX.Direct3D11.Buffer(device,
  Utilities.SizeOf<ConstantBuffers.PerObject>(),
  ResourceUsage.Default, BindFlags.ConstantBuffer,
  CpuAccessFlags.None, ResourceOptionFlags.None, 0));
```

```
perFrameBuffer = ToDispose(new Buffer(device,
    Utilities.SizeOf<ConstantBuffers.PerFrame>(),
    ResourceUsage.Default, BindFlags.ConstantBuffer,
    CpuAccessFlags.None, ResourceOptionFlags.None, 0));
```

20. In the same method, we bind them to the shaders (note that we now bind a buffer to the pixel shader as well).

```
// Set our vertex constant buffers
context.VertexShader.SetConstantBuffer(0, perObjectBuffer);
context.VertexShader.SetConstantBuffer(1, perFrameBuffer);
// Set our pixel constant buffers
context.PixelShader.SetConstantBuffer(1, perFrameBuffer);
```

21. Within our render loop, we can now change the value of the buffers to an instance of one of the structures we have defined. First is the `PerFrame` constant buffer.

```
// Extract camera position from view matrix
var camPosition = Matrix.Transpose(
    Matrix.Invert(viewMatrix)).Column4;
cameraPosition = new Vector3(
    camPosition.X, camPosition.Y, camPosition.Z);

// Update the per frame constant buffer
var perFrame = new ConstantBuffers.PerFrame();
perFrame.CameraPosition = cameraPosition;
context.UpdateSubresource(ref perFrame, perFrameBuffer);
```

22. Before each call to the renderer's `Render` method, change the code to use our `PerObject` structure. Here we show the code for the quad:

```
var perObject = new ConstantBuffers.PerObject();
perObject.World = quad.World * worldMatrix;
perObject.WorldInverseTranspose = Matrix.Transpose(Matrix.
Invert(perObject.World));
perObject.WorldViewProjection = perObject.World * viewProjection;
perObject.Transpose();
context.UpdateSubresource(ref perObject, perObjectBuffer);
```

23. Setting the depth pixel shader as the active pixel shader will result in the output as shown in the following screenshot. The completed example in the downloadable code bundle, provided with this book on Packt's website, binds `z-key` to toggle the depth shader.

The output of depth

How it works...

As the normal vector is a vector and not a point, when we are transforming it into world space using our matrix, we must be careful that we are performing either of the following:

  ▸ Either using 0 in the W component of a four-component vector when multiplying with the 4 x 4 matrix or multiplying a three-component vector with a 3 x 3 matrix (in our vertex shader here, we are casting our matrix to a `float3x3` variable)

  ▸ Multiply with the inverse transpose of the `World` matrix, especially when non-uniform scaling is involved (or always use uniform scaling)

This ensures that the normal vector is still pointing in the correct direction despite the affine transformations; for example, if the normal vector that points one unit up the y axis is translated by x1, y2, and z3, it is still pointing up the y axis. So, no matter where in the space the normal vector is, it is still pointing in the same direction.

> It is also important to keep track of whether a normal vector is normalized or not. Normalizing in a shader comes at a cost, and the normal vector that the pixel shader receives is not guaranteed to be normalized.

We have reorganized our shaders so that we can re-use the structures defined between multiple shaders. The example provided here is the use of the `SimplePS` and `DepthPS` pixel shaders, although we shall shortly see more examples using different lighting techniques.

The vertex shader now calculates a number of additional properties to pass to the pixel shader. The `WorldNormal` and `WorldPosition` properties of the pixel shader input are both important properties for determining the correct lighting. Although our pixel shaders do not yet make use of this information, we will be able to use the `PerFrame` constant buffer to retrieve the current camera's position to create the vector that points from the current `WorldPosition` to the camera (in world space).

As already discussed, in order to support non-uniform scaling, the normal must be transformed using the inverse transpose of the `World` matrix and excluding the homogeneous `W` component.

Using C# structures with HLSL constant buffers

In HLSL, data is packed into 4 bytes in such a way that it does not cross a 16-byte boundary. When creating our structures for use with a constant buffer, it is important that we take this memory layout into consideration.

For example, given a constant buffer with two `floats` and a `float3` variable, we must layout our structure in C# so that it matches the valid memory layout as shown in the following figure:.

An **incorrect** structure for this would be defined like this:

```
[StructLayout(LayoutKind.Sequential, Pack = 1)]
struct IncorrectStruct {
    public float a;
    public float b;
    public Vector3 c;
}
```

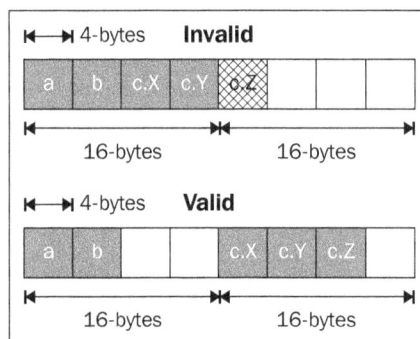

Invalid and valid memory layouts for the HLSL buffer

Two methods of defining the correct structure are using padding fields or explicitly defining the structure layout. It is important to note that the total size of the structure must be divisible by 16 bytes. Therefore, when using padding fields, you may actually need to use one of these methods at the end of the structure, as in `CorrectStructA` in the following code. The explicit layout requires the field offsets to be provided and that the size takes into consideration the 4 bytes at the end, as shown in `CorrectStructB`.

```
[StructLayout(LayoutKind.Sequential, Pack = 1)]
struct CorrectStructA {
    public float a;
    public float b;
    Vector2 _padding0;
    public Vector3 c;
    float _padding1;
}


[StructLayout(LayoutKind.Explicit, Size = 32)]
struct CorrectStructB {
    [FieldOffset(0)]
    public float a;
    [FieldOffset(4)]
    public float b;
    [FieldOffset(16)]
    public Vector3 c;
}
```

The problem with using the explicit layout is that it can be difficult to maintain and can easily go wrong; therefore, we have used the padding approach in our code. When trying to use an incorrect structure, you will have bleeding of values between fields; alternatively, in the case of an incorrect total size, you will receive a **The parameter is incorrect** error message when attempting to create the buffer.

It is also possible to control the packing within the HLSL structures themselves using the `packoffset` HLSL keyword.

See also

- ▶ Chapter 1, *Getting Started with Direct3D*, shows how to get started with the Visual Studio graphics debugger
- ▶ The following link provides more information on the why and how of the inverse transpose matrix for normal transformations: `http://www.arcsynthesis.org/gltut/Illumination/Tut09%20Normal%20Transformation.html`

- ▶ For more information on HLSL constant buffer packing rules, refer to the following link: `http://msdn.microsoft.com/en-us/library/windows/desktop/bb509632(v=vs.85).aspx`

- ▶ For more details on how to use the `packoffset` HLSL keyword, refer to the following link: `http://msdn.microsoft.com/en-us/library/windows/desktop/bb509581(v=vs.85).aspx`

Adding material and lighting

The most important properties for a mesh, other than the vertices themselves, are material and lighting. With the ability to specify the texture, color, and the way the surface behaves with lighting, we can generate much more realistic scenes.

In the previous recipe, we have already added two of the three input vectors needed for calculating the lighting:

- ▶ View direction (calculated from the camera's location)

- ▶ Surface normal

The final input vector is **light direction**. For this sample, we are going to create a simple directional light, that is, a light that has a constant direction anywhere in the scene (like the sun). We will define this light with a color and direction.

We also introduce the following material properties:

- ▶ **Ambient light color**: The ambient reflection is a constant ambient-lighting value. This is a simple, approximate representation of light that has bounced around a room and is lighting the back of the object, providing the **indirect light**. This value is not based on any of the three input vectors and will be provided by our material properties.

- ▶ **Diffuse reflection color**: Diffuse reflection is the reflection of light from a diffuse surface where the ray is reflected from the surface in random directions. In a 3D real-time rendering, we only approximate this light model. We will instead say that the light is reflected from the surface equally in all directions (*Luna 2012, p280*). This means that regardless of the viewer's angle, the amount of light reflected from a point on the surface is constant.

- ▶ **Material diffuse color**: This is multiplied with the vertex color within the vertex shader to give the final pixel-diffused color. The intensity of this value represents the amount of **direct light** that the light provides to the surface and is determined using the light direction and surface normal with Lambert's cosine law.

▶ **Specular reflection color and power (shininess of the surface)**: Specular reflection represents the amount of perfectly reflected light that bounces off the surface of an object. The material's specular color represents the color of this reflected light, and the specular power represents the exponent of the equation that determines how shiny the surface is (the higher the value, the shinier the surface, and therefore, the smaller the **specular highlight**). The specular amount is calculated using all three input vectors.

▶ **Emissive light color**: The emissive lighting value is a constant that represents the emitted light from the surface. This value is not based on any of the input vectors and is not affected by the light color. The value of this constant is controlled via the material properties.

From the three input vectors and the previous material properties, we determine the four lighting output components: the ambient reflection, diffuse reflection, specular reflection, and emissive lighting.

Getting ready

For this recipe, we need the vertices to include a normal vector and the supporting changes from the previous recipe.

The completed project can be found in the companion code as `Ch02_02MaterialAndLighting`.

How to do it...

The first thing we will do is make changes to `Shaders\Common.hlsl` to include a new per material constant buffer and add directional light to the per frame constant buffer to store the light's color and direction.

1. First add a new structure for the `directional light` class; this must be placed before the `PerFrame` structure.

```
// A simple directional light (e.g. the sun)
struct DirectionalLight
{
    float4 Color;
    float3 Direction;
};
```

2. Now we will update the `PerFrame` structure to include the light.

```
cbuffer PerFrame: register (b1)
{
    DirectionalLight Light;
    float3 CameraPosition;
};
```

3. Finally, we add a new constant buffer for the material properties (note that the slot number used is 2).

```
cbuffer PerMaterial : register (b2)
{
    float4 MaterialAmbient;
    float4 MaterialDiffuse;
    float4 MaterialSpecular;
    float MaterialSpecularPower;
    bool HasTexture;
    float4 MaterialEmissive;
    float4 UVTransform;
};
```

> A good practice would be to render objects sorted by their material, saving on pipeline changes and constant buffer updates.

4. Next, we will combine the vertex color and material diffuse and pass the result to the pixel shader by modifying the vertex shader. Find the appropriate line in `Shaders\VS.hlsl` and add the highlighted code:

```
result.Diffuse = vertex.Color * MaterialDiffuse;
```

> If we do not set a vertex color or material diffuse, the color will be black as the colors are multiplied. Therefore, it is important that both are provided with a value. If the diffused color should have no impact upon the final color, for example, the texture sample provides all the necessary surface colors, the vertex and material diffuse colors should be set to white (1.0f, 1.0f, 1.0f, and 1.0f). Alternatively, if the vertex color is to be ignored, provide the correct brightness, some grayscale value, and vice versa.

5. Also within the vertex shader, we apply the material's `UVTransform` matrix to the UV coordinates. The following code shows how this is done:

```
/ Apply material UV transformation
result.TextureUV = mul(float4(vertex.TextureUV.x,
    vertex.TextureUV.y, 0, 1), (float4x2)UVTransform).xy;
```

6. Within `ConstantBuffers.cs`, we need to update the `PerFrame` structure to also include the directional light and to create a new structure, `PerMaterial`, while keeping in mind the HLSL 16-byte alignment.

```
[StructLayout(LayoutKind.Sequential, Pack = 1)]
public struct DirectionalLight
{
```

```
        public SharpDX.Color4 Color;
        public SharpDX.Vector3 Direction;
        float _padding0;
}
[StructLayout(LayoutKind.Sequential, Pack = 1)]
public struct PerFrame
{
        public DirectionalLight Light;
        ...
}
[StructLayout(LayoutKind.Sequential, Pack = 1)]
public struct PerMaterial
{
        public Color4 Ambient;
        public Color4 Diffuse;
        public Color4 Specular;
        public float SpecularPower;
        public uint HasTexture; // Has texture 0 false, 1 true
        Vector2 _padding0;
        public Color4 Emissive;
        public Matrix UVTransform; // Support UV transforms
}
```

7. Within our D3DApp class, create a new private member field, perMaterialBuffer, and initialize the constant buffer in CreateDeviceDependentResources. As the material constant buffer will be used by both the vertex and pixel shaders, assign the buffer to each of them using SetConstantBuffer with the slot 2.

    We're now ready to update the render loop.

8. Update the per material constant buffer with the following lines of code.

```
var perMaterial = new ConstantBuffers.PerMaterial();
perMaterial.Ambient = new Color4(0.2f);
perMaterial.Diffuse = Color.White;
perMaterial.Emissive = new Color4(0);
perMaterial.Specular = Color.White;
perMaterial.SpecularPower = 20f;
perMaterial.HasTexture = 0;
perMaterial.UVTransform = Matrix.Identity;
context.UpdateSubresource(ref perMaterial, perMaterialBuffer);
```

9. Now update the `perFrame` variable with the following lines of code.

```
perFrame.Light.Color = Color.White;
var lightDir = Vector3.Transform(new Vector3(1f, -1f, -1f),
    worldMatrix);
perFrame.Light.Direction = new Vector3(lightDir.X,
    lightDir.Y, lightDir.Z);
```

10. Compile and run (*F5*) the code. The output should still be the same as the previous recipe; however, it is worth double checking that the shaders are compiling correctly.

> The shader compilation will throw an exception with line numbers and the description of any syntax errors. Depending on the error, it may also provide correct examples of usage.

We will now implement three lighting shaders: diffuse (using Lambert's cosine law), Phong, and Blinn-Phong.

Implementing diffuse shaders

Follow the given steps for implementing diffuse shaders:

1. In `Common.hlsl`, add the following function to determine the diffuse reflection:

```
float3 Lambert(float4 pixelDiffuse, float3 normal, float3 toLight)
{
// Calculate diffuse color (Lambert's Cosine Law - dot
// product of light and normal). Saturate to clamp the
// value within 0 to 1.
    float3 diffuseAmount = saturate(dot(normal, toLight))
    return pixelDiffuse.rgb * diffuseAmount;
}
```

2. Create a new shader file `Shaders\DiffusePS.hlsl` (again, remember the encoding), add the include directive `#include "Common.hlsl"`, and then declare a texture and texture sampler:

```
Texture2D Texture0 : register(t0);
SamplerState Sampler : register(s0);
```

3. Within a `PSMain` function, include this code:

```
// After interpolation the values are not necessarily
// normalized
float3 normal = normalize(pixel.WorldNormal);
float3 toEye = normalize(CameraPosition -
    pixel.WorldPosition);
float3 toLight = normalize(-Light.Direction);

// Texture sample (use white if no texture)
float4 sample = (float4)1.0f;
```

```
if (HasTexture)
    sample = Texture0.Sample(Sampler, pixel.TextureUV);

float3 ambient = MaterialAmbient.rgb;
float3 emissive = MaterialEmissive.rgb;
float3 diffuse = Lambert(pixel.Diffuse, normal, toLight);

// Calculate final color component
float3 color = (saturate(ambient+diffuse) * sample.rgb) * Light.
Color.rgb + emissive;
// We saturate ambient+diffuse to ensure there is no over-
// brightness on the texture sample if the sum is greater
// than 1 (we would not do this for HDR rendering)

// Calculate final alpha value
float alpha = pixel.Diffuse.a * sample.a;
return float4(color, alpha);
```

4. Within `D3DApp.CreateDeviceDependentResources`, create the pixel shader as per the simple and depth pixel shaders.

Implementing Phong shaders

Follow the given steps for implementing Phong shaders:

1. In `Common.hlsl`, we will now add a function for determining specular reflection using the Phong reflection model.

```
float3 SpecularPhong(float3 normal, float3 toLight, float3 toEye)
{
    // R = reflect(i,n) => R = i - 2 * n * dot(i,n)
    float3 reflection = reflect(-toLight, normal);

    // Calculate the specular amount (smaller specular power =
    // larger specular highlight) Cannot allow a power of 0
    // otherwise the model will appear black and white
    float specularAmount = pow(saturate(dot(reflection,toEye)), ma
x(MaterialSpecularPower,0.00001f));
    return MaterialSpecular.rgb * specularAmount;
}
```

2. Create a new shader file `Shaders\PhongPS.hlsl`. After the include directive, create the `PSMain` function with the same contents as the diffuse shader, except for the following two changes for calculating the color component:

```
float3 specular = SpecularPhong(normal, toLight, toEye);
float3 color = (saturate(ambient+diffuse) * sample.rgb + specular)
* Light.Color.rgb + emissive;
```

3. Within `D3DApp.CreateDeviceDependentResources`, create the pixel shader as per the simple and depth pixel shaders.

Implementing Blinn-Phong shaders

Follow the given steps for implementing Blinn-Phong shaders:

1. This time in `Common.hlsl`, we will create a pixel shader that uses the Blinn-Phong shading model. This is similar to the Phong reflection model; however, instead of the costly reflection calculation per pixel, we use a half-way vector.

```
float3 SpecularBlinnPhong(float3 normal, float3 toLight, float3
toEye) {
  // Calculate the half vector
  float3 halfway = normalize(toLight + toEye);
  // Saturate is used to prevent backface light reflection
  // Calculate specular (smaller power = larger highlight)
  float specularAmount = pow(saturate(dot(normal,
    halfway)), max(MaterialSpecularPower,0.00001f));
  return MaterialSpecular.rgb * specularAmount;
}
```

2. Create the shader file, `Shaders\BlinnPhongPS.hlsl`. After the include directives, `Texture2D` and `SamplerState`, add the `PSMain` function as per the Phong shader, except in this case, call `SpecularBlinnPhong` instead of `SpecularPhong`. Again, create the pixel shader object in your `D3DApp` class.

3. The final output of each material/lighting shader is shown in sequence in the following screenshot. The downloadable sample code binds the number keys *1*, *2*, *3*, and *4* to each of these in order.

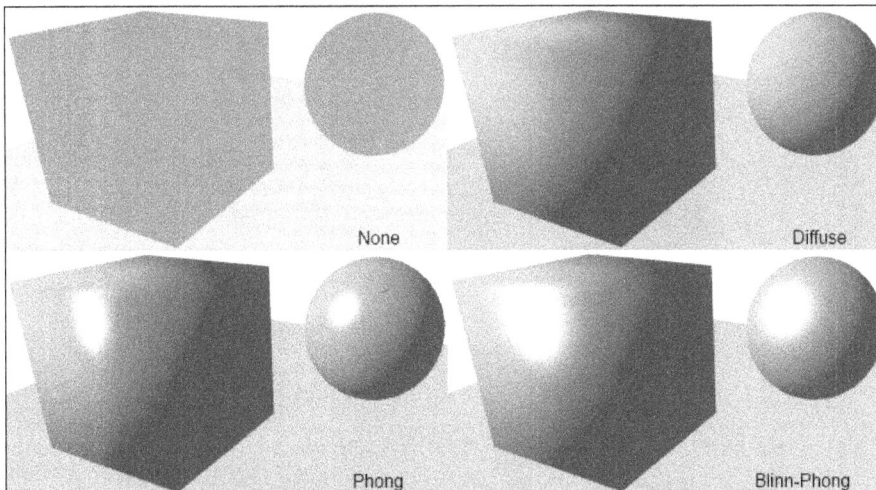

Material and lighting output comparison – None, diffuse, Phong, and Blinn-Phong

How it works...

We first added the light's color and direction to our per frame constant buffer. This groups the camera location and light together as in most situations they will not change between the start and end of a frame. The new per material buffer on the other hand could change many times per frame but not necessarily for each object.

We have set the light's direction in world space as we are performing all our light calculations in this space.

We have added a new structure for storing material properties. These properties are based on the information that we will be loading from the Visual Studio graphics content pipeline CMO file.

UV mapping

By adding the UV transformation matrix to the per material constant buffer, we have completed support for UV mapping for Visual Studio CMO meshes. The UV transform is used to rotate or flip the vertex UV coordinates. This is necessary depending on how the mesh has been converted by the Visual Studio graphics content pipeline. It can also be useful to use the UV transform when changing a mesh vertex's winding order.

UV mapping is the process of unwrapping a mesh and assigning 2D texture coordinates to vertices in such a way that when rendered in 3D space, the texture wraps around the object. This process is performed within the 3D modeling software and looks something like the following screenshot. From a rendering point of view, we are interested in the UV coordinates assigned and the UV transform applied to the mesh.

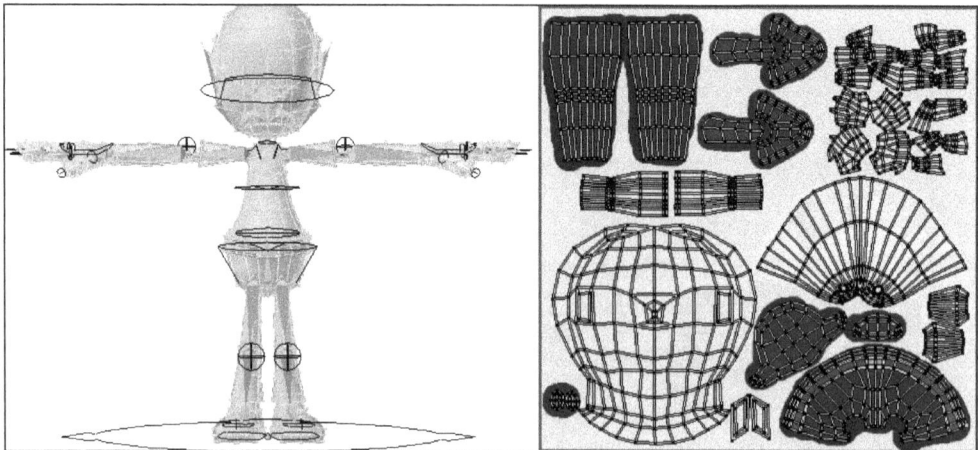

UV mapping within Blender (www.blender.org)

When performing the UV unwrapping process, it is important to consider the impact that **mip-mapping** will have on the final render result as this can lead to color bleeding. Mip-mapping is the process of sampling from lower resolution versions of a texture to control the level of detail for objects that are further away. For example, if a UV coordinate borders two colors with little room to wiggle at a lower resolution, the two colors may get blended together.

> **Mipmaps** can be created for a DDS texture within the Visual Studio graphics editor or at runtime when loading a texture by configuring the texture description with the `ResourceOptionFlags.GenerateMipMaps` flag.
>
> ```
> var desc = new Texture2DDescription();
> ...
> desc.OptionsFlags = ResourceOptionFlags.
> GenerateMipMaps;
> ```

Lighting

In our common shader file, we have implemented three lighting formulas. The Lambert function calculates the diffuse reflection using Lambert's Cosine law, while the `SpecularPhong` and `SpecularBlinnPhong` methods calculate the specular reflection using the Phong and Blinn-Phong models respectively. Our pixel shaders then combine the components for ambient light, emissive light, and diffuse, and in the case of the two specular light models, specular reflection.

Blinn-Phong is a modification of the Phong reflection model that produces a slightly larger specular highlight when using the same specular power as Phong. This can easily be corrected by increasing the specular power when using the Blinn-Phong shader. The Blinn-Phong shader generally produces more desirable results than the Phong method (see `http://people.csail.mit.edu/wojciech/BRDFValidation/index.html`).

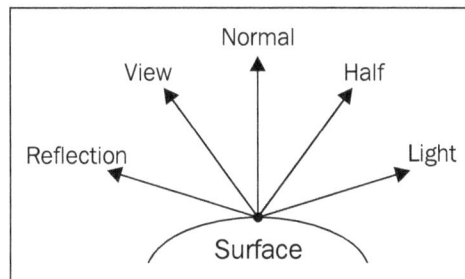

Unit vectors used in the calculation of Phong and Blinn-Phong specular reflection

Both specular formulas use the normal, light, and view unit vectors shown in the previous figure (note that the vector directions for **Light** and **View** are the vectors **towards** the light and view). The Phong model requires the calculation of a reflection vector (using the normal and the from-light vector, and not to-light vector). The dot product of the reflection vector and view vector (or the eye vector) are then used to determine the specular amount (along with the specular power material constant).

```
float3 Reflection = -Light - 2 * Normal * dot(Light,Normal)
```

Blinn-Phong uses the vector halfway between the view and the light instead; this is then used in the dot product between the normal and halfway vectors.

```
float3 halfway = normalize(Light + View);
```

Although Blinn-Phong is less efficient than pure Phong (as the normalization contains a square root calculation) for directional lights, the halfway vector can be calculated outside of the pixel shader as it does not rely on the normal vector. In most other cases where lights are not treated to be at infinity (as in directional lights), the Phong model will be faster.

```
float3 normalizedV = v / sqrt(dot(v, v));
```

There's more...

Currently we are saturating the result of the lighting operations to keep the value within the 0.0 to 1.0 range. If instead, we are supporting **high-dynamic-range** (**HDR**) rendering, we could choose a render target format that supports more than 8 bits per component (for example, `Format.R16G16B16A16_Float`) and stores a larger range of values. To display the result, this technique requires further processing called **tone mapping** to map colors from HDR to a lower dynamic range that matches the capabilities of the display device.

Included in the companion source code is an additional project (*ChO3_02WithCubeMapping. csproj*) that demonstrates how to sample a **texture cube** (or **cube map**) using `float4 sample = CubeMap.Sample(SamplerClamp, normal);`.

The support for sampling the texture cube was added by the following methods:

- ▸ Creating a cube map texture (within a DDS) by importing each of the six 512 x 512 textures into the DirectX Texture Tool (`DxTex.exe`) found in the June 2010 DirectX SDK
- ▸ Adding the texture and sampler state in the cube and sphere renderers

▶ Sampling the `TextureCube` method in the pixel shader, passing the normal vector as the UVW coordinate

Cube mapping with diffuse and specular highlights

> Texture cube UVW coordinates are unit vectors pointing from the center of the object to the surface where it is mapped to one of the six textures of the cube map by the sampler within the pixel shader.

See also

▶ *Chapter 6, Adding Surface Detail with Normal and Displacement Mapping,* demonstrates how to add support for normal mapping

▶ For more information about implementing other types of lights, including volumetric lights, see *Chapter 10, Implementing Deferred Rendering*

Using a right-handed coordinate system

Up to this point, we have used a left-handed coordinate system, where the z axis points away from the view. The Visual Studio graphics content pipeline assumes a right-handed coordinate system when producing `.cmo` files. For the resulting 3D models we use for the remainder of this book, use a clockwise vertex winding order. The difference between left-handed and right-handed coordinates can be seen in the following figure:

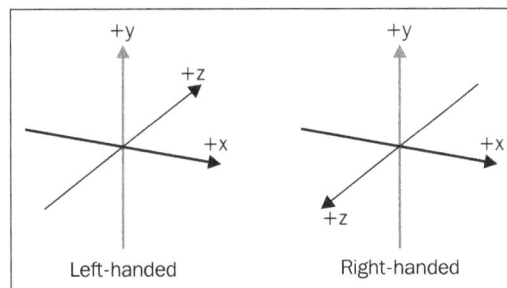

Left-handed versus right-handed Cartesian coordinates – note that the z axis is reversed

In this recipe, we will look at the changes necessary to use a right-handed coordinate system and what this means for our 3D assets. This recipe can be applied to any SharpDX Direct3D application.

How to do it...

We will first step through the changes to the view and projection setup and then look at the changes necessary to the vertices within the simple `QuadRenderer` class.

1. When creating the view matrix, use `SharpDX.Matrix.LookAtRH` instead of `SharpDX.Matrix.LookAtLH` as shown in the following code:

```
// Create the view matrix from our camera position, look
// target and up direction
var viewMatrix = Matrix.LookAtRH(cameraPosition, cameraTarget,
cameraUp);
```

2. When creating the projection matrix, use `SharpDX.Matrix.PerspectiveFovRH` instead of `SharpDX.Matrix.PerspectiveFovLH` as shown in the following code snippet:

```
var projectionMatrix = Matrix.PerspectiveFovRH(
    (float)Math.PI / 3f, Width / (float)Height, 0.5f, 100f);
```

3. Depending on how the 3D assets were authored and exported, it may be necessary to create a rasterizer state that correctly reflects the vertex winding order. The following example applies back-face culling with a clockwise vertex winding order representing front faces:

```
var rasterizerState = ToDispose(new RasterizerState(device, new
RasterizerStateDescription()
{
    FillMode = FillMode.Solid,
    CullMode = CullMode.Back,
    IsFrontCounterClockwise = false,
}));
```

> For assets requiring a counter-clockwise winding order, a rasterizer state with `IsFrontCounterClockwise` set to `true` can be used.

4. When initializing the vertices for a mesh, it may also be desirable to reverse the vertex winding direction or to set the `IsFrontCounterClockwise` property to `true` in the rasterizer state description. For example, to render the quad from the *Rendering a cube and sphere* recipe in a right-handed coordinate system, we can change the order of the indices as follows:

```
new ushort[] {
    0, 2, 1, // instead of 0, 1, 2
    2, 0, 3  // instead of 2, 3, 0
}
```

How it works...

By creating our view and projection matrices in a right-handed coordinate system, with the x axis still pointing to the right, the positive z axis now extends towards the viewer. Although we refer to the z axis, any setup where a positive axis points towards the viewer is considered a right-handed Cartesian coordinate system. It is also common for 3D modeling software to use a coordinate system where the y axis points towards/away from the viewer and the z axis points up. Depending on the vertex data, simply reordering the vertices may not be sufficient. UV coordinates may need adjusting, or normal vectors updated. The `PerMaterial` buffer has a UV transform matrix that can be used to adjust UV coordinates; this is covered further in the next recipe: *Loading a static mesh from a file*.

See also

▶ The following information on 3D coordinate systems for DirectX on MSDN provides more information on how to work with different coordinate systems: `http://msdn.microsoft.com/en-us/library/windows/desktop/bb324490%28v=vs.85%29.aspx`

Loading a static mesh from a file

In this recipe, we will create a mesh renderer that renders meshes loaded from a compiled mesh object (`.CMO`) file. We will use the Visual Studio graphics content pipeline to compile an Autodesk FBX model that has been exported from the open source 3D modeling and animation software, Blender (`blender.org`).

The class `Common.Mesh` within the provided sample framework will be used to load the `.CMO` file format and to store the loaded mesh. The loaded mesh will contain the vertex and index buffers along with material and lighting parameters and can also include the name of textures and pixel shaders to use.

Getting ready

This recipe assumes that a right-handed coordinate system is being used; see the previous recipe, *Using a right-handed coordinate system*.

Before we get started, there are a few files we need from the downloaded package and a class within the Common project we will review.

1. The Common.Mesh class is a C# implementation for deserializing the compiled mesh object (.CMO) that is generated by the Visual Studio graphics content pipeline. Most notably, this class includes the following static method: Common.Mesh. LoadFromFile. This class is partly based on a C# port of the ModelLoadCMO class in DirectXTK (https://directxtk.codeplex.com).

2. The MeshContentTask.targets and MeshContentTask.props files must be copied to the same directory as your solution file.

3. The Ch03_02LoadMesh\Male_base_mesh.fbx file is the example mesh we will be loading for this recipe.

4. Alternatively, you can export any selected objects within Blender to Autodesk FBX by navigating to **File | Export | Autodesk FBX (.fbx)** within Blender.

5. On the resulting export configuration panel, tick **Selected Objects** and select **–Z Forward** (for right-handed coordinates) as shown in the following screenshot:

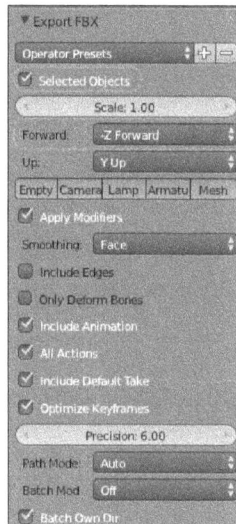

Blender Export FBX configuration for use with Visual Studio graphics content pipeline

6. Enter a filename and click on **Export FBX**.

The completed project for this recipe can be found in the code bundle of this chapter, *Ch03_03LoadMesh*, downloadable from Packt's website.

How to do it...

We will begin by adding the additional build targets and then including the FBX model and checking that it correctly compiles.

1. First we need to install the additional build targets in to our project file. Unload your project by right-clicking on the project in the Solution Explorer and selecting **Unload Project**.

2. Next, right-click on the project again and select **Edit ProjectName.csproj**.

3. We need to insert the following code into the project file just before the closing `</Project>` tag. Here we are assuming that the additional build target files are located in the directory above this project.

   ```
   <Import Project="..\MeshContentTask.targets" />
   ```

4. Right-click on the project and select **Reload Project**.

5. Now, add the `Male_base_mesh.fbx` file into the project directory and include it in the project.

6. Select the FBX file within the Solution Explorer and then within the **Build Action** in the **Properties** window, select **MeshContentTask**.

7. Build the project (*F6*) and confirm that in the build output directory, there is the compiled mesh file: `bin\Debug\Male_base_mesh.cmo` (or the `bin\Debug\AppX` directory for Windows Store apps). Any messages from the content pipeline will also appear in the build output window.

> The modified `MeshContentTask.*` files are based upon the Visual Studio 2012 Update 2 and Visual Studio 2013 releases. If for some reason they are not working correctly for you, a copy of the compiled mesh object is included in `Ch03_03LoadMesh\Male_base_mesh.cmo`. This can then be included in the project. Once this is done, select **Copy if newer** as the copy for the output directory option.

Mesh Renderer

Now that we have our compiled mesh, we need to create a mesh renderer.

1. Follow the steps given in the *Creating a Direct3D renderer class* recipe in *Chapter 2, Rendering with Direct3D*, to create our `MeshRenderer` class.

2. Add the following private member fields and public property:

   ```
   // The vertex buffer
   List<Buffer> vertexBuffers = new List<Buffer>();
   // The index buffer
   ```

```
List<Buffer> indexBuffers = new List<Buffer>();
// Texture resources
List<ShaderResourceView> textureViews = new
    List<ShaderResourceView>();
// Control sampling behavior with this state
SamplerState samplerState;
// The loaded mesh
Common.Mesh mesh;
public Common.Mesh Mesh { get { return this.mesh; } }

// The per material buffer to use so that the mesh
// parameters can be used
public Buffer PerMaterialBuffer { get; set; }
```

3. Next, we will create a single constructor that accepts a Visual Studio graphics content pipeline CMO mesh via a `Common.Mesh` instance.

```
public MeshRenderer(Common.Mesh mesh)
{
    this.mesh = mesh;
}
```

4. Override `CreateDeviceDependentResources` with the following code. First release the existing vertex, index buffers, and texture views.

```
// Dispose of each vertex, index buffer and texture
vertexBuffers.ForEach(vb => RemoveAndDispose(ref vb));
vertexBuffers.Clear();
indexBuffers.ForEach(ib => RemoveAndDispose(ref ib));
indexBuffers.Clear();
textureViews.ForEach(tv => RemoveAndDispose(ref tv));
textureViews.Clear();
RemoveAndDispose(ref samplerState);
```

5. We read each of the vertex buffers from the CMO file into a new buffer.

```
// Initialize vertex buffers
for (int indx = 0; indx < mesh.VertexBuffers.Count; indx++)
{
    var vb = mesh.VertexBuffers[indx];
    Vertex[] vertices = new Vertex[vb.Length];
    for (var i = 0; i < vb.Length; i++)
    {
        // Create vertex
```

```
        vertices[i] = new Vertex(vb[i].Position,
            vb[i].Normal, vb[i].Color, vb[i].UV);
    }
    vertexBuffers.Add(ToDispose(Buffer.Create(device,
      BindFlags.VertexBuffer, vertices.ToArray())));
    vertexBuffers[vertexBuffers.Count - 1].DebugName =
      "VertexBuffer_" + indx.ToString();
}
```

6. Next we load each of the index buffers.

```
// Initialize index buffers
foreach (var ib in mesh.IndexBuffers)
{
    indexBuffers.Add(ToDispose(Buffer.Create(device,
      BindFlags.IndexBuffer, ib)));
    indexBuffers[indexBuffers.Count - 1].DebugName =
      "IndexBuffer_" + (indexBuffers.Count - 1).ToString();
}
```

7. And lastly, create **Shader Resource Views** (**SRVs**) for each of the textures and a default sampler state.

```
// Initialize texture views
// The CMO file format supports up to 8 per material
foreach (var m in mesh.Materials)
{
    // Diffuse Color
    for (var i = 0; i < m.Textures.Length; i++)
    {
        if (SharpDX.IO.NativeFile.Exists(m.Textures[i]))
            textureViews.Add(ToDispose(
              ShaderResourceView.FromFile(
                device, m.Textures[i])));
        else
            textureViews.Add(null);
    }
}
// Create our sampler state
samplerState = ToDispose(new SamplerState(device, new
SamplerStateDescription() {
    AddressU = TextureAddressMode.Clamp,
    AddressV = TextureAddressMode.Clamp,
    AddressW = TextureAddressMode.Clamp,
```

```
        BorderColor = new Color4(0, 0, 0, 0),
        ComparisonFunction = Comparison.Never,
        Filter = Filter.MinMagMipLinear,
        MaximumAnisotropy = 16,
        MaximumLod = float.MaxValue,
        MinimumLod = 0,
        MipLodBias = 0.0f
    }));
```

8. We can now implement the `DoRender` method to render our mesh. We will be rendering the model's submeshes grouped by material, so we begin by iterating the mesh's available materials. After retrieving the submeshes for the material, we update the `PerMaterialBuffer` instance and then render the submesh as shown in the following code:

```
// Draw sub-meshes grouped by material
for (var mIndx = 0; mIndx < mesh.Materials.Count; mIndx++)
{
    // If the material buffer is assigned and submeshes
    // user the material, update the PerMaterialBuffer
    if (PerMaterialBuffer != null &&
        subMeshesForMaterial.Length > 0)
    {
        ... update material buffer
    }
    // For each sub-mesh
    foreach (var subMesh in subMeshesForMaterial)
    {
        ... render each sub-mesh
    }
}
```

9. We update the material buffer and assign any textures if `PerMaterialBuffer` is assigned. If the first texture view is not null, we will set the `HasTexture` property of the `PerMaterial` buffer to `true`.

```
// update the PerMaterialBuffer constant buffer
var material = new ConstantBuffers.PerMaterial()
{
    Ambient = new Color4(mesh.Materials[mIndx].Ambient),
    Diffuse = new Color4(mesh.Materials[mIndx].Diffuse),
    Emissive = new Color4(mesh.Materials[mIndx].Emissive),
    Specular = new Color4(mesh.Materials[mIndx].Specular),
    SpecularPower = mesh.Materials[mIndx].SpecularPower,
    UVTransform = mesh.Materials[mIndx].UVTransform,
};
```

```
// Bind textures to the pixel shader
int texIndxOffset = mIndx * Common.Mesh.MaxTextures;
material.HasTexture = (uint)(textureViews[texIndxOffset] !=
    null ? 1 : 0); // 0=false
context.PixelShader.SetShaderResources(0,
    textureViews.GetRange(texIndxOffset,
    Common.Mesh.MaxTextures).ToArray());

// Set texture sampler state
context.PixelShader.SetSampler(0, samplerState);

// Update material buffer
context.UpdateSubresource(ref material, PerMaterialBuffer);
```

10. To render each submesh, we set the vertex and index buffers in the **Input Assembler** (**IA**) and then draw the vertices.

```
// Ensure the vert                        ex buffer and index
buffers are in range
if (subMesh.VertexBufferIndex < vertexBuffers.Count && subMesh.
IndexBufferIndex < indexBuffers.Count)
{
    // Retrieve and set the vertex and index buffers
    var vertexBuffer = vertexBuffers[
        (int)subMesh.VertexBufferIndex];
    context.InputAssembler.SetVertexBuffers(0, new
        VertexBufferBinding(vertexBuffer,
            Utilities.SizeOf<Vertex>(), 0));
    context.InputAssembler.SetIndexBuffer(indexBuffers[
        (int)subMesh.IndexBufferIndex], Format.R16_UInt, 0);
    // Set topology
    context.InputAssembler.PrimitiveTopology =
        SharpDX.Direct3D.PrimitiveTopology.TriangleList;
}
// Draw the sub-mesh (includes the triangle count)
// The submesh has a start index into the vertex buffer
context.DrawIndexed((int)subMesh.PrimCount * 3,
    (int)subMesh.StartIndex, 0);
```

Now we can load and render our mesh within our D3DApp class.

11. Within `D3DApp.Run()`, where we have created our previous renders, insert the following code to load the mesh file and then create the mesh renderer.

```
// Create and initialize the mesh renderer
var loadedMesh =
    Common.Mesh.LoadFromFile("Male_base_mesh.cmo");
var mesh = ToDispose(new MeshRenderer(loadedMesh.First()));
mesh.Initialize(this);
mesh.World = Matrix.Identity;
```

> For Windows Store apps, use `Common.Mesh.LoadFromFileAsync`.

12. And finally within the render loop, we update the `PerObject` constant buffer, set the `PerMaterialBuffer` property of the mesh renderer, and then tell it to render.

```
// Update the matrices
perObject.World = mesh.World * worldMatrix;
...
context.UpdateSubresource(ref perObject, perObjectBuffer);
// Provide with material constant buffer
mesh.PerMaterialBuffer = perMaterialBuffer;
// Render the mesh
mesh.Render();
```

13. Compile and run (*F5*) the previous code, and we should now see something like the following screenshot (note that you may want to change the default pixel shader to Blinn-Phong first):

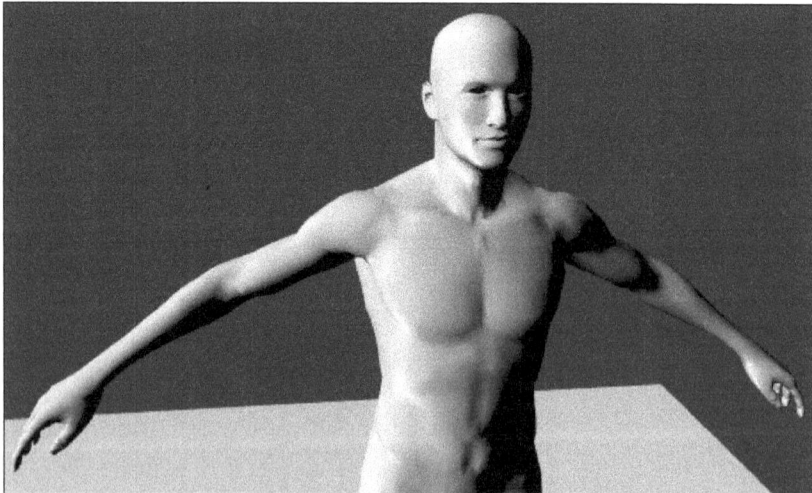

Final output of the mesh renderer

How it works...

The Visual Studio graphics content pipeline uses `[VSInstallDir]\Common7\IDE\` `Extensions\Microsoft\VsGraphics\vsgraphics.exe` to display models/scenes and also to compile them into objects ready for consumption in your application at runtime. Unfortunately, Microsoft has only provided MSBuild targets for C++ projects; however, with a few tweaks of the original MSBuild target files (also located in the same directory), we can now do the same for our C# projects.

The compiled mesh object file structure may include multiple vertex buffers, index buffers, submeshes, materials, texture references, the pixel shaders used, bones, and animations. The exact binary file layout is shown within the comments in the `Common\Mesh.cs` class file. The mesh class uses a `BinaryReader` instance and some helpful extension methods to load the CMO file.

> The `MeshContentTask` method supports compiling Autodesk FBX (`.fbx`), Collada (`.dae`), and Wavefront (`.obj`), to compile mesh objects (`.CMO`).

Our mesh renderer is now available to manage the rendering tasks for the mesh object's vertex and index buffers, materials, and textures. This renderer simply iterates the available materials, updating the material buffer and then for each submesh that uses this material, it loads the appropriate vertex and index buffers.

Currently, our solution is grouping materials that are used within a single mesh and its submeshes. For a full-engine implementation, it would be more likely that materials are shared between different meshes and therefore it would be necessary to correctly group multiple meshes that use a material.

You can open the FBX file within Visual Studio and play with the material settings to see how they affect the final render. At this point, it is also worth trying to use models that include textures.

There's more...

You will find two more content pipeline MSBuild targets that have been converted to work with C# projects in the downloaded code: one for compiling images (*ImageContentTask*) and one for compiling shader graphs (the `.dgls` files) to shader byte code (*ShaderGraphContentTask*).

Note that many downloaded meshes may have counter-clockwise vertex winding. When debugging rendering issues, it can sometimes be helpful to try disabling back-face culling in the rasterizer state. This is done as shown in the following code snippet:

```
// No culling
context.Rasterizer.State = ToDispose(new RasterizerState(device, new
RasterizerStateDescription() {
    FillMode = FillMode.Solid,
    CullMode = CullMode.None,
}));
```

See also

▶ In *Chapter 4, Animating Meshes with Vertex Skinning,* we extend the mesh renderer to support animating our mesh, using a mesh's bones to perform vertex skinning.

▶ For more information about working with the Visual Studio graphics content pipeline, see `http://msdn.microsoft.com/en-us/library/vstudio/hh315737.aspx`.

▶ For instructions and general guidelines on how to export Blender scenes to Autodesk FBX scenes, see `http://blog.diabolicalgame.co.uk/2011/07/exporting-animated-models-from-blender.html`. These instructions target the XNA content pipeline; however, most of the steps still apply, especially with regards to the tips for preparing the Blender scene for export.

▶ A large number of high quality Blender models/scenes are available for download under various Creative Commons licenses from `www.blendswap.com`.

▶ The Visual Studio graphics content pipeline build targets for C# can also be found online at `http://spazzarama.com/2013/11/20/visual-studio-graphics-content-pipeline-csharp-projects/`.

4

Animating Meshes with Vertex Skinning

In this chapter, we will cover the following topics:

- ▶ Preparing the vertex shader and buffers for vertex skinning
- ▶ Loading bones in the mesh renderer
- ▶ Animating bones

Introduction

In this chapter, we will see how a bone structure can be used to make the skin of our model (in this case, our vertices) move, producing a dynamic mesh that we can manipulate into poses or use for playing back animations.

Using the Visual Studio graphics content pipeline, we will learn how to make use of the skin and bone information stored within a **compiled mesh object** (**CMO**).

Preparing the vertex shader and buffers for vertex skinning

In this recipe, we will update our vertex structure, constant buffers, and vertex shader to support the transforming of vertices based on an underlying bone structure.

The key component of **vertex skinning** or **skinning** is the hierarchy of pose and movement that is produced by a bone structure or skeleton within a mesh (also known as an **armature**). As we know from basic anatomy, a skeleton provides, among other functions, a mechanism for transmitting muscular forces. It is a collection of bones, each connected to another.

We apply the same concept to the armature of a mesh. We have a root bone, and each subsequent bone is parented by the root bone or another bone that ultimately resolves it's parentage to this root bone. In this manner, if we move the root bone, the whole body moves with it; but if we move the shoulder, then only the arm moves with it.

The left-most figure in the following screenshot shows an example of an armature of a simple mesh that has been divided into four segments. In this example, the root bone is the bottom-most bone, and each subsequent bone is parented by it's previous bone. The position or pose shown in this figure is referred to as the **bind pose** or **rest pose**, and it represents the default starting transformation of each bone at the time the mesh was bound to the armature or rigged.

Simply having an armature in place is not enough for it to apply forces upon the skin. We must bind the mesh to the armature and specify how each of the bones will influence the vertices. By applying weights, known as **bone-weights** or **blend-weights**, to the vertex of each of the influencing bones, our armature will be able to influence the placement of vertices.

In the following screenshot, the right-most figure shows how the vertices' bone-weights have been applied in relation to the top-most bone in the hierarchy. The cooler the color, lesser the influence of the bone on the vertex (where the blue color at the bottom is 0.0); and the warmer the color, the greater the influence of the bone (where the red color at the top is 1.0). As seen from the gradual cooling of the bone-weights toward the next bone, it is clear that more than one bone can have an influence upon a vertex.

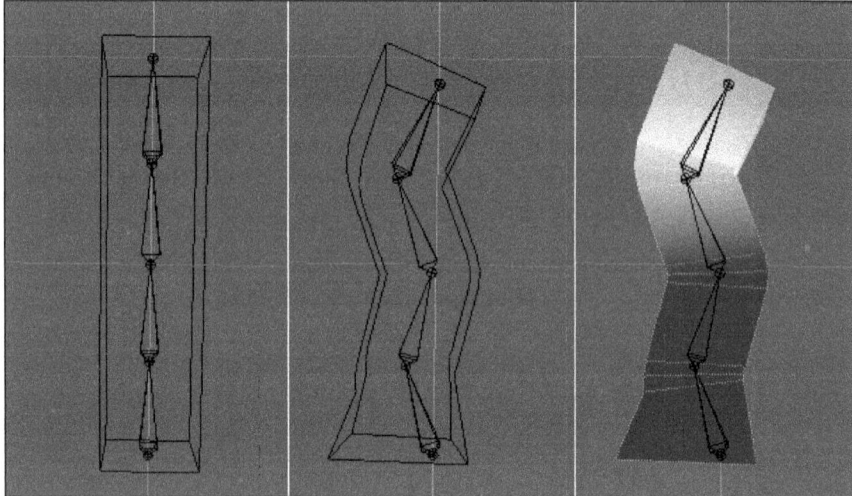

Impact of bones upon the vertices of a mesh (from left to right: bind pose, a pose, and bone-weights)

Getting ready

We can apply this recipe to any of our Direct3D applications. It is assumed that a class descending from the `D3DApplicationBase` abstract class is being used, the C# vertex structure is contained within the `Vertex` structure, and the C# structures for the constant buffers are defined in `ConstantBuffers.cs`.

How to do it...

We will start by updating our C# vertex structure. So go ahead and open the `Vertex.cs` file for editing.

1. Update the member fields of the `Vertex` class to include a new property that will store the skinning information for the vertex.

```
public Vector3 Position;
public Vector3 Normal;
public Color Color;
public Vector2 UV;
public Common.Mesh.SkinningVertex Skin;
```

2. The `SkinningVertex` structure is based upon the internal format of a CMO file, and it is included within the `Common.Mesh` class. For completeness, the `SkinningVertex` structure is shown in the following code snippet:

```
[StructLayout(LayoutKind.Sequential, Pack = 1)]
public struct SkinningVertex
{
    public uint BoneIndex0;
    public uint BoneIndex1;
    public uint BoneIndex2;
    public uint BoneIndex3;
    public float BoneWeight0;
    public float BoneWeight1;
    public float BoneWeight2;
    public float BoneWeight3;
}
```

A CMO file supports up to four bone indices (unsigned integers) and four bone weights (floats) that together add up to 1.0. Also, four bone indices and weights fit nicely within a 4-component HLSL such as `uint4` and `float4` respectively.

3. Add an appropriate constructor to the `Vertex` structure. This allows us to initialize the `Skin` property we had added previously.

4. As always, after updating the vertex structure, we need to change the input layout that is passed to the **Input Assembler** (**IA**) stage. Within the `D3DApp.CreateDeviceDependentResources` method, change the definition of the input layout to include the new vertex properties.

```
vertexLayout = ToDispose(new InputLayout(device,
  vsBytecode.GetPart(ShaderBytecodePart.InputSignatureBlob),
new[]
{
  new InputElement("SV_POSITION",0,Format.R32G32B32_Float,
    0,0),
  new InputElement("NORMAL", 0,
    Format.R32G32B32_Float,12,0),
  new InputElement("COLOR", 0, Format.R8G8B8A8_UNorm,
    24,0),
  new InputElement("TEXCOORD", 0, Format.R32G32_Float,
    28,0),
// "SkinIndices"
  new InputElement("BLENDINDICES", 0, Format.R32G32B32A32_UInt,
    36, 0),
// "SkinWeights"
  new InputElement("BLENDWEIGHT", 0, Format.R32G32B32A32_Float,
    52, 0),
}));
```

5. To complete our vertex structure changes, we need to update the vertex shader and pixel shader inputs within `.\Shaders\Common.hlsl`.

6. Change the `VertexShaderInput` structure to include the two new vertex properties.

```
uint4 SkinIndices : BLENDINDICES; // blend indices
float4 SkinWeights : BLENDWEIGHT; // blend weights
```

7. To store the list of bone influences (matrices) that will be used within the vertex shader, we need to create a new constant buffer. This buffer will be updated *per armature*.

```
// Constant buffer to hold our skin matrices for each bone.
// Note: 1024*64 = max bytes for constant buffers in SM4/5
cbuffer PerArmature : register(b3)
{
  float4x4 Bones[1024];
};
```

With our shader structures and constant buffers in place, we will update the vertex shader in `\Shaders\VS.hlsl` to apply the vertex skinning.

8. Create a new HLSL method called `SkinVertex`.

```
void SkinVertex(float4 weights, uint4 bones,
          inout float4 position, inout float3 normal)
{
  // If there are skin weights apply vertex skinning
  if (weights.x != 0)
  {
    // Calculate the skin transform combining up to
    // four bone influences
    float4x4 skinTransform =
    Bones[bones.x] * weights.x +
    Bones[bones.y] * weights.y +
    Bones[bones.z] * weights.z +
    Bones[bones.w] * weights.w;

    // Apply skinning to vertex and normal
    position = mul(position, skinTransform);

    // We assume here that the skin transform includes
    // only uniform scaling (if any)
    normal = mul(normal, (float3x3)skinTransform);

  }
```

9. Immediately before applying the `WorldViewProjection` matrix to the vertex position, call the new `SkinVertex` method as shown in the following code:

```
// Apply vertex skinning if any
SkinVertex(vertex.SkinWeights, vertex.SkinIndices,
    vertex.Position, vertex.Normal);
```

We are done with our shaders for the moment. As we have just added a new constant buffer, we need to open `ConstantBuffers.cs` and make the appropriate changes.

10. Create a new class to store our *per armature* data. Note that we are using `class` here instead of `struct`, as we will be passing through the `Bones` array when updating the constant buffer. This simplifies the marshalling of the structure to the Direct3D buffer, and we can initialize the array more easily.

```
// Per armature/skeleton constant buffer
public class PerArmature
{
  // The maximum number of bones supported by the shader
  public const int MaxBones = 1024;
  public Matrix[] Bones;
```

```
      public PerArmature()
      {
        Bones = new Matrix[MaxBones];
      }

      public static int Size()
      {
        return Utilities.SizeOf<Matrix>() * MaxBones;
      }
    }
```

11. Within the `D3DApp.CreateDeviceDependentResources` method, initialize a new `SharpDX.Direct3D11.Buffer` field member as shown in the following screenshot. We use the `PerArmature.Size()` method to determine the correct buffer size.

```
perArmatureBuffer = ToDispose(new Buffer(device,
    ConstantBuffers.PerArmature.Size(), ResourceUsage.Default,
    BindFlags.ConstantBuffer, CpuAccessFlags.None,
    ResourceOptionFlags.None, 0));
```

12. Now assign the buffer to the fourth vertex shader constant buffer slot.

```
context.VertexShader.SetConstantBuffer(3,
    perArmatureBuffer);
```

This completes the changes necessary to support vertex skinning in our vertex shader.

How it works...

In order to apply the bone influences on our vertices, we must be able to pass through the bone indices and the weighting of the influence they have on the current vertex. For this purpose, we will re-use the existing structure defined within `Common.Mesh`.

Our implementation supports up to four bone influences per vertex. This is not only the maximum number supported by the CMO file format produced by Visual Studio, but the four bone indices and weights fit conveniently within a HLSL `uint4` and `float4` as you can see from the input layout we defined for the IA stage and the updated HLSL vertex structure.

As already discussed, the key component of skinning is the hierarchy of transformations that is produced from the bones of an armature. These transformations or skin matrices are implemented using the trusty old 4 x 4 **affine transformation matrix**. However, instead of transforming from the local object space to world space as we have done previously, we will be applying these transformations in bone space.

[🖊 A bone's affine transformation matrix is able to influence a vertex's translation, rotation, and scale.]

The transformation to bone space involves calculating the current translation and rotation for each bone, as well as its scale against its parent bone. This initial transform is now in the bind pose or rest pose space. To bring the transform into bone space, we apply the inverse bind pose matrix of the bone. The following figure shows the bones at rest (in the top-left), and in various poses for the remaining layouts.

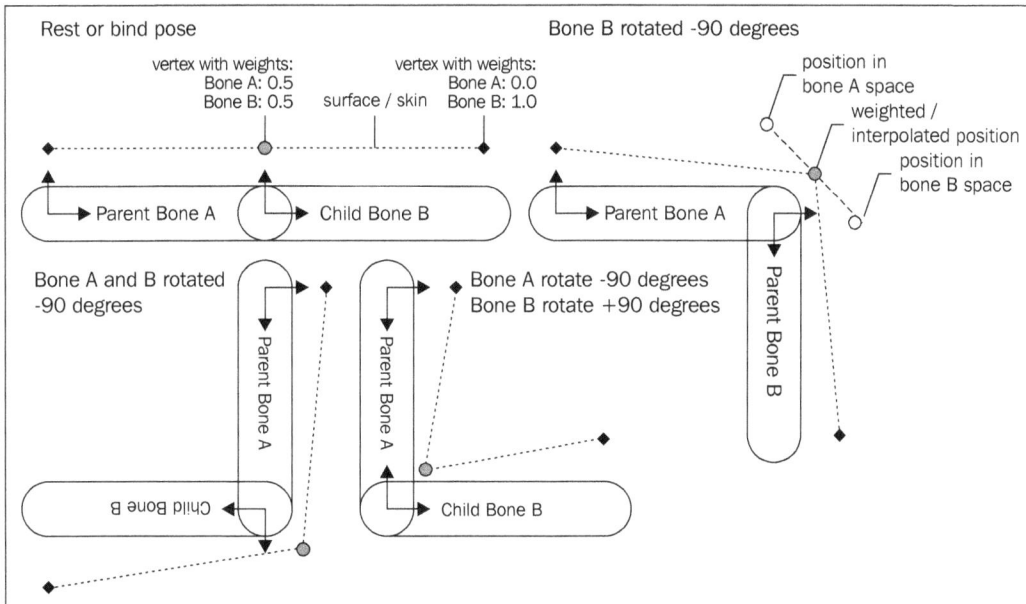

Blending of bone influences upon a vertex, and relationship between parent/child bones

This resulting **skin matrix** for each bone is what we are storing in the `PerArmature` constant buffer, and it is the matrix that we refer to within the vertex shader.

Within the vertex shader, we blend the bone influences together based upon their weight. The previous figure shows how the central vertex is influenced equally by the two bones, by using a weighting of `0.5` for each bone. The following pseudocode shows how the final transform matrix for this vertex would be calculated from the skin matrices of bone `A` and `B`.

```
float4x4 transform = Bones[A] * 0.5 +
  Bones[B] * 0.5;
```

In order to reduce the memory bandwidth, the number of bones should be reduced to a number that reflects more realistically the maximum number of bones within the models used (for example, between 64 and 100). The value of 1024 is used in this recipe to highlight the fact that this is the maximum number of 4 x 4 matrices that can be stored within a constant buffer in Shader Model 4/5 (or 65,536 bytes). In contrast, Shader Model 3 supports 256 constant float registers that can hold a single float4 component, or a maximum of sixty-four 4 x 4 matrices. This is shared between other floating point data. So, the actual number available would be less.

> There are tricks to increase the number of bones, such as using 4 x 3 matrices, as bones rarely require non-affine transformations. For DirectX 11 class hardware, there is probably no need; although, perhaps on some mobile devices or if you must support older hardware, it may still be something to consider.

With the armature's skin matrices in place, we can apply the vertex skinning within the vertex shader. For each of the bone influences (specified in `SkinIndices`), the skin transform matrix is retrieved and multiplied by the bone-weight (stored in `SkinWeights`). These four matrices are then added together to determine the final skin transform for this vertex.

```
float4x4 skinTransform = Bones[bones.x] * weights.x +
   Bones[bones.y] * weights.y +
   Bones[bones.z] * weights.z +
   Bones[bones.w] * weights.w;
// Apply skinning to vertex and normal
position = mul(position, skinTransform);
normal = mul(normal, (float3x3)skinTransform);
```

We then apply the skin transform to the vertex position and vertex normal. The normal transformation presented here will only work if the bone matrices always contain uniform scaling. For this to work with non-uniform scaling, it requires the usage of an inverse transpose of the matrix as described in the *Preparing the vertex and constant buffers for material and lighting* recipe in *Chapter 3, Rendering Meshes*.

If the first bone has a weight of zero, we are skipping this process. This is important because we are using this vertex shader for meshes whether or not they have any bones. A very small performance improvement can possibly be gained by splitting the vertex shader into two and choosing which shader to use on the CPU per mesh instead of making the decision within a single vertex shader for each vertex. There is, however, a performance overhead when switching shaders; so your results may vary.

The result of applying a skin matrix of zero upon all of our vertices will place them all at the origin. In the case of triangle primitives, this will result in no output. This symptom can indicate that the `PerArmature` constant buffer hasn't been updated correctly.

> Debugging incorrect vertex placement is sometimes easier by changing the IA primitive topology to a point list and changing the background color of the scene to white or black (depending on the expected vertex color).

There's more...

Performing vertex skinning results in a constant per-vertex performance hit. Therefore, it is desirable to have as few vertices as possible in large scenes that have multiple armatures.

A common technique of getting around the limitations of a lower maximum bone count on older hardware was implementing **bone partitioning**, whereby the mesh is broken up into smaller parts that share the same subset of bones. Each part is then drawn separately.

See also

> ▸ The *Loading bones in the mesh renderer* recipe provides an implementation for loading the bones from a CMO mesh within a mesh renderer

Loading bones in the mesh renderer

In this recipe, we will modify the mesh renderer to support transforming vertices based on the underlying bone structure. This necessitates the loading of the armature from the loaded mesh. This is required in order to implement mesh animations.

The Visual Studio graphics content pipeline includes bones and animations from Autodesk FBX models in the resulting CMO file. Bones are stored in the file as an array of bones, consisting of a parent index and the inverse bind pose, the bind pose, and bone local transform matrices. The root bone in a hierarchy of bones has a parent index of -1.

Getting ready

We will be using a new Autodesk FBX model along with a texture file that can be found in the downloaded content. The precompiled mesh file and texture are also included.

In this example, we will need the `MeshRenderer` class and the graphics content pipeline's build targets in place that were created in the *Loading a static mesh from a file* recipe in *Chapter 3*, *Rendering Meshes*. We will also require the vertex shader from the previous recipe, *Preparing the vertex shader and buffers for vertex skinning*.

> ▸ The completed project for this recipe (`Ch04_01VertexSkinning`) includes a new axis-grid renderer for the x and z axes, which can be optionally included.

▸ From the downloaded source, copy `.\Ch04_01VertexSkinning\Character.fbx` to the project directory and include it in the project. The build action needs to be changed to `MeshContentTask`.

▸ Also, copy `.\Ch04_01VertexSkinning\Character.png` to the project directory. You can include it in the project if you want. There is no need to apply a build task to this item as it will already be processed by `MeshContentTask`.

> The compiled character mesh (`.cmo`) and character texture (`.dds`) can be found in the same location if there are issues with the VS compilation process. Simply add these to the project instead and select **Copy if newer**.

How to do it...

We will now update our mesh renderer so that it loads the bone information from the `Common.Mesh` class that we have been using for loading the CMO files.

1. First, add a new public property that provides access to the `PerArmature` buffer we added in the previous recipe.

```
// The per armature constant buffer to use
public Buffer PerArmatureBuffer { get; set; }
```

2. Now, within the `MeshRenderer.CreateDeviceDependentResources` method, we can load the skinning information for the vertices. Update the existing vertex buffer initialization code so that we are now including the `SkinningVertex` structure.

```
// Initialize vertex buffers
for (int indx = 0; indx < mesh.VertexBuffers.Count; indx++)
{
  ...
  for (var i = 0; i < vb.Length; i++)
  {
    // Retrieve skinning information for vertex
    Common.Mesh.SkinningVertex skin = new
      Common.Mesh.SkinningVertex();
    if (mesh.SkinningVertexBuffers.Count > 0)
      skin = mesh.SkinningVertexBuffers[indx][i];

    // Create vertex
    vertices[i] = new Vertex(vb[i].Position,
    vb[i].Normal, vb[i].Color, vb[i].UV, skin);

  ...
}
```

3. Within the `MeshRenderer.DoRender` method, we will now calculate the skin transforms for each of the bones, and then update the armature constant buffer. Let's add this code just before the existing material loop.

```
// Calculate skin matrices for each bone
ConstantBuffers.PerArmature skinMatrices = new ConstantBuffers.
PerArmature();
if (mesh.Bones != null)
{
  ... Calculate skin matrices
}
// Update constant buffer with skin matrices of each bone
context.UpdateSubresource(skinMatrices.Bones,
  PerArmatureBuffer);

// Draw sub-meshes grouped by material
for (var mIndx = 0; mIndx < mesh.Materials.Count; mIndx++)
...
```

Within the previous `if` statement, we will perform the following operations:

1. First, we load the bone's local transform (which is currently in the bone's local bind pose/rest pose space) using the following code snippet:

```
// Retrieve each bone's local transform
for (var i = 0; i < mesh.Bones.Count; i++)
{
  skinMatrices.Bones[i] = mesh.Bones[i].BoneLocalTransform;
}
```

2. Next, we apply the transform of the parent bone upon each child bone, making the assumption that each parent bone appears before its children in the list of bones.

```
// TODO: Load bone transforms from animation frames here

// Apply parent bone transforms.
// We assume here that the first bone has no parent
// and that each parent bone appears before children
for (var i = 1; i < mesh.Bones.Count; i++)
{
  var bone = mesh.Bones[i];
  // ParentIndex == -1 means this is a root bone
  if (bone.ParentIndex > -1)
  {
```

```
        // Retrieve and apply parent bone transform
        var parentTransform =
          skinMatrices.Bones[bone.ParentIndex];
        skinMatrices.Bones[i] = (skinMatrices.Bones[i] *
          parentTransform);
    }
}
```

> If the mesh's bones do not match the previous assumptions, then the rendered mesh may end up looking strange in the final render. See the screenshot in the *How it works...* section that shows the result of using invalid skin transforms.

3. Then, we convert the transform from bind pose space into bone space by using the inverse of the bind pose for the bone loaded with the mesh.

```
// Change the bone transform from rest pose space into bone space
// (using the inverse of the bind/rest pose)
for (var i = 0; i < mesh.Bones.Count; i++)
{
  skinMatrices.Bones[i] =
  Matrix.Transpose(mesh.Bones[i].InvBindPose *
  skinMatrices.Bones[i]);
}
// TODO: Check need to loop animation here
```

4. Finally, we must update `D3DApp.Run` so that we are loading the correct mesh and passing in the armature buffer when rendering. Instead of limiting the rendering to only the first mesh found in the loaded CMO file, we will instead create a mesh renderer for each mesh.

5. Change the initialization of the mesh renderer to the following code:

```
// Create and initialize the mesh renderers
var loadedMesh = Common.Mesh.LoadFromFile("Character.cmo");
List<MeshRenderer> meshes = new List<MeshRenderer>();
meshes.AddRange((from mesh in loadedMesh
    select ToDispose(new MeshRenderer(mesh))));
meshes.ForEach(m => m.Initialize(this));
var meshWorld = Matrix.Identity;
```

6. Replace the rendering of the mesh within the render loop with:

```
foreach (var m in meshes)
{
  ... update perObjectBuffer
```

```
   m.PerMaterialBuffer = perMaterialBuffer;
   m.PerArmatureBuffer = perArmatureBuffer;
   m.Render();
}
```

7. Compile and run (*F5*). You should see something like the first figure of the following screenshot (while using the Blinn-Phong shader). The second figure shows what the armature looks like within the Blender.

   Although the character here is static and indeed appears exactly as it would had we not loaded any bones, it will in fact move with the bones when animated.

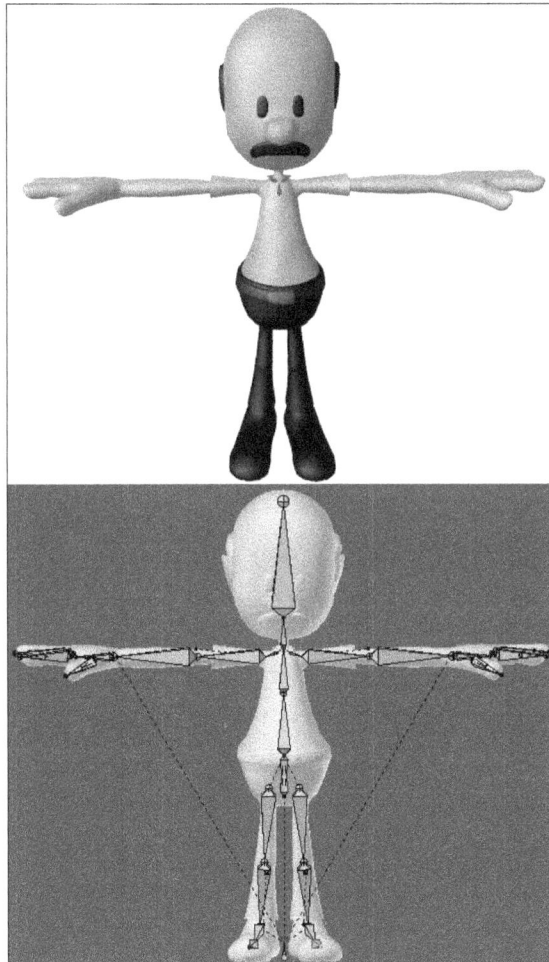

Render output in bind pose (top) and armature in Blender (bottom). Model by Rui Teixeira @ blendswap.com

How it works...

As already covered in the *Loading a static mesh from a file* recipe in *Chapter 3, Rendering Meshes*, the sample rendering framework's `Common.Mesh` class supports loading a CMO file, including the bones and animations.

The structure that stores the hierarchy of bones within a CMO and their representation in the `Common.Mesh` class is shown within the following code extracted from `Common\Mesh.cs`:

```
public class Mesh {
  ...
  [StructLayout(LayoutKind.Sequential, Pack = 1)]
  public struct Bone
  {
    public int ParentIndex; // Indexes into Mesh.Bones
    public Matrix InvBindPose;
    public Matrix BindPose;
    public Matrix BoneLocalTransform;
  };
  ...
  // Flat list of all bones
  public List<Bone> Bones { get; private set; }
  // Bone name is stored in Mesh.BoneNames (indexes match
  // between Bones and BoneNames)
  public List<string> BoneNames { get; private set; }
}
```

The `Mesh.Bone.ParentIndex` property links the bones to their immediate parent, with root bones having a parent index of `-1`.

We calculate the bone skin matrices within our mesh renderer by first loading the bone's local transform, then applying the parent transform, and finally applying the inverse bind pose.

Removing the code that applies the inverse bind pose will result in a mesh that looks like the following figure. This may also happen if the parent bones appear after the children or for some reason the transforms are incorrect.

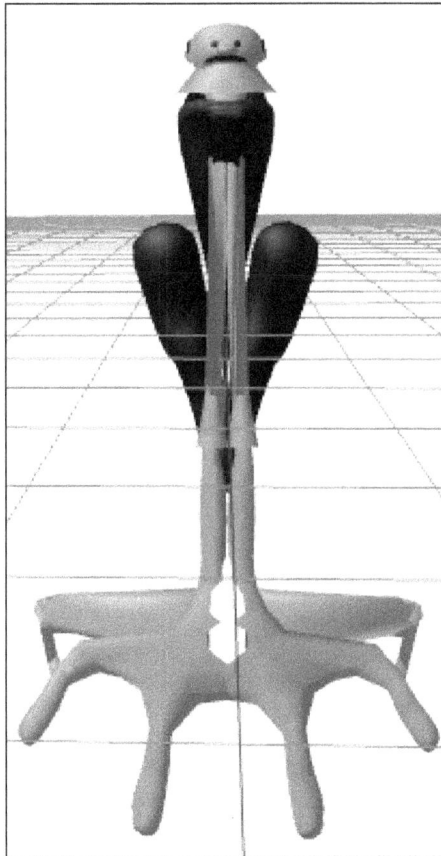

Result of incorrect bone skin transforms

As we can see from the previous figure, it is important to be in the correct space when applying transformation matrices; otherwise, when rotations are applied to an object, it will pivot around the origin within the wrong space. For example, applying a rotation matrix to a ball will not cause it to rotate on its own axis if the ball is within world space, but around the origin of the scene instead. To correctly rotate the ball, first transform it into its local space. To demonstrate the problem, the figure on the left-hand side of the following diagram shows how a rotation and translation is applied upon an object directly within world space. On the right-hand side, the object is first translated to its local space. This works in the same manner for our bones, and this is why we must use the bone's inverse bind pose matrix to transform into bone space.

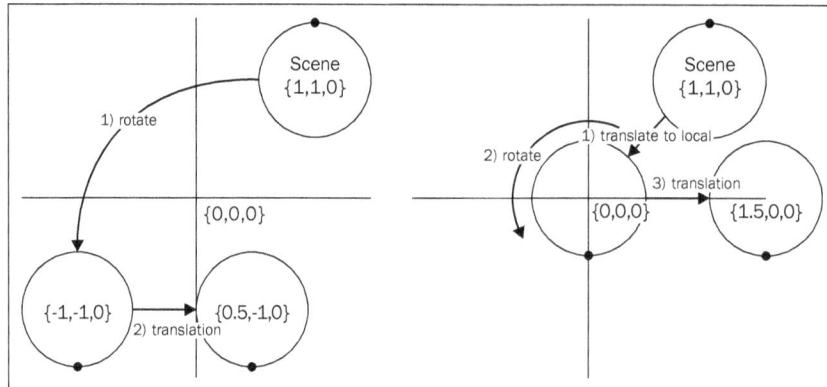

Left: an object being rotated directly in world space. Right: the same object correctly rotated within its local/model space

There's more...

Rigging is the process of binding an armature to a static model. This process usually involves creating a hierarchical bone structure that roughly reflects the shape of the static model. The amount of influence that the individual bones have on the vertices is then determined either automatically through some proximity algorithm in the authoring tool or by manual weight painting.

See also

▸ The models used in this book have been prepared using Blender, an open source 3D modeling and animation tool available at `www.blender.org`. There are plenty of great tutorials on rigging models within Blender available on YouTube. A number of great models can be found at `www.blendswap.com`.

▸ The *Animating bones* recipe takes our mesh renderer to the next step and adds support for animating our bones.

Animating bones

With an armature loaded and our vertex skinning in place, we are now ready to playback bone animations. In this recipe, we will access the animation's keyframes that are loaded from the first animation in a mesh, and playback within a loop.

Getting ready

For this recipe, we will continue from where we left off in the *Loading bones in the mesh renderer* recipe.

The completed project for this recipe, called `Ch04_02Animate`, is available within the companion source code provided with this book's code bundle. It is available on Packt website.

How to do it...

We will start by adding a few new properties to our mesh renderer.

1. Open `MeshRenderer.cs` and add the following code:

```
// Create and allow access to a timer
System.Diagnostics.Stopwatch clock = new System.Diagnostics.
Stopwatch();
public System.Diagnostics.Stopwatch Clock
{
  get { return clock; }
  set { clock = value; }
}
// The currently active animation (allows nulls)
public Mesh.Animation? CurrentAnimation { get; set; }

// Play once or loop the animation?
public bool PlayOnce { get; set; }
```

2. At the start of our `MeshRenderer.DoRender` method, calculate the number of seconds elapsed:

```
var time = clock.ElapsedMilliseconds / 1000.0f;
```

3. In place of the first `TODO` comment that we added in the previous recipe for loading bone transforms, add the following code:

```
// Load bone transforms from animation frames
if (CurrentAnimation.HasValue)
{
```

```
    // Keep track of the last key-frame used for bones
    Mesh.Keyframe?[] lastKeyForBones =
      new Mesh.Keyframe?[mesh.Bones.Count];
    // Keep track of bone interpolation
    bool[] lerpedBones = new bool[mesh.Bones.Count];
    for (var i = 0; i <
      CurrentAnimation.Value.Keyframes.Count; i++)
    {
      // Retrieve current key-frame
      var frame = CurrentAnimation.Value.Keyframes[i];
      // If the current frame is not in the future
      if (frame.Time <= time)
      {
        // Retrieve transform from current key-frame
        skinMatrices.Bones[frame.BoneIndex] =
          frame.Transform;
        // Keep track of last key-frame for bone
        // for interpolation with future frame
        lastKeyForBones[frame.BoneIndex] = frame;
      }
      // Otherwise frame is in future check interpolation
      else
      {
        ... perform frame interpolation
      }
    }
}
```

4. To provide smoother animations, we will interpolate the current keyframe for each bone with the next key-frame for each bone. We will use the following code:

```
// Only interpolate a bone's key-frames ONCE
if (!lerpedBones[frame.BoneIndex])
{
  // Retrieve the previous key-frame for bone
  Mesh.Keyframe prevFrame;
  if (lastKeyForBones[frame.BoneIndex] != null)
    prevFrame =
      lastKeyForBones[frame.BoneIndex].Value;
  else
    continue; // nothing to interpolate
  // Make sure we only interpolate with
  // one future key-frame for this bone
  lerpedBones[frame.BoneIndex] = true;
```

```
// Calculate time difference between frames
var frameLength = frame.Time - prevKeyForBone.Time;
var timeDiff = time - prevKeyForBone.Time;
var amount = timeDiff / frameLength;

// Interpolation using Lerp on scale and translation,
// and Slerp on Rotation (Quaternion)
Vector3 t1, t2;   // Translation
Quaternion q1, q2;// Rotation
float s1, s2;     // Scale
// Decompose the previous key-frame's transform
prevFrame.Transform.DecomposeUniformScale(out s1,
  out q1, out t1);
// Decompose the current key-frame's transform
frame.Transform.DecomposeUniformScale(out s2,
  out q2, out t2);

// Perform interpolation and reconstruct matrix
skinMatrices.Bones[frame.BoneIndex] =
  Matrix.Scaling(MathUtil.Lerp(s1, s2, amount)) *
Matrix.RotationQuaternion(
  Quaternion.Slerp(q1, q2, amount)) *
  Matrix.Translation(Vector3.Lerp(t1, t2, amount));
}
```

5. And finally, in place of the second TODO comment regarding the animation loop, insert the following code:

```
// Check if need to loop animation
if (!PlayOnce && CurrentAnimation.HasValue &&
  CurrentAnimation.Value.EndTime <= time)
{
  this.Clock.Restart();
}
```

6. To start our animation, add the following code to the D3DApp.Run method just after we finish loading and initializing our mesh renderers:

```
// Set first animation as the current animation and start
foreach (var m in meshes) {
  if (m.Mesh.Animations != null && m.Mesh.Animations.Any())
    m.CurrentAnimation = m.Mesh.Animations.First().Value;
  m.Clock.Start();
}
```

> The animations are stored by name in a dictionary. Therefore, the original name of the animation from the 3D authoring tool can be used to retrieve the appropriate animation. For example, `mesh.Animations["Walk"];`

7. Simply compile and run (*F5*) the project. You will see that our character is now following an animation that moves through the poses, as shown in the sequence in the following screenshot:

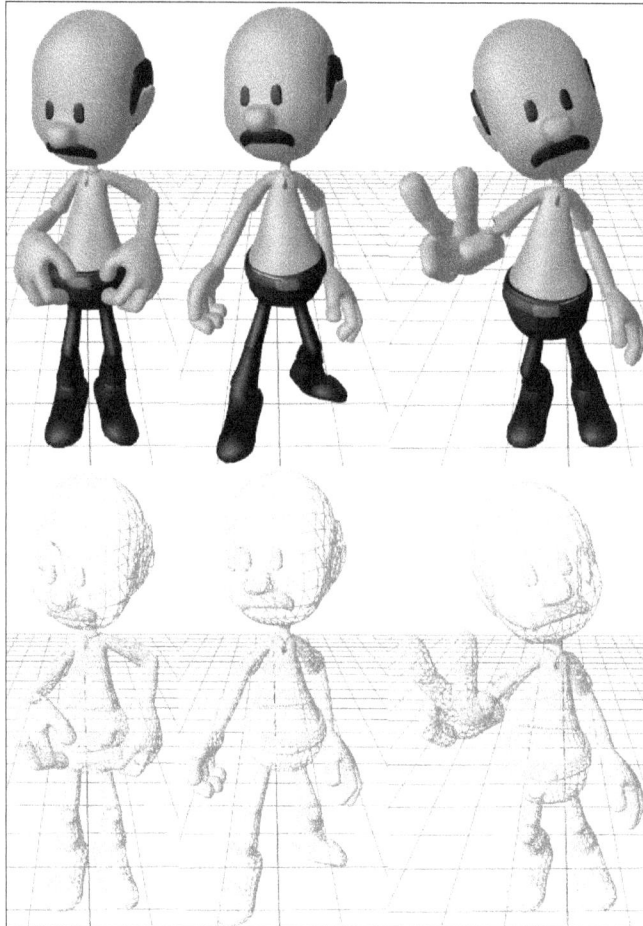

The three poses used in our animation sequence.

How it works...

As you can see, all the hard work has already been completed in the two previous recipes.

Along with the bones, the CMO file includes a list of animations for manipulating these bones. Each animation consists of a start and end time, and a list of key-frames. These are loaded into the `Common.Mesh.Animations` property. The structure of these objects within the CMO file and how they are represented in the `Common.Mesh` class is shown in the following code extracted from `Common\Mesh.cs`.

```
public class Mesh {
  ...
  [StructLayout(LayoutKind.Sequential, Pack = 1)]
  public struct Keyframe
  {
    public uint BoneIndex;
    public float Time;
    public Matrix Transform;
  };

  [StructLayout(LayoutKind.Sequential, Pack = 1)]
  public struct Animation
  {
    public float StartTime;
    public float EndTime;
    public List<Keyframe> Keyframes;
  };
  ...
  // Named list of bone animations
  public Dictionary<string, Animation> Animations { get; }
}
```

What we're doing in this recipe is retrieving the key-frames of an animation that was created within the original scene by using Blender. When exporting the scene to Autodesk FBX from Blender, the option to include animations was selected. The Visual Studio graphics content pipeline has then preserved these animations when creating the compiled mesh.

Our mesh class loads the animation key-frames (which are basically a set of frame times), bone transforms (or **animation transforms**), and bone indices. We iterate these frames up to the current frame time and replace the existing bone's local transform with that of the key-frame. We then interpolate each bone's current key-frame with its next future key-frame based on the amount of time that has lapsed between the two frames.

To produce a smoother animation without artefacts introduced from the linear interpolation of rotation matrices, we have decomposed our transformation matrices for the two key-frames into its translation, rotation, and scale components. The translation is stored within `Vector3`, the uniform scale within a `float` variable, and finally the rotation component is now stored within a **quaternion**.

```
prevFrame.Transform.DecomposeUniformScale(out s1, out q1, out t1);
frame.Transform.DecomposeUniformScale(out s2, out q2, out t2);
```

A quaternion is an alternative mathematical entity used to represent rotations. The use of quaternion has advantages over rotation matrices in numerous situations because they require less storage, fewer arithmetic operations for concatenation, and quaternions are more easily interpolated (which is most important for this recipe). **Spherical linear interpolation** is used here as the method for interpolating the quaternions because regular linear interpolation does not trace out the arc between q1 and q2 at a constant rate (*Lengyel, 2012, pp. 80-87*).

Using linear interpolation between two matrices with the `SharpDX.Matrix.Lerp` method would not necessarily result in a correct rotation matrix. It may work fine if the key-frames are close together and there are no large movements; however, it would be necessary to use either normalized linear interpolation or spherical linear interpolation to get correct results. Both of these operations are more efficient when using quaternions.

We **linearly interpolate** (**lerp**) between the two scale floats (s1 and s2) and the two translation vectors (t1 and t2). Then we perform **spherical linear interpolation** (**Slerp**) between the two quaternions (q1 and q2). The matrix is then reconstructed from the interpolated scale, rotation, and translation.

```
// Perform interpolation and reconstruct matrix
skinMatrices.Bones[frame.BoneIndex] =
  Matrix.Scaling(MathUtil.Lerp(s1, s2, amount)) *
  Matrix.RotationQuaternion(
    Quaternion.Slerp(q1, q2, amount)) *
  Matrix.Translation(Vector3.Lerp(t1, t2, amount));
```

To ensure that we end up with the correct result, multiply the matrices in the following order: first apply scale, then rotate, and finally translate.

> To exaggerate the effect of the frame smoothing, try slowing down the animation. For example, to get 1sec of the animation equal to 10secs, use the following code:
> ```
> // Calculate elapsed seconds as 1sec = 10sec
> var time = clock.ElapsedMilliseconds / 10000.0f;
> ```

Finally, we do a simple check to see whether we have reached the end of the animation sequence; and if looping is enabled, we reset the timer.

```
if (!PlayOnce && CurrentAnimation.HasValue &&
  CurrentAnimation.Value.EndTime <= time)
{
  this.Clock.Restart();
}
```

By allowing the `CurrentAnimation` variable to be defined, and if the animation will be looped, it is possible for the calling code to determine which animation in the mesh will be played and when it will start/stop.

There's more...

Animation blending is possible by interpolating between frames from different animation sequences over a period of time. This is similar to how we have implemented the smoothing between frames in this recipe. For example, a walking sequence blending into a jumping animation when a character jumps.

It is possible to apply transforms manually to animate the bone by performing the transform against a bone's bind pose. For example, applying a rotation to the bone's bind pose matrix will apply the rotation to the bone relative to its bind position. This would take place irrespective of where we have applied the animation frame transforms in this recipe. This is still a tricky process, and it is much easier to bake animations using a 3D modeling software.

Another option that can be used instead of baking animations or manual transformations is **ragdoll physics**, a type of procedural animation. This technique is named so due to the fact that characters using the system would typically fall into a heap like a toy rag doll. Ragdoll physics involves using a physics solver that takes into consideration collisions and the constraints built into each of the joints in a collection of **rigid bodies** that make up the character. This can allow a character to respond more dynamically to its environment. For example, if a character were to be hit by a bus or trip down some stairs, it may flop and bounce around realistically.

As already mentioned, getting models to work as expected after three conversions (`.blend`, `.fbx`, and then `.cmo`) can be quite tricky at times. For any large scale development, it would be worth investigating using other formats directly, or by using a custom structure that aligns with the projects requirements more closely.

The types of issues that can be encountered include, among others, incorrect normals, inconsistent vertex winding between meshes, and issues with coordinate handedness (that is, right-handed instead of left-handed). When choosing a 3D modeling package, be sure that it has the flexibility to apply custom export logic. Blender supports the extension of the export modules by editing the applicable Python script.

5
Applying Hardware Tessellation

In this chapter, we will cover the following topics:

▸ Preparing the vertex shader and buffers for tessellation

▸ Tessellating a triangle and quad

▸ Tessellating bicubic Bezier surfaces

▸ Refining meshes with Phong tessellation

▸ Optimizing tessellation through back-face culling and dynamic Level-of-Detail

Introduction

Tessellation is the process of tiling/dicing a plane with one or more geometric shapes, for example, the creation of mosaics. In Direct3D 11, this process refers to the division of geometry into smaller triangles according to an algorithm and a tessellation factor. Hardware tessellation is available in Shader Model 5.0 and, therefore, hardware must support a Direct3D feature level of 11_0 or higher.

When applying tessellation, we are submitting a control point *patch* to the input assembler using one of the available control point input topologies (supporting up to 32 control points per patch). A patch is a Direct3D primitive made up of a list of control points. For example, we can re-use our existing meshes, made up of triangle lists, for tessellation by using the `PrimitiveTopology.PatchListWith3ControlPoints` enumeration value (natively, `D3D11_PRIMITIVE_3_CONTROL_POINT_PATCH`). What each control point does or means is entirely up to the implementation within the hull and domain shaders; the tessellator itself does not use the control points as it doesn't know how to interpret them.

As already covered in *Chapter 1*, *Getting Started with Direct3D*, the tessellation stages of the graphics pipeline are made up of two programmable shader stages and one fixed function stage—the hull shader, tessellator, and domain shader stages. Similar to the geometry shader, the tessellation stages are able to generate additional vertices. However, the vertices tend to be a part of the same surface, whereas a geometry shader might be used to create an entirely new unrelated shape or copies of the existing primitive.

Using tessellation can reduce the memory bandwidth by allowing the use of lower quality meshes with fewer vertices, while still maintaining the high quality detailed meshes in the final render. The flexibility gained through the programmable stages of the tessellation pipeline allows multiple uses from supporting dynamic **Level-of-Detail** (**LoD**), to rendering parametric surfaces from a single control point.

Preparing the vertex shader and buffers for tessellation

In this recipe, we will update the constant buffers to accept the tessellation parameters, and update the vertex shader to output a structure for input into the hull shaders in the next few recipes in this chapter.

Getting ready

For this recipe, we can begin with any Direct3D project with an existing vertex shader, the `PerObject` and `PerFrame` constant buffers, and their C# counterparts in `ConstantBuffers.cs`.

The completed source code for this recipe can be found within the `Ch05_01TessellationPrimitives` project, contained within the companion source code.

How to do it...

We will first update our **HLSL** (**High-level Shader Language**) and C# structures, and then make a new vertex shader to use with the tessellation pipeline.

1. Update the `PerObject` constant buffer within `Common.hlsl` to include the following property:

   ```
   // Matrix to take world coordinates to view/projection
   // Used in the domain shader
   float4x4 ViewProjection;
   ```

> As mentioned in the recipe, *Rendering a cube and sphere*, in *Chapter 3*, *Rendering Meshes*, the `ViewProjection` matrix should ideally be placed within the `PerFrame` constant buffer. Here, for simplicity, we continue to group the matrices within the `PerObject` constant buffer.

2. Update the corresponding structure in `ConstantBuffers.cs` to include `public Matrix ViewProjection;` remember that it also needs to be transposed in the `Transpose` method.

3. To reflect the desired tessellation factor, update the `perFrame` constant buffer in `Common.hlsl` to include a new member named `float TessellationFactor`.

4. In the corresponding `PerFrame` structure in the `ConstantBuffers.cs` file, we add `public float TessellationFactor;` remember to keep in mind the 16-byte alignment and to match the layout with the HLSL structure.

5. Jump over to the `D3DApp` render loop and locate where the `perObject.WorldViewProjection` property is set and add the following:

    ```
    perObject.ViewProjection = viewProjection;
    ```

6. Then, find where the `perFrame.CameraPosition` property is updated and add the following:

    ```
    perFrame.TessellationFactor = tessellationFactor;
    ```

> The `tessellationFactor` variable is a `float` value that is set between `1.0f` and `64.0f`. The completed sample maps the +/- keys to increase/decrease the value.

We are now done with the changes to `Common.hlsl` and the constant buffers.

7. Next, let's create the `Shaders\CommonTess.hlsl` file that houses the common shader structures and functions used by our tessellation shader code. Now, we will add the following HLSL structures:

    1. The `HullShaderInput` structure, a subset of the existing vertex structure input, is as shown in the following code snippet:

        ```
        struct HullShaderInput
        {
            float3 WorldPosition : POSITION;
            float4 Diffuse : COLOR;
            float2 TextureUV: TEXCOORD0;
            float3 WorldNormal : TEXCOORD1;
        };
        ```

2. The common domain shader input structure is as follows:

```
// Max 32 outputs
struct DS_ControlPointInput {
    float3 Position : BEZIERPOS;
    float4 Diffuse : COLOR0;
};
```

8. With the prerequisites in place, let us create a new vertex shader for use with the tessellation pipeline.

   1. With `VS.hlsl` open, add a new include directive:

      ```
      #include "CommonTess.hlsl"
      ```

   2. Create a copy of your existing vertex shader function and name it as `VSPassThruTessellate`. Then, change the return type to `HullShaderInput`.

9. Update the vertex shader to set the four properties of the preceding `HullShaderInput` structure. We will continue to apply the `PerObject.World` transform to the `position` and `normal` variables.

How it works...

As the domain shader will now be performing the multiplication of the position by the `ViewProjection` matrix and it is easier to work with the vertices in world space, we need to ensure our *per object* structures in `Common.hlsl` and `ConstantBuffers.cs` include a copy of our `ViewProjection` matrix to take the position from world space to view/projection space (or clip space).

The vertex shader now simply passes through the vertex attributes within world space to be processed by the hull and domain shaders.

Tessellating a triangle and quad

In this recipe, we will perform tessellation upon a triangle and a quad patch. We will create the hull and domain shaders that are necessary to use the triangle and quad tessellation domains, respectively.

As the fixed function tessellation stage is used to define new vertices, it is necessary to move some of the vertex shader code into the applicable domain shader, such as applying the `ViewProjection` matrix and calculating the interpolated vertex normal and texture coordinates.

We will update the `CommonTess.hlsl` shader code to perform barycentric interpolation, to calculate the attributes for new vertices in a triangle domain, and bilinear interpolation to interpolate between the four attributes within the quad domain.

Getting ready

We will continue from the previous recipe, *Preparing the vertex shader and buffers for tessellation*.

For this recipe, we will also re-use the triangle and quad renderers from the recipe *Rendering primitives* in *Chapter 2, Rendering with Direct3D*, along with the `Texture2.png` texture.

1. Add the `Texture2.png` texture, and the `TriangleRenderer.cs` and `QuadRenderer.cs` renderers to your project.

2. Update the quad and triangle renderers to use the `Vertex` structure for the vertices, passing in the vertex positions and UV coordinates as appropriate.

3. The vertex winding will also need to be reversed, as these renderers were created for a left-handed coordinate system.

> Remember to update the vertex binding in order to use the size of the `Vertex` structure.

The completed project for this recipe can be found in `Ch05_01TessellationPrimitives` within the downloaded companion code.

How to do it...

We will begin by creating the interpolation functions necessary for the `tri` and `quad` domains within `Shaders\CommonTess.hlsl`. We will then implement the hull and domain shaders, and finally update the renderers. Perform the following steps:

1. First add a new HLSL function `BarycentricInterpolate` to `CommonTess.hlsl`. As we may need to interpolate `float2`, `float3`, and `float4` values, we will add a number of overloaded versions of this function. For convenience, we can accept the inputs as individual parameters or as an array. The following code snippet shows the `float3` version; you need to do the same using `float2` and `float4`:

```
float3 BarycentricInterpolate(float3 v0, float3 v1,
    float3 v2, float3 barycentric)
{
    return barycentric.z * v0 + barycentric.x * v1 +
```

```
            barycentric.y * v2;
    }
    float3 BarycentricInterpolate(float3 v[3],
        float3 barycentric)
    {
        return BarycentricInterpolate(v[0], v[1], v[2],
          barycentric);
    }
```

2. To perform bilinear interpolation between the four values of a quad domain, add a `Bilerp` function to `CommonTess.hlsl`. Again, we will need to interpolate between `float2` and `float3` values. The following code snippet shows the implementation for the four `float3` values; you need to do the same using `float2` and `float4`:

```
float3 Bilerp(float3 v[4], float2 uv)
{
    // bilerp the float3 values
    float3 side1 = lerp( v[0], v[1], uv.x );
    float3 side2 = lerp( v[3], v[2], uv.x );
    return lerp( side1, side2, uv.y );
}
```

3. The hull shader constant data that is generated for a triangle patch will use the following structure, which we also add to `CommonTess.hlsl`:

```
// Max 32 outputs
struct HS_TrianglePatchConstant {
    float EdgeTessFactor[3] : SV_TessFactor;
    float InsideTessFactor : SV_InsideTessFactor;

    float2 TextureUV[3]: TEXCOORD0;
    float3 WorldNormal[3] : TEXCOORD3;
};
```

4. Lastly, to support the hull shader constant data for a quad patch, add the following HLSL structure:

```
// Max 32 outputs
struct HS_QuadPatchConstant {
    float EdgeTessFactor[4] : SV_TessFactor;
    float InsideTessFactor[2] : SV_InsideTessFactor;
    float2 TextureUV[4]: TEXCOORD0;
    float3 WorldNormal[4] : TEXCOORD4;
};
```

5. Create a new shader file named `Shaders\TessellateTri.hlsl`; this will contain our triangle tessellation hull shaders, hull shader patch constant function, and domain shader.

> Remember that the file encoding needs to be changed to **Western European (Windows) – Codepage 1252**, and select **Copy if newer**.

6. Add the following `include` directives to the start of the code:

```
#include "Common.hlsl"
#include "CommonTess.hlsl"
```

7. For simplicity, we will create four hull shaders, one for each of the available partitioning methods, `HS_TrianglesInteger`, `HS_TrianglesFractionalOdd`, `HS_TrianglesFractionalEven`, and `HS_TrianglesPow2`. Each of these functions is identical, except for the name and the partitioning type attribute applied.

```
[domain("tri")] // Triangle domain for our shader
[partitioning("integer")] // Partitioning type
[outputtopology("triangle_ccw")] // winding order
[outputcontrolpoints(3)] // Number of points for each patch
// The constant hull shader function
[patchconstantfunc("HS_TrianglesConstant")]
DS_ControlPointInput HS_TrianglesInteger(
                    InputPatch<HullShaderInput, 3> patch,
                    uint id : SV_OutputControlPointID,
                    uint patchID : SV_PrimitiveID )
{
    DS_ControlPointInput result = (DS_ControlPointInput)0;
    result.Position = patch[id].WorldPosition;
    result.Diffuse = patch[id].Diffuse;
    return result;
}
```

8. Here, we have shown the `integer` partitioning type function; repeat the preceding step for each of the following partitioning types (substituting the partitioning attribute and changing the function name accordingly): `fractional_odd`, `fractional_even`, and `pow2`.

> This could also be achieved by defining a conditional macro, for example:
> ```
> #define HS_PARTITIONING "integer"
> ```
> This can also be specified as a parameter to the HLSL compiler when compiling the shader code.

9. Next, we will add the patch constant function, which will be executed only once for each patch; this is the same function used by each of the hull shaders and is referenced in the hull shader with the `patchconstantfunc` attribute.

```
// Triangle patch constant function
// (executes once for each triangle patch)
HS_TrianglePatchConstant HS_TrianglesConstant(
  InputPatch<HullShaderInput, 3> patch)
{
    HS_TrianglePatchConstant result =
        (HS_TrianglePatchConstant)0;

    // Determine the rounded tess factor
    float3 roundedEdgeTessFactor;
    float roundedInsideTessFactor, insideTessFactor;
    ProcessTriTessFactorsMax((float3)TessellationFactor,
        1.0, roundedEdgeTessFactor, roundedInsideTessFactor,
        insideTessFactor);

    // Apply the edge and inside tessellation factors
    result.EdgeTessFactor[0] = roundedEdgeTessFactor.x;
    result.EdgeTessFactor[1] = roundedEdgeTessFactor.y;
    result.EdgeTessFactor[2] = roundedEdgeTessFactor.z;
    result.InsideTessFactor = roundedInsideTessFactor;

    // Apply constant information
    [unroll]
    for (uint i = 0; i < 3; i++)
    {
        result.TextureUV[i] = patch[i].TextureUV;
        result.WorldNormal[i] = patch[i].WorldNormal;
    }

    return result;
}
```

10. Next, we will add the domain shader. This shader performs the necessary barycentric interpolation, and then returns the pixel shader input structure. The final transformation to clip space with the view/projection matrix is also performed here:

```
// This domain shader applies control point weighting to
// the barycentric coords produced by the fixed function
// tessellator stage
[domain("tri")]
```

```
PixelShaderInput DS_Triangles(HS_TrianglePatchConstant
constantData, const OutputPatch<DS_ControlPointInput, 3> patch,
float3 barycentricCoords : SV_DomainLocation)
{
    PixelShaderInput result = (PixelShaderInput)0;
    // Interpolate using barycentric coordinates
    float3 position = BarycentricInterpolate(
        patch[0].Position, patch[1].Position,
        patch[2].Position, barycentricCoords);
    // Interpolate the array of UV coords
    float2 UV = BarycentricInterpolate(
        constantData.TextureUV, barycentricCoords);
    float4 diffuse = BarycentricInterpolate(
        patch[0].Diffuse, patch[1].Diffuse,
        patch[2].Diffuse, barycentricCoords);
    // Interpolate the array of normals
    float3 normal = BarycentricInterpolate(
        constantData.WorldNormal, barycentricCoords);
    // Prepare pixel shader input:
    // Transform world position to view-projection
    result.Position = mul( float4(position,1),
        ViewProjection );

    result.Diffuse = diffuse;
    result.TextureUV = UV;
    result.WorldNormal = normal;
    result.WorldPosition = position;

    return result;
}
```

We will now create a quad domain hull and domain shader that accepts four control points.

11. Create a new shader file named `Shaders\TessellateQuad.hlsl` and set the encoding, build action, and add the `include` directives as per the preceding triangle tessellator.

12. Now, we will create a hull shader for each of the tessellation partitioning methods as before. The hull shader for the `integer` partitioning type is shown as follows; create one for each of the partitioning types as before. The differences from the triangle hull shader are highlighted:

```
[domain("quad")] // Quad domain for our shader
[partitioning("integer")] // Partitioning type
```

```
[outputtopology("triangle_ccw")] // order of the tris
[outputcontrolpoints(4)] // Number of times called for patch
// The constant hull shader function
[patchconstantfunc("HS_QuadsConstant")] DS_ControlPointInput HS_
QuadsInteger(
                        InputPatch<HullShaderInput, 4> patch,
                        uint id : SV_OutputControlPointID,
                        uint patchID : SV_PrimitiveID)
{
    DS_ControlPointInput result = (DS_ControlPointInput)0;
    result.Position = patch[id].WorldPosition;
    result.Diffuse = patch[id].Diffuse;
    return result;
}
```

13. Now, add the quad patch constant function. Here, the changes from the triangle tessellator are highlighted:

```
HS_QuadPatchConstant HS_QuadsConstant(
    InputPatch<HullShaderInput, 4> patch)
{
    HS_QuadPatchConstant result = (HS_QuadPatchConstant)0;

    // Perform rounding
    float4 roundedEdgeTessFactor;
    float2 roundedInsideTessFactor, insideTessFactor;
    Process2DQuadTessFactorsMax((float4)TessellationFactor, 1.0,
roundedEdgeTessFactor, roundedInsideTessFactor, insideTessFactor);

    // Apply the edge and inside tessellation factors
    result.EdgeTessFactor[0] = roundedEdgeTessFactor.x;
    result.EdgeTessFactor[1] = roundedEdgeTessFactor.y;
    result.EdgeTessFactor[2] = roundedEdgeTessFactor.z;
    result.EdgeTessFactor[3] = roundedEdgeTessFactor.w;

    result.InsideTessFactor[0] = roundedInsideTessFactor.x;
    result.InsideTessFactor[1] = roundedInsideTessFactor.y;

    // Apply constant information
    [unroll]
    for (uint i = 0; i < 4; i++)
    {
        result.TextureUV[i] = patch[i].TextureUV;
        result.WorldNormal[i] = patch[i].WorldNormal;
    }

    return result;
}
```

14. And finally, we will add the quad domain shader. This time, we will perform a bilinear interpolation using the `Bilerp` function from `CommonTess.hlsl`:

```
// Applies control point weighting with bilinear
// interpolation
[domain("quad")]
PixelShaderInput DS_Quads(
    HS_QuadPatchConstant constantData,
    const OutputPatch<DS_ControlPointInput, 4> patch,
    float2 uv : SV_DomainLocation)
{
    PixelShaderInput result = (PixelShaderInput)0;

    // Interpolate using bilerp
    float4 c[4];
    float3 p[4];
    [unroll]
    for(uint i=0;i<4;i++) {
        p[i] = patch[i].Position;
        c[i] = patch[i].Diffuse;
    }
    float3 position = Bilerp(p, uv);
    float2 UV = Bilerp(constantData.TextureUV, uv);
    float4 diffuse = Bilerp(c, uv);
    float3 normal = Bilerp(constantData.WorldNormal, uv);

    // Prepare pixel shader input:
    ...SNIP as per the triangle tessellator domain shader
    return result;
}
```

15. Within the `D3DApp.CreateDeviceDependentResources` method, compile the `TessellateTri.hlsl` and `TessellateQuad.hlsl` shader functions, using the `hs_5_0` shader profile for each of the hull shader functions, and `ds_5_0` for the domain shader function.

16. We will also need to provide access to the `PerObject` and `PerFrame` constant buffers within the hull and domain shaders. To do this, add the following code to the `D3DApp.CreateDeviceDependentResources` method:

```
// Set our hull/domain shader constant buffers
context.HullShader.SetConstantBuffer(0, perObjectBuffer);
context.HullShader.SetConstantBuffer(1, perFrameBuffer);
context.DomainShader.SetConstantBuffer(0, perObjectBuffer);
context.DomainShader.SetConstantBuffer(1, perFrameBuffer);
```

Lastly, we need to update the renderers, so that they pass through the correct input topology.

17. For the `TriangleRenderer` C# class, change the `DoRender` method to set the `PrimitiveTopology` enumeration to a patch list with three control points:

```
context.InputAssembler.PrimitiveTopology =
    PrimitiveTopology.PatchListWith3ControlPoints;
```

18. For the `QuadRenderer` class, we do not need an index buffer. Instead, we will use the following code in the `DoRender` method to set up the patch topology and draw the vertices:

```
context.InputAssembler.PrimitiveTopology =
    PrimitiveTopology.PatchListWith4ControlPoints;
context.InputAssembler.SetVertexBuffers(0, quadBinding);
context.Draw(4, 0);
```

19. Create an instance of our renderers within `D3DApp.Run`, and add a call to their `Render` method within the render loop.

20. Add the `TriangleRenderer` and `QuadRenderer` classes to the render loop:

```
// TRIANGLE
context.VertexShader.Set(tessellateVertexShader);
context.HullShader.Set(activeTriTessellator);
context.DomainShader.Set(tessellateTriDomainShader);
triangle.Render();
// QUAD
context.VertexShader.Set(tessellateVertexShader);
context.HullShader.Set(activeQuadTessellator);
context.DomainShader.Set(tessellateQuadDomainShader);
quad.Render();

...
// RESET SHADERS
context.VertexShader.Set(vertexShader);
context.HullShader.Set(null);
context.DomainShader.Set(null);
```

Attempting to use the wrong primitive topology type with the hull/domain shader may result in an unexpected behavior; therefore, we clear the shaders to ensure that they don't interfere with other renderers.
For example, on a test machine, it was possible to crash the display driver subsystem by specifying a standard triangle list while a hull shader was set.

21. In the preceding code, `active*Tessellator` is one of the applicable `integer`, `pow2` hull shaders. The completed project maps keys from *F1* to *F4* to the different partitioning types. Compiling and running the application will produce results similar to those shown in the following sequence of figures:

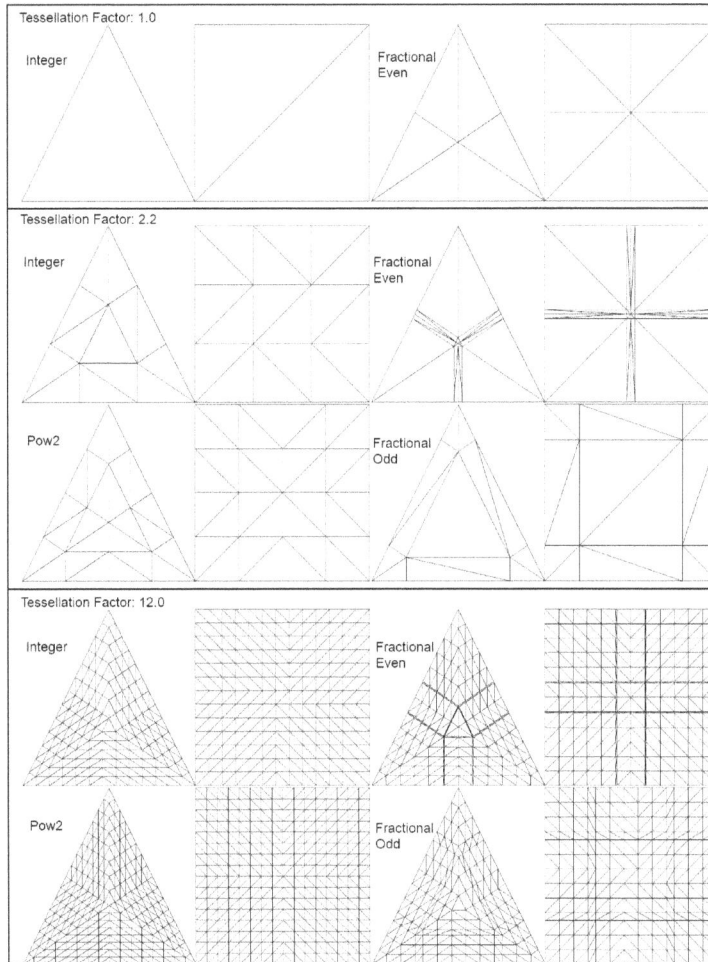

Examples of each of the partitioning methods with varying tessellation factors. Applying a tessellation factor of 0 will cull the primitive, while setting the [maxtessfactor] attribute of the hull shader will limit the maximum tessellation factor.

How it works...

As already covered in *Chapter 1, Getting Started with Direct3D*, the tessellation phase of the graphics pipeline incorporates three distinct stages, the hull shader, the fixed function tessellator, and the domain shader.

The hull shader is made of two shader functions: the hull shader itself that is responsible for outputting per control point properties, and the patch constant function that is responsible for outputting per patch properties and tessellation factor that will be used by the fixed function tessellator stage. Both the methods have access to the entire input patch. After the fixed function tessellator stage is processed, the new geometry is passed to the domain shader, where the attributes of each new control point can be determined.

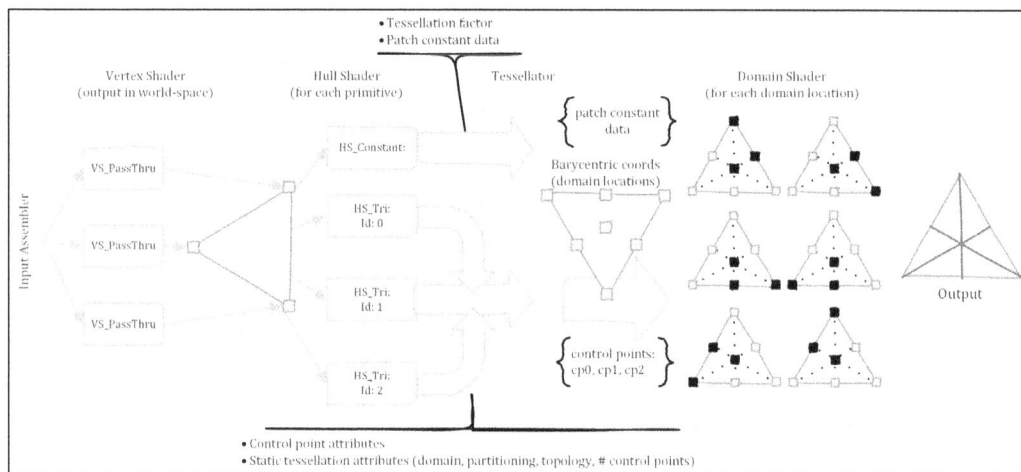

Tessellation pipeline for a triangle domain

While creating the triangle hull shader, we have indicated with the `domain` attribute that the domain of the tessellator is triangles, and this instructs the fixed function tessellator stage to generate barycentric coordinates as the `SV_DomainLocation` parameter that is passed to the domain shader. This `domain` attribute must be consistent across the hull and domain shaders currently bound to the pipeline.

```
[domain("tri")]
```

The impact of the `partitioning` attribute upon the tessellator is shown in the previous example output. You can see that depending on the selected `partitioning` method and for the same tessellation factor, additional geometry of varying amount is generated at different locations. This is best experienced by seeing the tessellation factor slowly increasing in time.

The `integer` and `pow2` methods will increase the number of primitives generated based on the current whole number or power of two respectively, while showing no change for the values in between. Whereas the `fractional_even` and `fractional_odd` methods will show a gradual increase of the tessellation level between the whole numbers—with odd numbers starting from the outside edges and even the center. As more or less geometry is generated with changes in the tessellation factor, `integer` and `pow2` will show *popping* geometry, while the fractional partitioning schemes can result in *swimming* geometry. These two behaviors are important to consider while you are using dynamic levels of tessellation:

```
[partitioning("fractional_odd")]
```

The `outputtopology` attribute controls, whether the output primitive topology is a triangle (clockwise or counter-clockwise), a point or a line, as shown in the following code snippet:

```
[outputtopology("triangle_cw")]   // triangle clockwise
[outputtopology("triangle_ccw")]  // triangle counter-clockwise
[outputtopology("point")]         // point
[outputtopology("line")]          // line
```

The `outputcontrolpoints` attribute value defines how many times the hull shader will be called for each input patch. Each hull shader execution is passed an ID through the `SV_OutputControlPointID` input semantic and the input patch, and it returns a single control point. The complete list of control points for the primitive will be passed on to the domain shader by the fixed function tessellator stage. This can be seen in the preceding pipeline diagram. The last attribute, `patchconstantfunc`, tells the tessellator pipeline which function is the counterpart of the hull shader. This function is required and is used to define the edge and internal tessellation factors of the patch along with any other patch attributes.

```
[patchconstantfunc("HS_TrianglesConstant")]
```

The body of our hull shader is simply retrieving the control point from the input patch and passing this information to the result. By using the `SV_OutputControlPointID` parameter, it is possible to load additional information for the control points from precalculated textures or buffers.

The constant function of the hull shader patch must provide the tessellation factor for the patch. In our example, this is a constant value that is provided in the `perFrame` constant buffer.

Although it is possible to provide multiple tessellation factors (left, right, top, and bottom, depending on the domain), we are providing a constant tessellation factor across all the edges by casting `TessellationFactor float` to a `float3` for `tri` domain or `float4` for the `quad` domain. We use the built-in HLSL functions to round the tessellation factor. This ensures that the values used for the inside and outside edges are correct for the specified `partitioning` method.

```
ProcessTriTessFactorsMax((float3)TessellationFactor, 1.0,
    roundedEdgeTessFactor, roundedInsideTessFactor,
      insideTessFactor);
Process2DQuadTessFactorsMax((float4)TessellationFactor, 1.0,
    roundedEdgeTessFactor, roundedInsideTessFactor,
      insideTessFactor);
```

The last part of the hull shader constant function returns data to be shared across all the control points of the patch. The maximum number of outputs supported for a structure involved in the tessellation pipeline is 32 `float4` properties, allowing a total of 1024 bytes per patch (remember that the structure will be padded to 16 bytes). Generally the amount of information should be kept to a minimum, and it may be necessary to use buffers or texture sampling to load additional data.

The domain shader is called for each newly created output control point in each patch by the fixed function tessellator stage. This shader is responsible for generating appropriate texture coordinates, and so on, across the newly created geometry. The result is then output to the pixel shader.

Our two renderers use two different interpolation techniques: barycentric interpolation (for the `tri` domain), and bilinear interpolation (for the `quad` domain with four control points).

There's more...

Controlling the tessellation factors for individual outside and inside edges within the hull shader constant function is especially useful while performing screen adaptive tessellation. This form of adaptive tessellation determines the tessellation factor for an edge based upon the length of the edge within screen space.

See also

We cover culling of primitives within the tessellation pipeline in the recipe, *Optimizing tessellation through back-face culling and dynamic Level-of-Detail*, later in this chapter.

Tessellating bicubic Bezier surfaces

In this recipe, we will perform tessellation upon a bicubic Bezier control patch using the tessellation stages of the graphics pipeline. This tessellation will use the quad domain of the tessellator. We will update the CommonTess.hlsl shader code to include the methods to perform bicubic interpolation of the Bezier control points using **De Casteljau's algorithm** to subdivide a Bezier curve at an arbitrary point along the curve.

Getting ready

We will continue on from the earlier recipe, *Preparing the vertex shader and buffers for tessellation*.

How to do it...

We will first implement the shader code for tessellating our Bezier control points. We will then implement a renderer for a bicubic Bezier surface. Consider the following steps:

1. First within CommonTess.hlsl, we add the hull shader constant data structure to be generated for a Bezier patch:

```
// Max 32 outputs
struct HS_BezierPatchConstant {
    float EdgeTessFactor[4] : SV_TessFactor;
    float InsideTessFactor[2] : SV_InsideTessFactor;

    float2 TextureUV[16]: TEXCOORD0;
};
```

2. Then, we add a new function for bicubic interpolation to CommonTess.hlsl. As with the previous recipe, we will implement the interpolation for float2 and float3 variables. The following code shows the implementation for float3:

```
// Calculate point upon Bezier curve and return
void DeCasteljau(float u, float3 p0, float3 p1, float3 p2, float3 p3, out float3 p, out float3 t)
{
    float3 q0 = lerp(p0, p1, u);
    float3 q1 = lerp(p1, p2, u);
    float3 q2 = lerp(p2, p3, u);
```

```
        float3 r0 = lerp(q0, q1, u);
        float3 r1 = lerp(q1, q2, u);
        t = r0 - r1; // tangent
        p = lerp(r0, r1, u);
}
// Bicubic interpolation of cubic Bezier surface
void DeCasteljauBicubic(float2 uv, float3 p[16], out float3
result, out float3 normal)
{
        // Interpolated values (e.g. points)
        float3 p0, p1, p2, p3;
        // Tangents (derivatives)
        float3 t0, t1, t2, t3;
        // Calculate tangent and positions along each curve
        DeCasteljau(uv.x, p[ 0], p[ 1], p[ 2], p[ 3], p0, t0);
        DeCasteljau(uv.x, p[ 4], p[ 5], p[ 6], p[ 7], p1, t1);
        DeCasteljau(uv.x, p[ 8], p[ 9], p[10], p[11], p2, t2);
        DeCasteljau(uv.x, p[12], p[13], p[14], p[15], p3, t3);
        // Calculate final position and tangents across surface
        float3 du, dv, tmp;
        DeCasteljau(uv.y, p0, p1, p2, p3, result, dv);
        DeCasteljau(uv.y, t0, t1, t2, t3, du, tmp);
        // du represents tangent
        // dv represents bitangent
        normal = normalize(cross(du, dv));
}
```

> A difference in the implementation of `float2` support is that we will not calculate the normal vector.

3. Create a new shader file named `Shaders\TessellateBezier.hlsl`, as per the `quad` example provided in the previous recipe.

4. The hull shaders are identical to the `quad` hull shaders, except that the number of input and output control points is now `16` instead of `4`, and the names should begin with `HS_Bezier` (for example, `HS_BezierInteger`). The `patchconstantfunc` attribute should also be changed to `HS_BezierConstant`.

5. The Bezier patch constant function, as shown in the following code snippet, is very similar to the `quad` example:

```
HS_BezierPatchConstant HS_BezierConstant(InputPatch<HullShaderInp
ut, 16> patch)
{
```

```
HS_BezierPatchConstant result =
    (HS_BezierPatchConstant)0;
// Perform rounding
...SNIP as per quad patch constant function above

// Apply constant information
[unroll]
for (uint I = 0; i < 16; i++)
{
    result.TextureUV[i] = patch[i].TextureUV;
}
return result;
}
```

6. Next, we create the Bezier patch domain shader. This time, we will use bicubic Bezier surface interpolation with the `DeCasteljauBicubic` function within `CommonTess.hlsl`. The domain shader code for the Bezier surface is as follows:

```
// Applies control point weighting using Bezier bicubic
// interpolation
[domain(""quad"")]
PixelShaderInput DS_Bezier( HS_BezierPatchConstant constantData,
  const OutputPatch<DS_ControlPointInput, 16> patch,
    float2 uv : SV_DomainLocation )
{
    PixelShaderInput result = (PixelShaderInput)0;
    // input Colors
    float3 c[16];
    // input Control points
    float3 p[16];
    [unroll]
    for(uint i=0;i<16;i++) {
        p[i] = patch[i].Position;
        c[i] = patch[i].Diffuse.rgb;
    }
    float3 position, normal;
    // Perform De Casteljau bicubic interpolation of
    // positions then output final position and normal
    DeCasteljauBicubic(uv, p, position, normal);
    // Perform De Casteljau bicubic interpolation of UV
    DeCasteljauBicubic(uv, constantData.TextureUV,
        result.TextureUV);
```

```
        // Calculate diffuse color with consideration of all 16
        // control points (using alpha from only the first)
        float3 color, c1;
        DeCasteljauBicubic(uv, c, color, c1);
        float4 diffuse = float4(color, patch[0].Diffuse.a);
        // Prepare pixel shader input:
        // Transform world position to view-projection
        result.Position = mul(float4(position, 1),
            ViewProjection);
        result.Diffuse = diffuse;
        result.WorldNormal = normal;
        result.WorldPosition = position;
        return result;
}
```

7. Add a new C# renderer class named `BezierPatchRenderer` with the appropriate
    SharpDX `using` directives. This renderer will be used to render a 16 control point
    Bezier surface.

8. Within the `BezierPatchRenderer.CreateDeviceDependentResources`
    override, we will add the following code to define the 16 control points:

```
// Create the cubic Bezier surface
// Note: the normals are calculated from the Bezier surface
vertexBuffer = ToDispose(Buffer.Create(device, BindFlags.
VertexBuffer, new[] {
    //          x, y, z          u, v texture coord
    new Vertex(-1, 0, 1,         0, 0),
    new Vertex(-0.34f, 0, 1,     1, 0),
    new Vertex(0.34f, 0, 1,      2, 0),
    new Vertex(1, 0, 1,          3, 0),

    new Vertex(-1, 0, 0.34f,       0, 1),
    new Vertex(-0.34f, 2, 0.34f,1, 1),
    new Vertex(0.34f, 2, 0.34f, 2, 1),
    new Vertex(1, 0, 0.34f,        3, 1),

    new Vertex(-1, 0, -0.34f,       0, 2),
    new Vertex(-0.34f, 2, -0.34f, 1, 2),
    new Vertex(0.34f, 2, -0.34f,  2, 2),
    new Vertex(1, 0, -0.34f,        3, 2),

    new Vertex(-1, 0, -1,       0, 3),
    new Vertex(-0.34f, 0, -1, 1, 3),
    new Vertex(0.34f, 0, -1,  2, 3),
    new Vertex(1, 0, -1,        3, 3),}));
vertexBinding = new VertexBufferBinding(vertexBuffer,
  Utilities.SizeOf<Vertex>(), 0);
```

9. We can load the control points from a file, such as for the famous Utah Teapot (refer to the link in the *See also* section). The following diagram shows how the vertices match the control points of a cubic Bezier surface:

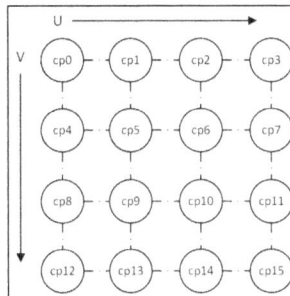

Cubic Bezier surface control point layout

10. Finally, within the `DoRender` override, we will draw the surface with the following code:

```
// Tell the IA we are using a list of patches with 16
// control points each
context.InputAssembler.PrimitiveTopology =
  PrimitiveTopology.PatchListWith16ControlPoints;
// Pass in the vertices
context.InputAssembler.SetVertexBuffers(0, vertexBinding);
context.Draw(16, 0);
```

> The completed sample within the downloaded content includes the options to enable a second and third draw sequence for the Bezier patch that outputs the control points as `PointList` and `LineList`. This can be helpful to visualize how the control points impact the final result.

11. Within the `D3DApp.CreateDeviceDependentResources` method, compile the shader methods as per the triangle and quad shader code from the previous recipe.

12. Lastly, render the Bezier surface, as shown in the previous recipe. Remember to reset the vertex, hull, and domain shaders afterwards.

13. In the completed project, the *Backspace* key is mapped to toggle between the renderers. The following screenshot shows the Bezier output:

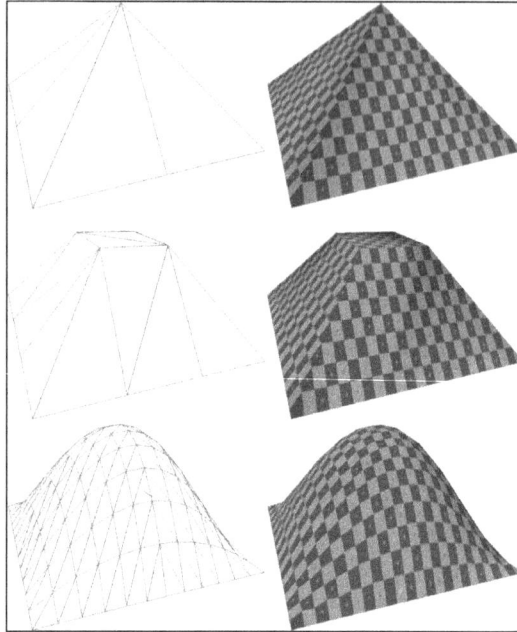

Bezier patch with integer partitioning and tessellation factors from top to bottom of: 1.2, 2.0, and 12.0

How it works...

In this recipe, we use bicubic interpolation of Bezier patches (for a `quad` domain with 16 control points), which can be used as a method for approximating **Catmull-Clark** subdivision surfaces (Loop and Schaefer 2008).

The bicubic Bezier surface consists of four rows of Bezier curves using four control points each. The interpolation across the Bezier surface works by first linear interpolating (**lerp**) each of the Bezier curves, and then linear interpolating the results of these four curves. The following diagram shows how this works for a single Bezier curve with a lerp value of 0.5:

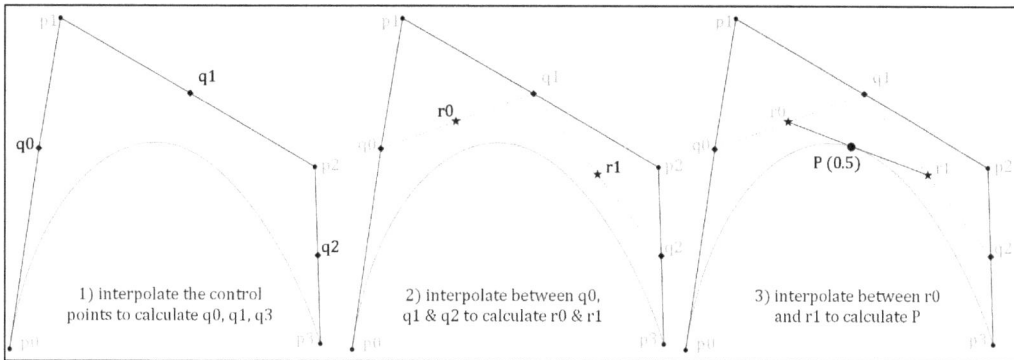

Using De Casteljau's algorithm to calculate a point upon a Bezier curve where u == 0.5

The following diagram shows the control points used to generate our cubic Bezier surface:

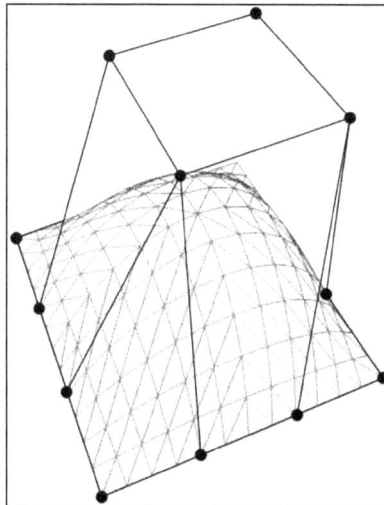

Bezier patch showing lines between 12 of the 16 control points

There's more...

At this point, we have only scratched the surface of what can be done with tessellation. With the exception of the Bezier patch, our tessellation has only created additional triangles, and they have not been displaced or otherwise manipulated to improve the level of detail. For example, if we were to apply the triangle tessellation against a 3D mesh, we would see that the mesh remains in the same shape albeit with a denser distribution of triangles.

Parametric surfaces

By implementing a domain shader for parametric shapes, it is possible to generate complex shapes with minimal memory bandwidth, for example, a single control point can be used to create a sphere. By passing a single control point using the primitive topology, `PrimitiveTopology.PatchListWith1ControlPoints`, and duplicating the `Quad` renderer HLSL while changing the hull and domain shaders in order to accept a single input and output control point, we can implement a range of parametric surfaces. The domain shader provides two parameters for our equations via the `SV_DomainLocation` (UV) parameter.

The completed project includes the parametric renderer along with shader source code:

```
PixelShaderInput DS_Parametric( HS_QuadPatchConstant constantData,
const OutputPatch<DS_ControlPointInput, 1> patch, float2 uv : SV_
DomainLocation )
{
    PixelShaderInput result = (PixelShaderInput)0;
    float PI2 = 6.28318530;
    float PI = 3.14159265;
    float S = PI2 * uv.x;
    float T = PI2 * uv.y;
    float sinS, cosS, sinT, cosT;
    sincos(S, sinS, cosS);
    sincos(T, sinT, cosT);

    // Torus
    float R1 = 0.5; // radius of ring
    float R2 = 0.25;// radius of tube
    float R3 = (R1 + R2 * cosT);
    float3 torusPos = float3(R3 * cosS, R3 * sinS, R2 * sinT);
    float3 position = torusPos;
    float4 diffuse = float4(normalize(position)+0.4, 1);
    float3 normal = normalize(position);

    // Prepare pixel shader input:
    // Transform to World-view-projection
    result.Position = mul(float4(position,1),WorldViewProjection);
    result.Diffuse = diffuse;
    result.WorldNormal = normal;
    result.WorldPosition = position;
    return result;
}
```

The previous domain shader code renders a torus, as shown in the following screenshot:

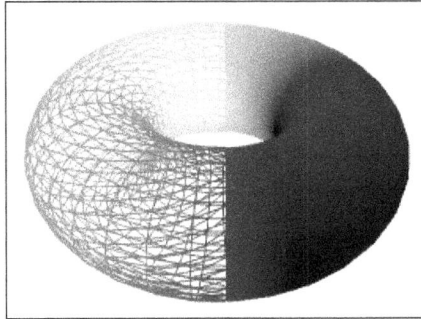

Render of a torus using a parametric surface domain shader (wireframe on the left and solid on the right)

It is also possible to implement the parametric surfaces directly within the vertex shader with no vertex buffers, and with the use of the `SV_VertexId` input semantic to index into a shader resource or as input into some function. This may result in an even faster generation of the parametric geometry as compared to the tessellation pipeline, although it would also require additional logic to be implemented either on CPU or within further shader functions.

See also

Bezier surface patches for the famous **Utah Teapot** can be found at: `http://www.holmes3d.net/graphics/teapot/`. These can be loaded directly into a vertex buffer for use with this recipe. Remember that every four vertices represent a Bezier curve, and there are four curves to a patch giving 16 control points per patch.

Refining meshes with Phong tessellation

In this recipe, we will implement a simple technique for the local refinement of triangle meshes through tessellation—Phong tessellation. This technique, put forward by Boubekeur and Alexa in 2008, follows the same principles as Phong shading (thus the name) and normal mapping, but instead of improving the perceived *visual smoothness* of flat surfaces, it improves the actual smoothness of contours and silhouettes.

Phong tessellation is computationally inexpensive when compared to algorithms for approximating Catmull-Clark subdivision surfaces. It still achieves smooth silhouettes and more importantly, it can be locally implemented on the tessellation hardware without requiring any additional precalculated weights/control points or specially prepared meshes unlike bicubic Bezier patches or Gregory patches.

This means that most existing triangulated meshes will work *reasonably* well with Phong tessellation with few or no changes to the original mesh.

Getting ready

For this recipe, we will be continuing on from the recipe, *Tessellating a triangle and quad*, and will be using the completed mesh renderer C# class from *Chapter 4, Animating Meshes with Vertex Skinning*.

The completed project for this recipe can be found in the `Ch05_02TessellatedMesh` project within the companion source code.

How to do it...

We will first update the `MeshRenderer` class to supply a patch list with three control points. Then, we will continue to implement a Phong tessellation domain shader. Consider the following steps:

1. Create a copy of the `MeshRenderer` class named `TessellatedMeshRenderer`, so that we don't get confused between the two classes later on.

2. Find the location at which the primitive topology is set, and change it to the following:

```
// Set topology
context.InputAssembler.PrimitiveTopology =
  SharpDX.Direct3D.PrimitiveTopology
    .PatchListWith3ControlPoints;
```

This is all that we need to change in order to prepare the mesh renderer for the tessellation pipeline.

3. We will use the triangle hull shaders from the previous project and use a modified version of the domain shader to implement the Phong tessellation.

> The `Character.cmo` model from *Chapter 4, Animating Meshes with Vertex Skinning*, requires the tessellation winding order to be `triangle_cw`.

4. Create a new shader file called `Shaders\TessellatePhong.hlsl`, and remember to change the encoding and build action.

5. Open the new shader file and add the following `include` directives:

```
#include "Common.hlsl"
#include "CommonTess.hlsl"
```

6. Next, we will add a new function for orthogonally projecting a point on to a plane, as follows:

```
// Orthogonal projection on to plane
// v2_projected = v2 - dot(v2-v1, n) * n;
```

```
float3 ProjectOntoPlane(float3 planeNormal, float3 planePoint,
float3 pointToProject)
{
    return pointToProject - dot(pointToProject-planePoint,
        planeNormal) * planeNormal;
}
```

7. Finally, we create the new domain shader. Begin by copying the existing triangle domain shader from the recipe, *Tessellating a triangle and quad*, and rename to `DS_PhongTessellation`.

8. Within the new domain shader, after the code that performs the barycentric interpolation, we insert the following Phong tessellation logic:

```
// Interpolate using barycentric coordinates
...SNIP - existing triangle domain shader code
// BEGIN Phong Tessellation
// Orthogonal projection in the tangent planes
float3 posProjectedU =
  ProjectOntoPlane(constantData.WorldNormal[0],
    patch[0].Position, position);
float3 posProjectedV =
  ProjectOntoPlane(constantData.WorldNormal[1],
    patch[1].Position, position);
float3 posProjectedW =
  ProjectOntoPlane(constantData.WorldNormal[2],
    patch[2].Position, position);


// Interpolate the projected points
position = BarycentricInterpolate(posProjectedU,
  posProjectedV, posProjectedW, barycentricCoords);
// END Phong Tessellation
// Transform world position to view-projection
...SNIP - existing triangle domain shader code
```

9. Within `D3DApp.CreateDeviceDependentResources`, compile the new domain shader. Remember to use the `ds_5_0` shader profile.

10. Within the render loop, ensure that the `Character.cmo` mesh is being loaded correctly into a `TessellatedMeshRenderer` instance, and update the mesh rendering section of the render loop with the following code:

```
context.VertexShader.Set(tessellateVertexShader);
context.HullShader.Set(activeTriTessellator);
if (usePhongTessellation)
    context.DomainShader.Set(tessellatePhongDomainShader);
else
```

```
        context.DomainShader.Set(tessellateTriDomainShader);

meshes.ForEach((m) =>
{
    m.PerMaterialBuffer = perMaterialBuffer;
    m.PerArmatureBuffer = perArmatureBuffer;
    m.Render();
});
```

> The completed example maps the *F5* key to toggle Phong tessellation.

11. Compiling and running (*F5*) the project will result in the same character animation present at the end of *Chapter 4, Animating Meshes with Vertex Skinning*; however, if you look carefully at the silhouette, changing the tessellation level now improves the smoothness.

The following screenshot shows the results of using an `integer` partitioning type with Phong tessellation active and a tessellation factor of 1.0 (equivalent to no tessellation), 2.0, and 3.0:

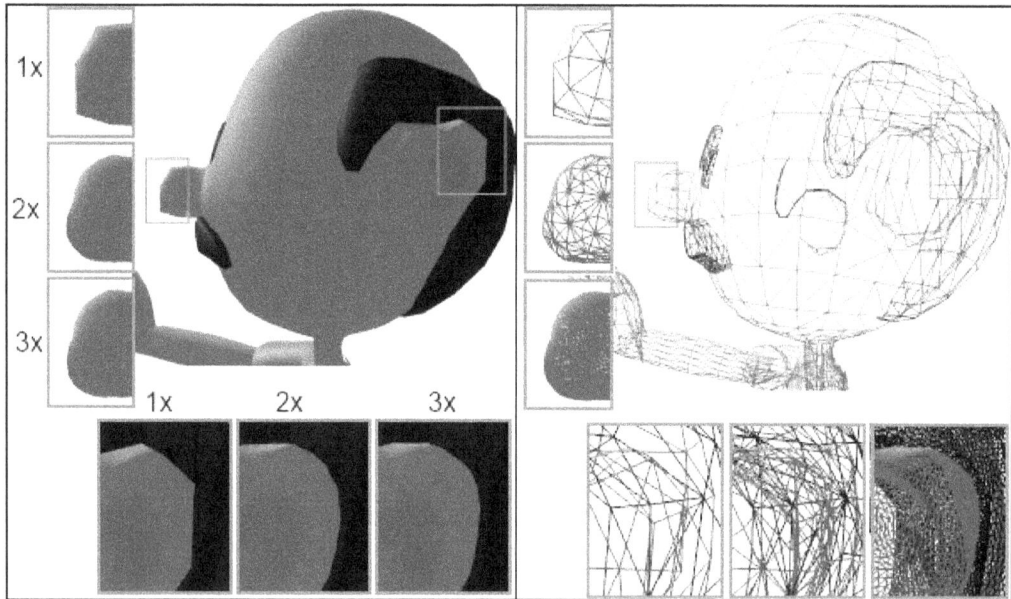

Phong tessellation at work

How it works...

In the preceding screenshot, the impact of Phong tessellation upon contours and silhouettes (the ear and nose) is quite clear. With only a small increase in the tessellation factor, a fairly smooth surface is quickly possible.

As shown in the following diagram, calculating the vertex displacement in Phong tessellation is done by:

1. Computing `p1` as the position on the flat surface (as per the previous triangle domain shader using barycentric interpolation):

   ```
   float3 p1 = BarycentricInterpolate(v0, v1, v2, baryUVW);
   ```

2. Projecting `p1` orthogonally to the tangent plane of each of the triangle vertices' normal vectors (outputting `Proj1`, `Proj2`, and `Proj3`):

   ```
   float3 proj1 = ProjectOntoPlane(n0, v0, p1);
   float3 proj2 = ProjectOntoPlane(n1, v1, p1);
   float3 proj3 = ProjectOntoPlane(n2, v2, p1);
   ```

3. And finally, computing the barycentric interpolation of the three projected points that gives us our final position of `P1`:

   ```
   P1 = BarycentricInterpolate(proj1, proj2, proj3, baryUVW);
   ```

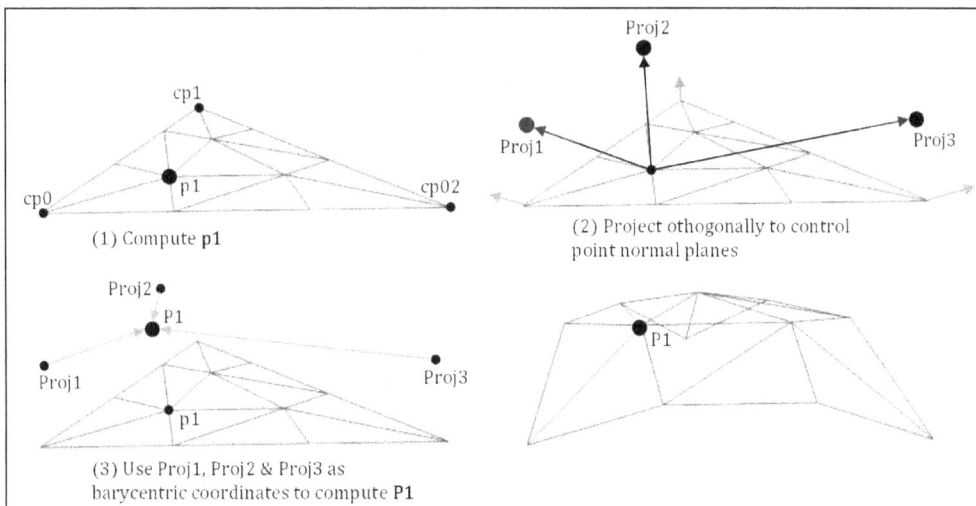

Calculation of the new vertex's displacement for Phong tessellation

The character mesh is already fairly smooth, so in order to see a more dramatic result, the completed example includes a very low polygon frog character with only 60 triangles. The following screenshot shows the frog rendered at varying tessellation levels:

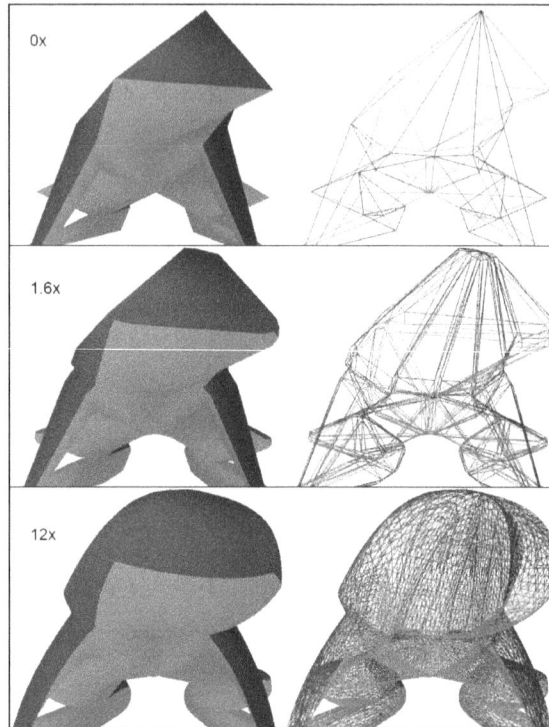

Low-poly frog (60 triangles) with no tessellation (top), Phong tessellation and fractional odd partitioning with tessellation factor of 1.6 (middle) and 12.0 (bottom). Original model by kednar @ blendswap.com

Reviewing the impact of Phong tessellation for the preceding screenshots of the character and frog highlights the following issues:

▸ The number of primitives increases quite significantly and it will be necessary to cull some primitives or use an adaptive Level–of-Detail to prevent performance issues.

▸ Although the model does not need to be authored with tessellation in mind, it is still beneficial if it has been. For example, to maintain a crease or hard edge in some instances, it will now be necessary to include additional primitives to ensure that the Phong tessellation process does not curve them off too much, as we saw happening to the preceding frog mesh.

▸ Unless there are additional details to be incorporated (for example, displacement mapping), the benefits of Phong tessellation only lie with the smoother contours and silhouettes (which is its purpose in the first place). Therefore, to improve the performance, we may only need to tessellate the contours.

There's more...

It is important to note that the low-poly mesh has already been transformed (by the animation code) into the appropriate pose before the tessellation, and therefore, we have been able to increase the smoothness of the mesh (especially for contours and silhouettes) without increasing the animation cost.

There are a number of other techniques that can be used for mesh refinement or subdivision. Curved PN Triangles (Vlachos, Peters et al. 2001) is one such technique that also allows local mesh refinement with similar results to Phong tessellation; however, this is a more computationally expensive algorithm (Boubekeur and Alexa 2008). This algorithm does keep the vertices closer to the original bounding mesh as opposed to Phong tessellation's more bulging appearance. Other implementations such as **Approximating Catmull-Clark Subdivision Surfaces with Bicubic Patches** (Loop and Schaefer 2008), or **Approximating subdivision surfaces with Gregory patches for hardware tessellation** (Loop, Schaefer et al. 2009) may provide more flexibility and more exact results. However, they also require significant additional asset workflow or some preprocessing to implement and incur a larger computational cost.

See also

  ▸ *Chapter 6, Adding Surface Detail with Normal and Displacement Mapping*, will look into more detail at tessellation and displacement mapping

  ▸ Refer to the Phong tessellation paper and video at: `http://perso.telecom-paristech.fr/~boubek/papers/PhongTessellation/`

  ▸ Refer to *Approximating Subdivision Surfaces with Gregory Patches for Hardware Tessellation* at: `http://research.microsoft.com/en-us/um/people/cloop/sga09.pdf`

  ▸ Refer to the implementation of Curved PN Triangles that can be found within `Shaders\TessellatePNTri.hlsl` for comparison.

Optimizing tessellation through back-face culling and dynamic Level-of-Detail

As we saw in the previous recipe, the number of generated triangles from tessellation can be quite high, and the most obvious optimization is to exclude any triangles that are facing away from the camera. This is called **back-face culling**. We will also look at how we may implement dynamic **Level-of-Detail** (**LoD**) by changing the tessellation levels, depending on whether the triangles are silhouetted or aligned roughly perpendicular to the camera view.

We will continue on from the point where we left off with the *Refining meshes with Phong tessellation* recipe.

> All the code for implementing the back-face culling methods and dynamic LoD is included as comments within the `HS_TrianglesConstant` function in `TessellateTri.hlsl` for the `Ch05_02TessellatedMesh` project.

How to do it...

We will implement two methods of back-face culling, and then incorporate a reduction of the tessellation factor for non-silhouette faces.

Back-face culling using face normal vectors

Consider the following steps:

1. After loading the project from our previous recipe, open `Shaders\TessellateTri.hlsl`.

2. Locate the `HS_TrianglesConstant` function, and modify it to include the following code:

```
...SNIP
HS_TrianglePatchConstant result = (HS_TrianglePatchConstant)0;
// Backface culling - using face normal
// Calculate face normal
float3 edge0 = patch[1].WorldPosition -
               patch[0].WorldPosition;
float3 edge2 = patch[2].WorldPosition -
               patch[0].WorldPosition;
float3 faceNormal = normalize(cross(edge2, edge0));
// Create view vector
float3 view = normalize(CameraPosition -
                        patch[0].WorldPosition);
// If cosine(angle) < -0.25
if (dot(view, faceNormal) < -0.25) {
    result.EdgeTessFactor[0] = 0;
    result.EdgeTessFactor[1] = 0;
```

```
        result.EdgeTessFactor[2] = 0;
        result.InsideTessFactor = 0;
        return result; // culled, so no further processing
    }
    // end: backface culling
    ...SNIP rest of function excluded from listing
```

3. Running the project and switching to wireframe (the *F* key in the provided code)
    will show that the back-facing triangles are no longer rendered. The following
    screenshot shows the output.

> The sample project has disabled back-face culling within the rasterizer state
> (RasterizerStateDescription.CullMode = CullMode.None),
> so that this can be tested correctly.

Back-face culling using vertex normal vectors

Consider the following steps:

1. Comment out or remove the previous code for back-face culling based
    on the face normal, and include the following code instead:

```
...SNIP
HS_TrianglePatchConstant result = (HS_TrianglePatchConstant)0;
// Backface culling - using Vertex normals
bool backFacing = true; // default to cull
[unroll]
for (uint j = 0; j < 3; j++)
{
    // Create view vector
    float3 view = normalize(CameraPosition -
                            patch[j].WorldPosition);
    float a = dot(view, patch[j].WorldNormal);
    if (a >= -0.125) {
        backFacing = false; // do not cull patch
    }
}
if (backFacing) {
    result.EdgeTessFactor[0] = 0;
    result.EdgeTessFactor[1] = 0;
    result.EdgeTessFactor[2] = 0;
    result.InsideTessFactor = 0;
```

```
            return result; // culled, so no further processing
    }
    // end: backface culling
    ...SNIP rest of function excluded from listing
```

2. Running the project now, we see a very similar result. However, if you look closely at the two renders, the culling based on the face normal will sometimes remove a partially visible triangle whereas using the vertex normal does not (circled in the following screenshot). This is especially noticeable in low-poly models, where a larger angle threshold is necessary. By increasing the angle threshold, we can address the issue.

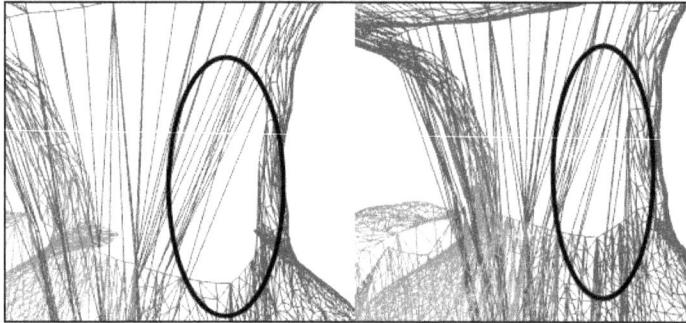

Back-face culling (left using the face normal and right by checking all vertex normals)

Dynamic Level-of-Detail (LoD) near silhouettes

We will now take advantage of Phong tessellation to improve contours and silhouettes, while minimizing the number of triangles generated elsewhere. We do this by reducing the tessellation factor on surfaces that are facing more directly to the camera.

1. First, implement back-face culling, as described earlier, using vertex normals.

2. If the dot product is larger than 0.125, we will set a multiplier variable to reduce the inside tessellation factor by 0.25 of the full tessellation factor. Otherwise, we will leave the `insideMultiplier` value as `1.0f`:

```
float insideMultiplier = 0.25f;
...
result.InsideTessFactor = roundedInsideTessFactor *
                          insideMultiplier;
```

How it works...

By calculating the face normal, we were able to determine if, on average, the triangle was facing towards or away from the camera. If a face is within the viewing threshold's cosine angle, we keep the patch (in this case, larger than -0.25), otherwise it is discarded before it even reaches the rasterizer stage (remember to turn off back-face culling in the rasterizer to test this). Setting the patch tessellation factor to zero tells the fixed function tessellator stage to discard the patch. This method of using the face normals occasionally results in some visual artifacts, such as partially visible triangles popping in and out, that is, where one of the three vertices' normals is within the threshold and the other two are not. The more the source mesh is detailed, the smaller threshold necessary to remove the artifact.

In our second approach, we look at each vertex's normal. If any of the normals are within the threshold, we keep the patch; otherwise, we set the tessellation factor to zero in order to tell the fixed function tessellator stage to discard the patch.

A couple of benefits to this approach are that the popping of triangles is mostly fixed, and the threshold can be reduced resulting in even fewer extraneous triangles. In the example of the vertex normal, we were able to use -0.125 (or 97.18 degrees), whereas the face normal approach needed -0.25 for the same model (or 104.5 degrees). This approach does have a slightly higher cost.

Finally, we have implemented a very basic dynamic LoD within the patch constant function. Rather than applying the modifier to the edge and inner tessellation factors, we have only changed the inside factor. This is because the neighboring/adjacent edges must have the same tessellation factor in order to maintain water tightness; otherwise, the resulting mesh will have visible seams (especially near curves). We have done this to keep the example simple and fast. It is important to note that this method of dynamic LoD does not work well with the `fractional_odd` partitioning type, due to the additional inside vertices that are nearer to the edges.

It is important to remember that tessellation is not free; it should be used wisely where tessellation will benefit the image quality the most.

There's more...

Tessellation can be optimized in many ways and we have only covered a few of them. Other options might include analyzing the complexity of a patch's location in a displacement map or using a feature complexity map (feature adaptive), frustum culling, checking the triangle size, distance, or based on edge length, and screen adaptive.

▸ For more information about calculating watertight positions, normals, and UV coordinates, refer to Efficient substitutes for subdivision surfaces in feature-quality games Tianyun Ni, ACM SIGGRAPH ASIA 2010 Courses

▸ Refer to the *Optimizing tessellation based on displacement decal (displacement adaptive tessellation)* recipe in *Chapter 6, Adding Surface Detail with Normal and Displacement Mapping*

▸ Refer to Adaptive Tessellation of Bezier Surfaces Based on Displacement Maps by Espino, F. J., et al. in WSCG (Short Papers). 2005. available at: `http://ac.usc.es/system/files/gac2005-c01.pdf.gz`

▸ Refer to Feature Adaptive Rendering of Loop Subdivision Surfaces on GPU at: `http://www.cad.zju.edu.cn/home/jqfeng/papers/TR_FAGRL.pdf`

6
Adding Surface Detail with Normal and Displacement Mapping

In this chapter, we will cover the following topics:

- ▸ Referencing multiple textures in a material
- ▸ Adding surface detail with normal mapping
- ▸ Adding surface detail with displacement mapping
- ▸ Implementing displacement decals
- ▸ Optimizing tessellation based on displacement decal (displacement adaptive tessellation)

Introduction

Displacement mapping is the process of displacing vertices (usually created via the process of tessellation) based upon the information sampled from a height map texture. This process extends upon traditional normal mapping to provide additional detail to the surface. Displacement mapping is not a replacement for normal mapping. They both work together to produce a more realistic result. While normal mapping manipulates lighting to give the appearance of a more irregular surface, displacement mapping will physically manipulate the mesh to give it additional 3D detail—especially noticeable for silhouettes, contours, and therefore shadows. The example output shown in *Adding surface detail with normal mapping* highlights the impact of normal and displacement mapping both separately and when combined.

In this chapter, we will learn how to use these techniques together to produce more realistic real-time rendering results, and then see how to extend the process to implement local deformations such as footprints or scratch marks.

Referencing multiple textures in a material

In this recipe, we will create a Visual Shader Graph for use with our models that accepts multiple textures. This is necessary to include multiple textures, such as the diffuse texture and the normal and displacement maps, within the same material.

How to do it...

In order to specify multiple textures for the materials in our models with the Visual Studio graphics content pipeline, we need to implement a new Visual Shader Graph (`.dgsl` file) that allows the selection of additional textures:

1. Start by right-clicking on the project and selecting **Add \ New Item...**.

2. Click on the **Graphics** node, and then click on **Visual Shader Graph (.dgsl)**. We will name the file `MultipleTextures.dgsl`.

> In order to improve the preview of the models when using this shader graph, you can copy the existing `phong.dgsl` from `\Common7\IDE\Extensions\Microsoft\VsGraphics\Assets\Effects\` located in the Visual Studio installation directory (the default being `C:\Program Files (x86)\Microsoft Visual Studio 11.0` for VS 2012 or `C:\Program Files (x86)\Microsoft Visual Studio 12.0` for VS 2013)

3. With the shader graph open, click within the dark background so as to unselect any graph nodes.

4. Now, in the **properties** window, we simply need to change the **Access** property of **Texture1** through to **Texture8** to **Public Access**.

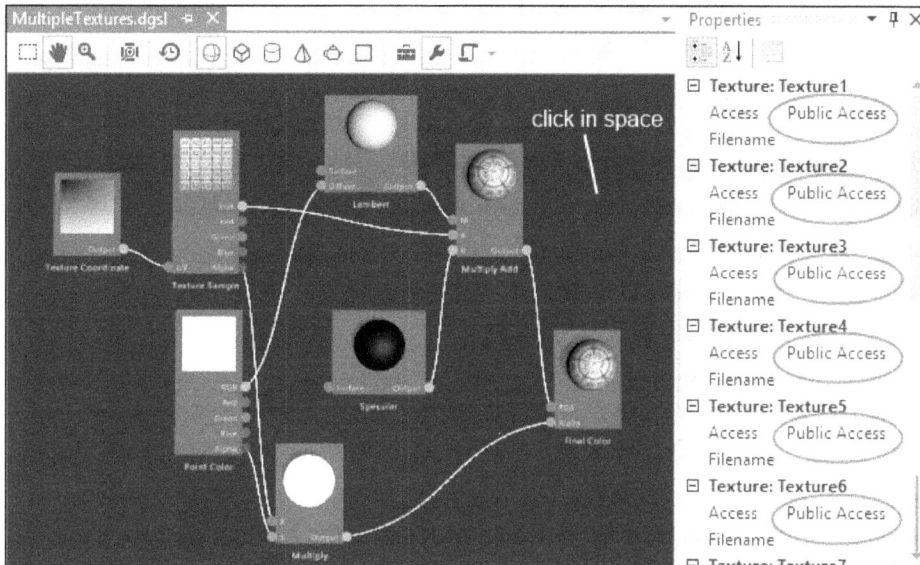

Editing the DGSL to enable multiple textures per material in a Visual Studio 3D Scene (.fbx)

5. At this point, we will also make the additional lighting variables visible to our models if they aren't already visible. Scroll down the list of shader graph properties and change the **Access** to **Public Access** for **Variable:MaterialAmbient**.

> Although the graphics content pipeline supports compiling the shader graph to HLSL for us (it requires manual tweaking to support Feature Level 9 x devices), we aren't using this within our recipes as we require a little more control and want to delve deeper into the underlying shader code. This is especially the case when implementing tessellation and displacement mapping.

6. When editing models with materials that require multiple textures within a **3D Scene (.fbx)**, we can now reference the `MultipleTextures.dgsl` shader graph in an object's **Effect** property and provide the name of a file for each of the texture properties as necessary.

How it works...

By changing the texture properties in the DGSL file to **Public Access**, we make the corresponding texture properties visible within the 3D Scene (.fbx) graphics editor. The Visual Studio graphics content pipeline will then convert the assigned textures to DDS textures, and copy them to the output directory along with the compiled mesh (.cmo) file.

Adding surface detail with normal mapping

Normal mapping allows us to perturb normal vectors so that the light bounces from the surface in the correct direction, making the appearance of additional detail on the surface where otherwise there is not. We have already added support for loading multiple textures for a mesh, both in the `MeshRenderer` class in the *Loading a static mesh from a file* recipe in *Chapter 3, Rendering Meshes*, and within models in the previous recipe *Referencing multiple textures in a material* with the Visual Studio graphics content pipeline. Now, we need to update our shaders to sample the normal map and calculate the final normal direction.

Here, we will update the vertex structure and shaders to support passing a vertex's **tangent** vector from the loaded mesh in order to calculate the new normal direction. We also look at the changes necessary to support normal mapping within the tessellation pipeline if that is in use.

Getting ready

In this recipe, we will begin with the completed mesh renderer class from *Chapter 4, Animating Meshes with Vertex Skinning*.

We will be using a number of new models along with some new textures. These assets are available with the completed project in the companion download. The completed version of this recipe is available from the companion code as `Ch06_01DisplacementMapping`. These models also require the use of `MultipleTextures.dgsl` that we created in the previous *Referencing multiple textures in a material* recipe with the Visual Studio graphics content pipeline.

To add the models for this recipe, follow these steps:

1. With the Visual Studio shader graph `MultipleTextures.dgsl` in place, we can add the new 3D scenes from the downloaded content. Go ahead and add `Cube.fbx`, `Plane.fbx`, and `Tree.fbx` along with their textures to the root of our project directory. The `*.fbx` files need to be included in the project, and have the `MeshContentTask` applied as explained in *Chapter 3, Rendering Meshes*.

2. Within `D3DApp.Run`, change the existing mesh loading code to the following:

```
// Create and initialize the mesh renderer
var loadedMesh = Common.Mesh.LoadFromFile("Tree.cmo");
loadedMesh.AddRange(Common.Mesh.LoadFromFile("Plane.cmo"));
loadedMesh.AddRange(Common.Mesh.LoadFromFile("Cube.cmo"));
```

3. At this point, you should be able to compile the project and view the models. The completed sample maps the *Backspace* key to cycle through the loaded meshes.

How to do it...

As we have often done in previous recipes, we will begin by updating our constant buffers and structures. Then, we will start updating our shaders and C# rendering code:

1. We need to modify our per material constant buffer to indicate whether a normal map is available. The updated `PerMaterial` HLSL structure in `Shaders\Common.hlsl` is as follows:

```
cbuffer PerMaterial : register (b2)
{
...
    bool HasTexture;
    bool HasNormalMap;
    float4 MaterialEmissive;
    float4x4 UVTransform;
};
```

2. The updated `ConstantBuffers.PerMaterial` structure within `ConstantBuffers.cs` is as follows (note that we changed the padding property):

```
public struct PerMaterial {
...
    public uint HasTexture;     // (0 false, 1 true)
    public uint HasNormalMap;   // (0 false, 1 true)
    float _padding0;
    public Color4 Emissive;
    public Matrix UVTransform;
}
```

> Note that we have not placed the new property at the end of the buffer. Instead, we are adding them in such a way that we can efficiently pack data, given the HLSL 16-byte data alignment.
>
> A `bool` in HLSL is 4 bytes, and a `uint` 0 and 1 map to the `false` and `true` values respectively.

3. Next, we will modify the vertex structure by adding a new `Tangent` property to the end of the `VertexShaderInput` structure in `Shaders\Common.hlsl`.

```
struct VertexShaderInput {
...
    float4 Tangent: TANGENT; // for normal mapping
};
```

4. Now, let's add a new `WorldTangent` property to the end of the `PixelShaderInput` structure within `Shaders\Common.hlsl`.

```
struct PixelShaderInput {
...
    float4 WorldTangent: TANGENT; // for normal mapping
};
```

5. Next, we will modify the vertex skinning (if any) to skin the tangent vector.

```
void SkinVertex(float4 weights, uint4 bones, inout float4
   position, inout float3 normal, inout float4 tangent) {
    // If there are skin weights apply vertex skinning
    if (weights.x != 0)
    {
... SNIP
        // also for the tangent (the w component contains
        // the handedness used for calculating bitangent)
        tangent = float4(mul(tangent.xyz,
                        (float3x3)skinTransform),
                          tangent.w);
    }
}
```

6. Within each vertex shader in `Shaders\VS.hlsl`, we add the input tangent to the parameter list of `SkinVertex`. Then, we will apply the same transform matrix as per the `WorldNormal` property. The new code is highlighted in the following code:

```
... SNIP vertex shader code
// Apply vertex skinning if any
SkinVertex(vertex.SkinWeights, vertex.SkinIndices, vertex.
Position, vertex.Normal, vertex.Tangent);
... SNIP vertex shader code
result.WorldNormal = mul(vertex.Normal, (float3x3)
WorldInverseTranspose);
result.WorldTangent = float4(mul(vertex.Tangent.xyz,
   (float3x3)WorldInverseTranspose), vertex.Tangent.w);
... SNIP vertex shader code
```

7. In order to support normal mapping in our tessellation pipeline, let's add the new `WorldTangent` property to the end of the `HullShaderInput` and `DS_ControlPointInput` structures within `Shaders\CommonTess.hlsl`. Any other implementations such as the `DS_PNControlPointInput` structure within `TessellatePNTri.hlsl` can also be updated.

```
struct HullShaderInput / DS_ControlPointInput / etc {
...
    float4 WorldTangent: TANGENT; // for normal mapping
};
```

8. For each hull shader, we must pass the `Tangent` property from the patch to the control point. The updated `HS_TrianglesInteger` function from `TessellateTri.hlsl` is shown as follows:

```
//... attributes domain, partitioning, etc
DS_ControlPointInput HS_TrianglesInteger(
        InputPatch<HullShaderInput, 3> patch,
        uint id : SV_OutputControlPointID,
        uint patchID : SV_PrimitiveID ) {
    DS_ControlPointInput result = (DS_ControlPointInput)0;
    result.Position = patch[id].WorldPosition;
    result.WorldTangent = patch[id].WorldTangent;
    return result;
}
```

9. Within each domain shader, we must interpolate the tangent in the same way that the normal is interpolated, and then assign the tangent to `PixelShaderInput.Tangent`. The code for the triangle and Phong tessellation shaders would look something like the following:

```
    PixelShaderInput result = (PixelShaderInput)0;
...SNIP
    float3 normal = BarycentricInterpolate(constantData.
WorldNormal, barycentricCoords);
    float3 tangent = BarycentricInterpolate(patch[0].WorldTangent,
patch[1].WorldTangent, patch[2].WorldTangent, barycentricCoords);
...SNIP
    result.WorldNormal = normal;
    result.WorldPosition = position;
    result.WorldTangent = tangent;
...SNIP

}
```

10. Next, we need to update the `Vertex` structure within `Vertex.cs` to include the `Tangent` property. The constructors will also need to be updated to reflect this. The complete `Vertex` structure members are shown here with the changes highlighted:

```
public Vector3 Position;
public Vector3 Normal;
public Color Color;
public Vector2 UV;
public Common.Mesh.SkinningVertex Skin;
public Vector4 Tangent;
```

11. Now, we tell the input assembler stage what our updated input layout for the vertex structure looks like. This change is highlighted in the next code snippet, and is made within `D3DApp.CreateDeviceDependentResources`.

```
// Layout from VertexShader input signature
vertexLayout = ToDispose(new InputLayout(device, ShaderSignature.
GetInputSignature(vertexShaderBytecode),
new[] {
// "SV_Position" = vertex coordinate in object space
new InputElement("SV_Position",0, Format.R32G32B32_Float,
                  0, 0),
...
// "TANGENT" = tangent vector, from loaded Mesh
new InputElement("TANGENT", 0,
  Format.R32G32B32A32_Float,68,0),
}));
```

12. Lastly, we need to use the `Tangent` property of the mesh in `MeshRenderer.CreateDeviceDependentResources` when creating the vertex buffer.

```
for (var i = 0; i < vb.Length; i++) {
...
// Create vertex
vertices[i] = new Vertex(vb[i].Position, vb[i].Normal,
  vb[i].Color, vb[i].UV, skin, vb[i].Tangent);
}
```

With the tangent data now available to the pipeline, we can update each pixel shader to perform the normal mapping.

13. First, we add the new function `ApplyNormalMap` within `Shaders\Common.hlsl`. This will allow us to adjust the normal direction using a normal map sample.

```
float3 ApplyNormalMap(float3 normal, float4 tangent,
                      float3 normalSample) {
    // Remap normalSample to the range (-1,1)
    normalSample = (2.0 * normalSample) - 1.0;
```

```
        // Ensure tangent is orthogonal to normal vector
        // Gram-Schmidt orthogonalize
        float3 T = normalize(tangent - normal *
                            dot(normal, tangent));
        // Create the Bitangent
        float3 bitangent = cross(normal, T) * tangent.w;

        // Create TBN matrix to transform from tangent space
        float3x3 TBN = float3x3(T, bitangent, normal);
        return normalize(mul(normalSample, TBN));
    }
```

14. Within the Diffuse, Blinn-Phong, and Phong pixel shaders, add a new input texture for the normal map (using the second texture slot `t1`). Then, update the `PSMain` function to adjust the normal prior to any lighting calculations.

```
Texture2D Texture0 : register(t0);
Texture2D NormalMap : register(t1);
SamplerState Sampler : register(s0);

float4 PSMain(PixelShaderInput pixel) : SV_Target
{
    // Normalize our vectors as they are not
    // guaranteed to be unit vectors after interpolation
    float3 normal = normalize(pixel.WorldNormal);
    float3 tangent = normalize(pixel.WorldTangent.xyz);
    float3 toEye = normalize(CameraPosition -
                            pixel.WorldPosition);
    float3 toLight = normalize(-Light.Direction);

    // If there is a normal map, apply it
    if (HasNormalMap)
        normal = ApplyNormalMap(normal,
            float4(tangent, pixel.WorldTangent.w),
            NormalMap.Sample(Sampler,
            pixel.TextureUV).rgb);
    // Texture sample here (use white if no texture)
    float4 sample = (float4)1.0f;
    if (HasTexture)
        sample = Texture0.Sample(Sampler, pixel.TextureUV);
    ...
}
```

> Performing the normal transformation to world space within the pixel shader as we are doing within `ApplyNormalMap` is a suboptimal solution with regards to performance in certain circumstances.
>
> While it's useful to have the flexibility gained by using `HasNormalMap` and `HasTexture` when trying out different techniques, it is more efficient to have multiple shaders that may or may not support normal mapping or textures (as appropriate).

Last of all, we need to update our `MeshRenderer` class to update the `HasNormalMap` constant buffer property.

15. Add a new public property to the `MeshRenderer` class.

    ```
    public bool EnableNormalMap { get; set; }
    ```

16. Initialize this property within the constructor.

    ```
    this.EnableNormalMap = true;
    ```

17. We can now update the `MeshRenderer.DoRender` function so that when we are applying the mesh's materials to the per material constant buffer, we are now also updating the `PerMaterial.HasNormalMap` property. Here, we are assuming that the normal map is assigned to the second texture of the material within the mesh file. The changes are highlighted in the following code snippet:

    ```
    protected override void DoRender() {
    ...
    int texIndxOffset = mIndx * Common.Mesh.MaxTextures;
    material.HasTexture = (uint)(textureViews[texIndxOffset] !=
        null ? 1 : 0); // 0=false
    material.HasNormalMap = (uint)(EnableNormalMap &&
        textureViews[texIndxOffset+1] != null ? 1 : 0);
    // Bind textures to the pixel shader
    context.PixelShader.SetShaderResources(0,
        textureViews.GetRange(texIndxOffset,
            Common.Mesh.MaxTextures).ToArray());
    ...
    // Update material buffer
    context.UpdateSubresource(ref material, PerMaterialBuffer);
    ...
    }
    ```

18. The results of normal mapping are visible in the right-hand side images of the tree log render image in the *Adding surface detail with displacement mapping* recipe. The following figure highlights the differences between normal mapping only (left), displacement mapping only (center), and displacement mapping with normal mapping (right).

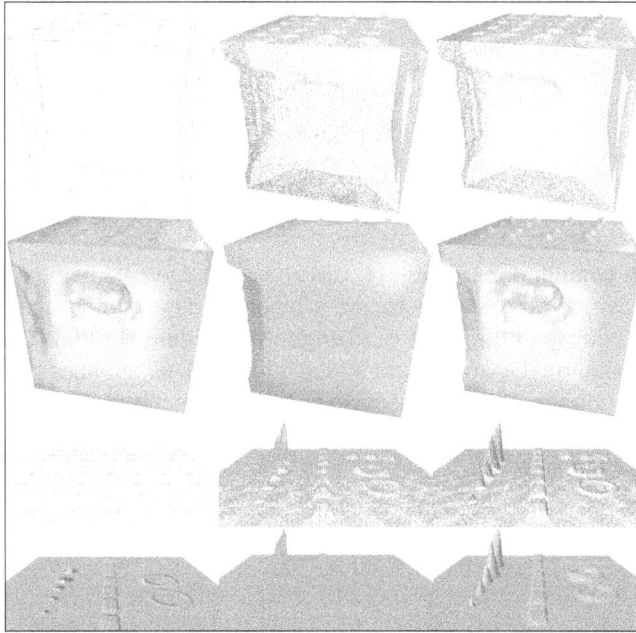

Comparison of normal mapping (left), displacement mapping (center), and displacement mapping with normal mapping (right). Cube displacement scale is 0.69, and plane displacement scale 0.5—tessellation factor of 8.0 for middle and right.

How it works...

Using a normal map gives us additional directional information about a normal that allows us to simulate surface detail. When viewed straight-on the illusion is quite convincing; however, it falls short where there are silhouettes or contours (in the top-left cube in the previous figure, the left edge and the top are obviously incomplete, whereas the side facing us looks correct).

Normal maps are usually in tangent space (also known as vertex space), which is aligned to the tangent plane and normal vector at a vertex. The normal, tangent, and bitangent are all vectors that are at right angles to each other (orthogonal). The tangent and bitangent are usually used in relation to the texture map, with the tangent pointing along the u axis and bitangent pointing along the V axis.

The following diagram shows the coordinate systems for texture and tangent space:

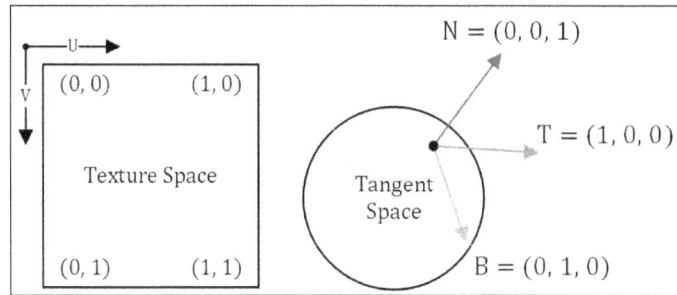

Texture space in Direct3D (left) and tangent space (right). The completed project for this recipe maps the *N* key to toggle rendering of the normal, tangent, and bitangent vectors.

The tangents for the **compiled mesh object** (**CMO**) models are calculated during compilation. From the normal vector and tangent vector, we are able to determine the bitangent vector (also known as binormal), and therefore our **Tangent Bitangent Normal** (**TBN**) matrix for transforming from the normal map tangent space into world/object space or vice versa. The meshes also include the handedness of the bitangent vector within the tangent vector, allowing us to correctly calculate the direction of the bitangent vector as can be seen in point **B** in the following calculations:

$$
\begin{aligned}
&\text{A)}\ \ T' = T_{xyz} - N'\left(N' \cdot T_{xyz}\right) \\
&\text{B)}\ \ B' = (N' \times T')T_w \\
&\text{C)}\ \ \begin{bmatrix} T'_x & T'_y & T'_z \\ B'_x & B'_y & B'_z \\ N'_x & N'_y & N'_z \end{bmatrix}
\end{aligned}
$$

A) Orthogonalization of tangent vector N to normal vector N, B) Calculating the bitangent vector, C) Resulting TBN matrix

The Microsoft .cmo file format stores a fourth component in the tangent vector to indicate the handedness of the tangent. Therefore, we have used `float4` instead of `float3`. This would not be used within a streamlined asset workflow. Instead, all shaders and assets would be built with the same handedness in mind.

By using a normal map that is stored in tangent space, we sample the red, green, and blue channels (x, y, and z respectively); and then transform the sample into world space using the current pixel's normal and tangent vectors. We first remap the normal sample from the range (0, 1) to (-1, 1) as the color data stored in the texture is packed between 0 and 1.

```
// Remap normalSample to the range -1,1
normalSample = (2.0 * normalSample) - 1.0;
```

Next, we will ensure that the tangent vector is orthogonal (perpendicular) to the normal vector with the Gram-Schmidt process (*Lengyel, 2001*). Then, we will determine the bitangent (perpendicular to both the normal and tangent) by calculating the cross product of the normal and tangent vectors.

```
// Ensure tangent is orthogonal to normal- Gram-Schmidt
float3 T = normalize(tangent - normal * dot(normal, tangent));
// Create the Bitangent
float3 bitangent = cross(normal, T);
```

The following diagram illustrates this orthonormalization process:

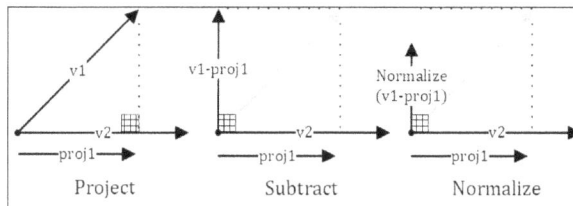

To make v1 orthogonal to v2, project v1 onto v2, then subtract from v1, and then normalize.

In this recipe, both our normal and tangent are in world space. Therefore, so is the bitangent and the resulting TBN matrix.

With the tangent, bitangent, and normal unit vectors, we are able to construct the 3 x 3 TBN matrix to transform the sampled normal from tangent space into world space. Note that when researching this topic, you will come across many instances where the matrix is used in the other direction. It all depends in what space the basis vectors are in, for example, tangent space T, B, and N or world space T, B, and N.

```
float3x3 TBN = float3x3(tangent, bitangent, normal);
return normalize(mul(normalSample, TBN));
```

For simplicity, our examples have used the tangent and normal vectors in world coordinates. Traditionally, the best practice has been to keep these in tangent space, sample the normal, and calculate the lighting in tangent space. Since we also need the normal in world space to implement the vertex displacement, we have left the lighting calculations in world space. This brings with it a performance hit when used with normal mapping, as we are transforming the sampled normal to world coordinates (in `ApplyNormalMap`) for every pixel in every frame rather than calculating the tangent camera and light directions for each vertex.

A version of `Ch06_01DisplacementMapping` is available in the downloaded content that implements normal mapping by using tangent space instead. A comparison of the source code will show the necessary changes. The project is called `Ch06_01DisplacementMapping_TangentSpace`.

There's more...

As mentioned previously, it is important to consider whether to perform the lighting calculations for normal mapping in tangent space or world space. This will greatly reduce the number of matrix operations performed within the pixel shader. However, it can also increase the amount of information needed in the `PixelShaderInput`, and it can introduce some additional complexity to our vertex, hull, domain and geometry shaders.

See also

> ▸ For information about manually calculating tangents for an arbitrary mesh, refer to `http://www.terathon.com/code/tangent.html`

Adding surface detail with displacement mapping

In this recipe, we will use displacement mapping via the tessellation pipeline to add additional geometric detail to an otherwise smooth or flat surface. This is the key technique used for approximating the detail on high-poly meshes using a low-poly version of the same mesh.

Displacement mapping uses a displacement map texture (also known as a height map) that consists of a single channel that is used to control the amount to displace a vertex. Depending on the method of construction, this height map can have a midpoint that allows the vertex to be lowered/raised, or the map may only support displacement in one direction. A displacement map will generally use the same UV coordinates as the diffuse texture and normal map. We will make changes to our existing tessellation shaders and incorporate displacement mapping to the solution to improve the surface detail of the final render.

Getting ready

In this recipe, we require the normal mapping changes we made in the *Adding surface detail with normal mapping* recipe, including the additional assets that were added within the *Getting ready* section—these include the displacement maps.

We will also need to implement the changes necessary to support tessellation from the previous chapter's recipe *Mesh refinement with Phong Tessellation*.

How to do it...

As we have often done in previous recipes, we will begin by updating our constant buffers, and then move on to updating our shaders and C# rendering code:

1. We need to modify our per material constant buffer to indicate which displacement scale to apply (if any), zero being the equivalent of no displacement. The updated `PerMaterial` HLSL structure in `Shaders\Common.hlsl` is as follows:

```
cbuffer PerMaterial : register (b2)
{
    ...
    bool HasNormalMap;
    float DisplaceScale;
    float4 MaterialEmissive;
    float4x4 UVTransform;
};
```

2. And the updated ConstantBuffers.PerMaterial structure within ConstantBuffers.cs is as follows (note that we replaced the padding property):

```
public struct PerMaterial
{
    ...
    public uint HasNormalMap;  // (0 false, 1 true)
    public float DisplaceScale;// displacement scale
    public Color4 Emissive;
    public Matrix UVTransform;
}
```

3. At the start of `Shaders\CommonTess.hlsl`, add our input displacement texture.

```
Texture2D DisplacementMap : register(t0);
SamplerState Sampler : register(s0);
```

4. We will add our `CalculateDisplacement` HLSL function to the end of this file. This will be used by each of the domain shaders to apply the vertex displacement.

```
// Simple displacement calculation from displacement map
// If DisplaceScale is 0 no displacement takes place
// The float3 result should be added to the vertex position
float3 CalculateDisplacement(float2 UV, float3 normal)
{
    // Skip displacement sampling if 0 multiplier
    if (DisplaceScale == 0)
        return 0;
```

```
        // Choose the most detailed mipmap level
        const float mipLevel = 1.0f;

        // Sample height map - using R channel
        float height = DisplacementMap.SampleLevel(Sampler, UV,
                                                    mipLevel).r;
        // remap height from 0 to 1, to -1 to 1
        height = (2 * height) - 1;

        // Return offset along normal.
        return height * DisplaceScale * normal;
    }
```

5. Within each domain shader, just prior to applying the `ViewProjection` matrix to the new vertex position, we can apply the displacement function.

```
... existing domain shader code
// Perform displacement
position += CalculateDisplacement(UV, normal);

// Transform world position to view-projection
result.Position = mul(float4(position,1), ViewProjection );
... existing domain shader code
```

6. To use our models with displacement mapping, we need to create a copy of `TessellatedMeshRenderer.cs` from the previous chapter and call it `DisplacedMeshRenderer.cs`. Then, we need to incorporate the changes from the previous recipe *Adding surface detail with normal mapping*.

7. Add a new property `DisplacementScale` to `DisplacedMeshRenderer`.

```
public float DisplacementScale { get; set; }
```

8. Initialize the default value for `DisplacementScale` within the constructor.

```
this.DisplacementScale = 1.0f;
```

9. We now update the `DisplacedMeshRenderer.DoRender` function; so that when applying the mesh's materials to the per material constant buffer, we are also binding the displacement map and updating the `PerMaterial.DisplacementScale` property. We will assume that the third texture is the displacement map.

```
int texIndxOffset = mIndx * Common.Mesh.MaxTextures;
...
material.HasNormalMap = (uint)(EnableNormalMap &&
    textureViews[texIndxOffset+1] != null ? 1 : 0);
material.DisplaceScale = (textureViews[texIndxOffset+2] !=
    null ? DisplacementScale : 0);
```

```
// If displace scale > 0 then assign texture resource
if (material.DisplaceScale > 0)
{
    context.DomainShader.SetShaderResources(0,
        textureViews[texIndxOffset+2]);
    context.DomainShader.SetSampler(0, samplerState);
}
...
// Update material buffer
context.UpdateSubresource(ref material, PerMaterialBuffer);
```

Now, we will update D3DApp.cs to bind the per material constant buffer to the domain shader stage, and use our new mesh renderer and properties in the render loop.

1. First, add the perMaterialBuffer constant buffer to the domain shader stage within D3DApp.CreateDeviceDependentResources (or the applicable location where the pipeline state was initialized).

   ```
   context.DomainShader.SetConstantBuffer(0, perObjectBuffer);
   context.DomainShader.SetConstantBuffer(1, perFrameBuffer);
   context.DomainShader.SetConstantBuffer(2,
     perMaterialBuffer);
   context.DomainShader.Set(tessellateTriDomainShader);
   ```

2. Within D3DApp.Run, change the creation of the mesh renderers to use the new DisplacedMeshRenderer.

   ```
   List<DisplacedMeshRenderer> meshes = new
     List<DisplacedMeshRenderer>();
   meshes.AddRange((from mesh in loadedMesh
       select ToDispose(new DisplacedMeshRenderer(mesh))));
   ```

3. And lastly, we will change the mesh rendering within the render loop so that we are setting the mesh properties with our desired values.

   ```
   var m = meshes[meshIndex]; // show one mesh at a time
   m.EnableNormalMap = enableNormalMap;
   m.DisplacementScale = displacementScale;
   m.PerMaterialBuffer = perMaterialBuffer;
   m.PerArmatureBuffer = perArmatureBuffer;
   m.Render();
   ```

> The completed sample maps *Shift +/-* to increase and decrease the displacement scale and *Shift + N* to toggle the normal map on/off.

At this point, it is possible to compile and run the project to see displacement mapping in action. The bottom right image (**D**) of the following figure shows an example of the result:

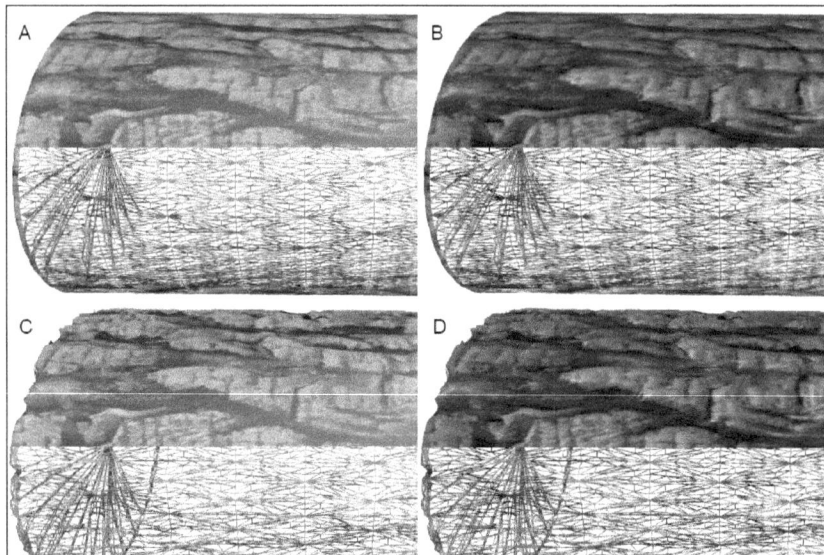

Tree log render: (A) no displacement and with a tessellation factor of 2.0, (B) as per A, but with normal mapping applied, (C) as per A, but with displacement mapping applied and using a displacement scale of 0.020, (D) as per C, but with normal mapping applied.

How it works...

Displacement mapping modifies the structure of the mesh in the direction of the normal. Looking at the tree log render and the comparison of normal and displacement mapping in the previous recipe, it is clear that normal mapping or displacement mapping alone are not enough. However, when combined together, they can have a profound impact on the scene. We have combined these techniques by first modifying our model's material to support multiple textures in addition to the diffuse texture (refer to the *Referencing multiple textures in a material with the Visual Studio graphics content pipeline* recipe), the normal map, and the displacement or height map. We then sample these textures within the pixel shader and domain shader respectively.

> It is important to note that too many small triangles can impact the GPUs ability to process many pixel shaders in parallel resulting in adverse performance. This is where dynamic level of detail and other tessellation optimizations become quite important.

In our recipe, we will support moving the vectors outwards if the value sampled from the displacement map is larger than 0.5, and inwards if it is less. In an optimized asset workflow, it may be desirable to support a single direction only. Moving excessively in either direction can result in problems. Moving too far outwards can cause the object to be too large to fit inside its bounding box, resulting in issues with geometry intersections; whereas, moving too far inwards can result in degenerate, thin, and strange-looking meshes. Applying both displacement directions within the one displacement map can make it more difficult to fine tune these artifacts.

When our domain shader is processing newly created vertices from the fixed function tessellation stage, we sample the displacement map for the given UV coordinates. If the value is closer to black, we push the vertices in the opposite direction of the normal; and if the value is closer to white, we pull the vertices out in the direction of the normal. Note that the normal used here must be in *world space*.

```
// Perform displacement
position += CalculateDisplacement(UV, normal);
```

The distance that the vertices are moved depends not only on the sampled displacement value, but also on the value of the newly created `DisplaceScale` property in the per material constant buffer. The meshes used in this project all require different scales for optimal display. Ideally, this value would be stored with the mesh, or the models and displacement maps would all be created with the same scale in mind.

```
// Sample height map - using Red channel
float height = DisplacementMap.SampleLevel(Sampler, UV, mipLevel).r;

// remap height from 0 to 1, to -1 to 1 (with midlevel offset)
... SNIP
// Return offset along normal.
return height * DisplaceScale * normal;
```

The smoothness and quality of the resulting mesh depends on the original base mesh, the tessellation factor, method of tessellation and the displacement scale. The following skull jaw figure shows the data from the displacement and normal maps that affect the mapping process:

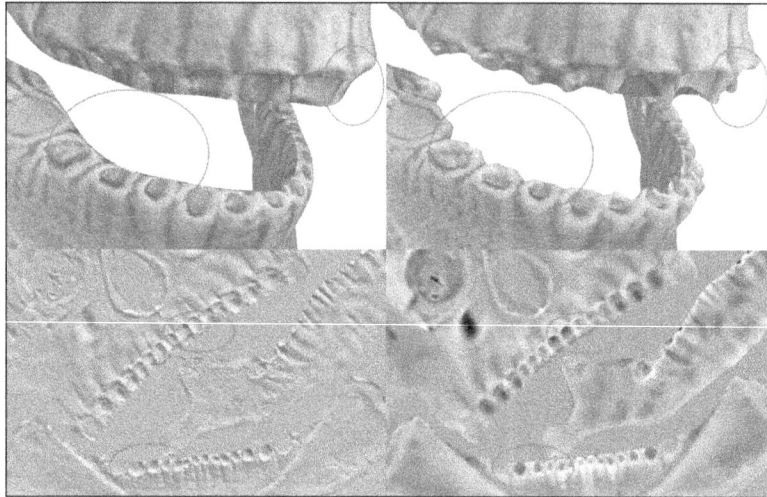

Skull jaw showing the impact of normal (left) and displacement (right) maps (displacement scale 0.020),—using the *Backspace* key within the completed project cycles through the available models

The displacement and normal maps for the models used in this recipe were generated by baking the normals and displacement between too meshes into textures within Blender. This is done by creating a low-poly version of a model by decimating it, then selecting the high and low-poly versions, and running the baking functions.

The displacement process presented in this recipe cannot add detail under the displaced vertices; for example, the simple plane we have rendered includes a spiral like cone in the original model. However, the displacement map does not include enough information to produce the same output. Instead, it results in a stretched region under the overhanging geometry as shown in the following figure. Therefore, it is necessary for the base model to contain enough geometry to approximate the final surface topology, and then the displacement can be applied for the final touches.

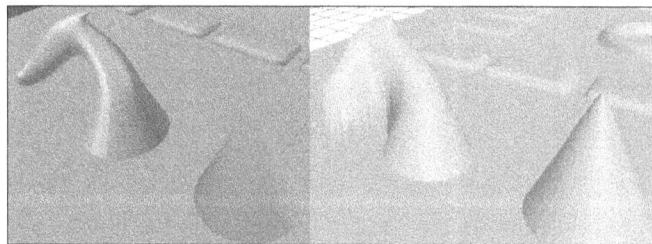

Comparison of missing 3D detail in the left cone between original model (left) and displaced render (right)

There's more...

Displacement mapping provides maximum impact around edges and contours. As we have seen with normal mapping, when we are looking straight at a surface, it does not necessarily require additional geometry to make it look realistic. Another pixel technique that can simulate additional surface detail without modifying the underlying geometry is **parallax occlusion mapping**.

Parallax occlusion mapping uses a height map like displacement mapping. By sampling within a maximum radius from the current UV coordinate, the algorithm will use the height map to determine if another sample occludes it; and if so, will use its UV coordinate instead. This is a useful approach that produces more than sufficient results in many cases, while being faster than tessellation and displacement mapping. However, this technique does not create additional geometry around edges. By combining displacement mapping (with only contours being displaced) and parallax occlusion mapping, it may be possible to achieve a similar visual effect while still allowing a reduction in the amount of tessellation needed.

You may have noticed that we only sample the red channel of the displacement map, and the red, green, and blue channels of the normal map. This means that we could add the displacement map into the alpha channel of the normal map. Whether this is of benefit really depends on the asset workflow and specifics of the implementation. However, it could reduce the number of texture slots used. Although **Shader Model 4** (**SM4**) or later supports 128 texture slots, there is a maximum of eight textures that can be assigned to a material in the Microsoft .cmo file format. Of course this becomes less of an issue when using a purpose built mesh/material format.

The displacement height calculation could be modified to support a mid-level value that is provided as an additional `PerMaterial` constant buffer variable. This provides greater control over the displacement process. For example, if finer detail is required in the peaks, it may be useful to move the mid-level more towards the black end of the range, leaving additional room in the upper-half of the spectrum.

```
// remap height from 0 to 1, to -1 to 1 (with offset)
float midLevel = max(DisplaceMidLevel, 0.00001); // no zero
if (height > midLevel)
    // Remap the range between (midlevel,1) to (0,1)
    height = (height-midLevel) / (1 - midLevel);
else
    // Remap the range between (0,midlevel) to (-1,0)
    height = height / midLevel - 1;
```

See also

- *Chapter 5, Applying Hardware Tessellation*, provides more information on the hardware tessellation process

- The *Optimizing tessellation through back-face culling and dynamic Level-of-Detail* recipe in *Chapter 5, Applying Hardware Tessellation*, includes how to reduce the tessellation factor for nonsilhouette triangles

- Search on YouTube for *blender baking displacement* or *blender baking normals* for tutorials on how to bake normal and displacement maps in Blender

- The following link provides an overview of the decimate modifier (to produce a low-poly model from a high-poly model) within Blender: `http://wiki.blender.org/index.php/Doc:2.4/Manual/Modifiers/Generate/Decimate`

- MeshLab is a useful software for mesh manipulation (Visual Computing Lab of-ISTI-CNR at `http://meshlab.sourceforge.net/`)

- An overview and implementation of parallax occlusion mapping can be found at: `http://www.d3dcoder.net/Data/Resources/ParallaxOcclusion.pdf`

Implementing displacement decals

In this recipe, we will be creating a displacement decal in order to add dynamic detail to a mesh on the GPU in real-time. This technique combines hardware tessellation and displacement to implement local mesh deformations such as footsteps, bullet holes, and craters.

Getting reading

We are using three new textures that are available in the downloaded content for this recipe, `Crater_Diffuse.png`, `Crater_Displacement.png`, and `Crater_Normal.png`. The completed project can be found in the companion code `Ch06_02DisplacementDecals`.

How to do it...

We will begin by creating our new `Shaders\CommonDecal.hlsl` HLSL shader file. This will introduce a new constant buffer to hold the necessary information that will be applied to our decal, include the texture references we need, and house the functions to calculate our decal's displacement:

1. First, create a new HLSL file, `Shaders\CommonDecal.hlsl`; be sure to change the encoding or copy an existing HLSL file and clear the contents.

2. Within our new shader file, add the following global textures:

```
// To support decal displacement mapping
Texture2D DecalDisplacementMap : register(t2);
```

```
Texture2D DecalDiffuse : register(t3);
Texture2D DecalNormalMap : register(t4);
// Assumes that SamplerState Sampler : register(s0); exists
```

3. Now, add our new `DecalBuffer` constant buffer (note that we use the fifth constant buffer slot `b4`).

```
// Controls the decal displacement
cbuffer DecalBuffer : register(b4) {
    float DecalDisplaceScale; // If 0 no decal applied
    float3 DecalNormal;// If normal is 0 no decal applied
    float3 DecalTangent; // used to determine texcoord
    float3 DecalBitangent;// used to determine texcoord
    float3 DecalPosition; // decal position in local space
    float DecalRadius;    // decal size
}
```

4. We will create three new functions: one for sampling the normal, one for sampling the diffuse, and one for calculating the displacement.

```
float3 DecalNormalSample(float2 decalUV)
{
    return DecalNormalMap.Sample(Sampler, decalUV).rgb;
}


float4 DecalDiffuseSample(float2 decalUV)
{
    return DecalDiffuse.Sample(Sampler, decalUV).rgba;
}


// The float3 result should be added to the vertex position
float3 DecalDisplacement(float3 worldNormal, float3 worldPosition,
out float3 decalUV)
{
    float3 result = (float3)0;

    // Note: if the decalUV.z == 0 the pixel shader will
    // assume no decal map needs to be queried
    decalUV = (float3)0;

    // Skip displacement sampling if 0 multiplier or if the
    // decal normal is not set
    if (DecalDisplaceScale == 0 || (DecalNormal.x == 0.0 &&
            DecalNormal.y == 0.0 && DecalNormal.z == 0))
        return result;
```

```
    // Determine decal world position
    float3 decalPosWorld = mul(float4(DecalPosition, 1),
        World).xyz;
    // Calculate distance from vertex to decal
    float distanceToDecal = distance(worldPosition,
        decalPosWorld);

    // if distance to the decal position is within radius
    // then we need to perform displacement based on decal
    if (distanceToDecal <= DecalRadius)
    {
... SNIP see below
    }
    return result;
}
```

Within the `if (distanceToDecal <= DecalRadius) {...}` block of the `DecalDisplacement` function, if the distance to the decal from the current vertex is within the decal radius we need to do the following:

5. Determine the current decal UV coordinate based upon the decal's normal/tangent/bitangent and the difference between the vertex position and decal position.

```
// Convert vectors to world space
float3 dT = normalize(mul(DecalTangent,
    (float3x3)WorldInverseTranspose));
float3 dB = normalize(mul(DecalBitangent,
    (float3x3)WorldInverseTranspose));
float3 dN = normalize(mul(DecalNormal,
    (float3x3)WorldInverseTranspose));
float3x3 worldToDecal = float3x3(dT, dB, dN);

decalUV = mul(worldToDecal, worldPosition - decalPosWorld);
// Remap to range between 0 and 1
decalUV /= 2 * DecalRadius; // (-0.5,0.5)
decalUV += 0.5;  // (0,1)
// z=1 tells pixel shader to sample decal diffuse texture
decalUV.z = 1.0;
```

6. Sample the displacement value and perform the displacement in the same way as we did for regular displacement mapping.

```
// Choose the most detailed mipmap level
const float mipLevel = 1.0f;
// Sample height map - using R channel
```

```
float height = DecalDisplacementMap.SampleLevel(Sampler,
    decalUV.xy, mipLevel).r;

// remap height from (0,1) to (-1, 1)
height = (2 * height) - 1;

// Return offset along DecalNormal. This allows the decal
// to be applied at an angle to the surface, e.g. to allow
// the direction of a bullet to decide the direction of
// deformation. Using the worldNormal instead will result
// in uniform decals.
result = height * DecalDisplaceScale * dN;// worldNormal;
```

7. We now have the decal UV property that needs to be forwarded to the pixel shader. For this, we add a new property to the `PixelShaderInput` structure within `Common.hlsl`

   ```
   float3 DecalUV: TEXCOORD5; // .z==1 means there is a decal
   ```

   In the domain shaders that we want to support displacement decals, we can now add the following:

8. Include `CommonDecal.hlsl` after the other includes within the domain shader's HLSL file:

   ```
   #include "Common.hlsl"
   #include "CommonTess.hlsl"
   #include "CommonDecal.hlsl"
   ```

9. After the existing displacement code in the domain shader, add a call to the `DecalDisplacement` function we just created.

   ```
   // Perform displacement
   normal = normalize(normal);
   position += CalculateDisplacement(UV, normal);

   // Perform decal displacement
   position += DecalDisplacement(normal, position,
       result.DecalUV);
   ```

10. Next, we need to update each pixel shader that implements texture and normal map sampling (for example, `BlinnPhongPS.hlsl`, `DiffusePS.hlsl`, and `PhongPS.hlsl`).

11. Then, we include the `CommonDecal.hlsl` shader file after `Common.hlsl`.

12. After the normal and texture sampling, and before the lighting calculations, we can check if the decal has been applied to this fragment:

```
// Normal mapping
... SNIP
// Texture sample here (use white if no texture)
... SNIP

// Check if we have a decal .z == 1 means we do
if (pixel.DecalUV.z > 0.5)
{
    // Decal normal sample using the pixel.DecalUV and
    // apply to the existing normal. Note that we are
    // blending the existing normal map sample with the
    // decal normal sample
    normal = ApplyNormalMap(normal, pixel.WorldTangent,
        DecalNormalSample(pixel.DecalUV.xy));
    // Decal texture sample
    float4 decalDiffuse = DecalDiffuseSample(
        pixel.DecalUV.xy);
    // lerp the current sample and the decal diffuse, using
    // the alpha channel of the decal as 't'.
    sample = lerp(sample, float4(decalDiffuse.rgb,
        sample.a), decalDiffuse.a);
}
// Final color and lighting calculations
float3 ambient = MaterialAmbient.rgb;
...SNIP
```

We are nearly done. All we have to do now is create our C# decal constant buffer, assign it to the appropriate shader stages, load some decal textures, and then update the decal constant buffer subresource with the location, size, and normals.

13. Within `ConstantBuffers.cs`, add a new structure `DecalBuffer` with the equivalent properties we used in the HLSL structure. Note that we perform the appropriate padding to align correctly to 16 bytes:

```
// The decal constant buffer
[StructLayout(LayoutKind.Sequential, Pack = 1)]
public struct DecalBuffer
{
    public float DecalDisplaceScale; // If 0 no decal
    public Vector3 DecalNormal; // If 0 no decal
    public Vector3 DecalTangent;
    public float _padding0;
    public Vector3 DecalBitangent;
```

```
        public float _padding1;
        public Vector3 DecalPosition;
        public float DecalRadius;
    }
```

14. Within `D3DApp.cs`, create the new private member fields to hold the decal buffer and textures:

```
// A buffer that is used to update the displacement decal
Buffer decalBuffer;
ShaderResourceView decalDiffuse;
ShaderResourceView decalDisplacement;
ShaderResourceView decalNormal;
```

15. Within `D3DApp.CreateDeviceDependentResources`, add the obligatory `RemoveAndDispose` calls for these new properties; and after the existing constant buffers, initialize, the new resources as follows:

```
// Create the decal buffer
decalBuffer = ToDispose(new Buffer(device, Utilities.
SizeOf<ConstantBuffers.DecalBuffer>(), ResourceUsage.
Default, BindFlags.ConstantBuffer, CpuAccessFlags.None,
ResourceOptionFlags.None, 0));

// Load the decal textures
decalDiffuse      = ToDispose(ShaderResourceView.FromFile(
                    device, "Crater_Diffuse.png"));
decalDisplacement = ToDispose(ShaderResourceView.FromFile(
                    device, "Crater_Displacement.png"));
decalNormal       = ToDispose(ShaderResourceView.FromFile(
                    device, "Crater_Normal.png"));
```

16. Next, apply the constant buffer to the shader stages (remember that we used the `b4` constant buffer slot in the shader code):

```
// Add the decal buffer to the pixel, hull and domain
// shaders (it uses the 5th slot 0-indexed)
context.HullShader.SetConstantBuffer(4, decalBuffer);
context.DomainShader.SetConstantBuffer(4, decalBuffer);
context.PixelShader.SetConstantBuffer(4, decalBuffer);
```

17. As our `DisplacementMeshRenderer` class will clear the pixel shader resources, we will make its `textureViews` property publicly available so that we can assign the decal shader resources to the active mesh:

```
public List<ShaderResourceView> TextureViews
    { get { return textureViews; } }
```

18. Now, within the render loop prior to any draw calls, assign the shader resource views to the domain shader and the mesh's new `TextureView` property.

```
context.DomainShader.SetShaderResource(2,
    decalDisplacement);
...
var m = meshes[meshIndex];
// Assign decal textures to mesh pixel shader
// using registers t3 and t4
m.TextureViews[3] = decalDiffuse;
m.TextureViews[4] = decalNormal;
```

19. And lastly, we will hard code an example decal location within the render loop by updating the decal constant buffer as follows:

```
var decal = new ConstantBuffers.DecalBuffer();
decal.DecalDisplaceScale = 0.10f; // static scale for now
// Create orthonormalized normal/tangent/bitangent vectors
var decalVectors = new Vector3[3];
Vector3.Orthonormalize(decalVectors, new[] { new Vector3(0,
    0.5f, 0.5f), Vector3.UnitX, -Vector3.UnitY });
decal.DecalNormal = decalVectors[0];
decal.DecalTangent = decalVectors[1];    // U-axis of tex
decal.DecalBitangent = decalVectors[2]; // V-axis of tex
decal.DecalPosition = new Vector3(0, 1, 1);
decal.DecalRadius = 0.5f;
context.UpdateSubresource(ref decal, decalBuffer);
```

20. That's it! If we compile and run the project now, we will see that the displacement decal is modifying the existing surface to create a crater as per our textures. Note that the decal position must be located in the correct position so that it can be applied to the surface.

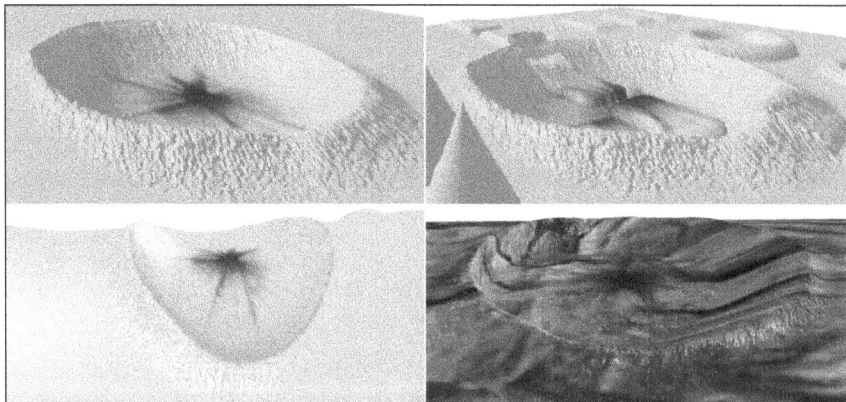

Displacement decal shown on plane (top-left), plane with displacement (top-right), corner of cube (bottom-left), and the tree log (bottom-right).

How it works...

Basically, displacement decals work in the same way as regular displacement mapping. The main differences are that the existence and location of the decal is dependent upon information passed into a constant buffer, and the UV coordinates for the displacement/ normal and diffuse sampling are determined based on the difference between the current vertex position and decal position.

Reviewing the tangent space that we covered in _Adding surface detail with normal mapping_, we can see how the normal, tangent, and bitangent vectors that we assign to the decal constant buffer are controlling the orientation (rotation and angle) of the decal on the surface it is applied.

The example decal position and tangent vectors in the code for this recipe will result in no decal appearing on the plane. This is not only due to the position not meeting the surface, but also because the angle of the decal will look odd. The following code snippet includes values that will appear on the plane in the example scene:

```
Vector3.Orthonormalize(decalVectors, new[] {
    new Vector3(0, 0.5f, 0.2f), Vector3.UnitX, Vector3.UnitZ });
decal.DecalPosition = new Vector3(0, 0, 0);
```

Our current implementation blends the two displacements together; although in certain circumstances, such as the crater shown previously, you may want to replace the existing displacement. This is easy enough to do; however, it is also necessary to blend the normal correctly, otherwise the two surfaces will appear disjointed. A solution for this is to include another channel in the decal displacement map that controls where and to what extent the decal overrides the existing displacement and normal (functioning like an alpha channel).

There's more...

The constant buffer could be easily extended to support multiple decals by changing it to an array of parameters. _Chapter 4, Animating Meshes with Vertex Skinning_, has an example of how to use arrays of elements in a constant buffer structure for the bones.

Currently we are just setting the decal properties directly in code; instead, we could have this event based (for example, mouse click) and determine the correct location from there. The decal constant buffer only needs to be updated when a decal is changed. If a significant number of decals need to be supported, then it may be a better option to store the decal properties within a regular buffer or texture.

Another interesting effect can be easily created by decreasing the decal displacement scale over time to simulate a fading decal (for example, a fading footstep). However, you will want to apply the same decay on the diffuse/normal texture samples.

Optimizing tessellation based on displacement decal (displacement adaptive tessellation)

By modifying our hull shader constant function, we can easily modify the tessellation factor based on whether or not a decal is located within the vicinity of a patch. This is also known as **displacement adaptive tessellation**.

Getting ready

Within the completed sample available for download in *Implementing displacement decals*, there is an additional function in `Shaders\CommonDecal.hlsl` that adds the provided tessellation factor to the appropriate edges and inside tessellation factors depending on whether the decal position and radius would impact the current patch.

```
void DecalTessellationFactor(float3 p[3], inout float3 edgeTessFactor,
inout float insideTessFactor, float tessellation)
```

How to do it...

To apply displacement adaptive tessellation to the triangle tessellation hull shader perform the following steps:

1. Update the triangle hull shader constant function `HS_TrianglesConstant` with the following highlighted changes:

```
...SNIP
ProcessTriTessFactorsMax((float3)TessellationFactor, 1.0,
roundedEdgeTessFactor, roundedInsideTessFactor, insideTessFactor);

float3 p[3];
[unroll]
for (uint j = 0; j < 3; j++)
    p[j] = patch[j].WorldPosition;
// Increase tessellation by 10 if decal
DecalTessellationFactor(p, roundedEdgeTessFactor,
    roundedInsideTessFactor, 10);

// Apply the edge and inside tessellation factors
result.EdgeTessFactor[0] = roundedEdgeTessFactor.x;
result.EdgeTessFactor[1] = roundedEdgeTessFactor.y;
result.EdgeTessFactor[2] = roundedEdgeTessFactor.z;
result.InsideTessFactor = roundedInsideTessFactor;
...SNIP
```

2. That's it. The resulting output with a base tessellation factor of 1.0 is shown in the following figure:

Example output of meshes with a tessellation increase of 10.0 for patches impacted by the displacement decal

How it works...

When we calculate the edge and inside tessellation factors, we are now adding 10.0 to the tessellation factor value if a decal happens to be located within range of the patch. The calculation correctly ignores edges that are not covered by the decal, and it generally results in crack free decal displacements. In situations where cracks appear, try using the inside tessellation factor only and discard the changes to the edges—or create a modified version of the `DecalTessellationFactor` method to exclude the edges or inside tessellation factor, as appropriate.

```
float3 ignoreEdge;
DecalTessellationFactor(p, ignoreEdge, roundedInsideTessFactor,
    10);
```

The `DecalTessellationFactor` method determines the tessellation factors for us using the Pythagorean Theorem to calculate the distance of each edge of the current patch (triangle) from the location of the decal as provided by the `DecalPosition` and `DecalRadius` properties in the decal constant buffer.

The example output shown previously uses a tessellation factor of 1.0 for all triangles not covered by a decal, and a tessellation factor of 11.0 for those that are. It can be seen that the increase in triangle count can be quite significant. Therefore, it is a good idea to apply the `maxtessfactor` attribute to your hull shaders, as shown in the following code snippet. This will prevent decals from increasing the tessellation factor beyond a certain limit, safeguarding performance:

```
[domain("tri")]
...
[maxtessfactor(12.0f)]
```

```
DS_ControlPointInput HS_TrianglesInteger(
    InputPatch<HullShaderInput, 3> patch,
                        uint id : SV_OutputControlPointID,
                        uint patchID : SV_PrimitiveID )
{ ... }
```

There's more...

The resulting triangles will benefit from a screen-based tessellation limit. This helps to prevent the occurrence of very small triangles by preventing the tessellation factor from increasing beyond certain limits depending on the triangle edge lengths of the screen. That is, when a triangle is far away from the view, and therefore small on the screen, the tessellation factor is reduced; and when the triangle is close, the tessellation factor is increased. If the triangle is at a glancing angle and the edge lengths are short, the tessellation factor would also be reduced.

7
Performing Image Processing Techniques

In this chapter, we will use compute shaders (or DirectCompute) for the following image processing techniques:

- ▸ Running a compute shader – desaturation (grayscale)
- ▸ Adjusting the contrast and brightness
- ▸ Implementing box blur using separable convolution filters
- ▸ Implementing a Gaussian blur filter
- ▸ Detecting edges with the Sobel edge-detection filter
- ▸ Calculating an image's luminance histogram

Introduction

Image processing is the process of applying a signal-processing technique against an input image. The input image is generally a two-dimensional signal with the output being either another image or any properties derived from the input signal.

During this chapter, we will implement a number of filtering techniques using **compute shaders** (also known as **DirectCompute**). Utilizing compute shaders for this process allows us to provide image processing in general applications, including non-UI applications, and in some cases is able to achieve a significant performance improvement over pixel shaders (most notably large radius filters). In some circumstances it may be desirable to implement the filter technique within a pixel shader by rendering to a screen-aligned quad, although we lose some of the unique capabilities of the compute shader when doing so—such an example might be small radius blurs where we can utilize the bilinear hardware support.

One of the main advantages of compute shaders over other solutions is that it is designed to integrate well with Direct3D, allowing them to be used for both compute-only applications as well as to augment graphics algorithms.

Running a compute shader – desaturation (grayscale)

The first task we will tackle is a simple conversion of an input image to grayscale (color desaturation); the input image can be an image file or any texture resource (such as a rendered scene). The formula is used in subsequent recipes for filters, such as the Sobel edge detector.

Getting ready

For this recipe we just need to have a Direct3D device and device context available, and an image to process. The image used for illustration here is available within the downloadable content from Packt's website.

How to do it...

First we will prepare our input and output shader resources. The compute shader will take a **Shader Resource View** (**SRV**) of a `Texture2D` variable as input and an **Unordered Access View** (**UAV**) of another `Texture2D` as output.

1. Load the source image into an SRV and retrieve the texture:

```
var srcTextureSRV = ShaderResourceView.FromFile(device,
    "Village.png");
var srcTexture = srcTextureSRV.ResourceAs<Texture2D>();
```

2. Initialize a new texture that is the same size as the original texture and create an unordered access view for it. Note that we are also setting a debug name:

```
var desc = srcTexture.Description;
desc.BindFlags = BindFlags.UnorderedAccess;
var target = new Texture2D(device, desc);
target.DebugName = "CSTarget";
var targetUAV = new UnorderedAccessView(device, target);
```

A compute shader cannot use an SRV and UAV of the same underlying texture resource at the same time. In fact, an SRV to the same texture as the UAV cannot be bound to any stage of the pipeline at the same time as running the compute shader. Doing so will result in a warning if the debug layer is active and will remove the SRV from the pipeline stage it is bound to. For simple processing, such as desaturation/contrast/brightness, we could however use the same UAV as the input and output.

Next we will create the HLSL compute shader, compile, and run it.

3. The complete compute shader source code is:

```
Texture2D<float4> input : register(t0);
RWTexture2D<float4> output : register(u0);

// used for RGB/sRGB color models
#define LUMINANCE_RGB float3(0.2125, 0.7154, 0.0721)
#define LUMINANCE(_V) dot(_V.rgb, LUMINANCE_RGB)

// Desaturate the input, the result is returned in output
[numthreads(THREADSX, THREADSY, 1)]
void DesaturateCS(uint groupIndex: SV_GroupIndex,
  uint3 groupId : SV_GroupID,
  uint3 groupThreadId: SV_GroupThreadID,
  uint3 dispatchThreadId : SV_DispatchThreadID)
{
  float4 sample = input[dispatchThreadId.xy];
  // Calculate the relative luminance
  float3 target = (float3)LUMINANCE(sample.rgb);
  output[dispatchThreadId.xy] = float4(target, sample.a);
}
```

4. We can add the previous shader code to a string variable easily by @-quoting (for example, `var hlslCode = @"…";`) to interpret the string as a literal value and ignore normal escaping rules (this also allows the string to span multiple lines).

5. With the previous shader source code within a string variable named `hlslCode`, we can now compile and run the shader as follows:

```
// Define the thread group size
SharpDX.Direct3D.ShaderMacro[] defines = new[] {
  new SharpDX.Direct3D.ShaderMacro("THREADSX", 16),
  new SharpDX.Direct3D.ShaderMacro("THREADSY", 4),
};
using (var bytecode = ShaderBytecode.Compile(hlslCode,
```

```
  "DesaturateCS", "cs_5_0", ShaderFlags.None,
  EffectFlags.None, defines, null))
using (var cs = new ComputeShader(device, bytecode))
{
  // Set the source resource
  context.ComputeShader.SetShaderResource(0,
    srcTextureSRV);
  // Set the destination resource
  context.ComputeShader.SetUnorderedAccessView(0,
    targetUAV);
  context.ComputeShader.Set(cs);
  // e.g. 640x480 -> Dispatch(40, 120, 1);
  context.Dispatch((int)Math.Ceiling(desc.Width / 16.0),
    (int)Math.Ceiling(desc.Height / 4.0), 1);
}
```

6. After running the previous code, the `target` texture now contains the desaturated image. We can use the graphics debugger to peek at the contents of the texture without having to render or save to a file. To do this, ensure that the project is configured to enable native code debugging (see *Chapter 1, Getting Started with Direct3D*) and run the project within the Visual Studio Graphics Debugger (*Alt + F5*). Pressing the *Print Screen* key will capture all resources and list them in the graphics object table where you can select the texture with the debug name `CSTarget` as shown in the following screenshot (a grayscale result when viewed within the Graphics Debugger of Visual Studio):

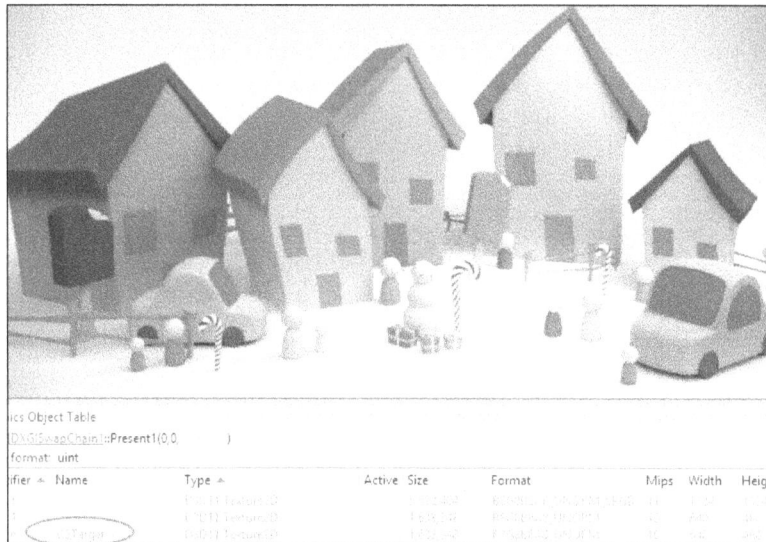

Grayscale result when viewed within the Graphics Debugger of Visual Studio

How it works...

We began by preparing the input and output resources, using an SRV as the input and a UAV as the output. By creating the target `Texture2D`, using the source image's texture description, we simply have to change the `desc.BindFlags` method to `BindFlags.UnorderedAccess`, and we are ready to create the texture and UAV.

After assigning the shader resources and compiling the compute shader, we dispatch a number of thread groups relative to the source image size. We use the `Ceiling` method to ensure that if the image dimensions are not evenly divisible by the thread group size, we are still covering the entire image (anything sampled outside the bounds of the SRV will be black and anything written will be discarded):

```
// 640x480 -> Dispatch(40, 120, 1);
context.Dispatch((int)Math.Ceiling(desc.Width / 16.0),
  (int)Math.Ceiling(desc.Height / 4.0), 1);
```

In our shader code, we have defined the input texture as we would for any SRV; it uses the first texture slot (`t0`). Our output resource is assigned to the first UAV slot (`u0`).

We have defined the number of threads per thread group to be 64 by specifying the `[numthreads(16,4,1)]` attribute. This size was defined by our shader macros `THREADSX` and `THREADSY`. The minimum recommended thread group size on AMD hardware is 64 and on NVidia hardware is 32. Generally, the thread group size should be a multiple of this minimum size. The maximum size supported by Shader Model 5 is 1024. The optimal thread group size varies depending on the hardware and what tasks the compute shader is performing. During performance tests, the optimal thread group sizes for this shader were 16x4x1 and 32x32x1.

Given a source image with the dimensions 640x480, we dispatch 40x120x1 groups of 16x4x1 threads. This effectively creates a thread for each pixel within the 640x480 source image.

Compute shader functions support the following input semantics: `SV_GroupID`, `SV_GroupThreadID`, `SV_DispatchThreadID`, and `SV_GroupIndex`. These values are used to identify the current thread and index into any resources required by the thread. The following diagram shows how each of these input semantics are calculated based on an image with the dimensions 640x480, using `[numthreads(32,32,1)]` for the number of threads per group, and dispatching the thread groups with `context.Dispatch(20,15,1)`.

Threads and thread groups execute in an undefined order with respect to each other during a single `Dispatch` call. There are thread synchronization commands for threads within the same thread group. These allow threads within the same thread group to communicate with each other using the thread group-shared memory.

Note that the number of groups in the x and y axes is determined by dividing the width of the image by the x axis threads/group count, and the height of the image by the y axis threads/group count. In this example, we only use a single slice (along the z axis). The following diagram shows the compute shader thread addressing for a thread group (large filled square) and a single thread (small filled square):

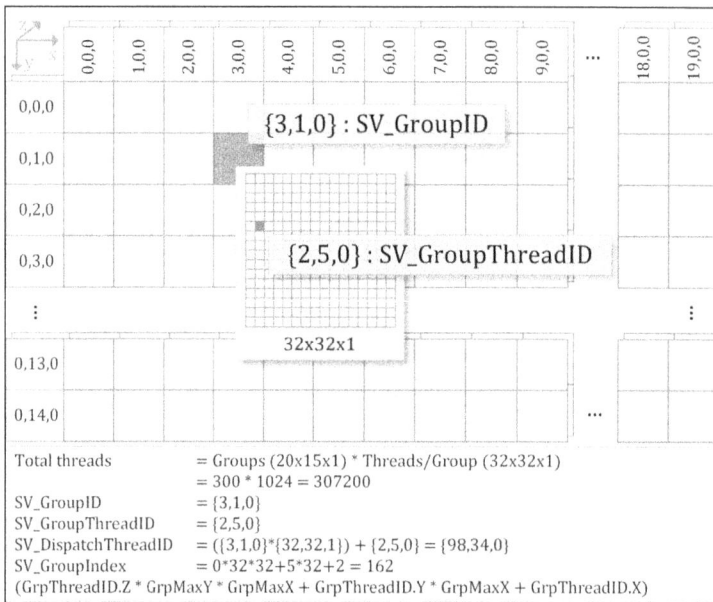

Compute shader thread addressing showing a thread group (large filled square) and a single thread (small filled square)

To sample from the source texture, we are using the pixel coordinate rather than a normalized UV coordinate (that is, for our 640x480 image we use 0-639 along the x axis rather than 0.0-1.0). This is done using the array access operator of the input texture `input []`. Because we have a single thread created for each pixel, the `dispatchThreadId` attribute matches the appropriate pixel's XY coordinate for the input and output image (see the previous diagram). As we are using a `Texture2D` variable rather than a `StructureBuffer` or `RawStructuredBuffer` variable for the input texture, we are still taking advantage of the texture-fetch hardware, which converts the image pixel RGBA data to a `float4` variable:

```
float4 sample = input[dispatchThreadId.xy];
```

Next, we determine the pixel's relative luminance (Y) by calculating the dot product of the linear RGB components with the appropriate coefficients (these depend on the colors that contribute the most to light intensity for the human eye and are based upon the ITU-R Recommendation BT.709):

```
Y = R * 0.2125 + G * 0.7154 + B * 0.0721;
Y = dot(sample.rgb, float3(0.2125,0.7154,0.0721));
```

If using sRGB input textures, the non-linear RGB components will be automatically linearized for you when sampling; however, writing back to the UAV will require a manual reapplication of the gamma correction because an sRGB texture cannot be bound to a UAV. This would look something similar to the following:

```
output[dispatchThreadId.xy] = pow(value, (1/2.2));
```

After calculating the relative luminance, we apply this to the red, green, and blue components of the result and write this value back to the appropriate location within the UAV—as we are using `RWTexture2D`, we take advantage of the video hardware's automatic conversion from `float4` to the appropriate pixel format. We have now desaturated the source pixel by 100 percent.

> The completed project for this chapter supports rendering the output back to the render target. It also supports using the render target as the input into the compute shaders as well as a number of sample images (*Ctrl* + */-* cycles through these).

There's more...

It is often useful to be able to apply a percentage of the effect upon the source image. For example, rather than a 100 percent desaturation, we might want to only apply 50 percent of the effect.

This can easily be achieved by **linearly interpolating** (**lerp**) between the original pixel and target pixel using the lerp HLSL intrinsic function. In fact, because linear interpolation can be extrapolated beyond the 0 to 1 range, we can use this approach to implement the reverse of desaturation and saturate the image.

We can add a constant buffer to the previous HLSL and create the equivalent structure in C# to pass in this information in the same way we can with vertex or pixel shaders.

1. Create a new constant buffer in the compute shader:

```
cbuffer ComputeConstants : register(b0)
{
    float Intensity;
};
```

2. The corresponding C# structure for the constant buffer is shown in the following code snippet:

```
[System.Runtime.InteropServices.StructLayout(System.Runtime.
InteropServices.LayoutKind.Sequential)]
public struct ComputeConstants
{
```

```
    public float Intensity;
    public Vector3 _padding0;
}
```

> [!NOTE]
> Remember that constant buffers are aligned to 16 bytes, so we need to include the additional `Vector3` padding property (12 bytes).

3. Create and update the constant buffer as shown here:

```
var computeBuffer = new Buffer(device,
   Utilities.SizeOf<ComputeConstants>(),
   ResourceUsage.Default, BindFlags.ConstantBuffer,
   CpuAccessFlags.None, ResourceOptionFlags.None, 0);
var constants = new ComputeConstants {
   Intensity = 0.5f
};
context.UpdateSubresource(ref constants, computeBuffer);
```

4. Next, set the constant buffer to the compute shader pipeline stage:

```
context.ComputeShader.SetConstantBuffer(0, computeBuffer);
```

5. And finally we change our compute shader code so that it interpolates the values, gradually adding gray to the result:

```
output[dispatchThreadId.xy] = float4(lerp(target, sample.rgb,
   Intensity), sample.a);
```

With the lerp in place, it is now possible to control the level of saturation/desaturation with negative/positive values for `Intensity`, respectively. The following figure shows the results of applying different interpolation amounts, starting with (**A**) normal image at 1.0, (**B**) half desaturated at 0.5, (**C**) oversaturated at 2.0, and (**D**) desaturated using 0.0:

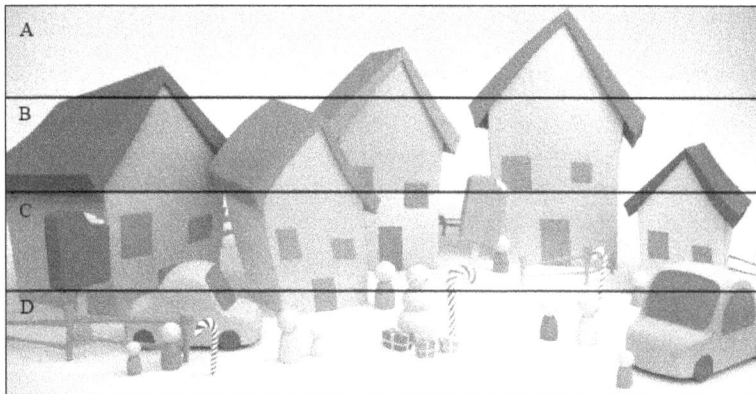

Various levels of saturation – A: original, B: half desaturation, C: 100 percent saturation, D: 100 percent desaturation

▸ The ITU-R Recommendation BT.709 can be found here: `http://www.itu.int/dms_pubrec/itu-r/rec/bt/R-REC-BT.709-5-200204-I!!PDF-E.pdf`

Adjusting the contrast and brightness

In this recipe we will adjust the contrast of the image by interpolating the color towards or away from gray, and adjusting the brightness by adding or removing the black color from the image. By moving the colors closer to gray (0.5, 0.5, 0.5), we are reducing the contrast, and by moving away in the positive direction we are increasing the contrast. Reducing the contrast by 100 percent will result in a totally gray image, while reducing by 200 percent, generates a negative image.

Getting ready

Begin with the resulting code from the previous recipe to adjust the color saturation levels, including the *There's more...* section for the interpolation of the source and target values.

How to do it...

First we will implement the contrast adjustment shader.

1. As we did in the *Running a compute shader – desaturation (grayscale)* recipe earlier in this chapter, add the following HLSL shader code to a string variable such as `hlslCode`. This will form our compute shader:

```
Texture2D<float4> input : register(t0);
RWTexture2D<float4> output : register(u0);
// Compute constant buffer
cbuffer ComputeConstants : register(b0)
{
  float LerpT;
};
// Lerp helper functions
float4 lerpKeepAlpha(float4 source, float3 target,
    float T)
{
  return float4(lerp(source.rgb, target, T), source.a);
}
float4 lerpKeepAlpha(float3 source, float4 target,
    float T)
{
```

```
      return float4(lerp(source, target.rgb, T), target.a);
}
// Adjust the image contrast
[numthreads(THREADSX, THREADSY, 1)]
void ContrastCS(uint groupIndex : SV_GroupIndex,
    uint3 groupId : SV_GroupID,
    uint3 groupThreadId: SV_GroupThreadID,
    uint3 dispatchThreadId : SV_DispatchThreadID)
{
  float4 sample = input[dispatchThreadId.xy];
  // Adjust contrast by moving towards or away from gray
  // Note: if LerpT == -1, we achieve a negative image
  //          LerpT == 0.0 will result in gray
  //          LerpT == 1.0 will result in no change
  //          LerpT >  1.0 will increase contrast
  float3 target = float3(0.5,0.5,0.5);
  output[dispatchThreadId.xy] = lerpKeepAlpha(target,
    sample, LerpT);
}
```

2. Next, we compile the shader as in the previous recipe; the only change is that we must update the constant buffer before dispatching the compute shader threads:

```
// Set the source resource
context.ComputeShader.SetShaderResource(0, srcTextureSRV);
// Set the destination resource
context.ComputeShader.SetUnorderedAccessView(0, targetUAV);
context.ComputeShader.Set(cs);

var computeBuffer = new Buffer(device, Utilities.
SizeOf<ComputeConstants>(), ResourceUsage.Default, BindFlags.
ConstantBuffer, CpuAccessFlags.None, ResourceOptionFlags.None, 0);

var constants = new ComputeConstants { LerpT = 0.5f };
context.UpdateSubresource(ref constants, computeBuffer);

// e.g. 640x480 -> Dispatch(20, 15, 1);
context.Dispatch(desc.Width / 32, desc.Height / 32, 1);
```

3. Next, we will implement a similar shader to adjust the brightness of the image. Everything is as per the ContrastCS shader; however, this time we set the target variable to black:

```
// Adjust brightness by adding or removing Black
// LerpT == 1.0 original image
// LerpT > 1.0 brightens
// LerpT < 1.0 darkens
```

```
float3 target = float3(0,0,0);
output[dispatchThreadId.xy] = lerpKeepAlpha(target, sample,
   LerpT);
```

4. The output of the contrast and brightness is shown in the following screenshot (Top (left to right): contrast 1.40, 0.6, -1.0 (negative); Bottom (left to right): brightness 0.70, 1.0 (original image), 1.4):

Top (left to right): contrast 1.40, 0.6, -1.0 (negative); Bottom (left to right): brightness 0.70, 1.0 (original image), 1.4

How it works...

Through the process of linear interpolation, we are able to add or remove levels of gray and black from the source image. By extrapolating the lerp, we are able to extend the effect past the standard 0-1 range.

We control the time (*t*) component of the lerp by updating a constant buffer that has been bound to the compute shader pipeline stage. To maintain the correct alpha for the initial sample, we exclude this component from the lerp, and add two helper functions to simplify the code.

Try experimenting with different LerpT values and different constants for the color that is being added/removed.

There's more...

Through a similar process as shown here, we can now perform any number of color manipulations within the compute shader.

Another simple example is applying a sepia tone to an image (sepia is a reddish brown color):

```
float4 sample = input[dispatchThreadId.xy];
float3 target;
target.r = saturate(dot(sample.rgb, float3(0.393, 0.769, 0.189)));
target.g = saturate(dot(sample.rgb, float3(0.349, 0.686, 0.168)));
target.b = saturate(dot(sample.rgb, float3(0.272, 0.534, 0.131)));

output[dispatchThreadId.xy]= lerpKeepAlpha(sample, target, LerpT);
```

See also

▸ The *Implementing box blur using separable convolution filters* recipe to learn how you can apply multiple filters in sequence

Implementing box blur using separable convolution filters

So far we have implemented some simple color manipulation techniques. Now we will create an image blur effect using a filter kernel. This technique will make more effective use of the compute shader thread groups by utilizing group shared memory and thread synchronization. Convolution filters can be used to apply a wide range of image processing effects, and among these effects, a number of them are separable, meaning that a 2D filter can be split into two 1D filters: the first representing the horizontal aspect of the filter, and the second representing the filter to be applied to the image vertically. These two 1D filters can then be processed in any order to produce the same result as the original 2D filter; however, the total number of texture reads required is significantly reduced.

How to do it...

Our blur operation will consist of two filters: horizontal and vertical blur filters that will be applied one after the other to produce the final blur. By adjusting the weights, we will be able to use the same shader for a box blur filter and a Gaussian blur filter.

> There are faster methods of implementing box blur and Gaussian blur filters; however, we can use the shader code presented here to implement a range of **separable convolution filters**. For blurs with smaller radiuses, a pixel shader version can be faster as we can take advantage of the bilinear hardware.

We'll begin with creating the horizontal blur compute shader.

1. The start of our shader code will introduce the input and output resources as before and in addition, we will use the `#define` macros to control the thread group size and filter tap.

```
Texture2D<float4> input : register(t0);
RWTexture2D<float4> output : register(u0);


#define FILTERTAP 5 // Must be ODD
// Note: at a thread group size of 1024, the maximum
// FILTERTAP possible is 33
#define FILTERRADIUS ((FILTERTAP-1)/2)
#define THREADSX 1024
#define THREADSY 1
// The total group size (DX11 max 1024)
#define GROUPSIZE (THREADSX * THREADSY)
```

2. Next, we will create our thread group shared memory. The shared memory needs to be large enough to store the samples for a complete thread group. Border threads at the start and end of the x axis for the thread group need to load an extra texel.

```
// Shared memory for storing thread group data for filters
// with enough room for
// GROUPSIZE + (THREADSY * FILTERRADIUS * 2)
// Max size of groupshared is 32KB
groupshared float4 FilterGroupMemX[GROUPSIZE + (THREADSY *
  FILTERRADIUS*2)];
```

3. Our last global variable is the blur filter kernel. For now we will configure the kernel as a simple box filter (where each texel under the kernel is given equal weight). It is important to note that the kernel must be of the same size as the filter-tap specified in `FILTERTAP` and that the middle element represents the kernel origin and therefore, the current texel.

```
static const float BlurKernel[FILTERTAP] =
  (float[FILTERTAP])(1.0/(FILTERTAP));
```

As we are only creating a 1D filter (for example, the horizontal and vertical filters are separated), we are using a *filter-tap x 1 convolution kernel*. Here we have used a shortcut to create the even weightings of a box filter by initializing the array with *1.0 / filter-tap*.

> As a general rule, the sum of all elements in the kernel must equal 1.0.

4. Next, we create our `BlurFilterHorizontalCS` compute shader method:

```
[numthreads(THREADSX, THREADSY, 1)]
void BlurFilterHorizontalCS(uint groupIndex: SV_GroupIndex,
  uint3 groupId : SV_GroupID,
  uint3 groupThreadId: SV_GroupThreadID,
  uint3 dispatchThreadId : SV_DispatchThreadID)
{ ... }
```

5. Within our compute shader, we have the following code:

```
// Calculate the correct index into FilterGroupMemX
uint offsetGroupIndex = groupIndex + (groupThreadId.y * 2 *
  FILTERRADIUS) + FILTERRADIUS;
// 1. Sample the current texel (clamp to max input coord)
FilterGroupMemX[offsetGroupIndex] =
  input[min(dispatchThreadId.xy, input.Length.xy - 1)];
// 2. If thread is within FILTERRADIUS of thread group
// boundary, sample an additional texel.
// 2a. additional texel @ dispatchThreadId.x - FILTERRADIUS
if (groupThreadId.x < FILTERRADIUS)
{  // Clamp out of bound samples that occur at image
  // borders (i.e. if x < 0, set to 0).
  int x = dispatchThreadId.x - FILTERRADIUS;
  FilterGroupMemX[offsetGroupIndex - FILTERRADIUS] =
    input[int2(max(x, 0), dispatchThreadId.y)];
}
// 2b. additional texel @ dispatchThreadId.x + FILTERRADIUS
if(groupThreadId.x >= THREADSX - FILTERRADIUS)
{  // Clamp out of bound samples that occur at image
  // borders (if x > imageWidth-1, set to imageWidth-1)
  int x = dispatchThreadId.x + FILTERRADIUS;
  FilterGroupMemX[offsetGroupIndex + FILTERRADIUS] =
    input[int2(min(x, input.Length.x - 1),
    dispatchThreadId.y)];
}
// 3. Wait for all threads in group to complete sampling
GroupMemoryBarrierWithGroupSync();
// 4. Apply blur kernel to the current texel using the
//    samples we have already loaded for this thread group
float4 result = float4(0, 0, 0, 0);
int centerPixel = offsetGroupIndex;
[unroll]
for(int i = -FILTERRADIUS; i <= FILTERRADIUS; ++i)
{  int j = centerPixel + i;
```

```
    result += BlurKernel[i + FILTERRADIUS] *
      FilterGroupMemX[j];
}
// Write the result to the output
output[dispatchThreadId.xy] = result;
```

This completes our horizontal filter. The vertical filter function
`BlurFilterVerticalCS` works similarly to the horizontal filter. The source for
the function can be found in the downloadable code for this chapter available on
Packt's website.

6. In order to run both the horizontal and vertical filters over the source image, it is
   necessary to use two texture resources and ping-pong between them.

7. We begin by changing our target resource description so that `desc.BindFlags` also
   indicates that the resource will be used as an SRV. We then create an SRV for the first
   target in addition to the UAV. Thereafter, define a second target (`target2`) with the
   same description, and create its SRV and UAV.

```
var srcTextureSRV = ShaderResourceView.FromFile(device,
  "Village.png");
var srcTexture = srcTextureSRV.ResourceAs<Texture2D>();
var desc = srcTexture.Description;
desc.BindFlags = BindFlags.ShaderResource |
  BindFlags.UnorderedAccess;

var target = new Texture2D(device, desc);
target.DebugName = "CSTarget";
var targetUAV = new UnorderedAccessView(device, target);
var targetSRV = new ShaderResourceView(device, target);

var target2 = new Texture2D(device, desc);
target2.DebugName = "CSTarget2";
var target2UAV = new UnorderedAccessView(device, target2);
var target2SRV = new ShaderResourceView(device, target2);
```

8. With our two resources ready, and the shader code for the horizontal and vertical
   shaders in the strings `horizHLSLCode` and `vertHLSLCode`, respectively, we need
   to compile both the horizontal and vertical shaders, and then dispatch the thread
   groups for each, switching the SRV and UAV each time.

```
// Compile the shaders
using (var horizBC = ShaderBytecode.Compile(horizHLSLCode,
  "BlurFilterHorizontalCS", "cs_5_0"))
using (var vertBC = ShaderBytecode.Compile(vertHLSLCode,
  "BlurFilterVerticalCS", "cs_5_0"))
using (var horizCS = new ComputeShader(device, horizBC))
```

```
using (var vertCS = new ComputeShader(device, vertBC))
{
  // The first source resource is the original image
  context.ComputeShader.SetShaderResource(0,
    srcTextureSRV);
  // The first destination resource is target
  context.ComputeShader.SetUnorderedAccessView(0,
    targetUAV);
  // Run the horizontal blur first (order doesn't matter)
  context.ComputeShader.Set(horizCS);
  context.Dispatch((int)Math.Ceiling(desc.Width / 1024.0),
    (int)Math.Ceiling(desc.Height / 1.0), 1);

  // We must set the compute shader stage SRV and UAV to
  // null between calls to the compute shader
  context.ComputeShader.SetShaderResource(0, null);
  context.ComputeShader.SetUnorderedAccessView(0, null);

  // The second source resource is the first target
  context.ComputeShader.SetShaderResource(0, targetSRV);
  // The second destination resource is target2
  context.ComputeShader.SetUnorderedAccessView(0,
    target2UAV);
  // Run the vertical blur
  context.ComputeShader.Set(vertCS);
  context.Dispatch((int)Math.Ceiling(desc.Width / 1.0),
    (int)Math.Ceiling(desc.Height / 1024.0), 1);

  // Set the compute shader stage SRV and UAV to null
  context.ComputeShader.SetShaderResource(0, null);
  context.ComputeShader.SetUnorderedAccessView(0, null);
}
```

An image processing renderer class (`ImageProcessingCS.cs`) for running multiple filters and a utility class for implementing the texture ping-pong (`TexturePingPong.cs`) is available within the downloadable code for this chapter (`Ch07_01ImageProcessing`) available on Packt's website.

9. The result of running both the horizontal and vertical blur filters is shown in the following figure comparing three filter sizes (3x3 (A), 5x5 (B), and 9x9 (C)):

Uniform box blur using varying kernel sizes: 3x3 (A), 5x5 (B), and 9x9 (C)

How it works...

To implement our blur filters, we use the convolution of two signals. This involves moving our first signal, a 2D matrix (called a **kernel** or **convolution matrix,** or sometimes a **mask**), from texel to texel over the source texture (our second signal). Usually the process replaces the original texel for the current kernel position (generally the central element of the kernel) with the sum of the products of the kernel elements with the texel underneath (see the following figure). This process is used to implement a range of other image filtering effects, such as edge detection and sharpening.

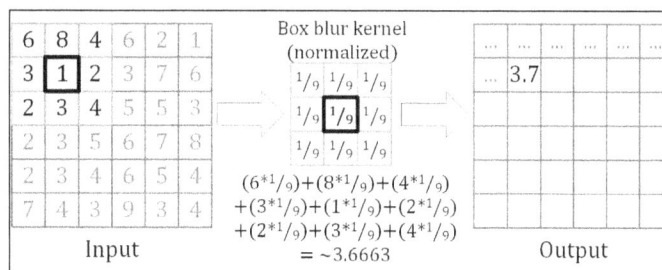

Convolution filter kernel (center) applied to input image, origin element is highlighted

The size of this kernel, and therefore the number of samples needed for the filter, is commonly referred to as the number of taps, that is, an **N-tap filter**. For example, a 3x3-tap filter will use a 3x3 kernel (and nine samples), whereas a 3-tap filter will use a 3x1 kernel (and three samples).

The box blur filter used in this recipe is separable, meaning that the vertical and horizontal components of the filter can be applied separately (one after the other) and still achieve the same result—generally this results in a much faster algorithm. For example, we can take the separable 3x3-tap box blur kernel shown in the previous figure and split it into two 3-tap kernels applied in two passes. The 3-tap horizontal kernel and 3-tap vertical kernel can be applied in any order (although the second filter must use the output of the first as its input). The final result is that instead of requiring nine samples per texel, the exact same output is achieved using only six samples per texel; for a 9x9, the difference is even greater, requiring only 18 samples per texel instead of 81. For smaller filters this is also possible within a pixel shader using a bilinear filter and the `Gather` texture sample command.

The coefficients of the resulting 1D filters must be normalized; therefore, instead of each texel contributing one ninth of the final result in the previous 3x3 box blur filter, each texel will contribute one third of the final result for the 3-tap horizontal/vertical filter.

To further reduce the number of samples required, we have taken advantage of the compute shader's local group shared memory. The actual number of samples is now close to two samples per texel instead of 6.6. Of course, the texture sampling isn't the only overhead; although the 32 KB shared memory sits closely with each of the SIMD units on the hardware, it still incurs a cost. We do this by first loading a texel into the group-shared memory for each thread within the group. After all threads in the current thread group have loaded their texel, each thread then applies the blur kernel to its texel accessing the cached values of neighboring texels from the group-shared memory. The following code snippet highlights the process:

```
// 1. Sample the texel for current thread and place in group
//    shared memory
...
// 2. Wait for all threads in group to complete sampling
GroupMemoryBarrierWithGroupSync();
// 3. Apply kernel to current texel, reading neighboring texels
//    from group shared memory. Write result to output UAV
...
```

To deal with the threads at the edge of the thread group, we need to load an additional `FILTERRADIUS*2` texels (that is, for a 5-tap blur, we need to load an additional texel for the first three and the last three threads on a row for the horizontal blur, or a column for the vertical blur). Our group-shared memory is set up to fit the thread's group size plus an additional (**THREADSY**`*FILTERRADIUS*2`) for the horizontal shader, and (**THREADSX**`*FILTERRADIUS*2`) for the vertical shader (see the outside elements in the following group-shared memory layout diagram):

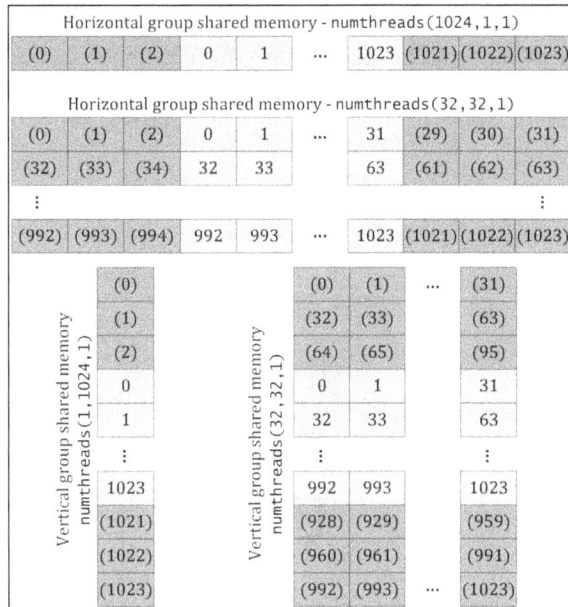

Layout of group-shared memory for horizontal and vertical filters for a 5-tap filter with varying thread group dimensions. The numbers represent which thread in the group loads the texel for that memory location where top-left is the 0th index. The outer cells indicate additional texels loaded from outside the bounds of the thread group.

If you recall the compute shader thread addressing figure in the explanation of the *Running a compute shader – desaturation (grayscale)* recipe, each thread group consists of up to a maximum of 1024 threads in Shader Model 5. These threads are given an ID based upon the number of groups dispatched and the dimensions within the `numthreads` attribute of the compute shader. Instead of a 32x32x1 or a 16x4x1 thread group, as we have used in the previous image processing recipes, in this recipe we have defined a thread group size to be 1024 threads wide (X-dimension) and one thread high (Y-dimension) for our `BlurFilterHorizontalCS` shader, and one thread wide and 1024 high for the `BlurFilterVerticalCS` shader. This means that for an ideal image size of 1024x1024, we sample *(1024*1024*2) + (1024*2*radius) + (1024*2*radius)* texels—with a filter radius of three (5-tap filter). This equates to 2.0117 samples per texel (2,109,440 total, a far cry from the approximately 6.29 million samples needed for a pixel shader implementation). Of course, this is the best case scenario; for a 1920x1080 image, the average samples per texel is 2.0119. This is due to the overlap of *2*radius between thread groups* (that is, we need two horizontal and vertical groups to cover the width/height respectively—although this could be alleviated by changing the thread dimensions). The previous figure shows the shared memory layout for the horizontal and vertical filters for a thread group with the dimensions 1024x1 and 1x1024, respectively, as well as a horizontal and vertical 32x32 thread group size to demonstrate the capabilities of the filter for dealing with 2D shared memory layouts.

> This implementation could be improved further to support sampling four texels per thread, although fewer threads would be possible due to the maximum thread group shared memory size.

The following figure shows the group-shared memory values during the convolution of a horizontal 3-tap box blur filter and image using this recipe:

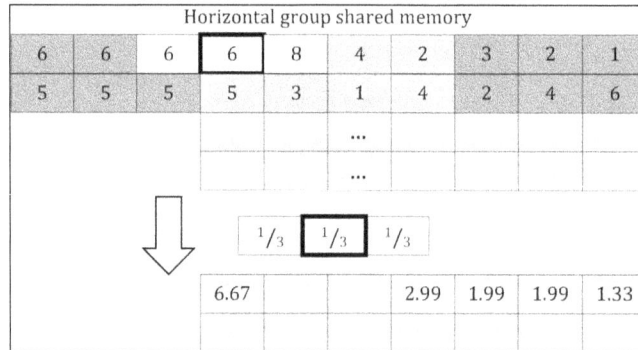

Convolution of horizontal 3-tap filter and image in progress showing the shared memory of two thread groups. Out-of-bound samples have been clamped.

Looking at the full 3x3 kernel in the *Convolution filter kernel (center) applied to input image* figure from earlier, it is apparent that the edge cases require some additional checking, that is, if the kernel is over the top-left pixel, the top and right side of the kernel will be outside the image bounds. This can be ignored but will result in some artifacts around borders—as an example, the box blur filter will gain a dark border around the right and bottom edges. Alternatively, we can clamp to the bounds of the input image, lending additional weight to border pixels (as we have done in this recipe, see the previous figure), or start the filter within the bounds of the image and produce a slightly smaller image on output. Clamping has the added benefit that we do not need to worry if the thread count does not exactly match the texel count, if there are a few extra it will not impact the result.

To allow us to accumulate multiple filters, we have created an additional texture. As the target textures must now also be used as input, we have enabled the shader resource binding flag. The example output of the *Implementing a Gaussian blur filter* recipe includes comparisons of filters that have been applied multiple times. With this *ping-pong* approach to textures, we can combine any number of filters together.

There's more...

If you are familiar with filters, you may have realized already that the `BlurFilterHorizontalCS` and `BlurFilterVerticalCS` methods can be used to apply any simple convolution filters provided they are separable.

For example, to apply the image sharpening filter using our existing filter methods:

1. Change the `FILTERTAP` method to `3` and the `BlurKernel` declaration to the following:

```
static const float BlurKernel[3] = {
  -0.3333333, 1.6666666, -0.3333333
};
```

2. And then run both the horizontal and vertical filters.

Original image on left, sharpened image on right (using lerp with T=2.0)

Implementing a Gaussian blur filter

In this recipe, we use the separability of the Gaussian blur convolution filter to apply a Gaussian blur in two passes for a vertical and horizontal Gaussian blur.

The Gaussian blur is used in many image processing and 3D graphics operations. The filter can be used to soften edges, apply blurring during depth of field operations, or for use within the Bloom lighting technique.

Getting ready

This recipe begins with the completed horizontal and vertical filter compute shaders and C# code to execute them from the *Implementing box blur using separable convolution filters* recipe.

How to do it...

By adjusting the kernel values, we can create a Gaussian blur filter. For each of the following kernels, the center weight (weight of current texel) is highlighted:

1. In order to create a 3-tap Gaussian blur, change the `BlurKernel` method of the horizontal and vertical compute shaders to:

```
#define FILTERTAP 3
...SNIP
static const float BlurKernel[FILTERTAP] = {
  0.2740686, 0.4518628, 0.2740686
};
```

2. For a 5-tap Gaussian blur, change the `BlurKernel` method of the horizontal and vertical compute shaders to:

```
#define FILTERTAP 5
...SNIP
static const float BlurKernel[FILTERTAP] = {
  0.1524691, 0.2218413, 0.2513791, 0.2218413, 0.1524691
};
```

3. And lastly, for a 9-tap Gaussian blur, use the following kernel:

```
#define FILTERTAP 9
...SNIP
static const float BlurKernel[9] = {
  0.08167442, 0.1016454, 0.1188356, 0.1305153, 0.1346584,
    0.1305153, 0.1188356, 0.1016454, 0.08167442
};
```

4. Executing both, the vertical and horizontal filters, will achieve the full Gaussian blur. The following image shows a comparison of the box and Gaussian blur filters at varying kernel sizes.

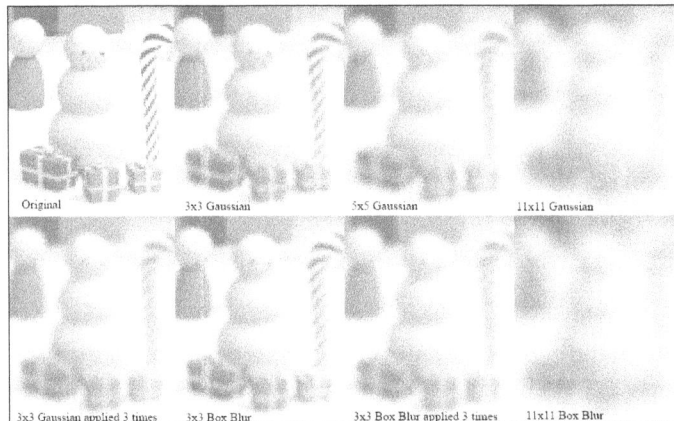

Comparison of box and Gaussian blur filters with varying kernel sizes.

The previous comparison of blur filter sizes and types shows how a box blur filter applied multiple times is able to approximate a Gaussian blur. In our blur recipes, this is of little consequence as our box blur filter and Gaussian blur filter have a similar cost.

How it works...

A Gaussian blur convolution kernel is a separable filter that is generated using the following Gaussian function formula. The weights of the kernel elements reduce as you move further away from the origin, meaning that the weighted average of the Gaussian blur is better at preserving the edge details than the box blur filter (see the previous comparison of the 11x11 Gaussian and box blur). The sum of the weights, as with most image filters, is 1.0.

$$G(x) = \frac{1}{\sqrt{2\pi\sigma^2}} e^{-\frac{x^2}{2\sigma^2}}$$

Gaussian blur formula in a single dimension, where σ (sigma) is the standard deviation of the Gaussian distribution (for example, blur radius) and x represents the distance from the origin

The previous formula can be implemented in C# for a given distance with the following code snippet:

```
var sigma = radius;
var twoSigmaSqrd = (2.0 * sigma * sigma);
var value = Math.Exp(-(distance*distance) / twoSigmaSqrd) /
  Math.Sqrt(twoSigmaSqrd));
```

When we specify a filter-tap size, we are effectively controlling the radius of the blur. For example, a 3-tap horizontal Gaussian blur has a radius of one, while a 9-tap filter has a radius of four. This is calculated by subtracting the origin pixel and dividing the result by two, for example, *(9-1) / 2 = 4*. Therefore, creating a Gaussian blur with a radius of nine requires a 19-tap filter.

The filter-tap size must be larger than one, an odd number, and no more than 33 depending on the thread group dimensions. The maximum size is dependent upon the maximum size of a compute shader's group-shared memory, which in Shader Model 5 is 32 KB.

The command-line project `ComputeGaussian.csproj` used to generate these Gaussian weights is included with the downloadable content for this Chapter, available on Packt's website. The weights used here were generated with the appropriate radius and a blur amount of `1.0`.

There's more...

By applying a blur multiple times, it is possible to approximate a larger radius blur; for example, a 9-tap filter applied three times results in a similar amount of blur compared to a single pass of a 27-tap blur filter.

Detecting edges with the Sobel edge-detection filter

In this recipe we will implement a single pass 3x3 Sobel convolution filter. This is the first convolution filter we will look at that does not implement a simple "sum of products" calculation as well as not being separable.

To keep things simple, this implementation has not undergone the same level of optimization as the separable convolution filter compute shaders; however, it would be a fairly simple task to modify it to work with the group-shared memory approach.

Getting ready

This recipe makes use of the constant buffer and the `lerpKeepAlpha` function that we implemented in the *Adjusting the contrast and brightness* recipe.

You will also use the `LUMINANCE` `#define` macro we created in the *Running a compute shader – desaturation (grayscale)* recipe.

How to do it...

We will implement two variations of the Sobel edge-detection compute shader, one will overlay the result onto the original image (producing an outlining effect), and the other will return the black and white result. Both use the same Sobel function to detect the edge.

1. Add the following HLSL code, for the Sobel edge overlay, to a string or HLSL shader file. We will implement the `SobelEdge` function used here, shortly.

```
#define THREADSX 32
#define THREADSY 32
// used for RGB/sRGB color models
#define LUMINANCE_RGB float3(0.2125, 0.7154, 0.0721)
#define LUMINANCE(_V) dot(_V.rgb, LUMINANCE_RGB)

[numthreads(THREADSX, THREADSY, 1)]
void SobelEdgeOverlayCS(uint groupIndex: SV_GroupIndex,
    uint3 groupId : SV_GroupID, uint3 groupThreadId:
    SV_GroupThreadID, uint3 dispatchThreadId :
    SV_DispatchThreadID)
{
    float4 sample = input[dispatchThreadId.xy];
    float threshold = 0.4f;
    float thickness = 1;
```

```
   float3 target = sample.rgb *
     SobelEdge(dispatchThreadId.xy, threshold, thickness);
   output[dispatchThreadId.xy] = lerpKeepAlpha(sample,
     target, LerpT);
}
```

Remember that the maximum total thread count is 1024.

2. Append the Sobel edge-detection shader without overlaying to the same HLSL file or string variable.

```
[numthreads(THREADSX, THREADSY, 1)]
void SobelEdgeCS(uint groupIndex: SV_GroupIndex, uint3
  groupId : SV_GroupID, uint3 groupThreadId:
  SV_GroupThreadID, uint3 dispatchThreadId :
  SV_DispatchThreadID)
{
  float threshold = 0.4f;
  float thickness = 1;
  output[dispatchThreadId.xy] = float4(
    (float3)SobelEdge(dispatchThreadId.xy, threshold,
    thickness), 1);
}
```

3. Now, we will create the shared `SobelEdge` HLSL function that applies the convolution kernel.

```
float SobelEdge(float2 coord, float threshold, float thickness)
{    // Sobel 3x3 tap filter: approximate magnitude
     // Cheaper than the full Sobel kernel evaluation
     // http://homepages.inf.ed.ac.uk/rbf/HIPR2/sobel.htm
     // -----------------------------
     // p1   p2   p3   | x
     // p4  (p5)  p6   | convolution kernel
     // p7   p8   p9   |
     // -----------------------------
     // Gx  = (p1 + 2 * p2 + p3) - (p7 + 2 * p8 + p9)
     // -----------------------------
     // p3   p6   p9   | y (x rotated counter cw)
     // p2  (p5)  p8   | convolution kernel
     // p1   p4   p7   |
     // -----------------------------
     // Gy  = (p3 + 2 * p6 + p9) - (p1 + 2 * p4 + p7)
     // -----------------------------
     // Formula:
```

```
// |G| = |Gx| + |Gy| => pow(G,2) = Gx*Gx + Gy*Gy
// |G| = |(p1 + 2 * p2 + p3) - (p7 + 2 * p8 + p9)| +
//       |(p3 + 2 * p6 + p9) - (p1 + 2 * p4 + p7)|
// p5 == current pixel,
// sample neighbors to create 3x3 kernel
float p1 = LUMINANCE(input[coord + float2(-thickness,
    -thickness)]);
float p2 = LUMINANCE(input[coord + float2( 0,
    -thickness)]);
float p3 = LUMINANCE(input[coord + float2( thickness,
    -thickness)]);
float p4 = LUMINANCE(input[coord + float2(-thickness,
    0)]);
float p6 = LUMINANCE(input[coord + float2( thickness,
    0)]);
float p7 = LUMINANCE(input[coord + float2(-thickness,
    thickness)]);
float p8 = LUMINANCE(input[coord + float2( 0,
    thickness)]);
float p9 = LUMINANCE(input[coord + float2( thickness,
    thickness)]);
```

4. Next we apply the Sobel formula on the values loaded for the kernel.

```
//float sobelX = (p1 + 2 * p2 + p3) - (p7 + 2 * p8 + p9);
//float sobelY = (p3 + 2 * p6 + p9) - (p1 + 2 * p4 + p7);
float sobelX = mad(2, p2, p1 + p3) - mad(2, p8, p7 + p9);
float sobelY = mad(2, p6, p3 + p9) - mad(2, p4, p1 + p7);
```

5. And finally, return the result based on the threshold.

```
float edgeSqr = (sobelX * sobelX + sobelY * sobelY);
float result = 1.0 - (edgeSqr > threshold * threshold);
// if (edgeSqr > threshold * threshold) { is edge }
return result; // black (0) = edge, otherwise white (1)
} // End SobelEdge
```

6. The result of applying the two Sobel edge-detection filters can be seen in the following figure:

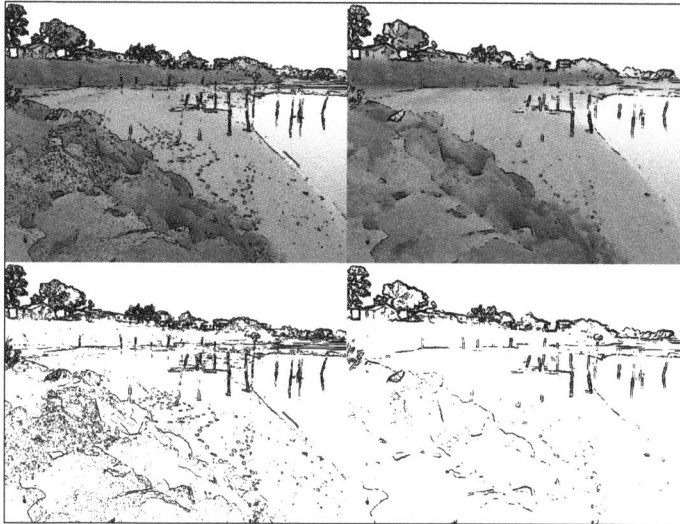

Left: Sobel filter, Right: 3x3 Blur + Sobel filter

How it works...

The Sobel filter is the combination of applying a formula to determine the gradient magnitude of two convolution kernels (the second is the first rotated counter-clockwise), and then checking the result against a provided threshold. If it passes the test, it is an edge (black), otherwise it is left blank (white).

The following formula is a faster approximation of the more complete Sobel gradient magnitude formula:

$$
\begin{bmatrix} P_1 & P_2 & P_3 \\ P_4 & P_5 & P_6 \\ P_7 & P_8 & P_9 \end{bmatrix} \quad \text{Convolution kernel (Pn = loaded texels)} \\ \text{P5 is origin (current) texel}
$$

$$|G| = |Gx| + |Gy| = Gx \times Gx + Gy \times Gy$$

$$|G| = |(P_1 + 2 \times P_2 + P_3) - (P_7 + 2 \times P_8 + P_9)| + \\ |(P_3 + 2 \times P_6 + P_9) - (P_1 + 2 \times P_4 + P_7)|$$

Faster approximation of the Sobel gradient magnitude formula

There's more...

By first applying blur to the source image, we are able to reduce the level of noise generated by the Sobel filter as shown in the right-hand example of the previous example output. This is where the *Implementing a Gaussian blur filter* recipe can be useful as this type of blur filter is better at preserving edges while still reducing noise within the source image.

See also

▶ The *Implementing box blur using separable convolution filters* recipe will cover how you can apply multiple filters one after another

Calculating an image's luminance histogram

In this recipe we will explore using a compute shader to gather characteristics from the source image and output to a buffer. The characteristic that we will be determining is the image's luminance histogram, that is, how many texels are there within the texture for each luminance value (mapped from 0.0-1.0 to 0-255).

We will also cover how to retrieve the data from the GPU and load it into an array that is accessible from the CPU.

How to do it...

We'll begin with the HLSL code necessary to calculate the histogram.

1. The input continues to be a `Texture2D` SRV; however, this time our output UAV will be `RWByteAddressBuffer`.

   ```
   Texture2D<float4> input : register(t0);
   RWByteAddressBuffer outputByteBuffer : register(u0);
   #define THREADSX 32
   #define THREADSY 32
   // used for RGB/sRGB color models
   #define LUMINANCE_RGB float3(0.2125, 0.7154, 0.0721)
   #define LUMINANCE(_V) dot(_V.rgb, LUMINANCE_RGB)
   ```

2. Our actual compute shader is quite simple:

   ```
   // Calculate the luminance histogram of the input
   // Output to outputByteBuffer
   [numthreads(THREADSX, THREADSY, 1)]
   void HistogramCS(uint groupIndex: SV_GroupIndex, uint3
   ```

```
  groupId : SV_GroupID, uint3 groupThreadId: SV_GroupThreadID,
uint3 dispatchThreadId :
  SV_DispatchThreadID)
{    float4 sample = input[dispatchThreadId.xy];
    // Calculate the Relative luminance (and map to 0-255)
    float luminance = LUMINANCE(sample.xyz) * 255.0;

    // Addressable as bytes, x4 to store 32-bit integers
    // Atomic increment of value at address.
    outputByteBuffer.InterlockedAdd((uint)luminance * 4,
       1);
}
```

3. In order to interact with this compute shader, we need to prepare a buffer to store the results. Note that we also create a buffer that is accessible from the CPU. The two properties that make the buffer accessible to the CPU are highlighted.

```
var histogramResult = new SharpDX.Direct3D11.Buffer(device,
  new BufferDescription
{
    BindFlags = BindFlags.UnorderedAccess,
    CpuAccessFlags = CpuAccessFlags.None,
    OptionFlags = ResourceOptionFlags.BufferAllowRawViews,
    Usage = ResourceUsage.Default,
    SizeInBytes = 256 * 4,
    StructureByteStride = 4
});
histogramResult.DebugName = "Histogram Result";

var histogramUAV = CreateBufferUAV(device, histogramResult);
// Create resource that can be read from the CPU for
// retrieving the histogram results
var cpuReadDesc = histogramResult.Description;
cpuReadDesc.OptionFlags = ResourceOptionFlags.None;
cpuReadDesc.BindFlags = BindFlags.None;
cpuReadDesc.CpuAccessFlags = CpuAccessFlags.Read;
cpuReadDesc.Usage = ResourceUsage.Staging;
var histogramCPU = new Buffer(device, cpuReadDesc);
histogramCPU.DebugName = "Histogram Result (CPU)";
```

4. We will wrap the logic to create the buffer's UAV into a reusable function called CreateBufferUAV.

```
public static UnorderedAccessView
  CreateBufferUAV(SharpDX.Direct3D11.Device device,
  SharpDX.Direct3D11.Buffer buffer)
{
```

```
UnorderedAccessViewDescription uavDesc = new
   UnorderedAccessViewDescription
   {
       Dimension = UnorderedAccessViewDimension.Buffer,
       Buffer = new UnorderedAccessViewDescription
           .BufferResource { FirstElement = 0 }
   };
   // If a raw buffer
   if ((buffer.Description.OptionFlags &
       ResourceOptionFlags.BufferAllowRawViews) ==
       ResourceOptionFlags.BufferAllowRawViews)
   {
       // A raw buffer requires R32_Typeless
       uavDesc.Format = Format.R32_Typeless;
       uavDesc.Buffer.Flags =
           UnorderedAccessViewBufferFlags.Raw;
       uavDesc.Buffer.ElementCount =
           buffer.Description.SizeInBytes / 4;
   }
   // else if a structured buffer
   else if ((buffer.Description.OptionFlags &
       ResourceOptionFlags.BufferStructured) ==
       ResourceOptionFlags.BufferStructured)
   {
       uavDesc.Format = Format.Unknown;
       uavDesc.Buffer.ElementCount =
           buffer.Description.SizeInBytes /
           buffer.Description.StructureByteStride;
   } else {
       throw new ArgumentException("Buffer must be raw or
           structured", "buffer");
   }
   // Create the UAV for this buffer
   return new UnorderedAccessView(device, buffer,
       uavDesc);
}
```

5. With the output resources in place, we can continue to load the image, and run with the previous `HistogramCS` shader code.

```
// Firstly clear the target UAV otherwise the value will
// accumulate between calls.
context.ClearUnorderedAccessView(histogramUAV, Int4.Zero);
// Load the image to process (this could be any compatible
// SRV).
```

```
var srcTextureSRV = ShaderResourceView.FromFile(device,
    "Village.png");
var srcTexture = srcTextureSRV.ResourceAs<Texture2D>();
var desc = srcTexture.Description;
// Compile the shaders
using (var bytecode = ShaderBytecode.Compile(hlslCode,
    "HistogramCS", "cs_5_0"))
using (var cs = new ComputeShader(device, bytecode))
{
    // The source resource is the original image
    context.ComputeShader.SetShaderResource(0,
        srcTextureSRV);
    // The destination resource is the histogramResult
    context.ComputeShader.SetUnorderedAccessView(0,
        histogramUAV);
    // Run the histogram shader
    context.ComputeShader.Set(cs);
    context.Dispatch((int)Math.Ceiling(desc.Width / 1024.0),
        (int)Math.Ceiling(desc.Height / 1.0), 1);

    // Set the compute shader stage SRV and UAV to null
    context.ComputeShader.SetShaderResource(0, null);
    context.ComputeShader.SetUnorderedAccessView(0, null);
...SNIP
}
```

6. Lastly, we copy the result into our CPU accessible resource and then load this into an array.

```
// Copy the result into our CPU accessible resource
context.CopyResource(histogramResult, histogramCPU);
// Retrieve histogram from GPU into int array
try
{   var databox = context.MapSubresource(histogramCPU, 0,
        MapMode.Read, SharpDX.Direct3D11.MapFlags.None);
    int[] intArray = new int[databox.RowPitch / sizeof(int)];
    System.Runtime.InteropServices.Marshal.Copy(
        databox.DataPointer, intArray, 0, intArray.Length);
    // intArray now contains the histogram data,
    // alternatively access databox.DataPointer directly
    // MapSubresource has a number of overrides that, one
    // provides a DataStream.
}
finally
{
```

```
            // We must unmap the subresource so it can be used
            // within the graphics pipeline again
            context.UnmapSubresource(histogramCPU, 0);
    }
```

7. The result of running the `HistogramCS` compute shader over the `Village.png` image is shown in the following chart:

Luminance histogram result exported to a chart

How it works...

We have already covered the calculation of the relative luminance itself; however, we now map the normalized luminance value to the 0-255 range. To determine the luminance histogram, we count how many texels there are within the source image at each relative luminance level.

We have done this by mapping an unstructured (raw) buffer to a byte address UAV as the output of the histogram shader. We then use the intrinsic `InterlockedAdd` method of the UAV to increment the appropriate index within the buffer for each texel based on its relative luminance. For example, a luminance of 255 (white), will result in the equivalent of `output[255]++;`, and a relative luminance of 127 (gray), will result in `output[127]++;`.

> The more threads there are, the more collisions with the interlock. By processing several pixels within a single thread, we can reduce the number of threads required, although this needs to be balanced with having enough threads to make effective use of the available hardware.

We have created a reusable function to create the UAV from a buffer. This simply determines if the buffer is a structured or raw buffer, and creates the UAV description accordingly with the appropriate size and element count based on the relevant byte stride (size of `uint` for raw or the size of the `buffer.Description.StructureByteStride` method for a structured buffer).

The interlocked methods on the `RWByteAddressBuffer` UAV allow us to write from multiple threads to the same buffer. Usually, a compute shader is only able to write to addresses reserved for the current thread. The range of interlocked operations include: `Add`, `AND`, `CompareExchange`, `CompareStore`, `Exchange`, `Max`, `Min`, `OR`, and `XOR`.

Once we have executed the shader function, we copy the result from the GPU `histogramResult` buffer into the `histogramCPU` resource that is accessible from the CPU. In order to be able to read the resource from the CPU, we have created the resource with the following settings:

```
cpuReadDesc.CpuAccessFlags = CpuAccessFlags.Read;
cpuReadDesc.Usage = ResourceUsage.Staging;
```

Once the result has been copied to the CPU accessible resource, we can then map it to a system memory location and read the data for whatever purpose we need. Transferring data from the GPU to CPU is slow and mapping the subresource can stall until the GPU is ready. C# can incur additional overhead if not careful, resulting in an extra memory copy operation. If the resource is correctly protected from further use, the actual reading of the data once mapped could potentially occur within another thread, but care must be taken, and the unmapping of the resource must be done in a thread-safe manner for the device context.

There's more...

It might be tempting to try to use the group-shared memory for the histogram calculation; however, our threads potentially need to write to any address and a thread is only allowed to write to its own region of the group memory without synchronization. Any thread synchronization would most likely defeat any potential performance gains. Reading from the same location in shared memory across multiple threads is allowed.

8

Incorporating Physics and Simulations

In this chapter, we will cover the following topics:

- ▸ Using a physics engine
- ▸ Simulating ocean waves
- ▸ Rendering particles

Introduction

In this chapter, we will look at implementing physics and simulations into our scene rendering. We will first look at a CPU-based physics engine, and then we will explore the power of the GPU to simulate waves and render millions of particles.

Using a physics engine

In this recipe, we will extend our existing mesh renderer to support the simulation of physics within a scene. We will continue to use the built-in Visual Studio graphics content pipeline, and rely on a simple mesh naming convention to designate static and dynamic objects within our scene.

For our physics engine, we will use **BulletSharp**, a .NET wrapper of the popular `Bullet Physics` library used in many AAA game and movie titles. Consider the following steps:

1. Download the `BulletSharp` library from `https://code.google.com/p/bulletsharp/`. It is also included in the `\External` folder within the downloadable content for this book.

2. Add a reference to the `\External\bulletsharp-2.82\Release SharpDX\BulletSharp.dll` assembly.

> Referencing the `SharpDX` version of the `BulletSharp` assembly uses the existing `SharpDX` vector and matrix structures.

3. We use an example scene to demonstrate the physics engine. This is available within the downloadable content.

4. A debug renderer class, `PhysicsDebugDraw`, is included in the completed project for debugging the rigid body shapes and constraints. This depends on `.\Shaders\PhysicsDebug.hlsl` and the `BufferedDebugDraw` class.

5. Finally, we will need a project that has the `MeshRenderer` class available.

We will begin by loading our 3D scene and generate their corresponding rigid bodies in the Bullet Physics Library.

1. Add the `PhysicsScene1.fbx` 3D scene to the project and set **Build Action** to **MeshContentTask**.

2. At the start of `D3DApp.Run` where we initialize our renderers, load `PhysicsScene1.cmo` (the compiled mesh object file) and create the `MeshRenderer` instances, as follows:

```
// Create and initialize the mesh renderer
var loadedMesh =
    Common.Mesh.LoadFromFile("PhysicsScene1.cmo");
List<MeshRenderer> meshes = new List<MeshRenderer>();
meshes.AddRange(from mesh in loadedMesh
                select ToDispose(new MeshRenderer(mesh)));
foreach (var m in meshes) {
  m.Initialize(this);
  m.World = Matrix.Identity;
}
var meshWorld = Matrix.Identity;
```

3. In order to make the physics engine update our mesh's world matrix, we will implement a class that is inherited from the `BulletSharp.MotionState` class.

```
using BulletSharp;
using SharpDX;
public class MeshMotionState: BulletSharp.MotionState
{
    public MeshRenderer Mesh { get; private set; }
    public MeshMotionState(MeshRenderer mesh)
    {
        Mesh = mesh;
    }
    // Retrieve or Sets the Mesh's world transform
    public override SharpDX.Matrix WorldTransform
    {
        get
        {
            return Mesh.World *  Matrix
                .Translation(Mesh.Mesh.Extent.Center);
        }
        set
        {
            Mesh.World = Matrix
                .Translation(-Mesh.Mesh.Extent.Center) *
                value;
        }
    }
}
```

4. After initializing the renderers and before the render loop, let's now initialize the physics engine within the `D3DApp.Run` method directly.

```
using BulletSharp;
...
DynamicsWorld world = null;
CollisionConfiguration defaultConfig =
    new DefaultCollisionConfiguration();
ConstraintSolver solver =
    new SequentialImpulseConstraintSolver();
BulletSharp.Dispatcher dispatcher =
    new CollisionDispatcher(defaultConfig);
BroadphaseInterface broadphase = new DbvtBroadphase();

// Function to initialize the world and rigid bodies for
// the loaded meshes. Done as an action so we can easily
```

```
// reset the simulation state.
Action initializePhysics = () =>
{
    RemoveAndDispose(ref world);
    // Initialize the Bullet Physics "world"
    world = ToDispose(new DiscreteDynamicsWorld(dispatcher,
        broadphase, solver, defaultConfig));
    world.Gravity = new Vector3(0, -10, 0);

    // For each mesh, create a RigidBody and add to "world"
    // for simulation
    meshes.ForEach(m =>
    {
        ... SNIP see below
    });
});
initializePhysics();
```

5. Within the `meshes.ForEach` loop in the previous code snippet, we'll initialize a rigid body for each mesh. Initially check to ensure that the mesh has a value for the `Name` attribute.

```
// We use the name of the mesh to determine the correct
// type of physics body to create
if (String.IsNullOrEmpty(m.Mesh.Name))
    return;
var name = m.Mesh.Name.ToLower();
var extent = m.Mesh.Extent;
BulletSharp.CollisionShape shape;
```

6. Next, we will determine whether to use a `BulletSharp` box or sphere collision shape, or to create one based on the mesh's vertices.

```
#region Create collision shape
if (name.Contains("box") || name.Contains("cube"))
{
    // Assumes the box/cube has an axis-aligned orientation
    shape = new BulletSharp.BoxShape(
        Math.Abs(extent.Max.Z - extent.Min.Z) / 2.0f,
        Math.Abs(extent.Max.Y - extent.Min.Y) / 2.0f,
        Math.Abs(extent.Max.X - extent.Min.X) / 2.0f);
}
else if (name.Contains("sphere"))
{
```

```
        shape = new BulletSharp.SphereShape(extent.Radius);
    }
    else // use mesh vertices directly
    {
        // for each SubMesh, merge the vertex and index
        // buffers to create a TriangleMeshShape for collisions
        List<Vector3> vertices = new List<Vector3>();
        List<int> indices = new List<int>();
        int vertexOffset = 0;
        foreach (var sm in m.Mesh.SubMeshes)
        {
            vertexOffset += vertices.Count;
            indices.AddRange(
                (from indx in m.Mesh.IndexBuffers
                [(int)sm.IndexBufferIndex]
                select vertexOffset + (int)indx));
            vertices.AddRange(
                (from v in m.Mesh
                .VertexBuffers[(int)sm.VertexBufferIndex]
                select v.Position - extent.Center));
        }
        // Create the collision shape
        shape = new BvhTriangleMeshShape(
            new TriangleIndexVertexArray(indices.ToArray(),
            vertices.ToArray()), true);
    }
    #endregion
```

7. At the end of the `intiailizePhysics` action, we will create the rigid body from the shape, determine if it is a dynamic or static shape (that is, whether it can be affected by collisions and gravity), and add it to the physics `world` object for simulation:

```
m.World = Matrix.Identity; // Reset mesh location
float mass; Vector3 vec;    // use radius as mass
shape.GetBoundingSphere(out vec, out mass);
// Create the rigid body, if static/kinematic set mass to 0
var body = new BulletSharp.RigidBody(
    new RigidBodyConstructionInfo(
        name.Contains("static") ? 0 : mass,
        new MeshMotionState(m),
        shape, shape.CalculateLocalInertia(mass)));
if (body.IsStaticObject)
{
```

```
        body.Restitution = 1f;
        body.Friction = 0.4f;
    }
    // Add to the simulation
    world.AddRigidBody(body);
```

8. In order to enable the debug drawing of bodies, you can include the following code (if you want) after having loaded all the bodies.

```
#if DEBUG
    world.DebugDrawer = ToDispose(
      new PhysicsDebugDraw(this.DeviceManager));
    world.DebugDrawer.DebugMode = DebugDrawModes.DrawAabb |
      DebugDrawModes.DrawWireframe;
#endif
```

With the physics world and bodies in place, we are ready to step through the simulation and apply the transformations to our mesh objects.

9. At the beginning of the D3DApp rendering loop, we will step forward the simulation in time. We will provide the last frame time, and also provide the maximum number of steps that the simulation will try to catch-up on, if it has fallen behind. We will use the default fixed time step of one sixtieth of a second.

```
var simTime = new System.Diagnostics.Stopwatch();
simTime.Start();
float time = 0.0f;
float timeStep = 0.0f;

#region Render loop
RenderLoop.Run(Window, () =>
{
    // Update simulation
    if (!paused)
    {
        if ((float)simTime.Elapsed.TotalSeconds < time)
        {   // Reset if the simTime is reset
            time = 0;
            timeStep = 0;
        }
        timeStep = ((float)simTime.Elapsed
            .TotalSeconds - time);
        time = (float)simTime.Elapsed.TotalSeconds;
        world.StepSimulation(timeStep, 7);
    }
    ... SNIP
});
```

> The completed sample maps the *P* key to pause/unpause the simulation, and maps the *R* key to reset the simulation with a call to the `initializePhysics()` method.

10. The `MeshMotionState` objects that we created for each mesh are already updating the mesh's `world` matrix, so now we just have to render the objects:

```
meshes.ForEach((m) =>
{
    perObject.World = m.World * worldMatrix;
    perObject.WorldInverseTranspose = Matrix
        .Transpose(Matrix.Invert(perObject.World));
    perObject.WorldViewProjection = perObject.World *
        viewProjection;
    perObject.ViewProjection = viewProjection;
    perObject.Transpose();
    context.UpdateSubresource(ref perObject,
        perObjectBuffer);

    // Provide the material constant buffer
    m.PerMaterialBuffer = perMaterialBuffer;
    m.PerArmatureBuffer = perArmatureBuffer;
    m.Render();
}
```

11. Lastly, we can render the debug layer (over the existing geometry) by using the following code snippet:

```
if (debugDraw)
{
    perObject.World = Matrix.Identity;
    ... as above
    perObject.Transpose();
    context.UpdateSubresource(ref perObject,
        perObjectBuffer);

    (world.DebugDrawer as PhysicsDebugDraw)
        .DrawDebugWorld(world);
    // Restore vertex/pixel shader and vertex layout
    context.VertexShader.Set(vertexShader);
    context.PixelShader.Set(pixelShader);
    context.InputAssembler.InputLayout = vertexLayout;
}
```

The completed sample maps the *E* key to toggle the debug renderer on and off. The following screenshot shows the final result with debug draw switched on:

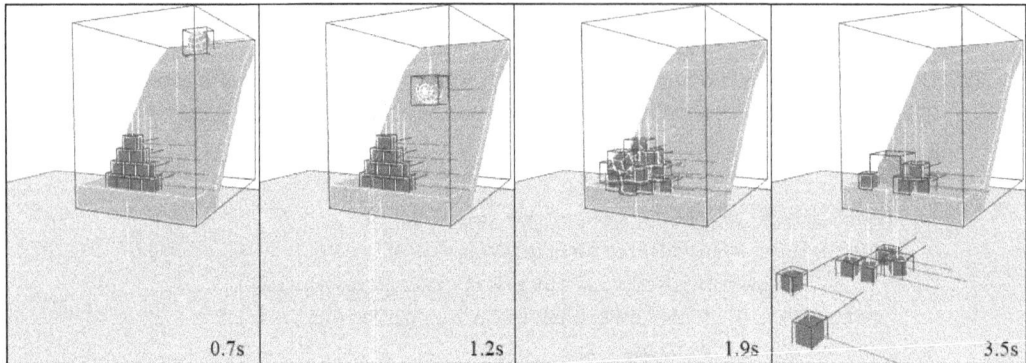

| 0.7s | 1.2s | 1.9s | 3.5s |

Physics debug render over 3.5 seconds

How it works...

A prominent part of the physics engine is **collision detection**. Collision detection typically involves two phases, a broad phase and a narrow phase. The broad phase detection is usually where the **axis-aligned bounding boxes** (**AABB**) of objects are checked for possible collisions, where false positives are allowed. Once the broad phase has been completed, and if one or more possible collisions have been detected, the narrow phase detection is run to determine where the two shapes are intersecting:

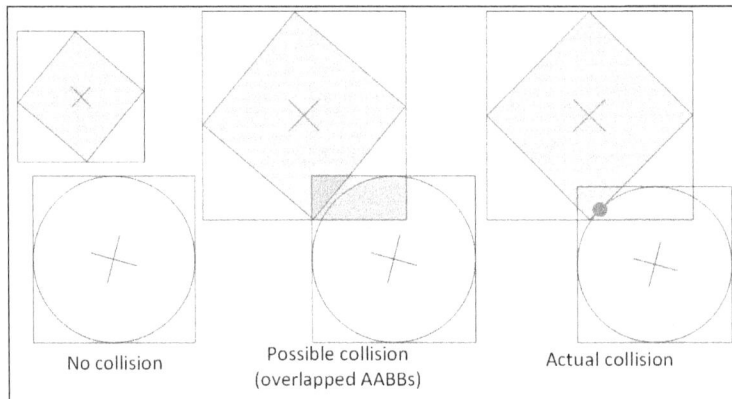

| No collision | Possible collision (overlapped AABBs) | Actual collision |

Collision detection: no collision (left), false positive broad-phase collision detected (center), and narrow-phase collision detected (right)

The 3D scene we have used in this recipe includes two static objects (the ramp and the floor) and eleven dynamic objects (a ball at the top of the ramp and 10 stacked boxes at the bottom). We have used a simple naming convention for the models in the scene, where the occurrence of the `box` or `cube` text in the name indicates that we will use the mesh's extent to define a box collision shape. For the names containing the text `sphere`, we create a sphere collision shape; and for everything else we will use the vertices to define a triangular mesh collision shape.

Any mesh in the scene with a name that contains `static` will be initialized as a static rigid body (unaffected by gravity and immovable), by giving a mass of zero to the rigid body. All the other shapes are created as dynamic rigid bodies.

During the render loop, we tell the physics world to *step* through the simulation. The amount of time taken by the last frame in seconds is used to determine how many substeps the simulation will attempt to catch up on. We have provided a value of seven as the maximum number of substeps, which is based on the following rule to prevent the simulation from losing time:

$$timeStep < maxSubSteps * fixedTimeStep$$

Rule for determining values for substeps and fixed time step for a given time step (frame time)

This means our simulation will continue to keep up until the frame rate slows to approximately 9 FPS (that is, *1/9 < 7 * 1/60*).

By default, the physics simulation uses a fixed time step of one-sixtieth of a second, that is, the simulation moves forward at one sixtieth of a second per step. If a higher frame rate is used by the render loop, for example, 120 FPS, then the simulation will be interpolating one in every two ticks. As we have just seen, running at a slower frame rate results in additional substeps being applied in an attempt to keep up.

Apart from the physics simulation itself and setting the time, the key to this implementation is the correct updating of each mesh's world affine transform matrix. The Bullet Physics library uses a `MotionState` object attached to each rigid body in order to update the transformation matrix of the underlying object. We have implemented our own `MeshMotionState` class that supports retrieving and updating of the `MeshRenderer.World` property.

The collision shapes in the scene have been created in a local model space (with origin at 0, 0, 0), although the corresponding mesh's are not necessarily centered at the origin (they are in scene space, not in model space). Therefore, our `MeshMotionState` class must translate the world matrix to and from scene space as appropriate. This is done by taking the mesh's extent (which is in scene space) and moving it back from its center point to the origin. The world matrix calculation for setting the `MeshMotionState.WorldTransform` property becomes: `Matrix.Translation(-m.Mesh.Extent.Center) * value`.

The Bullet Physics library not only supports rigid bodies, but also supports soft bodies, clothes, ropes, and constraints.

There's more...

In order to allow our character animations to have an impact within the physics of the simulated world, we can create a collision shape of bounding box for each bone in a character's rig. With a new class inheriting from `BulletSharp.MotionState`, we can retrieve each bone's current transform for the current frame in the animation. Using a kinematic rigid body allows us to apply forces to the world without them, in turn, affecting the bone's rigid body.

Due to the availability of a large number of threads and fast sorting capabilities of compute shaders (for example, bitonic sort), it is possible to significantly increase the speed of the broad- and narrow-phase collision detection for the rigid body collisions by implementing them within compute shaders. However, the entire simulation will probably need to be implemented on the GPU. This is because you will not want to do a part of the computation on the GPU and then read the results back to CPU. Since the CPU and GPU run asynchronously to each other, this can result in a lag or GPU/CPU underutilization.

See also

- Bullet Physics library homepage available at `http://bulletphysics.org`
- A soft body solver (for example, cloth) implemented with Direct3D 11 compute shaders within the Bullet Physics library 2.x available at `https://code.google.com/p/bullet/`
- OpenCL implementation of **Sweep and Prune** (**SAP**) broad-phase and **Separate Axis Theorem** (**SAT**) narrow-phase collision detection available at `https://github.com/erwincoumans/bullet3`
- *Stepping the World* available at `http://www.bulletphysics.org/mediawiki-1.5.8/index.php/Stepping_The_World`
- Example implementation of the bitonic sorting algorithm within a compute shader available at `http://code.msdn.microsoft.com/DirectCompute-Basic-Win32-7d5a7408`

Simulating ocean waves

In this recipe, we will look at a tried and tested technique for simulating ocean waves using a series of Gerstner waves at varying amplitudes, wave lengths, frequencies, and directions within a vertex shader (or domain shader).

Getting ready

For this recipe, we need to render a plane along the x and z axis. The completed solution uses an FBX scene with a simple subdivided mesh and UV coordinates for a normal map, however, a quad passed to the tessellation pipeline will also work; or better yet, a mesh generated in the vertex shader based on the `SV_VertexID` and `SV_InstanceID` input semantics.

A prerequisite is the mesh renderer and shaders that implement normal mapping as shown in the _Adding surface detail with normal mapping_ recipe of _Chapter 6, Adding Surface Detail with Normal and Displacement Mapping_.

How to do it...

As we will be generating sine waves over a period of time, we need to add a `Time` property to our `PerFrame` constant buffer. Then we will implement the vertex displacement within a vertex shader. Consider the following steps:

1. Within `Common.hlsl`, update the `PerFrame` structure (as shown in the highlighted section of the following code):

```
cbuffer PerFrame: register (b1)
{
    DirectionalLight Light;
    float3 CameraPosition;
    float Time;
};
```

2. Within your `ConstantBuffers.cs` file, update the matching `PerFrame` structure to include the time component.

```
[StructLayout(LayoutKind.Sequential, Pack = 1)]
public struct PerFrame
{
    public DirectionalLight Light;
    public SharpDX.Vector3 CameraPosition;
    public float Time;
}
```

3. Within the render loop, update the code for setting up the `perFrame` constant buffer, by setting up the `Time` property.

```
perFrame.CameraPosition = cameraPosition;
// Provide simulation time to shader
perFrame.Time = (float)simTime.Elapsed.TotalSeconds;
context.UpdateSubresource(ref perFrame, perFrameBuffer);
```

> The `simTime` variable is a `System.Diagnostics.Stopwatch` instance that has the *P* key mapped to pause/unpause the simulation in the completed sample.

4. Next, add the `SubdividedPlane.fbx` to your project, set the **Build Action** to **MeshContentTask**, and load it into a `MeshRenderer` instance. Alternatively, if you are using the tessellation pipeline, create a quad with a width (X-axis) and depth (Z-axis) of around 24 units and a tessellation factor in the range of approximately 10.0 to 20.0.

```
var loadedMesh =
    Common.Mesh.LoadFromFile("SubdividedPlane.cmo");
var waterMesh = ToDispose(new
    MeshRenderer(loadedMesh.First()));
waterMesh.Initialize(this);
```

Now, we can update the vertex shader to implement the displacement. If you are using the tessellation pipeline, the same changes will be made to your domain shader instead.

5. First, we will add a new HLSL function to our vertex shader file in order to generate the waveform.

```
void GerstnerWaveTessendorf(
    float waveLength,
    float speed,
    float amplitude,
    float steepness,
    float2 direction,
    in float3 position,
    inout float3 result,
    inout float3 normal,
    inout float3 tangent)
{
...SNIP see next steps
}
```

6. Within the preceding function, we will initialize the values for the Gerstner formula as follows:

```
float L = waveLength;// wave crest to crest
float A = amplitude; // wave height
float k = 2.0 * 3.1416 / L; // wave length
float kA = k*A;
float2 D = normalize(direction); // normalized direction
```

```
float2 K = D * k; // wave vector and magnitude (direction)
// peak/crest steepness, higher means steeper, but too much
// can cause the wave to become inside out at the top
// A value of zero results in a sine wave.
float Q = steepness;

// Calculate wave speed (frequency) from input
float S = speed * 0.5; // Speed 1 =~ 2m/s so halve first
float w = S * k; // Phase/frequency
float wT = w * Time;

// Calculate values for reuse
float KPwT = dot(K, position.xz)-wT;
float S0 = sin(KPwT);
float C0 = cos(KPwT);
```

7. Next, we will calculate the vertex offset from the provided direction and current vertex position.

```
// Calculate the vertex offset along the X and Z axes
float2 xz = position.xz - D*Q*A*S0;
// Calculate the vertex offset along the Y (up/down) axis
float y = A*C0;
```

8. Then, we need to calculate the new normal and tangent vectors, as follows:

```
// Calculate the tangent/bitangent/normal
// Bitangent
float3 B = float3(
    1-(Q * D.x * D.x * kA * C0),
    D.x * kA * S0,
    -(Q*D.x * D.y * kA * C0));
// Tangent
float3 T = float3(
    -(Q * D.x * D.y * kA * C0),
    D.y * kA * S0,
    1-(Q*D.y * D.y * kA * C0));
B = normalize(B);
T = normalize(T);
float3 N = cross(T, B);
```

9. And lastly, set the output values. Note that we are accumulating the results in order to call the method multiple times with varying parameters.

```
// Append the results
result.xz += xz;
```

```
result.y += y;
normal += N;
tangent += T;
```

With the Gerstner wave function in place, we can now displace the vertices within our vertex or domain shader.

10. The following is an example of the code that is necessary to generate gentle ocean waves. This should be inserted before any `WorldViewProjection` or `ViewProjection` transforms.

```
...SNIP
// Existing vertex shader code

float3 N = (float3)0; // normal
float3 T = (float3)0; // tangent
float3 waveOffset = (float3)0; // vertex xyz offset
float2 direction = float2(1, 0);

// Gentle ocean waves
GerstnerWaveTessendorf(8, 0.5, 0.3, 1, direction, vertex.Position,
  waveOffset, N, T);
GerstnerWaveTessendorf(4, 0.5, 0.4, 1, direction + float2(0, 0.5),
  vertex.Position, waveOffset, N, T);
GerstnerWaveTessendorf(3, 0.5, 0.3, 1, direction + float2(0, 1),
  vertex.Position, waveOffset, N, T);
GerstnerWaveTessendorf(2.5, 0.5, 0.2, 1, direction,
  vertex.Position, waveOffset, N, T);

vertex.Position.xyz += waveOffset;
vertex.Normal = normalize(N);
vertex.Tangent.xyz = normalize(T); // If using normal mapping

// Existing vertex shader code
result.Position = mul(vertex.Position, WorldViewProjection);
...SNIP
```

11. For larger and more choppy waves, you can try the following code instead:

```
// Choppy ocean waves
GerstnerWaveTessendorf(10, 2, 2.5, 0.5, direction,
  vertex.Position, waveOffset, N, T);
GerstnerWaveTessendorf(5, 1.2, 2, 1, direction,
  vertex.Position, waveOffset, N, T);
GerstnerWaveTessendorf(4, 2, 2, 1, direction + float2(0,
  1), vertex.Position, waveOffset, N, T);
```

```
GerstnerWaveTessendorf(4, 1, 0.5, 1, direction + float2(0,
  1), vertex.Position, waveOffset, N, T);
GerstnerWaveTessendorf(2.5, 2, 0.5, 1, direction +
  float2(0, 0.5), vertex.Position, waveOffset, N, T);
GerstnerWaveTessendorf(2, 2, 0.5, 1, direction,
  vertex.Position, waveOffset, N, T);
```

This completes our HLSL shader code.

12. Now, render the mesh within your render loop, and ensure that the correct vertex shader is assigned (if a new shader has been created, compile it within the appropriate location).

```
// If showing normal map
waterMesh.DisableNormalMap = disableNormalMap;
waterMesh.PerMaterialBuffer = perMaterialBuffer;
waterMesh.PerArmatureBuffer = perArmatureBuffer;
waterMesh.Render();
```

The completed project in the downloadable companion code maps the *Backspace* key to switch between the previous physics scene and this recipe. Pressing *Shift + N* toggles between the diffuse mapping as well as the diffuse and normal mapping, and the *N* key will toggle the display of the debug normal vectors. The final result of the gentle and choppy waves, is shown in the following diagram:

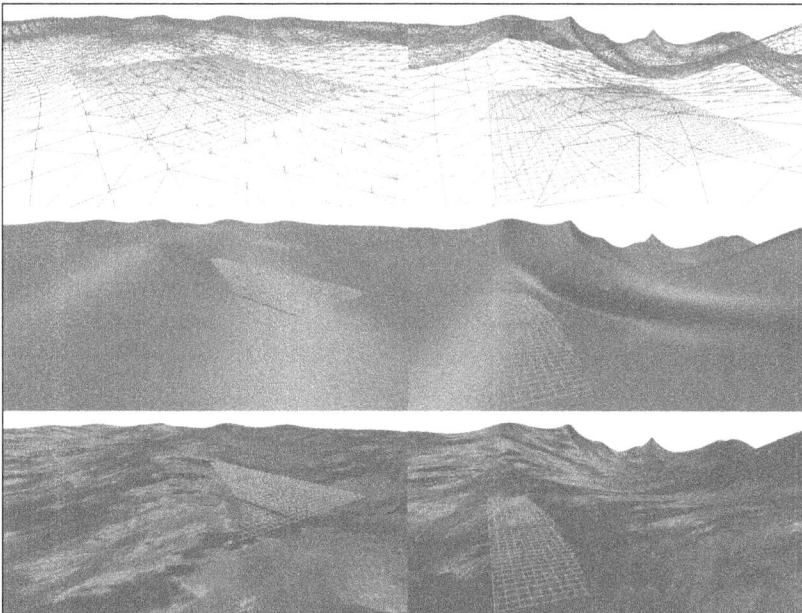

Multiple Gerstner waves: gentle ocean waves (left), choppy ocean waves (right), wireframe (top) with debug normal vectors (top-left), diffuse shader (middle), and diffuse + normal mapping (bottom).

How it works...

By combining multiple Gerstner waves of varying wave lengths and directions together, we have been able to produce a reasonable simulation of ocean waves. The Gerstner waves are an approximate solution to fluid dynamics, and our implementation is based upon the following formula, which in turn is based upon *Tessendorf 2004*.

$$k = \frac{2\pi}{\lambda}$$
$$K = \hat{D} \times k$$
$$xz = xz_0 - \left(\frac{K}{k}\right)QA\sin(K \cdot xz_0 - \omega t)$$
$$y = A\cos(K \cdot xz_0 - \omega t)$$

Where xz_0 is the current vertex XY position, D is the direction vector (normalized as $\hat{D}$), λ is the wavelength, Q is the steepness of the crest, A is the wave amplitude, ω is the frequency and finally t is time. xz holds the new horizontal displacement, and y the vertical.

Formula used to generate the Gerstner waves

A similar effect can be generated using multiple sine waves. However, the Gerstner waves not only displace the vertices vertically, but also horizontally. In order to produce a more natural result the vertices are displaced along the X and Z axes towards the crest of the wave, resulting in a sharper peak and smoother trough, we can control the amount of displacement through the steepness parameter of the `GerstnerWaveTessendorf` function.

The following screenshot shows three examples of waves, the first is a regular sine wave (Gerstner wave with a steepness of 0.0), the second is the same wave except with a steepness of 0.5, and the last is a wireframe of the same wave again with a steepness of 1.0. See how the vertices in the wireframe come closer along the length of the crest.

When comparing a single wave to the gentle and choppy waves, it is fairly obvious that a good simulation of a wave requires multiple waves of varying lengths, amplitudes, directions, and possibly frequencies; these different individual wave definitions are often referred to as **octaves**. By summing together the entire set of waves, we achieve a more realistic and varied result. The gentle waves are generated using four octaves, while the choppy waves are generated using six octaves.

Although we have generated the waves on the GPU, it is interesting to note that if we place a ship (similar to the one in the following screenshot – section D) , we still need to compute its movement as a part of the wider physics simulation. This would most likely occur on the CPU.

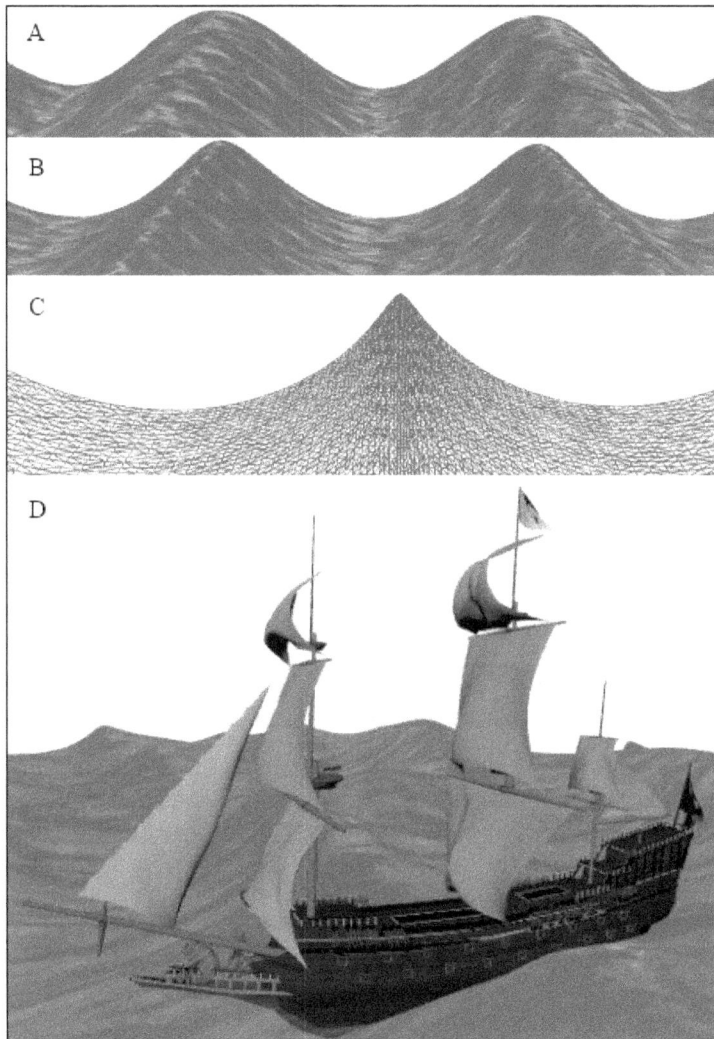

Three examples of a single wave with a length of 10 m and amplitude of 2.5 m, A) Crest steepness of 0.0, B) Crest steepness of 0.5, C) Steepness of 1.0, and D) A static ship on dynamic waves.

There's more...

There are a number of methods for simulating water, depending on whether it is shallow or deep, a lake or a river, and a realistic simulation or an approximation. One such method is the combination of the **Fast Fourier Transform** (**FFT**) and **Perlin Noise**.

In this recipe, we looked at the wave geometry. However, for a realistic water or ocean simulation, you must consider the caustics, refraction, reflectivity, dispersion, and interactivity as well.

Providing a static value for time, adding some texture, and playing with the amplitude could also produce interesting sand dunes or other terrain such as mountains or rolling hills.

See also

- For more information on implementing normal mapping, refer to *Chapter 6, Adding Surface Detail with Normal and Displacement Mapping*
- Vertex instancing and indirect draws are covered in the next recipe, *Rendering particles*

Rendering particles

In this recipe, we will implement a simple particle system on the GPU. Compute shaders will be used to generate and update the particles within append/consume buffers, and we will use the vertex shader input semantics, SV_VertexID and SV_InstanceID, to generate billboards from the particle points.

We will introduce blend states to deal with the alpha blending of particles. In order to render the particles without regard to the order, we will also disable writing to the depth buffer.

Getting ready

Let us start with one of the previous rendering projects used in the recipe, *Animating bones*, of *Chapter 4, Animating Meshes with Vertex Skinning*. In this recipe, we will make use of a modified version of the CreateBufferUAV C# function that we created in the *Calculating an image's luminance histogram* recipe of *Chapter 7, Performing Image Processing Techniques*.

The completed project and the following textures can be found in the downloadable companion code as well as the following textures for use within our particle renderer:

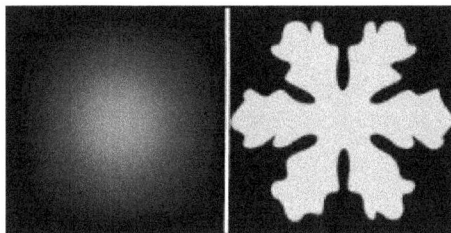

Two semitransparent particle textures (the transparent area is black). Particle on left-hand side and Snowflake on right-hand side

How to do it...

To begin with, we will add our new HLSL shader code, then create a particle renderer to run the compute shaders to generate/update the particles, and lastly render the particles:

1. Add four new HLSL source files, `Particle.hlsl`, `ParticleCS.hlsl`, `ParticlePS.hlsl`, and `ParticleVS.hlsl`. Include them in the project and select **Copy if newer** as the build action. Remember to change the text encoding or copy from the existing HLSL files (as described in the *Rendering primitives* recipe of *Chapter 2*, *Rendering with Direct3D*).

2. Within `Particle.hlsl`, add our particle constant buffers and structures.

```
// Particle system constants
cbuffer ParticleConstants : register(b0)
{
    float3 DomainBoundsMin;
    float ForceStrength;
    float3 DomainBoundsMax;
    float MaxLifetime;
    float3 ForceDirection;
    uint MaxParticles;
    float3 Attractor;
    float Radius;
};
// Particles per frame constant buffer
cbuffer ParticleFrame : register(b1)
{
```

```
        float Time;
        float FrameTime;
        uint RandomSeed;
        uint ParticleCount; // consume buffer count
    }
    // Represents a single particle
    struct Particle {
        float3 Position;
        float Radius;
        float3 OldPosition;
        float Energy;
    };
    // Pixel shader input
    struct PS_Input {
        float4 Position : SV_Position;
        float2 UV : TEXCOORD0;
        float Energy : ENERGY;
    };
```

3. Within `ParticleVS.hlsl`, we will create an instancing vertex shader that reads the particle for the current instance ID and computes the position for a quad.

```
#include "Common.hlsl"
#include "Particle.hlsl"
// Access to the particle buffer
StructuredBuffer<Particle> particles : register(t0);

// Computes the vertex position
float4 ComputePosition(in float3 pos, in float size,
                       in float2 vPos)
{
    // Create billboard (quad always facing the camera)
    float3 toEye = normalize(CameraPosition.xyz - pos);
    float3 up    = float3(0.0f, 1.0f, 0.0f);
    float3 right = cross(toEye, up);
    up           = cross(toEye, right);
    pos += (right * size * vPos.x) + (up * size * vPos.y);
    return mul(float4(pos, 1), WorldViewProjection);
}
PS_Input VSMain(in uint vertexID : SV_VertexID,
                in uint instanceID : SV_InstanceID)
{
```

```
    PS_Input result = (PS_Input)0;
    // Load particle using instance Id
    Particle p = particles[instanceID];
    // 0-1 Vertex strip layout
    //  /
    // 2-3
    result.UV = float2(vertexID & 1, (vertexID & 2) >> 1);
    result.Position = ComputePosition(p.Position, p.Radius,
        result.UV * float2(2, -2) + float2(-1, 1));
    result.Energy = p.Energy;
    return result;
}
```

4. Within `ParticlePS.hlsl`, we will sample the texture and create a fading value.

```
#include "Particle.hlsl"
Texture2D ParticleTexture : register(t0);
SamplerState linearSampler : register(s0);

float4 PSMain(PS_Input pixel) : SV_Target
{
    float4 result = ParticleTexture.Sample(linearSampler,
        pixel.TextureUV);
    // Fade-out as approaching the near clip plane
    // and as a particle loses energy between 1->0
    return float4(result.xyz,
        saturate(pixel.Energy) * result.w *
        pixel.Position.z * pixel.Position.z);
}
```

5. Within `ParticleCS.hlsl`, we will first add our particle's append/consume buffers, a method for applying forces to particles and methods for generating random numbers:

```
#include "Particle.hlsl"
// Append and consume buffers for particles
AppendStructuredBuffer<Particle> NewState : register(u0);
ConsumeStructuredBuffer<Particle> CurrentState :
    register(u1);

// Apply ForceDirection with ForceStrength to particle
void ApplyForces(inout Particle particle)
{
```

```
      // Forces
      float3 force = (float3)0;
      // Directional force
      force += normalize(ForceDirection) * ForceStrength;
      // Damping
      float windResist = 0.9;
      force *= windResist;
      particle.OldPosition = particle.Position;
      // Integration step
      particle.Position += force * FrameTime;
}
// Random Number Generator methods
uint rand_lcg(inout uint rng_state)
{   // Linear congruential generator
    rng_state = 1664525 * rng_state + 1013904223;
    return rng_state;
}
uint wang_hash(uint seed)
{   // Initialize a random seed
    seed = (seed ^ 61) ^ (seed >> 16);
    seed *= 9;
    seed = seed ^ (seed >> 4);
    seed *= 0x27d4eb2d;
    seed = seed ^ (seed >> 15);
    return seed;
}
```

6. Next, we will create the particle generator that inserts new particles into an append buffer.

```
[numthreads(THREADSX, 1, 1)]
void Generator(uint groupIndex: SV_GroupIndex,
    uint3 groupId : SV_GroupID, uint3 groupThreadId:
    SV_GroupThreadID, uint3 threadId : SV_DispatchThreadID)
{
    uint indx = threadId.x + threadId.y * THREADSX;
    Particle p = (Particle)0;

    // Initialize random seed
    uint rng_state = wang_hash(RandomSeed + indx);
    // Random float between [0, 1]
    float f0 = float(rand_lcg(rng_state)) *
        (1.0 / 4294967296.0);
```

```
        float f1 = float(rand_lcg(rng_state)) *
            (1.0 / 4294967296.0);
        float f2 = float(rand_lcg(rng_state)) *
            (1.0 / 4294967296.0);
        // Set properties of new particle
        p.Radius = Radius;
        p.Position.x = DomainBoundsMin.x + f0 *
            ((DomainBoundsMax.x - DomainBoundsMin.x) + 1);
        p.Position.z = DomainBoundsMin.z + f1 *
            ((DomainBoundsMax.z - DomainBoundsMin.z) + 1);
        p.Position.y = (DomainBoundsMax.y - 6) + f2 *
            ((DomainBoundsMax.y - (DomainBoundsMax.y-6)) + 1);
        p.OldPosition = p.Position;
        p.Energy = MaxLifetime;

    // Append the new particle to the output buffer
    NewState.Append(p);
}
```

7. Next, we will add a compute shader that takes the consume buffer to simulate falling snow.

```
[numthreads(THREADSX, THREADSY, 1)]
void Snowfall(uint groupIndex: SV_GroupIndex,
    uint3 groupId : SV_GroupID,
    uint3 groupThreadId: SV_GroupThreadID,
    uint3 threadId : SV_DispatchThreadID)
{
    uint indx = threadId.x + threadId.y * THREADSX;
    // Skip out of bounds threads
    if (indx >= ParticleCount)
        return;
    // Load/Consume particle
    Particle p = CurrentState.Consume();
    ApplyForces(p);

    // Ensure the particle does not´fall endlessly
    p.Position.y = max(p.Position.y, DomainBoundsMin.y);

    // Count down time to live
    p.Energy -= FrameTime;

    // If no longer falling only let sit for a second
```

```
        if (p.Position.y == p.OldPosition.y && p.Energy > 1.0f)
            p.Energy = 1.0f;
        if (p.Energy > 0) {
            // If particle is alive add back to append buffer
            NewState.Append(p);
        }
    }
}
```

This completes our HLSL code. Now, we will create our C# renderer class.

8. Add a new renderer class named `ParticleRenderer` that inherits from the `Common.RendererBase` instance, and implement an empty default constructor.

9. Within the `ParticleRenderer` class, we will define the C# structures for the HLSL structures declared earlier.

```
// Structure for particle
public struct Particle
{
    public Vector3 Position;
    public float Radius;
    public Vector3 OldPosition;
    public float Energy;
}
// Particle constants (updated on initialization)
public struct ParticleConstants
{
    public Vector3 DomainBoundsMin;
    public float ForceStrength;
    public Vector3 DomainBoundsMax;
    public float MaxLifetime;
    public Vector3 ForceDirection;
    public int MaxParticles;
    public Vector3 Attractor;
    public float Radius;
}
// particle constant buffer updated per frame
public struct ParticleFrame
{
    public float Time;
    public float FrameTime;
    public uint RandomSeed;
    // use CopyStructureCount for last component
    uint _padding0;
}
```

10. Within the `ParticleRenderer.CreateDeviceDependentResources` method, first override and reset the device resources using `RemoveAndDispose`, and then compile the vertex and pixel shaders `VSMain` and `PSMain` respectively.

11. Next, we will create the two blend states, as shown in the following code:

```
#region Blend States
var blendDesc = new BlendStateDescription() {
    IndependentBlendEnable = false,
    AlphaToCoverageEnable = false,
};
// Additive blend state that darkens when overlapped
blendDesc.RenderTarget[0] = new RenderTargetBlendDescription
{
    IsBlendEnabled = true,
    BlendOperation = BlendOperation.Add,
    AlphaBlendOperation = BlendOperation.Add,
    SourceBlend = BlendOption.SourceAlpha,
    DestinationBlend = BlendOption.InverseSourceAlpha,
    SourceAlphaBlend = BlendOption.One,
    DestinationAlphaBlend = BlendOption.Zero,
    RenderTargetWriteMask = ColorWriteMaskFlags.All
};
blendState = ToDispose(new BlendState(device, blendDesc));
// Additive blend state that lightens when overlapped
// (needs a dark background)
blendDesc.RenderTarget[0]
    .DestinationBlend = BlendOption.One;
blendStateLight = ToDispose(new BlendState(device,
    blendDesc));
#endregion
```

12. Next, we will create our depth stencil state that disables the write operation.

```
// depth stencil state to disable Z-buffer write
disableDepthWrite = ToDispose(new DepthStencilState(device,
new DepthStencilStateDescription {
    DepthComparison = Comparison.Less,
    DepthWriteMask = SharpDX.Direct3D11.DepthWriteMask.Zero,
    IsDepthEnabled = true,
    IsStencilEnabled = false
}));
```

13. In order to complete the `CreateDeviceDependentResources` method, we will create the particle constant buffers and load the particle textures.

```
// Create the per compute shader constant buffer
perComputeBuffer = ToDispose(new Buffer(device,
  Utilities.SizeOf<ParticleConstants>(),
  ResourceUsage.Default, BindFlags.ConstantBuffer,
  CpuAccessFlags.None, ResourceOptionFlags.None, 0));
// Create the particle frame buffer
perFrame = ToDispose(new Buffer(device,
  Utilities.SizeOf<ParticleFrame>(),
  ResourceUsage.Default, BindFlags.ConstantBuffer,
  CpuAccessFlags.None, ResourceOptionFlags.None, 0));
particleTextureSRV = ToDispose(ShaderResourceView
  .FromFile(device, "Particle.png"));
```

14. Copy the `CreateBufferUAV` function into the `ParticleRenderer` class created in the *Calculating an image's luminance histogram* recipe of *Chapter 7, Performing Image Processing Techniques*. We need to make the following highlighted changes to support the append/consume buffers:

```
public static UnorderedAccessView CreateBufferUAV(
    SharpDX.Direct3D11.Device device, Buffer buffer,
    UnorderedAccessViewBufferFlags flags =
    UnorderedAccessViewBufferFlags.None)
{
    . . .
    else if ((buffer.Description.OptionFlags &
        ResourceOptionFlags.BufferStructured) ==
        ResourceOptionFlags.BufferStructured)
    {
        uavDesc.Format = Format.Unknown;
        uavDesc.Buffer.Flags = flags;
        . . .
    }
    . . .
}
```

15. We will initialize our particle buffers and set the constants within a new function named `InitializeParticles`.

```
// Private member fields
Buffer indirectArgsBuffer;
List<Buffer> particleBuffers = new List<Buffer>();
List<ShaderResourceView> particleSRVs =
    new List<ShaderResourceView>();
```

```
List<UnorderedAccessView> particleUAVs =
    new List<UnorderedAccessView>();
public int ParticlesPerBatch = 16;
float limiter = 0f;
// Initialize the particle buffers
public void InitializeParticles(int maxParticles,
    float maxLifetime)
{
    ... RemoveAndDispose(...)
    this.Constants.MaxParticles = maxParticles;
    this.Constants.MaxLifetime = maxLifetime;
    // How often and how many particles to generate
    this.ParticlesPerBatch = (int)(maxParticles * 0.0128f);
    this.limiter = (float)(Math.Ceiling(ParticlesPerBatch /
        16.0) * 16.0 * maxLifetime) / (float)maxParticles;


    #region Create Buffers and Views
        ... SNIP see below
    #endregion

    // Update the ParticleConstants buffer
    device.ImmediateContext.UpdateSubresource(
        ref Constants, perComputeBuffer);
}
```

16. We will create the particle buffers and views with the following code:

```
// Create 2 buffers, these are our append/consume
// buffers and will be swapped each frame
particleBuffers.Add(
    ToDispose(new Buffer(device,
        Utilities.SizeOf<Particle>() * maxParticles,
        ResourceUsage.Default,
        BindFlags.ShaderResource |
        BindFlags.UnorderedAccess,
        CpuAccessFlags.None,
        ResourceOptionFlags.BufferStructured,
        Utilities.SizeOf<Particle>())));
particleBuffers.Add(...same as above...);
// Create a UAV and SRV for each particle buffer
particleUAVs.Add(ToDispose(CreateBufferUAV(device,
    particleBuffers[0],
    UnorderedAccessViewBufferFlags.Append)));
```

```
particleUAVs.Add(ToDispose(CreateBufferUAV(device,
    particleBuffers[1],
    UnorderedAccessViewBufferFlags.Append)));
particleSRVs.Add(ToDispose(new
    ShaderResourceView(device, particleBuffers[0])));
particleSRVs.Add(...particleBuffers[1]...);

// Set the starting number of particles to 0
context.ComputeShader.SetUnorderedAccessView(0,
    particleUAVs[0], 0);
context.ComputeShader.SetUnorderedAccessView(1,
    particleUAVs[1], 0);
```

17. And finally, we will create a buffer that will store the current consume buffer's particle count for input into the `DeviceContext.DrawInstancedIndirect` function within the render loop.

```
// Create particle count buffers:
var bufDesc = new BufferDescription {
    BindFlags = SharpDX.Direct3D11.BindFlags.ConstantBuffer,
    SizeInBytes = 4 * SharpDX.Utilities.SizeOf<uint>(),
    StructureByteStride = 0,
    Usage = ResourceUsage.Default,
    CpuAccessFlags = SharpDX.Direct3D11.CpuAccessFlags.None,
};
// Used as input to the context.DrawInstancedIndirect
// The 4 elements represent the 4 parameters
bufDesc.OptionFlags =
    ResourceOptionFlags.DrawIndirectArguments;
bufDesc.BindFlags = BindFlags.None;
indirectArgsBuffer = ToDispose(new Buffer(device,
    bufDesc));
// 4 vertices per instance (i.e. quad)
device.ImmediateContext.UpdateSubresource(new uint[4] { 4,
    0, 0, 0 }, particleCountIABuffer);
```

With all our resources initialized, we will now work on the compute shader's update stage.

18. Then, we will create a new method named `ParticleRenderer.Update`, as shown here:

```
float genTime = 0f; // time since Generator last run
public void Update(string generatorCS, string updaterCS)
{
    var append = particleUAVs[0];
```

```
var consume = particleUAVs[1];
// Assign UAV of particles
context.ComputeShader.SetUnorderedAccessView(0,
    append);
context.ComputeShader.SetUnorderedAccessView(1,
    consume);
// Update the constant buffers
// Generate the next random seed for particle generator
Frame.RandomSeed = (uint)random.Next(int.MinValue,
    int.MaxValue);
context.UpdateSubresource(ref Frame, perFrame);
// Copy current consume buffer count into perFrame
context.CopyStructureCount(perFrame, 4 * 3, consume);
context.ComputeShader.SetConstantBuffer(0,
    perComputeBuffer);
context.ComputeShader.SetConstantBuffer(1, perFrame);

// Update existing particles
UpdateCS(updaterCS, append, consume);
// Generate new particles (if reached limiter time)
genTime += Frame.FrameTime;
if (genTime > limiter) {
    genTime = 0;
    GenerateCS(generatorCS, append);
}
// Retrieve the particle count for the render phase
context.CopyStructureCount(indirectArgsBuffer, 4,
    append);
// Clear the shader and resources from pipeline stage
context.ComputeShader.SetUnorderedAccessViews(0, null,
    null, null);
context.ComputeShader.SetUnorderedAccessViews(1, null,
    null, null);
context.ComputeShader.Set(null);

// Flip UAVs/SRVs
particleUAVs[0] = consume; particleUAVs[1] = append;
var s = particleSRVs[0];
particleSRVs[0] = particleSRVs[1]; particleSRVs[1] = s;
}
```

19. We will now create the `ParticleRenderer.UpdateCS` function for compiling and running the particle simulation's update compute shader:

```
private void UpdateCS(string csName, UnorderedAccessView
    append, UnorderedAccessView consume)
{
    var context = this.DeviceManager.Direct3DContext;
    // Compile the shader if it isn't already
    if (!computeShaders.ContainsKey(csName))
        CompileComputeShader(csName);
    // Set the shader to run
    context.ComputeShader.Set(computeShaders[csName]);
    // Dispatch the compute shader thread groups
    context.Dispatch((int)Math.Ceiling(Constants
        .MaxParticles / (double)ThreadsX), 1, 1);
}
```

20. Next, we will create the `ParticleRenderer.GenerateCS` function for running the particle generator's compute shader.

```
public const int GeneratorThreadsX = 16;
private void GenerateCS(string name,
    UnorderedAccessView append)
{
    // Compile the shader if it isn't already
    if (!computeShaders.ContainsKey(name))
    {
        int oldThreadsX = ThreadsX;
        ThreadsX = GeneratorThreadsX;
        CompileComputeShader(name);
        ThreadsX = oldThreadsX;
    }
    // Set the shader to run
    context.ComputeShader.Set(computeShaders[name]);
    // Dispatch the compute shader thread groups
    context.Dispatch((int)Math.Ceiling(ParticlesPerBatch /
        16.0), 1, 1);
}
```

21. We will use the following `CompileComputeShader` function to compile our compute shaders on demand. This allows easy addition of more shaders.

```
public Dictionary<String, ComputeShader> computeShaders =
    new Dictionary<string, ComputeShader>();
public int ThreadsX = 128; // default thread group width
```

```
    public int ThreadsY = 1;    // default thread group height
    // Compile compute shader from file
    public void CompileComputeShader(string csFunction,
        string csFile = @"Shaders\ParticleCS.hlsl")
    {
        SharpDX.Direct3D.ShaderMacro[] defines = new[] {
            new SharpDX.Direct3D.ShaderMacro("THREADSX",
                ThreadsX),
            new SharpDX.Direct3D.ShaderMacro("THREADSY",
                ThreadsY),
        };
        using (var bytecode = HLSLCompiler.CompileFromFile(
            csFile, csFunction, "cs_5_0", defines))
        {
            computeShaders[csFunction] = ToDispose(new
                ComputeShader(this.DeviceManager
                    .Direct3DDevice, bytecode));
        }
    }
```

22. To complete our `ParticleRenderer` class, we will add the `DoRender` implementation. The following snippet shows the code to back up and restore the state of the pipeline:

```
protected override void DoRender()
{
    // Retrieve existing pipeline states for backup
    Color4 oldBlendFactor;
    int oldSampleMask;
    int oldStencil;
    var oldPSBufs
      =context.PixelShader.GetConstantBuffers(0,1);
    using (var oldVS = context.VertexShader.Get())
    using (var oldPS = context.PixelShader.Get())
    using (var oldGS = context.GeometryShader.Get())
    using (var oldSamp = context.PixelShader
        .GetSamplers(0, 1).FirstOrDefault())
    using (var oldBlendState = context.OutputMerger
        .GetBlendState(out oldBlendFactor, out oldSampleMask))
    using (var oldIA = context.InputAssembler.InputLayout)
    using (var oldDepth = context.OutputMerger
```

```
            .GetDepthStencilState(out oldStencil))
    {
...SNIP draw logic here

    // Restore previous pipeline state
    context.VertexShader.Set(oldVS);
    context.PixelShader.SetConstantBuffers(0, oldPSBufs);
    context.PixelShader.Set(oldPS);
    context.GeometryShader.Set(oldGS);
    context.PixelShader.SetSampler(0, oldSamp);
    context.InputAssembler.InputLayout = oldIA;

    // Restore previous blend and depth state
    context.OutputMerger.SetBlendState(oldBlendState,
      oldBlendFactor, oldSampleMask);
    context.OutputMerger.SetDepthStencilState(oldDepth,
      oldStencil);
    }
}
```

23. The draw logic for the preceding snippet is as follows:

```
// There is no input layout for this renderer
context.InputAssembler.InputLayout = null;
// The triangle strip input topology
context.InputAssembler.PrimitiveTopology =
    SharpDX.Direct3D.PrimitiveTopology.TriangleStrip;
// Disable depth write
context.OutputMerger
    .SetDepthStencilState(disableDepthWrite);
// Set the additive blend state
if (!UseLightenBlend)
    context.OutputMerger.SetBlendState(blendState, null,
        0xFFFFFFFF);
else
    context.OutputMerger.SetBlendState(blendStateLight,
        Color.White, 0xFFFFFFFF);
// Assign consume particle buffer SRV to vertex shader
context.VertexShader.SetShaderResource(0, particleSRVs[1]);
context.VertexShader.Set(vertexShader);

// Set pixel shader resources
context.PixelShader.SetShaderResource(0,
    particleTextureSRV);
```

```
context.PixelShader.SetSampler(0, linearSampler);
context.PixelShader.Set(pixelShader);

// Draw the number of quad instances stored in the
// indirectArgsBuffer. The vertex shader will rely upon
// the SV_VertexID and SV_InstanceID input semantics
context.DrawInstancedIndirect(indirectArgsBuffer, 0);
```

This completes our particle renderer class. Now it is ready to use in your D3DApp class.

24. Within D3DApp.Run, initialize an instance of our particle renderer with the following code snippet:

```
var particleSystem = ToDispose(new ParticleRenderer());
// Initialize renderer
particleSystem.Initialize(this);
var totalParticles = 100000;
particleSystem.Constants.DomainBoundsMax =
    new Vector3(20, 20, 20);
particleSystem.Constants.DomainBoundsMin =
    new Vector3(-20, 0, -20);
particleSystem.Constants.ForceDirection = -Vector3.UnitY;
// Gravity is normally ~9.8f, we want slower snowfall
particleSystem.Constants.ForceStrength = 1.8f;
// Initialize particle resources
particleSystem.InitializeParticles(totalParticles, 13f);
// Initialize simulation timer
var simTime = new System.Diagnostics.Stopwatch();
simTime.Start();
```

25. And lastly in the render loop which is in turn within D3DApp.Run, add the following code to update the particle simulation, and then render it:

```
// 1. Update the particle simulation
if (simTime.IsRunning)
{
    particleSystem.Frame.FrameTime = (float)simTime.Elapsed
        .TotalSeconds - particleSystem.Frame.Time);
    particleSystem.Constants.Time = (float)simTime.Elapsed
        .TotalSeconds;
    // Run the compute shaders (compiles if necessary)
    particleSystem.Update("Generator", "Snowfall");
}
// 2. Render the particles
particleSystem.Render();
```

An example of the final output is shown in the following screenshot:

Top-left: 100 k particles, Top-right: 500 k particles, Bottom-left: 1 million particles, Bottom-right: View of particle domain with 1 million particles

How it works...

We initialized two append/consume buffers and their corresponding views within `ParticleRenderer.InitializeParticles`. These buffers can contain up to the `MaxParticles` number of `Particle` structures. The initial number of items in the append/consume buffers is set to zero by assigning them to the pipeline and passing in `0`. If you want to initialize the particles on the CPU, the starting count can be provided here.

We have elected not to initialize any particles on the CPU. Instead we will create the particles in the `Generator` compute shader on the GPU to randomly disperse particles within the top two meters of our particle domain (as specified by the `DomainBoundsMin` and `DomainBoundsMax` properties of the constant buffer). We use two pseudo random number generators in our shader, as too much uniformity on either axis will result in visible gaps and patterns appearing between the particles. The generator adds the particles to the buffer by using `NewState.Append(newParticle)`.

The `ParticleRenderer.Update` method sets up the pipeline stage and executes the `GeneratorCS` and `UpdateCS` methods, which dispatch their respective compute shaders. We implemented a simple method of limiting the number of particles created, based upon the maximum number of particles, particle batch size, and the lifetime of the particles. The current number of particles is copied from the consume buffer and is applied to the `perFrame` constant buffer before updating the simulation.

The `Snowfall` compute shader applies the force that has been passed into the `ParticleConstants` constant buffer with a call to `ApplyForces`. This simply computes the current force vector and applies it to the particle's position, based on the current `FrameTime` value. Then, the `Snowfall` shader clamps the `Particle.Position.y` value to `DomainBoundsMin.y`; if the old and new Y positions are the same (that is, the particle is sitting on the ground), the `Particle.Energy` property is set to `1.0f`. To ensure that we do not try to create too many particles, we decreased their `Energy` property by the current `FrameTime` value. Once the amount of energy reaches zero, the particle is removed; otherwise, it is added into the `NewState` buffer.

The `DeviceContext.DrawInstancedIndirect` method allows us to generate our sprites or billboards by passing in a GPU-generated parameter list; the first two being the instance vertex count (always four for our quads) and number of instances. The instance count comes directly from the current consume buffer with a call to the `DeviceContext.CopyStructureCount` method. This allows our compute shaders to control the number of particles to be rendered.

By utilizing the vertex shader system value input semantics `SV_InstanceID` and `SV_VertexID`, we are able to index into the particle buffer directly and generate our camera-aligned quads without passing any additional information into the vertex shader. We compute the vertex UV coordinates and their positions based on the incoming `SV_VertexID` value. Another approach is to use a lookup table, saving approximately two instructions. The resulting camera-aligned quads (also known as **sprites** or **billboards**) will always face the camera.

Once the quad is rasterized and the fragments are sent to the pixel shader, we sample the texture and return the value. The texture used in the recipe is a white dot or snowflake shape with transparency. Multiplying this with any other color allows us to control the particle's final color. We also fade out the alpha as the particle approaches the near-clip plane, and during its final second of life.

To allow the particles to perform alpha-blending correctly, we have created an additive `BlendState` instance within our particle renderer. By setting the `blendDesc.RenderTarget[0].SourceBlend` to `BlendOption.SourceAlpha`, and `blendDesc.RenderTarget[0].DestinationBlend` to `BlendOption.InverseSourceAlpha`, we are telling the output merger stage to use the alpha component returned by the pixel shader, and merge with the render target accordingly. Given a source color of `(1, 1, 1, 0.5)` and destination color of `(0.6, 0.0, 0.6, 0.9)`, the blending calculation is as follows:

```
Final Color = (Source Color * BlendOption.SourceAlpha)
   BlendOperation.Add (Dest Color * BlendOption.InverseSourceAlpha)
Final Color = ((1, 1, 1) * 0.7) + ((0.6, 0.0, 0.6) * (1 - 0.7))
            = (0.7, 0.7, 0.7) + (0.18, 0.0, 0.18)
            = (0.88, 0.7, 0.88)
```

To ignore the draw order of the particles, we have disabled the depth buffer write in the output merger stage. If we don't do this, we would have darker or lighter squares around each particle (the size of the quad). Leaving the depth test enabled allows the particles to disappear behind other objects in the scene.

The completed project available for this recipe includes the following key mappings:

Key	Action
Backspace	Cycle between available compute shaders
Shift + Backspace	Switch between the blend states
Enter	Cycle between the loaded particle textures
B	Toggle between a light and dark background
+/- and *Shift* plus +/-	Increase or decrease the number of particles by 10,000 or 100,000 respectively (also resets the particles)
Mouse right-click	Change attractor location

There's more...

Our simple snowfall shader could be extended to allow the snow to land on objects within the scene by generating a top-down orthographic projection of the scene, and then sampling the resulting depth buffer to compare the particle's Y position against the top of the object underneath the particle's XZ location.

It is now quite easy to implement a range of particle simulations. For example, if we take the `GerstnerWaveTessendorf` function from the previous *Simulating ocean waves* recipe, we can make the particles form waves. This is shown in the following screenshot:

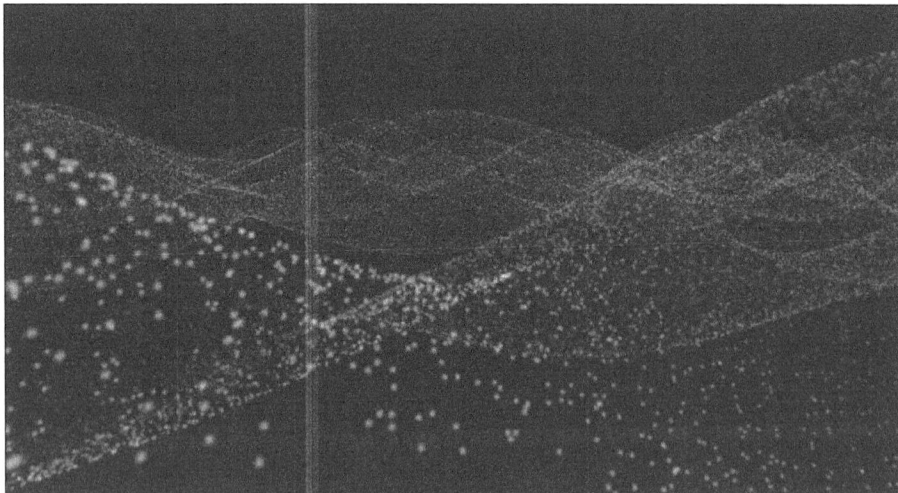

Particles with the Gerstner wave function applied.

By applying the lighten blend state, setting up the `Attractor` property of the `ParticleConstants` constant buffer, and using a compute shader that moves the particles around the attractor location, we can achieve something similar to the following screenshot:

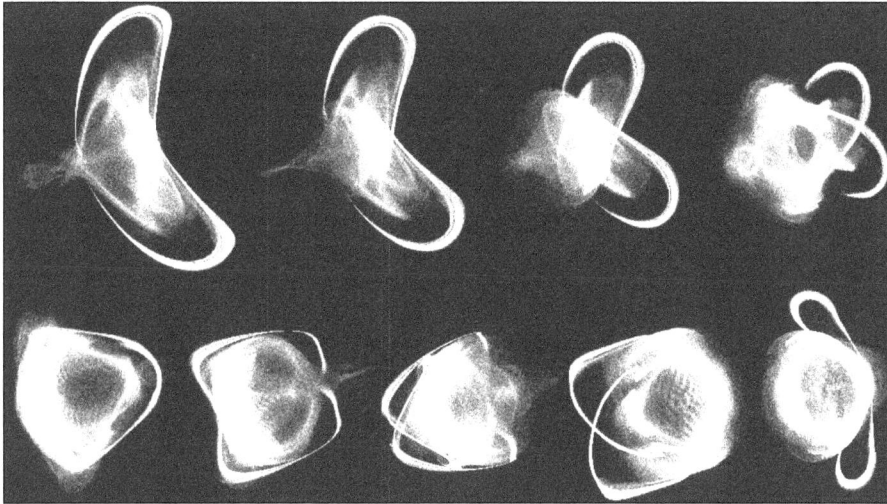

Sequential frames of 9 million particles moving towards and around an attractor location

See also

▸ *Chapter 7, Performing Image Processing Techniques*, for more information about running compute shaders and thread addressing

▸ Render target blend description is available at `http://msdn.microsoft.com/en-us/library/windows/desktop/hh404492(v=vs.85).aspx`

▸ *Quick and Easy GPU Random Numbers* at `http://www.reedbeta.com/blog/2013/01/12/quick-and-easy-gpu-random-numbers-in-d3d11/`

9
Rendering on Multiple Threads and Deferred Contexts

In this chapter, we will cover the following topics:

- ▶ Benchmarking multithreaded rendering
- ▶ Implementing multithreaded dynamic cubic environment mapping
- ▶ Implementing dual paraboloid environment mapping

Introduction

One of the improvements that came with Direct3D 11 is the improved multithreading support. This is facilitated through the use of deferred contexts, additional device contexts that are used to create a command list for future execution on the immediate context. Creating multiple deferred contexts allow us to prepare rendering commands on multiple threads at once, and therefore, take advantage of multiple CPU cores that are common on modern PCs.

In this chapter, we will look at how to implement multithreaded rendering and take a look at the impact on performance and under what circumstances it can provide us with benefits. We will then apply it to dynamic environment mapping, where we are performing multiple scene passes per frame. We will simulate additional CPU load (or CPU burn) by introducing additional matrix multiplications on the CPU within each thread. By increasing and decreasing the level of CPU burn, we will examine the impact on performance with and without multithreaded rendering enabled to gain an understanding of the circumstances in which it is beneficial to introduce multithreaded rendering. An introduction to the immediate and deferred contexts can be found in *Chapter 1, Getting Started with Direct3D*.

Benchmarking multithreaded rendering

In this recipe, we will introduce multithreaded rendering techniques and implement a simple benchmark application to analyze the performance of using multiple deferred contexts. We will render the same model multiple times, comparing the results between varying numbers of deferred contexts and the immediate context. We will introduce additional CPU processing overhead to compare GPU-bound and CPU-bound frame times.

Getting ready

We can begin with any completed rendering loop and apply the techniques presented in this recipe to it. However, for the purpose of this recipe, we will assume a starting point based upon the finished result from the *Animating bones* recipe in *Chapter 4*, *Animating Meshes with Vertex Skinning*.

How to do it...

In order to support multithreaded rendering, it is necessary to pass the `DeviceContext` deferred context instance that will receive the rendering commands for the renderer. We will implement support for starting a new thread for each deferred context and split the recording of rendering tasks between them.

1. The first change we will make to our renderer(s) is that we want it to support executing commands on a deferred context. So that a renderer can use the provided context, we will use the following `Render` override of `Common.RendererBase`:

   ```
   public void Render(SharpDX.Direct3D11.DeviceContext context)
   {
     if (Show)
       DoRender(context);
   }
   ```

2. Within appropriate renderer classes (for example, `MeshRenderer.cs`), we will change to the `RendererBase.DoRender` method override that accepts a `DeviceContext` parameter.

   ```
   protected override void DoRender(DeviceContext context) {
     ... SNIP - previous DoRender() code
   }
   ```

3. Within the `D3DApp` class, we need code for initializing the requested number of deferred context `DeviceContext` instances. This might look similar to the following code snippet:

   ```
   DeviceContext[] contextList;
   int threadCount = 2;
   ```

```
contextList = new DeviceContext[threadCount];
if (threadCount == 1) {
    // Use the immediate context if only 1 thread
    contextList[0] = this.DeviceManager
                        .Direct3DDevice.ImmediateContext;
} else {
    for (var i = 0; i < threadCount; i++)
    {
        contextList[i] = ToDispose(new DeviceContext(
            this.DeviceManager.Direct3DDevice));
        InitializeContext(contextList[i]);
    }
}
```

4. Within the previous code snippet, we are initializing the pipeline state for each new deferred context with a call to a new function named `InitializeContext`. Before the new context can be used for `Draw` calls, it must at least have a viewport and render target assigned. The following code snippet shows an example for representing this function in our simplistic, example-rendering framework:

```
protected void InitializeContext(DeviceContext context)
{
    // Tell the IA what the vertices will look like
    context.InputAssembler.InputLayout = vertexLayout;
    // Set the constant buffers for vertex shader stage
    context.VertexShader.SetConstantBuffer(0,
        perObjectBuffer);
    context.VertexShader.SetConstantBuffer(1,
        perFrameBuffer);
    context.VertexShader.SetConstantBuffer(2,
        perMaterialBuffer);
    context.VertexShader.SetConstantBuffer(3,
        perArmatureBuffer);
    // Set the default vertex shader to run
    context.VertexShader.Set(vertexShader);
    // Set our pixel shader constant buffers
    context.PixelShader
        .SetConstantBuffer(1, perFrameBuffer);
    context.PixelShader
        .SetConstantBuffer(2, perMaterialBuffer);
    // Set the default pixel shader to run
    context.PixelShader.Set(blinnPhongShader);
    // Set our depth stencil state
    context.OutputMerger
```

```
            .DepthStencilState = depthStencilState;
        // Set viewport
        context.Rasterizer.SetViewports(this.DeviceManager
            .Direct3DContext.Rasterizer.GetViewports());
        // Set render targets
        context.OutputMerger.SetTargets(this.DepthStencilView,
            this.RenderTargetView);
    }
```

5. In order to test the performance benefits or costs of multithreaded rendering within `D3DApp.Run`, we need to load a number of additional copies of a mesh (or perhaps load one very large scene). For loading the same model multiple times, let's create a grid of models using the same mesh and separate them by their `Mesh.Extent` property. The following code snippet can load simple or complex scenes and apply a `World` matrix to the `MeshRenderer` instances, laying them out in a grid:

```
// Create and initialize the mesh renderer
var loadedMesh = Common.Mesh.LoadFromFile("Character.cmo");
List<MeshRenderer> meshes = new List<MeshRenderer>();
int meshRows = 10;
int meshColumns = 10;

// Create duplicates of mesh separated by the extent
var minExtent = (from mesh in loadedMesh
    orderby new { mesh.Extent.Min.X, mesh.Extent.Min.Z }
    select mesh.Extent).First();
var maxExtent = (from mesh in loadedMesh
    orderby new { mesh.Extent.Max.X, mesh.Extent.Max.Z }
    descending select mesh.Extent).First();
var extentDiff = (maxExtent.Max - minExtent.Min);
// X-axis
for (int x = -(meshColumns/2); x < (meshColumns/2); x++)
{   // Z-axis
    for (int z = -(meshRows/2); z < (meshRows/2); z++)
    {
        var meshGroup = (from mesh in loadedMesh
          select ToDispose(new MeshRenderer(mesh))).ToList();
        // Reposition based on width/depth of combined extent
        foreach (var m in meshGroup)
        {
            m.World.TranslationVector = new Vector3(
                m.Mesh.Extent.Center.X + extentDiff.X * x,
                m.Mesh.Extent.Min.Y, m.Mesh.Extent.Center.Z +
                extentDiff.Z * z);
        }
```

```
        meshes.AddRange(meshGroup);
    }
}
// Initialize each mesh renderer
meshes.ForEach(m => m.Initialize(this));
```

To analyze the performance accurately, it is necessary to either disable the animation or pause on a particular frame. This is because the frames later in the animation will apply additional CPU load due to the increased number of bone matrix transformations that are necessary causing the frame times to increase and decrease at different times during the animation. It is also critical to run a release build.

We are now ready to update our rendering loop for multithreaded rendering.

6. At the start of the rendering loop in `D3DApp.Run`, we will retrieve the immediate context and the first context within the `contextList` array.

```
// Retrieve immediate context
var immediateContext = DeviceManager.Direct3DDevice
                          .ImmediateContext;
// Note: the context at index 0 is always executed first
var context = contextList[0];
```

7. All the operations within the main render loop are now taking place on the first device context within the `contextList` array, such as the following call to clear the render target:

```
// Clear render target view
context.ClearRenderTargetView(RenderTargetView,
  background);
```

Assuming all the contexts are using the same pipeline state, we only want to do this once and on the first context; otherwise, we will be clearing the results of other render contexts.

8. Towards the end of the render loop, where we normally call the `Render` method of our renderers, we will create a `System.Threading.Tasks.Task` instance for each render context, which will perform the render logic and then record its `SharpDX.Direct3D11.CommandList` value.

```
Task[] renderTasks = new Task[contextList.Length];
CommandList[] commands = new CommandList[contextList.Length];
for (var i = 0; i < contextList.Length; i++)
{
```

```
// Must store value of iterator in another variable
// otherwise all threads will end up using the last
// context.
var contextIndex = i;
renderTasks[i] = Task.Run(() => {
    // Retrieve render context for thread
    var renderContext = contextList[contextIndex];

    // TODO: regular render logic goes here

    // Create the command list
    if (contextList[contextIndex].TypeInfo ==
      DeviceContextType.Deferred)
    {
        commands[contextIndex] = contextList[contextIndex]
          .FinishCommandList(true);
    }
});
}
// Wait for all the tasks to complete
Task.WaitAll(renderTasks);
```

9. Next, we need to replay command lists on the immediate context. We are applying them in the order in which they are located within the contextList array.

```
// Replay the command lists on the immediate context
for (var i = 0; i < contextList.Length; i++)
{
    if (contextList[i].TypeInfo ==
        DeviceContextType.Deferred && commands[i] != null)
    {
        immediateContext.ExecuteCommandList(commands[i],
          false);
        commands[i].Dispose();
        commands[i] = null;
    }
}
```

10. The following code snippet shows an example of the logic that belongs to the preceding rendering task's loop. The only difference compared to our regular rendering process is that we are only rendering a portion of the available meshes for the current context, optionally simulating the additional CPU load, and we are calling the MeshRenderer.Render method with a context.

```
// Retrieve appropriate context
var renderContext = contextList[contextIndex];
// Create viewProjection matrix
```

```csharp
var viewProjection = Matrix.Multiply(viewMatrix,
  projectionMatrix);
// Determine the meshes to render for this context
int batchSize = (int)Math.Floor((double)meshes.Count /
  contextList.Length);
int startIndex = batchSize * contextIndex;
int endIndex = Math.Min(startIndex + batchSize,
  meshes.Count - 1);
// If the last context include remaining meshes due to
// the rounding above.
if (contextIndex == contextList.Length - 1)
    endIndex = meshes.Count - 1;
// Loop over the meshes for this context and render them
var perObject = new ConstantBuffers.PerObject();
for (var i = startIndex; i <= endIndex; i++)
{
    // Simulate additional CPU load
    for (var j = 0; j < additionalCPULoad; j++)
    {
        viewProjection = Matrix.Multiply(viewMatrix,
                                         projectionMatrix);
    }
    var m = meshes[i];
    // Update perObject constant buffer
    perObject.World = m.World * worldMatrix;
    perObject.WorldInverseTranspose = Matrix.Transpose(
        Matrix.Invert(perObject.World));
    perObject.WorldViewProjection = perObject.World *
      viewProjection;
    perObject.Transpose();
    renderContext.UpdateSubresource(ref perObject,
      perObjectBuffer);

    // Provide the material and armature constant buffer
    m.PerArmatureBuffer = perArmatureBuffer;
    m.PerMaterialBuffer = perMaterialBuffer;
    // Render the mesh using the provided DeviceContext
    m.Render(renderContext);
}
```

11. The following screenshot shows an example by running at a frame time of 8.2 ms with seven deferred contexts and threads. By comparison, rendering only on the immediate context on the same hardware configuration results in a frame time of 24.8 ms.

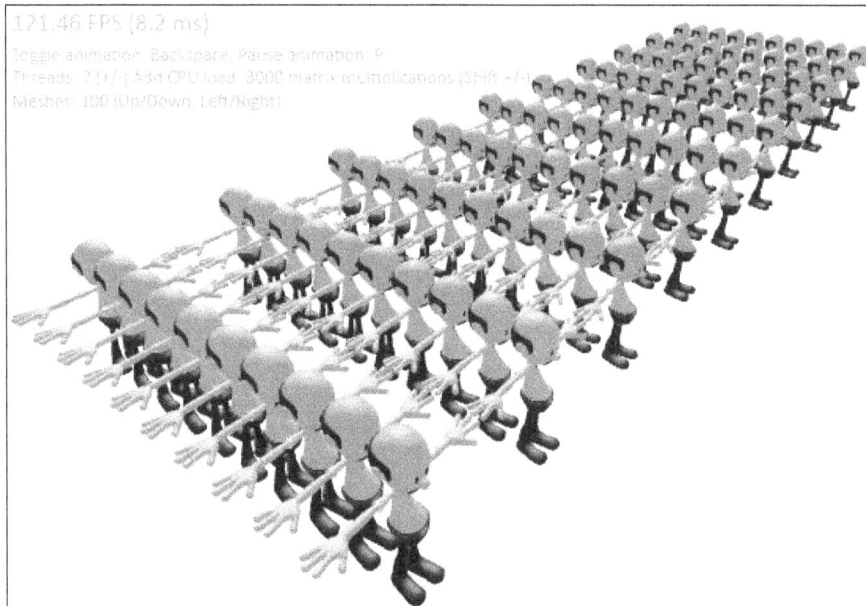

121.46 FPS (8.2 ms)
Toggle animation: Backspace, Pause animation: P
Threads: 7 (+/-) Add CPU load: 3000 matrix multiplications (Shift +/-)
Meshes: 100 (Up/Down, Left/Right)

Multithreaded rendering benchmark application running with 100 meshes, seven threads and deferred context instances, and an additional 3,000 matrix multiplications performed per mesh.

How it works...

A deferred context allows for a sequence of commands and state changes to be recorded and then packaged up into a command buffer for later execution on the Direct3D device's immediate context. We have implemented a method of creating a number of deferred contexts, starting with a new thread for each context and then splitting the load of rendering meshes across them. Our renderers are then able to use the deferred context to submit Direct3D commands by using the provided context instead of retrieving the `device.ImmediateContext` property directly. We implement this by calling the `Render(DeviceContext context)` function to support circumstances where the same instance of the renderer needs to be rendered multiple times in different threads. Before playing back the command lists on the immediate context, we first wait for all the threads to complete.

The process is outlined in the following diagram:

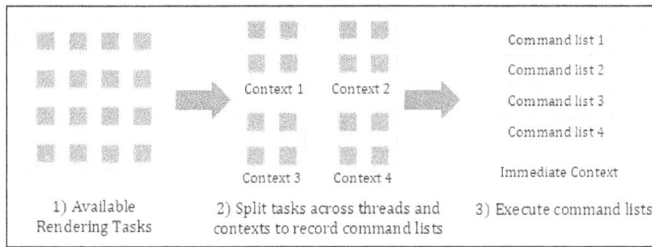

| 1) Available Rendering Tasks | 2) Split tasks across threads and contexts to record command lists | 3) Execute command lists |

Rendering across multiple deferred contexts

While setting up the deferred context, it is necessary to configure the pipeline state as you would for the immediate context. The deferred context begins with a default state, the equivalent of when the `DeviceContext.ClearState` method is called. When we create the `SharpDX.Direct3D11.CommandList` instance via a call to the `DeviceContext.FinishComandList(bool restoreState)` instance, we are passing in the `true` value so that the context's state remains as we have set it; otherwise, it reverts to its default state. Conversely, the `immediateContext.ExecuteCommandList` method is passed a `false` value because we don't need to preserve the immediate context state.

> Passing `true` to either `DeviceContext.FinishCommandList` or `DeviceContext.ExecuteCommandList` can potentially degrade the performance by introducing avoidable and inefficient state transitions. In order to throw away the current state, we need to call something similar to the `InitializeContext` method for each deferred context on every frame (or rendering pass).

Each context can have a different state applied depending on its purpose; in fact, this might be a convenient way of separating pipeline states for your rendering logic, for example, a deferred context with a different render target for shadow mapping, another for a lighting pass, and so on. Another example may be of a deferred context that is to be used only for preparing compute shaders in which there may be no need to set a viewport and render a target.

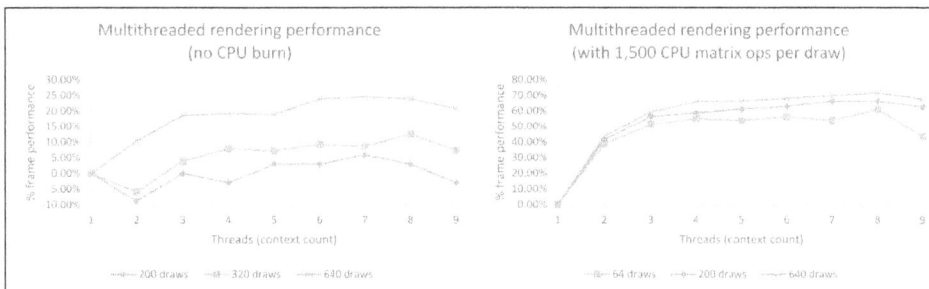

Multithreaded rendering performance as compared to single threaded (higher is better). Results with an AMD® Radeon HD 7950 on an Intel® i7-3770K.

> It is important to run any performance tests using a release
> build configuration and without the Direct3D debug layer to get
> accurate results.

By applying both GPU and CPU load, we are better able to identify where multithreaded
rendering might be beneficial. After reviewing the preceding graphs, it is apparent that unless
a certain amount of CPU load is present, there is only a small improvement in frame times;
in some cases, we even see a decrease in performance. The frame times have been
calculated using a 100-frame simple moving average.

There's more...

Another important feature of multithreading support in Direct3D 11 is that it also includes the
creation of Direct3D resources on multiple threads. This does not involve using immediate or
deferred contexts and is instead a feature of the Direct3D 11 device class. By creating resources
on multiple threads, we can decrease the initialization time of our Direct3D applications, and
importantly, for Windows 8, we are able to load and compile our resources asynchronously.

To identify the areas where multithreaded rendering has the most impact, it may be necessary
to employ the use of performance profilers or implement an in-application frame profiler.

GPUView is a CPU/GPU profiler included with the Windows Performance Toolkit; an overview
of using this profiling tool is available at `http://graphics.stanford.edu/~mdfisher/`
`GPUView.html`. The default install location for this tool on Windows 8 is `C:\Program`
`Files (x86)\Windows Kits\8.0\Windows Performance Toolkit\gpuview`.

To check whether multithreading is supported at the hardware/driver level, we can use the
following function:

```
// Determine if the hardware driver supports CommandLists
// If not, the Direct3D framework will emulate support.
bool createResourcesConcurrently;
bool nativeCommandListSupport;
device.CheckThreadingSupport(out createResourcesConcurrently, out
nativeCommandListSupport);
```

The `CheckThreadingSupport` function wraps the native API `ID3D11Device::CheckFeat`
`ureSupport` method, returning two Boolean values and indicating whether the driver natively
supports the creation of resources simultaneously on multiple threads or command lists.
If not supported, the Direct3D 11 API will emulate the behavior, albeit with potentially
smaller performance gains.

See also

▸ The *Loading and compiling resources asynchronously* recipe in *Chapter 11, Integrating Direct3D with XAML and Windows 8.1*

Implementing multithreaded dynamic cubic environment mapping

In this recipe, we will implement dynamic **cubic environment mapping** or **cube mapping** and explore how threading impacts the rendering performance. A **cube map** is commonly used for skyboxes with the camera located inside the cube. In this recipe, we will be using cube maps to implement reflections for objects. We will also be rendering directly to the cube map resource in order to implement dynamic reflections. In Direct3D, a cube map is implemented using a **texture cube**; this is a special texture array with six slices where each slice represents a face of the cube along an axis. The `TextureCube` HLSL shader resource provides built-in sampling support. The following figure shows a static cube map laid out flat, and the texture array indices are matched to the appropriate axis:

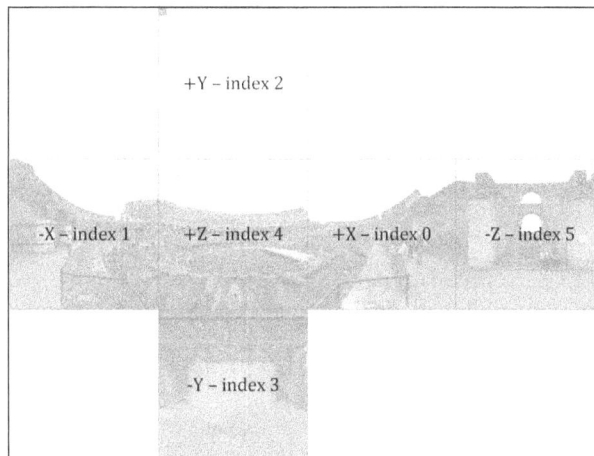

Static cubic environment map with texture array indices.

Note that the cube map is defined using a left-handed coordinate system (that is, **+Z** is forward, **+X** is to the right, and **+Y** is upward). Our recipe will, therefore require axis scaling and vertex winding changes when generating dynamic cube maps.

> The Collosseum cube map is by Emil Persson, who has a number of static cube map textures released under a Creative Commons Attribution 3.0 license available at `http://www.humus.name/index.php?page=Textures`.

Getting ready

For this recipe, we will start with the project from the previous recipe, *Benchmarking multithreaded rendering*. The scene file named `Scene.fbx`, used in the example screenshots, is available from the companion source download for this book. The completed project can also be found in the companion source named `Ch09_02DynamicCubeMapping`.

How to do it...

We will begin by creating the necessary HLSL code to generate and consume our cube maps. Generating the cube map will involve creating a new vertex shader (`VS_CubeMap`), geometry shader (`GS_CubeMap`), and pixel shader (`PS_CubeMap`); to consume cube maps, we will update the `PerMaterial` constant buffer and each pixel shader.

1. Firstly, we will update the `PerMaterial` constant buffer in `Shaders\Common.hlsl` to include a flag indicating whether a material is reflective and how reflective it is. This will be used by the pixel shaders.

   ```
   cbuffer PerMaterial : register (b2)
   {...
       bool IsReflective;
       float ReflectionAmount;
   ...};
   ```

   > Remember that HLSL structures are 16-byte aligned.

2. Create a new HLSL source file named `Shaders\CubeMap.hlsl`, and ensure that it has the correct encoding as described in *Chapter 2, Rendering with Direct3D*. Add the following `include` directive to use our existing constant buffers, vertex, and pixel structures:

   ```
   #include "Common.hlsl"
   ```

3. Add the following *per environment map* constant buffer to be updated using the fifth buffer slot, and define the geometry shader input to be the same as the pixel shader input:

   ```
   // Cube map ViewProjections for each face
   cbuffer PerEnvironmentMap : register(b4) {
       float4x4 CubeFaceViewProj[6];
   };
   // Use the PixelShaderInput as GeometryShaderInput
   #define GeometryShaderInput PixelShaderInput
   ```

4. The output from the geometry shader (and therefore, input to our new pixel shader) is exactly the same as the `PixelShaderInput` structure within `Shaders\Common.hlsl`, except that we have added one new property to control the render target (that is, the face of the cube map) used.

```
// Pixel Shader input structure (from Geometry Shader)
struct GS_CubeMapOutput
{   float4 Position : SV_Position;
...SNIP (existing PixelShaderInput structure properties)
    // Allows writing to multiple render targets
    uint RTIndex : SV_RenderTargetArrayIndex;
};
```

5. The new vertex shader is almost the same as the existing one in `Shaders\VS.hlsl`; however, we need to apply the `World` matrix transform on the `Position` property.

```
// Vertex shader cubemap function
GeometryShaderInput VS_CubeMap(VertexShaderInput vertex)
{   GeometryShaderInput result = (GeometryShaderInput)0;
...SNIP
    // Only apply world transform (not WorldViewProjection)
    result.Position = mul(vertex.Position, World);
...SNIP
}
```

6. The new geometry shader is where we use the geometry shader `instance` attribute of Shader Model 5 to execute the shader six times per input primitive (that is, six times per triangle).

```
[maxvertexcount(3)] // Outgoing vertex count (1 triangle)
[instance(6)] // Number of times to execute for each input
void GS_CubeMap(triangle GeometryShaderInput input[3],
    uint instanceId: SV_GSInstanceID,
    inout TriangleStream<GS_CubeMapOutput> stream)
{
    // Output the input triangle using the View/Projection
    // of the cube face identified by instanceId
    float4x4 viewProj = CubeFaceViewProj[instanceId];
    GS_CubeMapOutput output;

    // Assign the render target instance
    // i.e. 0 = +X-face, 1 = -X-face and so on
    output.RTIndex = instanceId;
    // In order to render correctly into a TextureCube we
    // must either:
```

```
        // 1) use a left-handed view/projection; OR
        // 2) use a right-handed view/projection with -1 X-
        //    axis scale
        // Our meshes assume a right-handed coordinate system
        // therefore both cases above require vertex winding
        // to be switched.
        uint3 idx = uint3(0,2,1);
        [unroll]
        for (int v = 0; v < 3; v++)
        {
            // Apply cube face view/projection
            output.Position =
                mul(input[idx[v]].Position, viewProj);
            // Copy other vertex properties as is
            output.WorldPosition = input[idx[v]].WorldPosition;
    ...SNIP
            // Append to the stream
            stream.Append(output);
        }
        stream.RestartStrip();
    }
```

> To achieve the best geometry shader performance, it is critical to try and minimize the amount of data passing in and out of the stage. The `PixelShaderInput` structure used in our recipes includes a number of additional properties for illustrative purposes that should be removed when not needed.

7. Add a new pixel shader for generating a cube map; this is a copy of our Blinn-Phong pixel shader. There are three differences highlighted in the following snippet from the original shader:

```
// Globals for texture sampling
Texture2D Texture0 : register(t0);
TextureCube Reflection : register(t1);
SamplerState Sampler : register(s0);

float4 PS_CubeMap(GS_CubeMapOutput pixel) : SV_Target
{
  // Normalize our vectors
  float3 normal = normalize(pixel.WorldNormal);
  float3 toEye = normalize(pixel.ToCamera);
...SNIP
```

```
    // Calculate reflection (if any)
    if (IsReflective) {
        float3 reflection = reflect(-toEye, normal);
        color = lerp(color, Reflection.Sample(Sampler,
                reflection).rgb, ReflectionAmount);
    }
    // Calculate final alpha value and return
    float alpha = pixel.Diffuse.a * sample.a;
    return float4(color, alpha);
}
```

8. Within each of our existing pixel shaders (for example, `BlinnPhongPS.hlsl`) that will implement reflections, add the highlighted changes (as shown in the preceding code snippet), except for the function signature. This includes the `TextureCube` shader resource and blending of the reflection sample.

9. This completes our HLSL source changes. We will now make the corresponding changes to the C# `PerMaterial` structure, create our `DynamicCubeMap` renderer class, and update our `MeshRenderer` class to use the cube map for reflections.

10. Within the `ConstantBuffers.cs` file, add the `IsReflective` and `ReflectionAmount` properties to the `PerMaterial` structure.

```
[StructLayout(LayoutKind.Sequential, Pack = 1)]
public struct PerMaterial {
...
    public uint IsReflective; //reflective (0 false, 1 true)
    public float ReflectionAmount; // how reflective? 0-1
...
}
```

11. Create a new renderer class descending from `Common.RendererBase` called `DynamicCubeMap`.

```
using SharpDX;
using SharpDX.DXGI;
using SharpDX.Direct3D11;
using Common;
using Buffer = SharpDX.Direct3D11.Buffer;
// Represents a dynamic cubic environment map (cube map)
public class DynamicCubeMap: Common.RendererBase
{
...
}
```

12. Create a new structure for storing the cube face camera view projections.

```
// Represents the camera for a cube face
// Note: the View matrix includes the current position
// Matrix.Transpose(Matrix.Invert(View)).Column4==Position
public struct CubeFaceCamera
{
    public Matrix View;
    public Matrix Projection;
}
```

13. Add the following private and public member fields and constructors to the
    DynamicCubeMap class:

```
// The cubic environment map texture array (6 slices)
Texture2D EnvMap;
// The RTV for all cube map faces (for single pass)
RenderTargetView EnvMapRTV;
// The DSV for all cube map faces (for single pass)
DepthStencilView EnvMapDSV;
// The TextureCube SRV for use by the mesh/renderer
public ShaderResourceView EnvMapSRV;

// The 'per cube map buffer' to be assigned to the geometry
// shader stage when rendering the cubemap. This will
// contain the 6 ViewProjection matrices for the cube map.
public Buffer PerEnvMapBuffer;

// The viewport based on Size x Size
ViewportF Viewport;

// The renderer instance using the cube map reflection
public RendererBase Reflector { get; set; }
// The cameras for each face of the cube
public CubeFaceCamera[] Cameras = new CubeFaceCamera[6];
// The cube map texture size (e.g. 256x256)
public int Size { get; private set; }

public DynamicCubeMap(int size = 256)
    : base()
{   // Set the cube map resolution (e.g. 256 x 256)
    Size = size;
}
```

14. Create an override for `DynamicCubeMap.CreateDeviceDependentResources` with the following code to reset the resources and to retrieve the device reference:

```
RemoveAndDispose(ref EnvMap);
RemoveAndDispose(ref EnvMapSRV);
RemoveAndDispose(ref EnvMapRTV);
RemoveAndDispose(ref EnvMapDSV);
RemoveAndDispose(ref PerEnvMapBuffer);
var device = this.DeviceManager.Direct3DDevice;
```

15. Within the same function, we will first initialize our `texture` array resource. The two important properties that define a resource compatible with the `TextureCube` HLSL shader resource are highlighted in the following code snippet:

```
// Create the cube map TextureCube (array of 6 textures)
var textureDesc = new Texture2DDescription()
{
    Format = Format.R8G8B8A8_UNorm,
    Height = this.Size,
    Width = this.Size,
    ArraySize = 6, // 6-sides of the cube
    BindFlags = BindFlags.ShaderResource |
      BindFlags.RenderTarget,
    OptionFlags = ResourceOptionFlags.GenerateMipMaps |
      ResourceOptionFlags.TextureCube,
    SampleDescription = new SampleDescription(1, 0),
    MipLevels = 0,
    Usage = ResourceUsage.Default,
    CpuAccessFlags = CpuAccessFlags.None,
};
EnvMap = ToDispose(new Texture2D(device, textureDesc));
```

16. Next, we will define the **Shader Resource View** (**SRV**) for the previous resource.

```
// Create the SRV for the texture cube
var descSRV = new ShaderResourceViewDescription();
descSRV.Format = textureDesc.Format;
descSRV.Dimension = SharpDX.Direct3D.ShaderResourceViewDimension.
TextureCube;
descSRV.TextureCube.MostDetailedMip = 0;
descSRV.TextureCube.MipLevels = -1;
EnvMapSRV = ToDispose(new ShaderResourceView(device, EnvMap,
descSRV));
```

17. After that, we will define the **Render Target View** (**RTV**) for our texture cube.

```
// Create the RTVs
var descRTV = new RenderTargetViewDescription();
descRTV.Format = textureDesc.Format;
descRTV.Dimension = RenderTargetViewDimension
  .Texture2DArray;
descRTV.Texture2DArray.MipSlice = 0;
// Single RTV array for single pass rendering
descRTV.Texture2DArray.FirstArraySlice = 0;
descRTV.Texture2DArray.ArraySize = 6;
EnvMapRTV = ToDispose(new RenderTargetView(device, EnvMap,
  descRTV));
```

18. And then, we will create the **Depth Stencil View** (**DSV**) for rendering our cube map.

```
// Create DSVs
using (var depth = new Texture2D(device, new Texture2DDescription
{   Format = Format.D32_Float,
    BindFlags = BindFlags.DepthStencil,
    Height = Size,
    Width = Size,
    Usage = ResourceUsage.Default,
    SampleDescription = new SampleDescription(1, 0),
    CpuAccessFlags = CpuAccessFlags.None,
    MipLevels = 1,
    OptionFlags = ResourceOptionFlags.TextureCube,
    ArraySize = 6 // 6-sides of the cube
}))
{   var descDSV = new DepthStencilViewDescription();
    descDSV.Format = depth.Description.Format;
    descDSV.Dimension = DepthStencilViewDimension
      .Texture2DArray;
    descDSV.Flags = DepthStencilViewFlags.None;
    descDSV.Texture2DArray.MipSlice = 0;
    // Single DSV array for single pass rendering
    descDSV.Texture2DArray.FirstArraySlice = 0;
    descDSV.Texture2DArray.ArraySize = 6;
    EnvMapDSV = ToDispose(new DepthStencilView(device,
      depth, descDSV));
}
```

19. Lastly, we will create the viewport and per environment map buffer.

```
// Create the viewport
Viewport = new Viewport(0, 0, Size, Size);
```

```
// Create the per environment map buffer (to store the 6
// ViewProjection matrices)
PerEnvMapBuffer = ToDispose(new Buffer(device,
    Utilities.SizeOf<Matrix>() * 6, ResourceUsage.Default,
    BindFlags.ConstantBuffer, CpuAccessFlags.None,
    ResourceOptionFlags.None, 0));
```

This completes the initialization of our cube map's Direct3D resources.

20. Still within the `DynamicCubeMap` class, we will create a new public method for updating the current camera positions.

```
// Update camera position for cube faces
public void SetViewPoint(Vector3 camera)
{   // The LookAt targets for view matrices
    var targets = new[] {
        camera + Vector3.UnitX, // +X
        camera - Vector3.UnitX, // -X
        camera + Vector3.UnitY, // +Y
        camera - Vector3.UnitY, // -Y
        camera + Vector3.UnitZ, // +Z
        camera - Vector3.UnitZ  // -Z
    };
    // The "up" vector for view matrices
    var upVectors = new[] {
        Vector3.UnitY, // +X
        Vector3.UnitY, // -X
        -Vector3.UnitZ,// +Y
        +Vector3.UnitZ,// -Y
        Vector3.UnitY, // +Z
        Vector3.UnitY, // -Z
    };
    // Create view and projection matrix for each face
    for (int i = 0; i < 6; i++)
    {
        Cameras[i].View = Matrix.LookAtRH(camera,
            targets[i],
            upVectors[i]) * Matrix.Scaling(-1, 1, 1);
        Cameras[i].Projection = Matrix.PerspectiveFovRH(
            (float)Math.PI * 0.5f, 1.0f, 0.1f, 100.0f);
    }
}
```

> To remain consistent, we have used a right-handed coordinate system for the view. However, the `TextureCube` resource will be a little backwards unless we also scale `-1` along the x axis. We will also need to reverse the vertex winding order (as we have done in the geometry shader `GS_CubeMap`) or switch the culling from back face to front face (or use no culling).

21. For the scene to be rendered in its entirety while generating the cube map, it is necessary to pass through `delegate` that will perform the rendering logic. Therefore, we will not use the `DynamicCubeMap.DoRender` override and instead create a new public function named `UpdateSinglePass`.

```
protected override void DoRender()
{
    throw new NotImplementedException("Use UpdateSinglePass
        instead.");
}
// Update the 6-sides of the cube map using a single pass
// via Geometry shader instancing with the provided context
// renderScene: The method that will render the scene
public void UpdateSinglePass(
    DeviceContext context,
    Action<DeviceContext, Matrix, Matrix, RenderTargetView,
        DepthStencilView, DynamicCubeMap> renderScene)
{
    // Don't render the reflector itself
    if (Reflector != null)
        Reflector.Show = false;

    // Prepare pipeline
    context.OutputMerger.SetRenderTargets(EnvMapDSV,
        EnvMapRTV);
    context.Rasterizer.SetViewport(Viewport);
    // Prepare the view projections
    Matrix[] viewProjections = new Matrix[6];
    for (var i = 0; i < 6; i++)
        viewProjections[i] = Matrix.Transpose(
            Cameras[i].View * Cameras[i].Projection);
    // Update perEnvMapBuffer with the ViewProjections
    context.UpdateSubresource(viewProjections,
        PerEnvMapBuffer);
    // Assign perEnvMapBuffer to the GS stage slot 4
    context.GeometryShader
```

```
                .SetConstantBuffer(4, PerEnvMapBuffer);
        // Render scene using the view, projection, RTV and DSV
        renderScene(context, Cameras[0].View,
          Cameras[0].Projection, EnvMapRTV, EnvMapDSV, this);
        // Unbind the RTV and DSV
        context.OutputMerger.ResetTargets();
        // Prepare the SRV mip levels
        context.GenerateMips(EnvMapSRV);
        // Re-enable the Reflector renderer
        if (Reflector != null)
            Reflector.Show = true;
    }
```

This completes our `DynamicCubeMap` renderer class. Next, we need to update the `MeshRenderer` class to consume `DyanamicCubeMap.EnvMapSRV`.

22. Within `MeshRenderer`, add a new public property for assigning a cube map.

```
public DynamicCubeMap EnvironmentMap { get; set; }
```

23. In the `MeshRenderer.DoRender` method, where the material constant buffer is prepared, add the following code to assign the cube map SRV:

```
...SNIP
// If this mesh has a cube map assigned set
// the material buffer accordingly
if (this.EnvironmentMap != null)
{
    material.IsReflective = 1;
    material.ReflectionAmount = 0.4f;
    context.PixelShader.SetShaderResource(1,
      this.EnvironmentMap.EnvMapSRV);
}

// Update material buffer
context.UpdateSubresource(ref material, PerMaterialBuffer);
...SNIP
```

For our final changes, we'll move over to `D3DApp.cs` where we will compile the `*_CubeMap` shaders, move our rendering logic into a reusable action, and implement threading.

24. We will compile the shaders in `CubeMap.hlsl` within `D3DApp.CreateDeviceDependentResources` as we have done in previous chapters. Compile the shader functions `VS_CubeMap`, `GS_CubeMap`, and `PS_CubeMap` using the `vs_5_0`, `gs_5_0`, and `ps_5_0` shader profiles respectively.

25. We need to perform most of our `DeviceContext` initialization within a `D3DApp.InitializationContext` function. However, we will be calling this for each context before each rendering pass and need to preserve the existing render targets under certain circumstances. In addition, the vertex, pixel, and geometry shaders change depending on whether we are rendering the cube map or the final scene.

```
VertexShader activeVertexShader = null;
GeometryShader activeGeometryShader = null;
PixelShader activePixelShader = null;


protected void InitializeContext(DeviceContext context,
                                 bool updateRenderTarget)
{
...SNIP
    // Set the default vertex shader to run
    context.VertexShader.Set(activeVertexShader);

    // Set the constant buffer for geometry shader stage
    context.GeometryShader.SetConstantBuffer(0,
        perObjectBuffer);
    context.GeometryShader.SetConstantBuffer(1,
        perFrameBuffer);
    // Set the geometry shader
    context.GeometryShader.Set(activeGeometryShader);
...SNIP
    // Set the pixel shader to run
    context.PixelShader.Set(activePixelShader);
...SNIP
// When rendering cube maps don't change the render target
    if (updateRenderTarget)
    {
      // Set viewport
      context.Rasterizer.SetViewport(this.Viewport);
      // Set render targets
      context.OutputMerger.SetTargets(this.DepthStencilView,
          this.RenderTargetView);
    }
}
```

26. Within `D3DApp.Run`, add a new local `List<DynamicCubeMap>` instance to keep track of the available cube maps.

```
// Keep track of list of cube maps
List<DynamicCubeMap> envMaps = new List<DynamicCubeMap>();
```

27. And then, for each mesh that supports reflections, create a new `DynamicCubeMap` instance and initialize.

```
// If MeshRenderer instance is reflective:
var mesh = ...some reflective MeshRenderer instance
var envMap = ToDispose(new DynamicCubeMap(256));
envMap.Reflector = mesh;
envMap.Initialize(this);
m.EnvironmentMap = envMap;
// Add to list of cube maps
envMaps.Add(envMap);
```

28. The bulk of our rendering loop will now be moved into a local anonymous method. In our simple example, this should be located before the start of the rendering loop as shown in the following code snippet:

```
// Action for rendering the entire scene
Action<DeviceContext, Matrix, Matrix, RenderTargetView,
DepthStencilView, DynamicCubeMap> renderScene =
(context, view, projection, rtv, dsv, envMap) =>
{
    // We must initialize the context every time we render
    // the scene as we are changing the state depending on
    // whether we are rendering a cube map or final scene
    InitializeContext(context, false);
    // We always need the immediate context
    var immediateContext = this.DeviceManager.Direct3DDevice
                            .ImmediateContext;
    // Clear depth stencil view
    context.ClearDepthStencilView(dsv,
        DepthStencilClearFlags.Depth |
        DepthStencilClearFlags.Stencil, 1.0f, 0);
    // Clear render target view
    context.ClearRenderTargetView(rtv, background);

    // Create viewProjection matrix
    var viewProjection = Matrix.Multiply(view, projection);

    // Extract camera position from view
    var camPosition = Matrix.Transpose(Matrix.Invert(view))
        .Column4;
    cameraPosition = new Vector3(camPosition.X,
        camPosition.Y, camPosition.Z);
    ...SNIP perform all rendering actions and multithreading
}
```

29. If the current pass of `renderScene` is rendering the environment map, it is necessary to assign the per environment map constant buffer to the geometry shader stage for each deferred context.

```
// If multithreaded
...
// If environment map is being rendered
if (envMap != null)
    renderContext.GeometryShader.SetConstantBuffer(4,
      envMap.PerEnvMapBuffer);
```

30. Finally, we will update our main rendering loop, `RenderLoop.Run(Window, () => { ... })`, to first render each cube map, then render the final scene, as shown in the following code:

```
// Retrieve immediate context
var context = DeviceManager.Direct3DContext;
#region Update environment maps
// Assign the environment map rendering shaders
activeVertexShader = envMapVSShader;
activeGeometryShader = envMapGSShader;
activePixelShader = envMapPSShader;

// Render each environment map
foreach (var envMap in envMaps)
{
  var mesh = envMap.Reflector as MeshRenderer;
  if (mesh != null)
  {
    // Calculate view point for reflector
    var center = Vector3.Transform(
        mesh.Mesh.Extent.Center, mesh.World * worldMatrix);
    envMap.SetViewPoint(new Vector3(center.X, center.Y,
      center.Z));
    // Render envmap in single full render pass using
    // geometry shader instancing.
    envMap.UpdateSinglePass(context, renderScene);
  }
}
#endregion

#region Render final scene
// Reset the vertex, geometry and pixel shader
activeVertexShader = vertexShader;
activeGeometryShader = null;
```

```
activePixelShader = blinnPhongShader;
// Initialize context (also resetting the render targets)
InitializeContext(context, true);
// Render the final scene
renderScene(context, viewMatrix, projectionMatrix,
    RenderTargetView, DepthStencilView, null);
#endregion
```

How it works...

The following screenshot shows the dynamic cube map from this recipe used with seven reflective surfaces. The 100 cubes in the sky are rotating around the y axis, and the cube maps are updated dynamically. The close up of the spheres illustrates how reflections include the reflections on other surfaces:

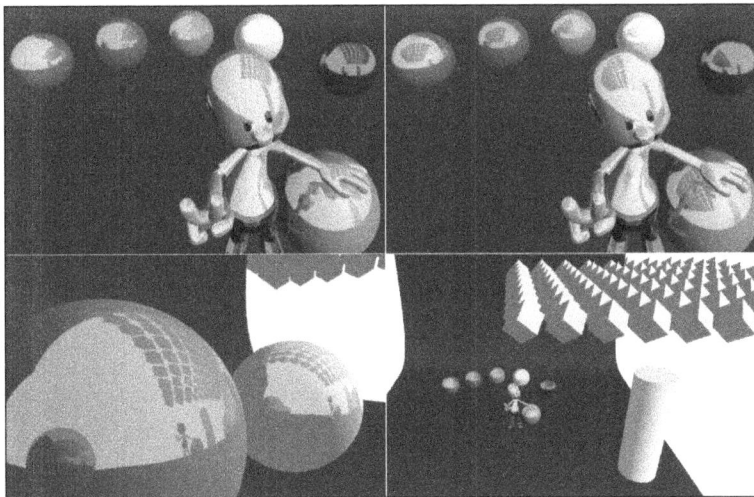

A scene with seven reflective surfaces using cubic environment maps

Rather than rendering the entire scene six times per cube map, we use multiple render targets and the `instance` attribute of the geometry shader to do this in a single render pass in a fraction of the time (approximately three to four times faster). For each triangle output from the vertex shader, the Direct3D pipeline calls the geometry shader six times as per the `instance` attribute. The `SV_GSInstanceID` input semantic contains the zero-based instance ID; this ID is used to index the view/projections that we calculated for each cube face. We indicate which render target to send the fragment to by setting the `SV_RenderTargetArrayIndex` input semantic (`GS_CubeMapOutput.RTIndex` in our example HLSL) to the value of the geometry shader's instance ID.

The following diagram outlines the process within the pipeline:

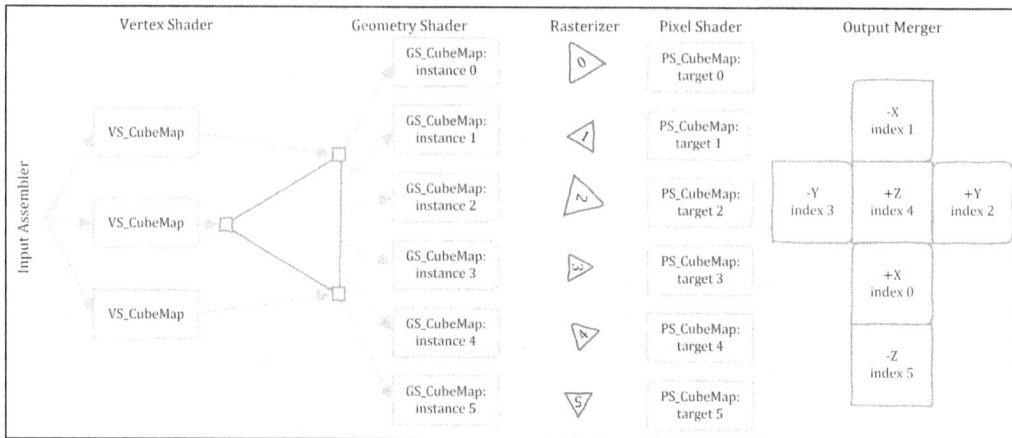

Direct3D pipeline view of cube map generation with geometry shader instancing

To calculate the reflection in our pixel shader, we use the intrinsic HLSL `reflect` function; this takes the camera direction and surface normal to compute a reflection vector. This reflection vector is used to sample the cube from its SRV as shown in the following diagram:

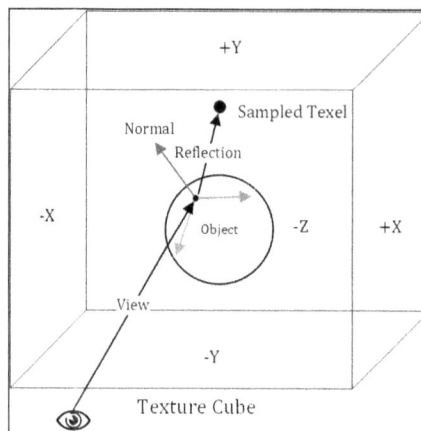

Sampling texture cube using reflection vector (right-handed coordinate system)

The view/projections are calculated for each face by taking the object's center point and creating "look at" view matrices for all the six faces. Because we are using a right-handed coordinate system, it is necessary for us to flip the x axis of the cube map view matrix by scaling the x axis by -1 and reversing the vertex winding order in the geometry shader. By implementing multithreaded deferred contexts, we can improve the performance when there is an increased CPU load or larger numbers of draw calls (for example, more reflective surfaces).

The following graph shows the performance impact of multithreading:

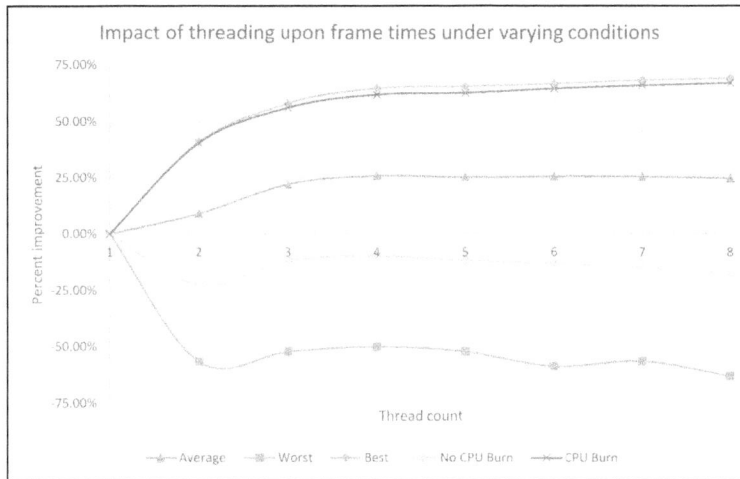

Impact of multithreaded cube map rendering with varying reflective surfaces, scene objects, CPU load, and threads.

The worst case scenario indicates a situation where there are two dynamic cube maps, no CPU load, and only 100 cubes reflecting in the sky. The best case scenario is of three dynamic cube maps with 2,000 matrix operations per mesh and 300 cubes in the sky. The impact of multithreading did not hit a positive result when there was no additional CPU load for 100 or 200 cubes in the sky but did for 300 cubes. It is clear that once there is enough CPU load, multithreaded rendering produces significant performance benefits; however, there are certain cases where it can have a detrimental effect.

There's more...

It is important to note that our implementation does not implement frustum culling or object occlusion. We also do not take into consideration whether or not a face of the cube map will be visible; however, this gets more complicated when you consider the reflections of reflections.

Within the completed companion project for this recipe, any mesh with a name containing `reflector` will have a cube map associated, any mesh name containing `rotate` will be rotated around the *y* axis, and adding a mesh name containing `replicate` will cause the object to be duplicated and arranged in a grid pattern. The same mesh can contain any or all of the three of these key words. There is also an implementation of the six-pass cube map for performance comparison.

Implementing dual paraboloid environment mapping

For this recipe, we extend the geometry shader's instancing approach to create environment maps that were introduced in the previous recipe, *Implementing multithreaded cubic environment mapping*, and generate a dual paraboloid environment map. A **dual paraboloid map** (**DPM**) requires only two render targets instead of the six used in the cube maps, therefore requiring less texture memory. However, there is also no built-in hardware support for sampling a DPM that instead requires a manual implementation of the sampling based on the reflection vector.

Getting ready

We will start with the finished result from the previous recipe, *Implementing multithreaded cubic environment mapping*.

How to do it...

In order to generate the dual paraboloid map, we will apply geometry instancing and fill two render targets. To sample the environment map for reflections, we will implement a new HLSL function that determines the location and the texture (half of the DPM) to sample.

1. We'll begin by creating two new HLSL files: `EnvironmentMap.hlsl` and `DualParaboloidMap.hlsl`. The first of these will include the common HLSL code for use when generating or sampling our environment maps. The second file will include the code necessary to generate our DPM.

2. Within the `EnvironmentMap.hlsl` file, add the reflection texture array and the following constant buffer:

```
// Texture array for Dual Paraboloid map
Texture2DArray Reflection : register(t1);

// Dual Paraboloid Map view and near/far distance
cbuffer PerEnvironmentMap : register(b4)
{
    float4x4 DualMapView; // for sampling
    float NearClip;       // for depth
    float FarClip;        // for depth
};
```

3. Unlike the `TextureCube` texture, there is no built-in support for sampling a paraboloid texture; therefore, we need to implement our own method.

```
float4 SampleEnvMap(SamplerState s, float3 R)
{
    // Transform to the Paraboloid view-space
    R = mul(R, (float3x3)DualMapView);
    float3 texCoord = (float3)0;
    texCoord.xy = (R.xy / (2*(1 + abs(R.z)))) + 0.5f;
    texCoord.y = 1-texCoord.y;

    if (R.z > 0) {
      texCoord.z = 0; // Front half (texture array index 0)
    } else {
      texCoord.z = 1; // Back half (texture array index 1)
    }

    return Reflection.Sample(s, texCoord.xyz);
}
```

4. Within the `DualParaboloidMap.hlsl` file, we add the following `include` directives and structures:

```
#include "Common.hlsl"
#include "EnvironmentMap.hlsl"

// Geometry shader input structure (from Vertex shader)
struct GS_DualMapInput
{
    float4 Position : SV_Position;
...SNIP - same as PixelShaderInput properties

    // Normalized Z for Paraboloid
    float DualMapZ: TEXCOORD4;
};

// Pixel Shader input structure (from Geometry Shader)
struct GS_DualMapOutput
{
    float4 Position : SV_Position;
...SNIP - same as PixelShaderInput properties

    // Normalized Z for Paraboloid
    float DualMapZ: TEXCOORD4;

    // Allows us to write to multiple render targets
    uint RTIndex : SV_RenderTargetArrayIndex;
};
```

5. The new vertex shader is an exact copy of our original vertex shader with the following highlighted changes:

```
GS_DualMapInput VS_DualMap(VertexShaderInput vertex)
{
    GS_DualMapInput result = (GS_DualMapInput)0;
...SNIP vertex skinning
// We use the Paraboloid's view within the
// WorldViewProjection with an Identity matrix for the
// projection.
    result.Position = mul(vertex.Position,
                          WorldViewProjection);
...SNIP set other vertex output properties
// We are relative to the DPM's view, the length of
// result.Position is the distance from Paraboloid's origin
// to result.Position
    float L = length(result.Position); // => for depth
    result.Position = result.Position / L; // normalize
    result.DualMapZ = result.Position.z; // Keep normalized
    // Scale depth to [0, 1]
    result.Position.z = (L - NearClip) / (FarClip - NearClip);
    result.Position.w = 1.0f; // No perspective distortion
    return result;
}
```

6. The instanced geometry shader is very similar to that used in the previous recipe, *Implementing multithreaded dynamic cubic environment mapping*. The differences are highlighted in the following code snippet:

```
[maxvertexcount(3)] // Outgoing vertex count (1 triangle)
[instance(2)] // Number of times to execute for each input
void GS_DualMap(triangle GS_DualMapInput input[3],
    uint instanceId: SV_GSInstanceID,
    inout TriangleStream<GS_DualMapOutput> stream)
{
    // Output the input triangle and calculate whether
    // the vertex is in the +ve or -ve half of the DPM
    GS_DualMapOutput output = (GS_DualMapOutput)0;

    // Assign the render target instance
    // i.e. 0 = front half, 1 = back half
    output.RTIndex = instanceId;

    // Direction (1.0f front, -1.0f back)
    float direction = 1.0f - instanceId*2;
```

```
    // Vertex winding
    uint3 indx = uint3(0,2,1);
    if (direction < 0)
        indx = uint3(0,1,2);

    [unroll]
    // for each input vertex
    for (int v = 0; v < 3; v++)
    {
        // Calculate the projection for the the DPM, taking
        // into consideration which half of the DPM we are
        // rendering.
        float projection = input[indx[v]].DualMapZ * direction
          + 1.0f;
        output.Position.xy = input[indx
          v]].Position.xy / projection;
        output.Position.z = input[indx[v]].Position.z;
        output.Position.w = 1; // no further perspective change
        output.DualMapZ = input[indx[v]].DualMapZ * direction;
        ...SNIP copy other vertex properties unchanged
        // Append to the stream
        stream.Append(output);
    }
    stream.RestartStrip();
}
```

7. Lastly, we will implement our modified pixel shader for generating the DPM.

```
float4 PS_DualMap(GS_DualMapOutput pixel) : SV_Target
{
    // Ignore this pixel if located behind.
    // We add a little additional room to ensure that
    // the two halves of the dual paraboloid meet at the
    // seams.
    clip(pixel.DualMapZ + 0.4f);
... SNIP pixel shader code
}
```

8. The existing pixel shaders will now implement DPM reflections by including the `EnvironmentMap.hlsl` file and using the following snippet:

```
// Calculate reflection (if any)
if (IsReflective) {
    float3 reflection = reflect(-toEye, normal);
    color = lerp(color, SampleEnvMap(Sampler, reflection),
                ReflectionAmount);
}
```

9. This completes our HLSL source code changes. Within our C# project, make a copy of the `DyanamicCubeMap.cs` file from the previous recipe, *Implementing multithreaded cubic environment mapping*, and name it `DualParaboloidMap.cs`.

10. Add the `PerEnvMap` structure and the `DualMapView` property to the new class.

```
public struct PerEnvMap
{
    public Matrix View;
    public float NearClip;
    public float FarClip;
    Vector2 _padding0;
}
public PerEnvMap DualMapView;
```

11. Within the `DualParaboloidMap.CreateDeviceDependentResources` method, change the texture creation so that it has an array size of 2 and is not a texture cube.

```
var textureDesc = new Texture2DDescription()
{
...
    ArraySize = 2, // 2-paraboloids
    OptionFlags = ResourceOptionFlags.GenerateMipMaps,
...
};
EnvMap = ToDispose(new Texture2D(device, textureDesc));
```

12. Next, we need to change the **Shader Resource View** (**SRV**) declaration to use a dimension of `Texture2DArray`.

```
// Create the SRV for the texture cube
var descSRV = new ShaderResourceViewDescription();
descSRV.Format = textureDesc.Format;
descSRV.Dimension = SharpDX.Direct3D
    .ShaderResourceViewDimension.Texture2DArray;
descSRV.Texture2DArray.MostDetailedMip = 0;
descSRV.Texture2DArray.MipLevels = -1;
descSRV.Texture2DArray.FirstArraySlice = 0;
descSRV.Texture2DArray.ArraySize = 2;
```

13. The creation of the **Render Target View** (**RTV**) needs to use a `descRTV. Texture2DArray.ArraySize` instance with a value of two instead of six.

14. The texture resource for the depth stencil will be a regular texture array with an array size of two.

```
using (var depth = new Texture2D(device, new Texture2DDescription
{
...
```

```
        OptionFlags = ResourceOptionFlags.None,
        ArraySize = 2 // 2-sides of the env map
}))
```

15. And the corresponding **Depth Stencil View** (**DSV**) is also initialized with an array size of `two`.

```
descDSV.Texture2DArray.ArraySize = 2;
EnvMapDSV = ToDispose(new DepthStencilView(device, depth,
    descDSV));
```

16. Lastly, the `DualParaboloidMap.PerEnvMapBuffer` property needs to be initialized with the size of the `PerEnvMap` structure.

```
PerEnvMapBuffer = ToDispose(new Buffer(device,
    Utilities.SizeOf<PerEnvMap>(), ResourceUsage.Default,
    BindFlags.ConstantBuffer, CpuAccessFlags.None,
    ResourceOptionFlags.None, 0));
```

17. The `SetViewPoint` method will now be changed to update the `DualParaboloidMap.DualMapView` property as follows:

```
public void SetViewPoint(Vector3 camera)
{
    this.DualMapView.View = Matrix.LookAtRH(camera, camera
      + Vector3.UnitZ Vector3.UnitY);
    this.DualMapView.NearClip = 0.0f;
    this.DualMapView.FarClip = 100.0f;
}
```

18. In order to complete the changes in the `DualParaboloidMap` class, we will change the `UpdateSinglePass` function with the following highlighted changes:

```
public void UpdateSinglePass(DeviceContext context,
  Action<DeviceContext, Matrix, Matrix, RenderTargetView,
  DepthStencilView, DualParaboloidMap> renderScene)
{
...
    context.Rasterizer.SetViewport(Viewport);

    // Update perCubeMap with the ViewProjections
    PerEnvMap pem = this.DualMapView;
    pem.View.Transpose(); // transpose the matrix for HLSL
    context.UpdateSubresource(ref pem, PerEnvMapBuffer);

    // Assign the buffer to the VS and PS stages at slot 4
    context.VertexShader.SetConstantBuffer(4, PerEnvMapBuffer);
    context.PixelShader.SetConstantBuffer(4, PerEnvMapBuffer);
```

```
// Render the scene using the view, projection, RTV and DSV
// Note that we use an identity matrix for the projection!
    renderScene(context, this.DualMapView.View,
      Matrix.Identity, EnvMapRTV, EnvMapDSV, this);
    // Unbind the RTV and DSV
    context.OutputMerger.ResetTargets();
    // Prepare the SRV mip levels
    context.GenerateMips(EnvMapSRV);
...
}
```

This completes the changes to the `DualParaboloidMap` class.

19. Within `MeshRenderer.cs`, change the type for the `EnvironmentMap` property.

```
public DualParaboloidMap EnvironmentMap { get; set; }
```

20. In the `MeshRenderer.DoRender` method, where the `IsReflective` property of the material constant buffer is prepared, make the following highlighted changes:

```
...SNIP
if (this.EnvironmentMap != null)
{
    material.IsReflective = 1;
    material.ReflectionAmount = 0.4f;
    context.PixelShader.SetShaderResource(1,
        this.EnvironmentMap.EnvMapSRV);
    // Assign the per dual map buffer to the PS
    // stage at slot 4
    context.PixelShader.SetConstantBuffer(4,
        this.EnvironmentMap.PerEnvMapBuffer);
}
...SNIP
```

21. Within the `D3DApp.CreateDeviceDependentResources` method, compile the `DualParaboloidMap.hlsl` shaders, namely, `VS_DualMap`, `GS_DualMap`, and `PS_DualMap`, using the `vs_5_0`, `gs_5_0`, and `ps_5_0` shader profiles respectively.

22. Next, change all of the remaining instances of `DynamicCubeMap` to `DualParaboloidMap` throughout the `D3DApp` class.

23. Our last change pertains to multithreaded rendering within the `renderScene` method, and for the thread `Task` delegate, it is necessary to assign the environment map constant buffer to vertex and pixel shaders.

```
// If multithreaded
...
// If we are rendering for an env map we must set the
// per environment map constant buffer.
```

```
if (envMap != null)
{
    renderContext.VertexShader.SetConstantBuffer(4,
        envMap.PerEnvMapBuffer);
    renderContext.PixelShader.SetConstantBuffer(4,
        envMap.PerEnvMapBuffer);
}
```

How it works...

The following screenshot shows the result of using dual paraboloid mapping using a similar scene as used in the previous recipe, *Implementing multithreaded cubic environment mapping*:

Results using the dual paraboloid mapping.

The DPM is generated by first applying the reflective surfaces' view affine transform to the vertices; this differs from the generation of the cubic environment map as there is only one view matrix required, and we can use the existing `WorldViewProjection` constant buffer property. Then, we calculate the distance from the vertex to the origin and prepare the *z* value for the depth buffer for further processing within the geometry shader (to apply the paraboloid projection). The implementation of the `GS_DualMap` geometry shader is similar to creating the cubic environment map; however, we are only generating two instances. As there is only one view, we can simply reverse the direction along the *z* axis for the second copy of each vertex. First, we determine the direction based on the current instance, set the vertex winding order accordingly, and then manually project the vertex onto the paraboloid.

```
// Project the xy based on which half of DPM we are in
float projection = input[indx[v]].DualMapZ * direction + 1.0f;
output.Position.xy = input[indx[v]].Position.xy / projection;
```

Within the `PS_DualMap` pixel shader, we simply skip the current pixel if it has a negative `DualMapZ` property. It may also be necessary to adjust the value slightly to include more pixels in the output; otherwise, you may get gaps along the hemisphere seam, for example, when directly looking down on one of the spheres in the example scene. To sample our DPM, we must take the reflection vector and transform it into the reflective surfaces' view-space, thus adding the `DualMapView` constant buffer property. This allows us to determine the UVW coordinates for the texture lookup. Based on the sign of the reflection's *z* value, we assign half of the dual paraboloid to it. We have separated the `DualMapView` property from the `WorldViewProjection` matrix so that we are able to sample other DPMs for the reflections of reflective surfaces. Compared to a cube map of the same resolution, a DPM requires one-third of the texture memory. The DPM does waste some of this space due to the curved images (the sampled portion is a parabola, as highlighted in the cross section of the following diagram), and as a result, the quality of the DPM is less than that of the cube map:

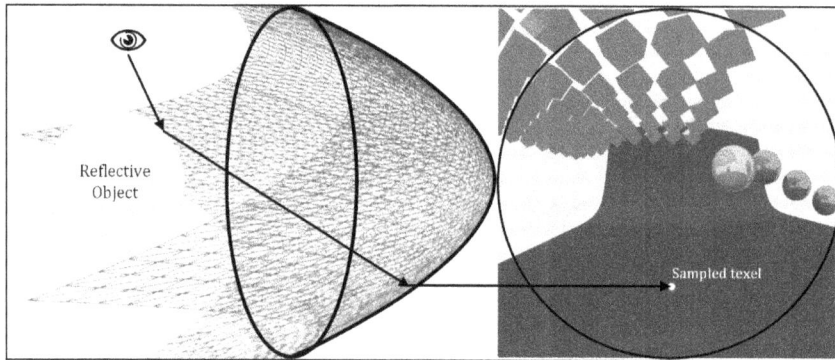

Visualization of sampling from one half of a dual paraboloid map, note the cross section.

Our simple test scene achieves a very similar performance for both dual paraboloid mapping and cubic environment mapping. Before geometry instancing and improvements in hardware support for cube mapping, we would have seen a greater performance difference between dual paraboloid and cube mapping. As it stands, fewer geometry instances are most likely offset by the increased sampling cost within the pixel shader.

The following table lists some pros and cons between the two methods. Note that both implementations presented here require Direct3D 10 or later.

	Dynamic cubic environment mapping	**Dual paraboloid environment mapping**
Pros	▶ Provides good quality and is seamless	▶ Uses less memory (two textures)
	▶ Supports hardware sampling	▶ Uses only up to two copies of a primitive
	▶ It is view independent	▶ It is view independent
Cons	▶ Larger memory use (six textures)	▶ Can be difficult to remove seams
	▶ Uses up to six copies of a primitive	▶ Custom sampling is required
		▶ There may be some distortion and the quality is lower than normal

See also

▶ *Practical Rendering and Computation with Direct3D 11* by *Jason Zink* and Dual Paraboloid Mapping at `http://members.gamedev.net/JasonZ/Paraboloid/DualParaboloidMappingInTheVertexShader.pdf`

▶ *View-independent Environment Maps* by *Wolfgang Heidrich* and *Hans-Peter Seidel (1998)* provides additional information on the underlying mathematics

10
Implementing Deferred Rendering

In this chapter, we will cover the following topics:

- ▸ Filling the G-Buffer
- ▸ Implementing a screen-aligned quad renderer
- ▸ Reading the G-Buffer
- ▸ Adding multiple lights
- ▸ Incorporating multisample anti-aliasing

Introduction

Deferred rendering refers to any rendering technique that defers the calculation of one or more components of a rendered frame to a screen-space operation using information that has been collected during one or more *attribute collection* passes.

One of the benefits of deferred rendering over forward rendering is that it can simplify and improve the performance of implementations using many lights and support better GPU utilization. It does, however, require extra texture memory for a G-Buffer, and can introduce complexities around the implementation of **multisample anti-aliasing** (**MSAA**) and transparencies.

There are a number of deferred rendering techniques with their own pros and cons. We will present a classic deferred rendering technique in this chapter. The same basic concepts can be applied across techniques although the number of rendering passes and/or the information recorded at each stage may vary. Other techniques such as tiled deferred rendering may also make use of compute shaders.

It is important to note that deferred rendering techniques require hardware support for **Multiple Render Targets** (**MRTs**). Direct3D feature level 9.3 supports four simultaneous render targets, while a feature level above 10 supports up to eight.

Filling the G-Buffer

A geometry buffer or G-Buffer is a collection of one or more textures that contain attributes of the current frame necessary to render the final scene at a later stage, usually within screen space. The attributes stored in the G-Buffer might consist of data, such as position, normal vectors, diffuse, and other material properties.

This recipe prepares a G-Buffer that collects the information needed for a **classic deferred rendering** technique (or **deferred shading**); however, the approach can be easily extended to cache information for any deferred technique.

Getting ready

We will need a scene with a number of objects and varying materials. We will use the `MeshRenderer` class and vertex structure from the *Adding surface detail with normal mapping* recipe in *Chapter 6, Adding Surface Detail with Normal and Displacement Mapping*. We will assume that the second and third texture slots in both the loaded meshes and the pixel shaders are used for normal maps and specular intensity maps, respectively.
The example scene used throughout this chapter is the *Sponza Model* made available to the public by Crytek at `http://www.crytek.com/cryengine/cryengine3/downloads`. The FBX version is available with the downloadable source for this chapter and the textures can be retrieved from the previous URL.

The render targets required and the layout of the G-Buffer that we will use in this recipe is shown in the following diagram. We will create three render targets and reconstruct the position data from the depth buffer and screen coordinates. Although we only pack the normals in this recipe, we could also pack everything into a single 128-bit render target.

	32-bit Render Target			
Render Target 0 R8G8B8A8_UNorm	Diffuse R	Diffuse G	Diffuse B	Specular Intensity
Render Target 1 R32_UInt	Normal X		Normal Y	
Render Target 2 R8G8B8A8_UNorm	Emissive R	Emissive G	Emissive B	Specular Power
Depth/Stencil R32G8X24_Typeless	Depth			

Example G-Buffer render target layout representing a single pixel

How to do it...

We will begin by creating a new class to manage rendering to the G-Buffer:

1. Let's create a new C# class, `GBuffer`, descending from `Common.RendererBase` and with the following public and private member fields:

```
// List of render target textures
public List<Texture2D> RTs = new List<Texture2D>();
// List of SRVs to the render targets
public List<ShaderResourceView> SRVs = new
  List<ShaderResourceView>();
// List of RTVs to the render targets
public List<RenderTargetView> RTVs = new
  List<RenderTargetView>();

// The Depth/Stencil buffer
public Texture2D DS0;
public ShaderResourceView DSSRV;
public DepthStencilView DSV;

// Dimensions
int width;
int height;

// The sample description (e.g. for MSAA)
SampleDescription sampleDescription;
// The Render target formats to be used
SharpDX.DXGI.Format[] RTFormats;
```

2. The only constructor initializes the width, height, and the number and format of render targets:

```
public GBuffer(int width, int height, SampleDescription
  sampleDesc, params SharpDX.DXGI.Format[] targetFormats)
{
    System.Diagnostics.Debug.Assert(targetFormats != null
      && targetFormats.Length > 0 && targetFormats.Length <
      9, "Between 1 and 8 render target formats must be
      provided");
    this.width = width;
    this.height = height;
    this.sampleDescription = sampleDesc;
    RTFormats = targetFormats;
}
```

> In Direct3D 11, render target formats are not required to have identical bits-per-element counts, that is a 32-bit render target can be used alongside a 64-bit one.

3. Within the `CreateDeviceDependentResources()` method, first clean up any resources and retrieve the device from the `DeviceManager` property:

```
RemoveAndDispose(ref DSSRV);
RemoveAndDispose(ref DSV);
RemoveAndDispose(ref DS0);

RTs.ForEach(rt => RemoveAndDispose(ref rt));
SRVs.ForEach(srv => RemoveAndDispose(ref srv));
RTVs.ForEach(rtv => RemoveAndDispose(ref rtv));
RTs.Clear();
SRVs.Clear();
RTVs.Clear();

var device = DeviceManager.Direct3DDevice;
```

4. Next, we will prepare the description for the render target textures, and the **Render Target Views** (**RTVs**) and **Shader Resource Views** (**SRVs**) for these textures:

```
// Render Target texture description
var texDesc = new Texture2DDescription();
texDesc.BindFlags = BindFlags.ShaderResource |
  BindFlags.RenderTarget;
texDesc.ArraySize = 1;
texDesc.CpuAccessFlags = CpuAccessFlags.None;
texDesc.Usage = ResourceUsage.Default;
texDesc.Width = width;
texDesc.Height = height;
texDesc.MipLevels = 1;
texDesc.SampleDescription = sampleDescription;

bool isMSAA = sampleDescription.Count > 1;

// Render Target View description
var rtvDesc = new RenderTargetViewDescription();
rtvDesc.Dimension = isMSAA ?
  RenderTargetViewDimension.Texture2DMultisampled :
  RenderTargetViewDimension.Texture2D;
rtvDesc.Texture2D.MipSlice = 0;
```

```
// SRV description for render targets
var srvDesc = new ShaderResourceViewDescription();
srvDesc.Format = SharpDX.DXGI.Format.R8G8B8A8_UNorm;
srvDesc.Dimension = isMSAA ? SharpDX.Direct3D.
  ShaderResourceViewDimension.Texture2DMultisampled :
  SharpDX.Direct3D.ShaderResourceViewDimension.Texture2D;
srvDesc.Texture2D.MipLevels = -1; // auto
srvDesc.Texture2D.MostDetailedMip = 0;
```

> All render targets and the depth stencil buffer used simultaneously for **Multiple Render Targets** (**MRTs**) must use the same underlying dimension (for example, `Texture2D` and `Texture3D`) and have the same value for `SampleDescription`.

5. We now need to create the corresponding texture, RTV and SRV, for each of the specified render target formats of the G-Buffer using the description objects we created previously:

```
// Create Render Target's texture (with SRV and RTV)
foreach (var format in RTFormats)
{
    texDesc.Format = format;
    srvDesc.Format = format;
    rtvDesc.Format = format;

    RTs.Add(ToDispose(new Texture2D(device, texDesc)));
    SRVs.Add(ToDispose(new ShaderResourceView(device,
        RTs.Last(), srvDesc)));
    RTVs.Add(ToDispose(new RenderTargetView(device,
        RTs.Last(), rtvDesc)));
}
```

6. To complete the `CreateDeviceDependentResources` method, we will create the depth stencil texture and **Depth Stencil View** (**DSV**), along with an SRV in order to access the depth buffer from our shaders:

```
// Create Depth/Stencil
texDesc.BindFlags = BindFlags.ShaderResource |
  BindFlags.DepthStencil;
// typeless so we can use as shader resource
texDesc.Format = SharpDX.DXGI.Format.R32G8X24_Typeless;
DS0 = ToDispose(new Texture2D(device, texDesc));
```

```
srvDesc.Format =
  SharpDX.DXGI.Format.R32_Float_X8X24_Typeless;
DSSRV = ToDispose(new ShaderResourceView(device, DS0,
  srvDesc));

// Depth Stencil View
var dsvDesc = new DepthStencilViewDescription();
dsvDesc.Flags = DepthStencilViewFlags.None;
dsvDesc.Dimension = isMSAA ?
  DepthStencilViewDimension.Texture2DMultisampled :
  DepthStencilViewDimension.Texture2D;
dsvDesc.Format = SharpDX.DXGI.Format.D32_Float_S8X24_UInt;
DSV = ToDispose(new DepthStencilView(device, DS0,
  dsvDesc));
```

7. Next, we create methods to bind and unbind the render targets to the pipeline and finally to clear the G-Buffer:

```
// Bind the render targets to the OutputMerger
public void Bind(DeviceContext1 context)
{
    context.OutputMerger.SetTargets(DSV, 0,
      new UnorderedAccessView [0], RTVs.ToArray());
}
// Unbind the render targets
public void Unbind(DeviceContext1 context)
{
    context.OutputMerger.ResetTargets();
}
// Clear the render targets and depth stencil
public void Clear(DeviceContext1 context, Color background)
{
    context.ClearDepthStencilView(DSV,
        DepthStencilClearFlags.Depth |
        DepthStencilClearFlags.Stencil, 1.0f, 0);

    foreach (var rtv in RTVs)
        context.ClearRenderTargetView(rtv, background);
}
```

This completes our generic GBuffer class. With this we can easily create new G-Buffer layouts depending on the specific rendering requirements.

8. Next, we will create the necessary shader code to fill the G-Buffer. First we will update the `PerObject` constant buffer within `Common.hlsl` to include the `View`, `InverseView`, `Projection`, and `InverseProjection` matrices shown as follows:

```
cbuffer PerObject : register(b0)
{
...
    // The view matrix
    float4x4 View;
    // The inverse view matrix
    float4x4 InverseView;
    // The projection matrix
    float4x4 Projection;
    // The inverse of the projection matrix
    float4x4 InverseProjection;
};
```

You may notice that these matrices are not necessarily changing per object, and perhaps should instead be moved to the `PerFrame` constant buffer. However, for simplicity we will continue to keep the affine transform matrices together.

9. We'll now put the logic for filling the G-Buffer into a new HLSL file named `FillGBuffer.hlsl`. Remember to use ANSI encoding as described in *Chapter 2, Rendering with Direct3D*.

10. Define the necessary input texture references, include the `Common.hlsl` HLSL file, and define our pixel shader output structure:

```
Texture2D Texture0 : register(t0);
Texture2D NormalMap: register(t1);
Texture2D SpecularMap: register(t2);
...
SamplerState Sampler : register(s0);

#include "Common.hlsl"

// From Vertex shader to PSFillGBuffer
struct GBufferPixelIn
{
    float4 Position : SV_Position;
    float4 Diffuse : COLOR;
    float2 TextureUV: TEXCOORD0;
    // view-space Normal and tangent
    float3 ViewNormal : TEXCOORD1;
    float4 ViewTangent : TANGENT; // .w handedness from CMO
};
```

```
// Pixel Shader output structure
struct GBufferOutput
{
    float4 Target0 : SV_Target0;
    uint   Target1 : SV_Target1;
    float4 Target2 : SV_Target2;
    // | -----------32 bits-----------|
    // | Diffuse (RGB) | SpecInt (A) | RT0
    // | Packed Normal--------------->| RT1
    // | Emissive (RGB) | SpecPwr (A) | RT2
};
```

11. We will be using view-space for our G-Buffer operations; therefore, we need to provide a new vertex shader that passes the normal and tangent vectors in view-space:

```
GBufferPixelIn VSFillGBuffer(VertexShaderInput vertex)
{
    GBufferPixelIn result = (GBufferPixelIn)0;
    result.Position = mul(vertex.Position,
        WorldViewProjection);
...
    // Transform normal/tangent into world view-space
    result.ViewNormal = mul(vertex.Normal,
        (float3x3)WorldInverseTranspose);
    result.ViewNormal = mul(result.ViewNormal, (float3x3)View);
    result.ViewTangent = float4(mul(vertex.Tangent.xyz,
        (float3x3)WorldInverseTranspose), vertex.Tangent.w);
    result.ViewTangent.xyz = mul(result.ViewTangent.xyz,
        (float3x3)View);
    return result;
}
```

12. We will use the following functions within our pixel shader to encode and pack our normal vectors into the second render target:

```
float2 EncodeAzimuthal(in float3 N)
{
    // Lambert azimuthal equal-area projection
    // with normalized N is equivalent to
    // Spheremap Transform but slightly faster
    //http://aras-p.info/texts/CompactNormalStorage.html
    float f = sqrt(8*N.z+8);
    return N.xy / f + 0.5;
}
```

```
uint PackNormal(in float3 N)
{
    float2 encN = EncodeAzimuthal(N);
    // Pack float2 into uint
    uint result = 0;
    result = f32tof16(encN.x);
    result |= f32tof16(encN.y) << 16;
    return result;
}
```

13. And finally, create the pixel shader to collect and output the attributes to the G-Buffer render targets:

```
GBufferOutput PSFillGBuffer(GBufferPixelIn pixel)
{
    // Normalize our vectors as they are not
    // guaranteed to be unit vectors after interpolation
    float3 normal = normalize(pixel.WorldNormal);
...
    float3 diffuse;
    float specIntensity;

... sample normal, texture and specular intensity

    GBufferOutput result = (GBufferOutput)0;
    result.Target0.xyz = diffuse;
    result.Target0.w = specIntensity;
    result.Target1 = PackNormal(normal);
    result.Target2.xyz = MaterialEmissive.rgb;
    // Specular Power normalized to 0-50 range
    result.Target2.w = MaterialSpecularPower / 50;

    // Return result
    return result;
}
```

14. Within `ConstantBuffers.cs`, we need to update the `PerObject` structure to include the additional matrices we defined in HLSL:

```
public struct PerObject {
...
    public Matrix ViewProjection;
    public Matrix View;
    public Matrix InverseView;
```

```
        public Matrix Projection;
        public Matrix InverseProjection;
// Transpose the matrices so that they are in column-major
// order for HLSL (in memory).
        internal void Transpose()
        {
...
            this.ViewProjection.Transpose();
            this.View.Transpose();
            this.InverseView.Transpose();
            this.Projection.Transpose();
            this.InverseProjection.Transpose();
        }
}
```

15. We are now ready to fill the G-Buffer within the `D3DApp` class. Compile the vertex and pixel shaders given previously within `CreateDeviceDependentResources` and assign each to a new property (for example, `fillGBufferVS` and `fillGBufferPS`).

16. Within the `D3DApp.Run` method, initialize a new `GBuffer` instance as shown in the following snippet:

```
GBuffer gbuffer = ToDispose(
    new GBuffer(this.RenderTargetSize.Width,
        this.RenderTargetSize.Height,
        new SampleDescription(1, 0),
        Format.R8G8B8A8_UNorm,
        Format.R32_UInt,
        Format.R8G8B8A8_UNorm));
gbuffer.Initialize(this);
```

17. Finally, within the render loop we set the vertex and pixel shader to `fillGBufferVS` and `fillGBufferPS`, prepare and bind the render targets of the G-Buffer, perform any rendering, and then restore the previous render targets:

```
...
context.VertexShader.Set(fillGBufferVS);
context.PixelShader.Set(fillGBufferPS);
gbuffer.Clear(context, new Color(0, 0, 0, 0));
gbuffer.Bind(context);

meshes.ForEach((m) =>
{
```

```
...
    perObject.View = viewMatrix;
    perObject.InverseView = Matrix.Invert(viewMatrix);
    perObject.Projection = projectionMatrix;
    perObject.InverseProjection = Matrix.Invert(projectionMatrix);
...
    m.Render();
}
gbuffer.Unbind(context);
// Optionally restore previous render targets
context.OutputMerger.SetRenderTargets(this.DepthStencilView
  , this.RenderTargetView);

... use G-Buffer for screen-space rendering
```

The following image shows the resulting G-Buffer contents:

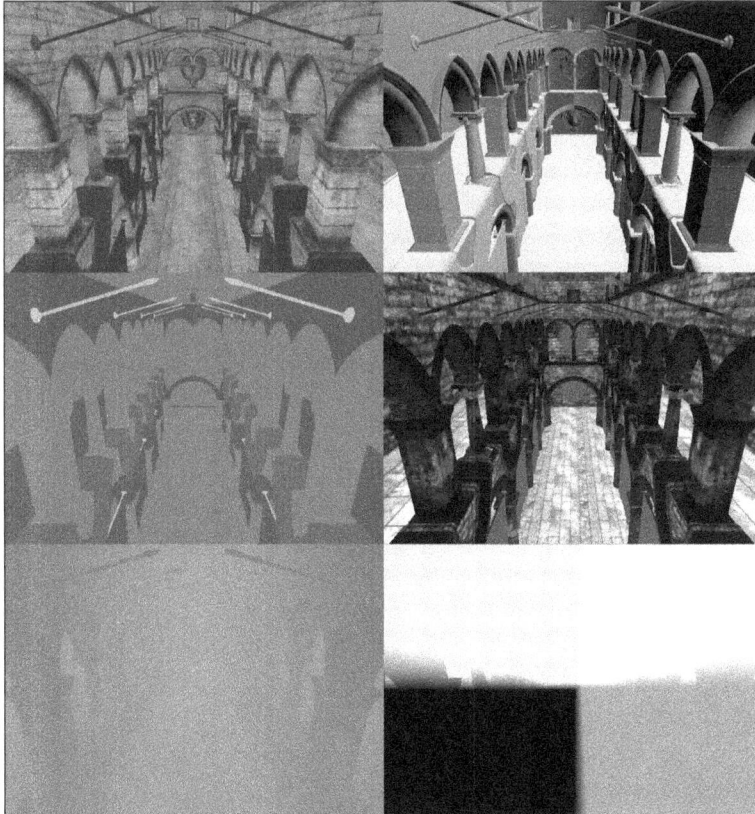

G-Buffer contents from top-left: diffuse/albedo, view-space normals, specular power, specular intensity, depth, and lastly view-space positions reconstructed from depth and screen coordinates (center is 0,0,0 or black).

How it works...

The `GBuffer` class is used to initialize a new render target for each DXGI format that is passed to the constructor. These render target textures are created with both the `BindFlags.ShaderResource` and `BindFlags.RenderTarget` binding flags specified, allowing them to be used as RTVs for our `PSFillGBuffer` pixel shader and also as SRVs for retrieving the G-Buffer attributes in our future deferred shaders.

This means that in our textures we can only use DXGI formats that are compatible with both RTVs and SRVs. For example, Direct3D 11.1 compatible hardware can optionally support the `SharpDX.DXGI.Format.R32G32B32_Float` format for render targets, whereas they must support the `SharpDX.DXGI.Format.R32G32B32A32_Float` format.

To check the format support at runtime, use the `Device.CheckFormatSupport` function, as shown in the following example:

```
FormatSupport fs = device.CheckFormatSupport(
    SharpDX.DXGI.Format.R32G32B32_Float);
if ((fs & FormatSupport.RenderTarget) ==
    FormatSupport.RenderTarget)
{
... format is supported for render targets
}
```

We also create a depth stencil buffer for the G-Buffer, using a `Typeless` format of `SharpDX.DXGI.Format.R32G8X24_Typeless` for the underlying texture, so that it can be used with both a DSV and an SRV. For the SRV, we then use `SharpDX.DXGI.Format.R32_Float_X8X24_Typeless` making the first 32 bits available within our shader while the remaining 32 bits are unused. The DSV uses a format of `SharpDX.DXGI.Format.D32_Float_S8X24_UInt`, utilizing the first 32 bits as the depth buffer, the next 8 bits as the stencil and leaving the remaining 24 bits unused. We have added the `View`, `InverseView`, `Projection`, and `InverseProjection` affine transform matrices to the `PerObject` structure so we can transform between view-space and world-space, and clip-space and view-space.

When we read the G-Buffer attributes again, we will be reconstructing the position into view-space. Rather than applying a transformation to bring the position to world space for lighting calculations, it is more efficient to leave them in view-space. This is why we have also transformed the normal and tangent vectors into view-space. It doesn't matter in what space the calculations are performed but generally, you want to do lighting in the space that requires the least amount of transformations and/or calculations.

For our `PSFillGBuffer` pixel shader, we have described the output structure `GBufferOutput` using the `SV_Target` output semantic on each property to control which render target is filled, using `SV_Target0` for the first render target, `SV_Target1` for the second, and so on up to a maximum of eight targets. The pixel shader performs standard operations, such as normal mapping and texture sampling, and then assigns the attributes to the appropriate render target property in the `GBufferOutput` structure.

In this recipe, we are encoding our normal vector so that we can reconstruct the Z component from the X and Y components, giving a higher precision for the same amount of space in the G-Buffer. There are a number of methods for compacting normal vectors. We have used an approach called **Lambert azimuthal equal-area projection** (**LAEAP**) that when used with normalized vectors is equivalent to sphere map transformations except with a slightly lower computing cost (*Compact Normal Storage for Small G-Buffers, Pranckevičius, 2009*). LAEAP is an azimuthal map projection commonly used in cartography for mapping the surface of a sphere to a flat disc; the projection and its inverse are shown in the following formula. As with other sphere map transformations, the direction of Z is preserved after encoding/decoding.

$$(X, Y) = \left(\sqrt{\frac{2}{1-z}} x, \sqrt{\frac{2}{1-z}} y \right) \qquad (x, y, z) = \left(\sqrt{1 - \frac{X^2 + Y^2}{4}} X, \sqrt{1 - \frac{X^2 + Y^2}{4}} Y, -1 + \frac{X^2 + Y^2}{2} \right)$$

Formula to project the normalized vector (x,y,z) of a sphere to (X,Y) on a plane and its inverse using Lambert azimuthal equal-area projection.

In addition to encoding our normal, we are then packing the encoded X and Y components into `uint`. Packing the encoded X and Y of the normal into `uint` is not required or even optimal, as we could easily use `SharpDX.DXGI.Format.R16G16_UNorm` for `SV_Target1` to store the `float2` directly. However, for demonstrative purposes, we have copied the X and Y components into the low and high bits of a `SharpDX.DXGI.Format.R32_UInt` texture using the `f32tof16` intrinsic HLSL function and bit shifting. This is a common method to pack as much information into the smallest G-Buffer possible. Using a similar technique, we could instead use a R32G32B32A32 format render target to pack our entire G-Buffer into a single render target.

You may have noticed that we are not outputting the position into the G-Buffer. In order to store the position with full precision, we would require 96 bits (3 x 32-bit floats), which on some hardware would require the use of a 128-bit texture (or a number of additional render targets). We could reduce the precision of the position; however, this may also introduce visual artifacts. Instead, with modern graphics pipelines, it is possible to read directly from the depth buffer. By using the depth buffer to reconstruct the position, we are able to save on bandwidth, one of the key limiting factors of modern graphics hardware.

We must also consider that because GPUs often handle the depth/stencil differently to other render targets (for example, hierarchical-Z/Hi-Z and compression), it may be worth using a dedicated depth texture in the G-Buffer instead of the depth/stencil, especially if you want to continue using the depth buffer later on. On modern hardware, we could use a single 128-bit render target to store our entire G-Buffer including depth.

There's more...

It is important to realize that there is no hard and fast rule as to how and what is stored within a G-Buffer (for example, we could also utilize unordered access views), or even how to implement deferred rendering. There are a range of deferred rendering approaches and alternatives, such as light prepass, tiled deferred rendering, light indexed deferred rendering, tile-based forward rendering, Forward+ and so on.

▶ Refer to the *Reading the G-Buffer* recipe to read the G-Buffer and reconstruct the position from depth

▶ *Compact Normal Storage for Small G-Buffers* at `http://aras-p.info/texts/CompactNormalStorage.html`

▶ *Inline format conversion reference* at `http://msdn.microsoft.com/en-us/library/windows/desktop/ff728753(v=vs.85).aspx`

▶ *Hardware support for Direct3D 10Level9 Formats* at `http://msdn.microsoft.com/en-us/library/windows/desktop/ff471324(v=vs.85).aspx`

▶ *Hardware support for Direct3D 11.1 Formats* at `http://msdn.microsoft.com/en-us/library/windows/desktop/hh404483(v=vs.85).aspx`

▶ *Interesting links on tiled forward shading techniques* at `http://aras-p.info/blog/2012/03/27/tiled-forward-shading-links/`

Implementing a screen-aligned quad renderer

Screen-aligned quads, also known as fullscreen quads, are a staple of deferred rendering techniques. They have traditionally been used to perform a range of screen-space operations, such as applying ambient lighting or implementing screen space ambient occlusion (SSAO), and provide a convenient method of addressing information within the G-Buffer.

Although image filtering and computation can be performed within compute shaders, the final result still needs to be presented to the screen, and this is usually through a screen-aligned quad. This recipe can be used where screen-space operations are required or visualization of textures is necessary.

How to do it...

We will begin by creating the vertex shader and its input and output structures. We'll then move onto creating the C# renderer class `ScreenAlignedQuadRenderer`:

1. Begin with a new HLSL shader file, `SAQuad.hlsl`, including `Common.hlsl` for the `PerObject` constant buffer matrices and adding the following new structures:

```
#include "Common.hlsl"

struct VertexIn
{
    float4 Position : SV_Position;
```

```
};

struct PixelIn
{
    float4 Position : SV_Position;
    float2 UV : TEXCOORD0;
};
```

2. Add a new vertex shader passing through the input positions unchanged, and calculate the UV coordinates from these:

```
// Screen-Aligned Quad: vertex shader main function
PixelIn VSMain(VertexIn vertex)
{
    PixelIn result = (PixelIn)0;

    // The input quad is expected in device coordinates
    // (i.e. 0,0 is center of screen, -1,1 top left, 1,-1
    // bottom right). Therefore no transformation!
    result.Position = vertex.Position;
    result.Position.w = 1.0f;

    // The UV coordinates are top-left 0,0 bottom-right 1,1
    result.UV.x = result.Position.x * 0.5 + 0.5;
    result.UV.y = result.Position.y * -0.5 + 0.5;

    return result;
}
```

3. Create a new C# class, `ScrenAlignedQuadRenderer`, descending from `Common.BaseRenderer`, and add the following private and public members and default constructor:

```
public class ScreenAlignedQuadRenderer :
  Common.RendererBase
{
    // The vertex shader
    VertexShader vertexShader;
    // The vertex layout for the IA
    InputLayout vertexLayout;
    // The vertex buffer
    Buffer vertexBuffer;
    // The vertex buffer binding
    VertexBufferBinding vertexBinding;
```

```
            // Pixel shader to assign to use
            public PixelShader Shader { get; set; }
            // Shader resources to bind to pixel shader
            public ShaderResourceView[] ShaderResources {get; set;}

            /// <summary>
            /// Default constructor
            /// </summary>
            public ScreenAlignedQuadRenderer()
            {
            }
    ...
    }
```

4. Within the overridden function `ScreenAlignedQuadRenderer.`
   `CreateDeviceDependentResources`, initialize the device resources
   as shown in the following snippet:

```
RemoveAndDispose(ref vertexShader);
RemoveAndDispose(ref vertexLayout);
RemoveAndDispose(ref vertexBuffer);

// Retrieve our SharpDX.Direct3D11.Device1 instance
var device = DeviceManager.Direct3DDevice;

ShaderFlags shaderFlags = ShaderFlags.None;
#if DEBUG
shaderFlags = ShaderFlags.Debug |
  ShaderFlags.SkipOptimization;
#endif
// Use our HLSL file include handler to resolve #include
  directives in the HLSL source
var includeHandler = new
  HLSLFileIncludeHandler(System.IO.Path.Combine
  (System.IO.Path.GetDirectoryName(System.Reflection.
  Assembly.GetEntryAssembly().Location), "Shaders"));

// Compile and create the vertex shader
using (var vertexShaderBytecode =
  ShaderBytecode.CompileFromFile(@"Shaders\SAQuad.hlsl",
    "VSMain", "vs_5_0", shaderFlags, EffectFlags.None, null,
    includeHandler))
```

```
{
    vertexShader = ToDispose(new VertexShader(device,
      vertexShaderBytecode));
    // Layout from VertexShader input signature
    vertexLayout = ToDispose(new InputLayout(device,

      ShaderSignature.GetInputSignature
      (vertexShaderBytecode),
    new[]
    {
        // "SV_Position"=vertex coordinate
        new InputElement("SV_Position", 0, Format.R32G32B32_Float,
0, 0),
    }));

    // Create vertex buffer
    vertexBuffer = ToDispose(Buffer.Create(device,
      BindFlags.VertexBuffer, new Vector3[] {
        /*  Position in normalized device coords */
        new Vector3(-1.0f, -1.0f, -1.0f),
        new Vector3(-1.0f, 1.0f, -1.0f),
        new Vector3(1.0f, -1.0f, -1.0f),
        new Vector3(1.0f, 1.0f, -1.0f),
    }));
    vertexBinding = new VertexBufferBinding(vertexBuffer,
      Utilities.SizeOf<Vector3>(), 0);
    // Triangle strip:
    // v1    v3
    // |\    |
    // | \ B|
    // | A\ |
    // |   \|
    // v0    v2
}
```

5. And finally, within protected override `void DoRender`, with the provided pixel shader and SRVs, draw the screen-aligned quad vertices:

```
var context = this.DeviceManager.Direct3DContext;
// Retrieve the existing shader and IA settings
using(var oldVertexLayout = context.InputAssembler.InputLayout)
using(var oldPixelShader = context.PixelShader.Get())
using(var oldVertexShader = context.VertexShader.Get())
{
```

```
            // Set pixel shader
            if (ShaderResources != null && ShaderResources.Length >
              0 && !ShaderResources[0].IsDisposed)
            {
                context.PixelShader.SetShaderResources(0,
                  ShaderResources);
            }
            // Set a default pixel shader
            if (Shader != null)
            {
                context.PixelShader.Set(Shader);
            }
            // Set vertex shader
            context.VertexShader.Set(vertexShader);

            // Update vertex layout to use
            context.InputAssembler.InputLayout = vertexLayout;

            // Tell the IA we are using a triangle strip
            context.InputAssembler.PrimitiveTopology =
                SharpDX.Direct3D.PrimitiveTopology.TriangleStrip;
            // Pass in the vertices (note: only 4 vertices)
            context.InputAssembler.SetVertexBuffers(0,
                vertexBinding);
            // Draw the 4 vertices that make up the triangle strip
            context.Draw(4, 0);

            // Unbind pixel shader resources
            if (ShaderResources != null && ShaderResources.Length >
                0)
            {
                context.PixelShader.SetShaderResources(0, new
                    ShaderResourceView[ShaderResources.Length]);
            }
            // Restore previous shader and IA settings
            context.PixelShader.Set(oldPixelShader);
            context.VertexShader.Set(oldVertexShader);
            context.InputAssembler.InputLayout = oldVertexLayout;
        }
```

This completes our `ScreenAlignedQuadRenderer` class.

How it works...

By using normalized device coordinates as the position of the input vertices, we can generate the UV coordinates within the vertex shader. Because the positions are already normalized device coordinates, there is also no need to apply any transformations. The following diagram shows the screen-aligned quad triangle-strip layout, and coordinates. In this recipe, we have used a Z value of -1.0f to represent the far clip plane. In a left-handed coordinate system, this would need to be 1.0f.

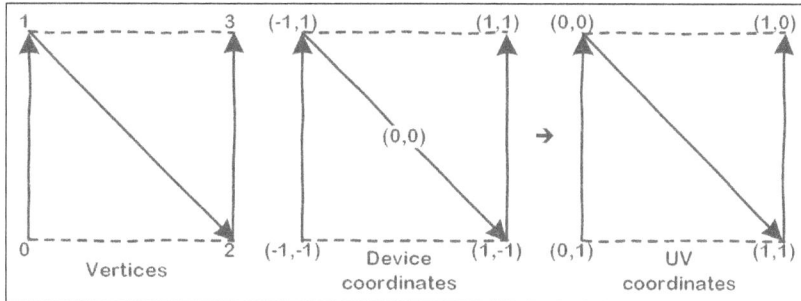

Screen-aligned Quad triangle-strip, positions in device coordinates, and generated UV texture coordinates

The DoRender method first backs up the current context state properties that are to be modified, then binds the provided SRVs to the pixel shader, sets the active pixel and vertex shader, and draws the four vertices of the quad's triangle strip. Finally, we restore the previous device context state so as to not interfere with any other renderers.

There's more...

The SV_Position input semantic of the PixelIn.Position property gives us the screen coordinates in pixels, for example, with a viewport of 640 x 480, this gives an X value in the range of 0-639 and a Y value in the range of 0-479. Assuming the texture is the same size as the viewport, this allows us to use the Texture2D.Load function to retrieve the SRV contents, as shown in the following snippet.

```
Texture2D<float4> Texture0 : register(t0);
float4 PSMain(PixelIn input) : SV_Target
{
    int3 screenPos = int3(pixel.Position.xy, 0);
    return Texture0.Load(screenPos);
}
```

The above pixel shader effectively copies the contents of Texture0 into the current RTV. Although we haven't used the UV coordinates above, for flexibility we will keep these properties in the PixelIn structure.

In order to render a multisampled input SRV to a MSAA render target, we can use the `pixel.Position` property along with the pixel shader `SV_SampleIndex` input semantic to sample all the source samples without any loops. This effectively tells the pipeline to run the pixel shader once for each sample rather than once for each pixel (that is, for an MSAA sample count of four, it runs the pixel shader four times instead of once). The following code snippet shows what this pixel shader might look like:

```
Texture2DMS<float4> TextureMS0 : register(t0);
float4 PSMainMultisample(PixelIn input,
    uint sampleIndex: SV_SampleIndex) : SV_Target
{
    int2 screenPos = int2(input.Position.xy);
    return TextureMS0.Load(screenPos, sampleIndex);
}
```

See also

▶ The screen-aligned quad can be useful to preview the results of the image processing recipes in *Chapter 7*, *Performing Image Processing Techniques*

▶ We also make use of this screen-aligned quad throughout the remainder of this chapter

▶ We use the multisampled anti-aliasing pixel shader shown here in the *Incorporating multisample anti-aliasing* recipe later in this chapter

Reading the G-Buffer

In this recipe, we will look at the HLSL shader code necessary to read from the G-Buffer's resources. We will then use the screen-aligned quad to implement a debug pixel shader for displaying information from the G-Buffer to screen.

Getting ready

We will follow on from where we left off with *Filling the G-Buffer* using the same G-Buffer layout as described in that recipe, and make use of the screen-aligned quad from *Implementing a screen-aligned quad renderer*.

How to do it...

First let's begin by outlining the HLSL code necessary to extract the attributes from the G-Buffer.

1. We'll start by defining a structure to store the loaded G-Buffer attributes in, as shown in the following HLSL code snippet:

```
// Structure for holding loaded G-Buffer attributes
struct GBufferAttributes
{
    float3 Position;
    float3 Normal;
    float3 Diffuse;
    float SpecularInt; // specular intensity
    float3 Emissive;
    float SpecularPower;
};
// Screen-aligned Quad PixelIn
struct PixelIn
{
    float4 Position : SV_Position;
    float2 UV : TEXCOORD0;
};
```

2. In order to unpack the normal, we will require the following functions:

```
float3 DecodeAzimuthal(in float2 enc)
{
    // Unproject Lambert azimuthal equal-area projection
    // http://aras-p.info/texts/CompactNormalStorage.html
    float2 fenc = enc*4-2;
    float f = dot(fenc,fenc);
    float g = sqrt(1-f/4);
    float3 n;
    n.xy = fenc*g;
    n.z = 1-f/2;
    return n;
}
float3 UnpackNormal(in uint packedN)
{
    // Unpack uint to float2
    float2 unpack;
    unpack.x = f16tof32(packedN);
    unpack.y = f16tof32(packedN >> 16);
    // Decode azimuthal (unproject)
    return DecodeAzimuthal(unpack);
}
```

3. The following function can then be called whenever we need to access the attributes of the G-Buffer:

```
void ExtractGBufferAttributes(in PixelIn pixel,
                             in Texture2D<float4> t0,
                             in Texture2D<uint> t1,
                             in Texture2D<float4> t2,
                             in Texture2D<float> t3,
                             out GBufferAttributes attrs)
{
    int3 screenPos = int3(pixel.Position.xy, 0);

    // Load diffuse RGB
    attrs.Diffuse = t0.Load(screenPos).xyz;
    // Specular Intensity
    attrs.SpecularInt = t0.Load(screenPos).w;
    // Unpack and decode the normal
    attrs.Normal = UnpackNormal(t1.Load(screenPos));
    // Retrieve the emissive light
    attrs.Emissive = t2.Load(screenPos).xyz;
    // Load the specular power and rescale to 0-50
    attrs.SpecularPower = t2.Load(screenPos).w * 50;
    // Retrieve non-linear depth
    float depth = t3.Load(screenPos);

    // Reconstruct the view-space position from viewport
    // position and depth
    // Convert UV coords to normalized device coordinates
    float x = pixel.UV.x * 2 - 1;
    float y = (1 - pixel.UV.y) * 2 - 1;
    // Unproject -> transform by inverse projection
    float4 posVS = mul(float4(x, y, depth, 1.0f),
        InverseProjection);
    // Perspective divide to get final view-space position
    attrs.Position = posVS.xyz / posVS.w;
}
```

4. Assuming the above structures and functions are now within an HLSL file, `GBuffer.hlsl`, we can define a pixel shader to be used with the screen-aligned quad to output the view-space normals as follows:

```
#include "Common.hlsl"
#include "GBuffer.hlsl"
// G-Buffer resources
```

```
Texture2D<float4> Texture0 : register(t0);
Texture2D<uint> Texture1 : register(t1);
Texture2D<float4> Texture2 : register(t2);
Texture2D<float> TextureDepth : register(t3);
// Render normals
float4 PS_GBufferNormal(PixelIn pixel) : SV_Target
{
    GBufferAttributes attrs;
    ExtractGBufferAttributes(pixel,
        Texture0, Texture1,
        Texture2, TextureDepth,
        attrs);
    return float4(attrs.Normal, 1);
}
```

5. Putting it all together within our `D3DApp` class in C# would look something like the following code snippet:

```
PixelShader gBufferNormalPS = ...;
ScreenAlignedQuad saQuad = new ScreenAlignedQuad();
saQuad.Initialize(this);
GBuffer gbuffer = ...;
gbuffer.Initialize(this);
// Assign G-Buffer resources to saQuad including depth
saQuad.ShaderResources = gbuffer.SRVs.ToArray()
    .Concat(new[] { gbuffer.DSSRV }).ToArray();
...
// Rendering loop
... Fill the G-Buffer
gbuffer.Unbind(context);


// Restore previous render targets
context.OutputMerger.SetRenderTargets(this.DepthStencilView,
this.RenderTargetView);
// Update the PerObject constant buffer
var perObject = new ConstantBuffers.PerObject();
...
perObject.View = viewMatrix;
perObject.InverseView = Matrix.Invert(viewMatrix);
perObject.Projection = projectionMatrix;
perObject.InverseProjection = Matrix.Invert(
    projectionMatrix);
```

```
        perObject.Transpose();
        context.UpdateSubresource(ref perObject, perObjectBuffer);

        context.PixelShader.SetConstantBuffer(0, perObjectBuffer);

        saQuad.Shader = gBufferNormalPS;
        saQuad.Render();
```

The result of running the above code will be similar to that shown in the top-right image of the G-Buffer contents from *Filling the G-Buffer*.

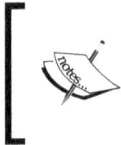

> There is an obvious difference between rendering a debug view of world-space and view-space normals. If you use view-space normals and rotate the camera, the color of the rendered normals will change, whereas world-space normals will remain static regardless of camera rotation.

How it works...

The C# render loop simply fills the G-Buffer and then renders a debug view of the normals by assigning the G-Buffer resources to a `ScreenAlignedQuadRenderer` instance along with our debug pixel shader. To make the additional matrices available within the pixel shader, we have bound `perObjectBuffer` to the first constant buffer slot of the pixel shader stage.

Retrieving the information from the G-Buffer within the pixel shader is quite self-explanatory. The pixel shader calls the `ExtractGBufferAttributes` HLSL function, passing in the textures to load the attributes from. When working with the G-Buffer, we generally have a one-to-one relationship between the rendered pixel and the value retrieved from the G-Buffer. Therefore we can use the `SV_Position` input semantic of the `PixelIn` structure to load the appropriate information from the provided shader resources using the `Texture2D.Load` function, bypassing the need to provide a sampler.

Unpacking the normal involves retrieving the low and high bits of the normal sample with bit shifting and the `f16tof32` HLSL intrinsic function. We then decode the azimuthal projected coordinate using the inverse of the Lambert azimuthal equal-area projection described in *Filling the G-Buffer*.

Reconstructing the position from depth involves a little bit more work. We do this by calculating the projected position. The X and Y values are derived from `pixel.UV` and using the existing non-linear depth sample as Z. We can then simply transform the position with the inverse of the projection matrix (the `PerObject.InverseProjection` matrix), and then apply the perspective divide to calculate our final view-space position.

See also

- ► The previous recipe *Implementing a screen-aligned quad renderer* includes more information about the use of the `SV_Position` input semantic

- ► For more in-depth details and examples of other ways in which you can calculate the position from non-linear and linear depth, see `http://mynameismjp.wordpress.com/2009/03/10/reconstructing-position-from-depth/` and `http://mynameismjp.wordpress.com/2010/09/05/position-from-depth-3/`

Adding multiple lights

In this recipe, we will implement a lighting pass that reads in the G-Buffer attributes while processing each light. The lights will be rendered using a light volume, where appropriate, in order to process only those pixels that lie within the bounds of the light. By utilizing an additive blend state, we can accumulate the light contribution for each light. When rendering many lights, it becomes important that we are only performing the expensive lighting operations on pixels that are actually affected by the current light. By implementing light volumes that approximate the light's range, shape, and attenuation, we can improve performance by utilizing the culling and clipping features of the graphics pipeline to limit the operations to pixels that require them.

A point light represents a light positioned in space with a limited range, and emits light equally in all directions. With this type of light, we are able to easily represent its area of effect with a bounding sphere, using the light position and range to translate and scale the sphere, accordingly. Our recipe will accept a mesh to be used for this purpose; this could be a simple box, sphere, or any other mesh.

Ambient and directional lights are both global lights that are rendered using a screen-aligned quad. The difference between the two is that the ambient light does not have a direction and, therefore, can be applied directly to the diffuse albedo stored in the G-Buffer without computing the angles between the light, surface, and eye, or calculating specular highlights.

Getting ready

We will make use of the HLSL functions we created in the previous recipe *Reading the G-Buffer*, along with the screen-aligned quad implementation.

How to do it...

We'll begin by creating the HLSL shaders that will read the G-Buffer and output the contribution of light based on a simple Blinn-Phong lighting model.

1. Create a new HLSL file named Lights.hlsl and add the G-Buffer texture references and functions that we created in the previous recipe to read the G-Buffer attributes.

2. Add the following additional HLSL structures:

```
struct LightStruct
{
    float3 Direction;
    uint Type; // 0=Ambient, 1=Direction, 2=Point
    float3 Position;
    float Range;
    float3 Color;
};
cbuffer PerLight : register(b4)
{
    LightStruct LightParams;
};
struct PixelIn // Same as SA Quad
{
    float4 Position : SV_Position;
    float2 UV : TEXCOORD0;
};
```

3. We need a new simple vertex shader that accepts the default vertex structure for rendering meshes, and outputs only the position and a UV coordinate based upon the final normalized device coordinate. This shader will be used to render any light volume meshes:

```
PixelIn VSLight(VertexShaderInput vertex)
{
    PixelIn result = (PixelIn)0;
    vertex.Position.w = 1.0f;
    result.Position = mul(vertex.Position,
      WorldViewProjection);
    // Determine UV from device coords
    result.UV.xy = result.Position.xy / result.Position.w;
    // The UV coords: top-left [0,0] bottom-right [1,1]
    result.UV.x = result.UV.x * 0.5 + 0.5;
    result.UV.y = result.UV.y * -0.5 + 0.5;

    return result;
}
```

4. As we will be supporting multiple light types with multiple pixel shaders we will split our light calculations into the following two functions. The first calculates the final light contribution from the lighting inputs and G-Buffer attributes. The second will prepare the light inputs: to eye vector, to light vector, half vector for Blinn-Phong, distance, and the light attenuation factor:

```
// Basic Lambert and BlinnPhong light contribution
float3 LightContribution(GBufferAttributes attrs, float3 V,
    float3 L, float3 H, float3 D, float attenuation)
{
    float NdotL = saturate(dot(attrs.Normal, L));
    if (NdotL <= 0)
        discard; // discard as no impact
    float NdotH = saturate(dot(attrs.Normal, H));

    // Lambert diffuse
    float3 diffuse = NdotL * LightParams.Color *
        attrs.Diffuse;
    // BlinnPhong specular term
    float specPower = max(attrs.SpecularPower,0.00001f);
    float3 specular = pow(NdotH, specPower) *
        attrs.SpecularInt * LightParams.Color;

    return (diffuse + specular) * attenuation +
        attrs.Emissive;
}
// Prepares the LightContribution inputs
void PrepareLightInputs(in float3 camera,
    in float3 position, in float3 N, in LightStruct light,
    out float3 V, out float3 L, out float3 H, out float D,
    out float attenuation)
{
    V = camera - position;
    L = light.Position - position;
    D = length(L);
    L /= D;
    H = normalize(L + V);
    // Simple light attenuation
    attenuation = max(1-D/light.Range, 0);
    attenuation *= attenuation;
}
```

5. We can then define the pixel shaders for each of the light types. The following snippet of code supports a **point light**:

```
float4 PSPointLight(in PixelIn pixel) : SV_Target
{
    float4 result = (float4)0;
    result.a = 1.0f;

    GBufferAttributes attrs;
    ExtractGBufferAttributes(pixel,
        Texture0, Texture1,
        Texture2, TextureDepth,
        attrs);
    float3 V, L, H;
    float D, attenuation;
    PrepareLightInputs((float3)0, attrs.Position,
        attrs.Normal, LightParams,
        V, L, H, D, attenuation);
    result.xyz = LightContribution(attrs, V, L, H, D,
        attenuation);
    return result;
}
```

6. The **directional light** simply overrides the `L` (to light) vector and sets the attenuation back to `1.0f` (no fall off).

```
float4 PSDirectionalLight(in PixelIn pixel) : SV_Target
{
...
    PrepareLightInputs((float3)0, attrs.Position,
        attrs.Normal, LightParams,
        V, L, H, D, attenuation);
    L = normalize(-LightParams.Direction);
    H = normalize(L + V);
    attenuation = 1.0f;
    result.xyz = LightContribution(attrs, V, L, H, D,
        attenuation);
    return result;
}
```

7. And lastly, we have our simple **ambient light** pixel shader.

```
float4 PSAmbientLight(in PixelIn pixel) : SV_Target
{
...
    result.xyz = attrs.Diffuse * LightParams.Color;
    return result;
}
```

We are now ready to move onto creating the `LightRenderer` class in our C# project, define some lights, and hook up the G-Buffer

8. First let's add the following C# light type enumeration and **PerLight** constant buffer structure for use in our renderer.

```
public enum LightType : uint
{
    Ambient = 0,
    Directional = 1,
    Point = 2,
}
[StructLayout(LayoutKind.Sequential)]
public struct PerLight
{
    public Vector3 Direction;
    public LightType Type;
    public Vector3 Position;
    public float Range;
    public Color4 Color;
}
```

9. Declare the `LightRenderer` class and add the following private and public member fields:

```
public class LightRenderer: Common.RendererBase
{
    #region Initialized by CreateDeviceDepenedentResources
    // PerLight constant buffer
    Buffer perLightBuffer;

    // Light texture and its RTV and SRV
    Texture2D lightBuffer;
    RenderTargetView RTV;
    public ShaderResourceView SRV;

    VertexShader vertexShader;
    PixelShader psAmbientLight;
    PixelShader psDirectionalLight;
    PixelShader psPointLight;

    RasterizerState rsCullBack;
    RasterizerState rsCullFront;
    RasterizerState rsWireframe;

    // Additive blend state
    BlendState blendStateAdd;
```

```
        // Depth stencil states
        DepthStencilState depthLessThan;
        DepthStencilState depthGreaterThan;
        DepthStencilState depthDisabled;
        // Read-only depth stencil view
        DepthStencilView DSVReadonly;
        #endregion

        // Initialized by caller
        public List<PerLight> Lights { get; private set; }
        public BoundingFrustum Frustum { get; set;}
        public ConstantBuffers.PerObject PerObject { get; set;}
        public Buffer PerObjectBuffer { get; set; }
    ...
    }
```

10. And then add the following constructor and additional field members:

```
MeshRenderer pointLightVolume;
ScreenAlignedQuadRenderer saQuad;
GBuffer gbuffer;
public LightRenderer(
    MeshRenderer pointLightVolume,
    ScreenAlignedQuadRenderer saQuad,
    GBuffer gbuffer)
{
    this.Lights = new List<PerLight>();
    this.pointLightVolume = pointLightVolume;
    this.saQuad = saQuad;
    this.gbuffer = gbuffer;
}
```

11. Now within the light renderer's `protected override void`
    `CreateDeviceDependentResources()` method, we will initialize the
    necessary Direct3D resources. First we use the G-Buffer depth buffer to
    determine the width/height and initialize the read-only **Depth Stencil View** (**DSV**).

```
... RemoveAndDispose(ref <all disposable resources>);
var device = this.DeviceManager.Direct3DDevice;
int width, height;
SampleDescription sampleDesc;
// Retrieve DSV from GBuffer, extract width/height then
// create a new read-only DSV
using (var depthTexture = gbuffer.DSV.ResourceAs<Texture2D>())
{
```

```
width = depthTexture.Description.Width;
height = depthTexture.Description.Height;
sampleDesc = depthTexture.Description
    .SampleDescription;
// Initialize read-only DSV
var dsvDesc = gbuffer.DSV.Description;
dsvDesc.Flags = DepthStencilViewFlags.ReadOnlyDepth |
  DepthStencilViewFlags.ReadOnlyStencil;
DSVReadonly = ToDispose(new DepthStencilView(device,
  depthTexture, dsvDesc));
}
// Check if GBuffer is multi-sampled
bool isMSAA = sampleDesc.Count > 1;
```

12. Next, we define the light render target texture and its **Render Target View** (**RTV**) and **Shader Resource View** (**SRV**). This is done exactly as we have done within the recipe *Filling the G-Buffer*.

```
// Initialize the light render target
var texDesc = new Texture2DDescription();
texDesc.BindFlags = BindFlags.ShaderResource | BindFlags.
RenderTarget;
...
texDesc.SampleDescription = sampleDesc;
texDesc.Format = Format.R8G8B8A8_UNorm;

lightBuffer = ToDispose(new Texture2D(device, texDesc));

// Render Target View description
var rtvDesc = new RenderTargetViewDescription();
...
RTV = ToDispose(new RenderTargetView(device, lightBuffer,
  rtvDesc));

// SRV description
var srvDesc = new ShaderResourceViewDescription();
...
SRV = ToDispose(new ShaderResourceView(device, lightBuffer,
  srvDesc));
```

13. To allow rendering multiple lights onto each other, we will use additive blending. The following code snippet shows how to initialize this blend state:

```
// Initialize additive blend state (assuming single RT)
BlendStateDescription bsDesc = new BlendStateDescription();
bsDesc.RenderTarget[0].IsBlendEnabled = true;
```

```
bsDesc.RenderTarget[0].AlphaBlendOperation =
  BlendOperation.Add;
bsDesc.RenderTarget[0].SourceAlphaBlend = BlendOption.One;
bsDesc.RenderTarget[0].DestinationAlphaBlend =
  BlendOption.One;
bsDesc.RenderTarget[0].BlendOperation = BlendOperation.Add;
bsDesc.RenderTarget[0].SourceBlend = BlendOption.One;
bsDesc.RenderTarget[0].DestinationBlend = BlendOption.One;
bsDesc.RenderTarget[0].RenderTargetWriteMask =
  ColorWriteMaskFlags.All;
blendStateAdd = ToDispose(new BlendState(device, bsDesc));
```

> As more lights overlap, it is quite possible for the accumulated light value to exceed the maximum `1.0f` supported by a `UNorm` format. In order to support **High Dynamic Range** (**HDR**), a larger bits-per-element format is required, and if you continue using a `UNorm` format, scaling will also be necessary.

14. Next, we have our rasterizer states. These are required so that we can easily control whether it is the front face or back face of the light volume that will be culled.

```
// Initialize rasterizer states
RasterizerStateDescription rsDesc = new
  RasterizerStateDescription();
rsDesc.FillMode = FillMode.Solid;
rsDesc.CullMode = CullMode.Back;
rsCullBack = ToDispose(new RasterizerState(device, rsDesc));
rsDesc.CullMode = CullMode.Front;
rsCullFront = ToDispose(new RasterizerState(device, rsDesc));
```

15. We now need to create three depth stencil states.

```
// Initialize depth state
var dsDesc = new DepthStencilStateDescription();
dsDesc.IsStencilEnabled = false;
dsDesc.IsDepthEnabled = true;
// Less-than depth comparison
dsDesc.DepthComparison = Comparison.Less;
depthLessThan = ToDispose(new DepthStencilState(device, dsDesc));
// Greater-than depth comparison
dsDesc.DepthComparison = Comparison.Greater;
depthGreaterThan = ToDispose(new DepthStencilState(device,
  dsDesc));
// Depth testing disabled
dsDesc.IsDepthEnabled = false;
depthDisabled = ToDispose(new DepthStencilState(device,
  dsDesc));
```

16. Finally, we create the `PerLight` constant buffer and initialize our shaders.

```
// Buffer to light parameters
perLightBuffer = ToDispose(new Buffer(device,
  Utilities.SizeOf<PerLight>(), ResourceUsage.Default,
  BindFlags.ConstantBuffer, CpuAccessFlags.None,
  ResourceOptionFlags.None, 0));
...
// Compile and create the vertex shader
using (var bytecode =
  ShaderBytecode.CompileFromFile(@"Shaders\Lights.hlsl",
  "VSLight", "vs_5_0", shaderFlags, EffectFlags.None, null,
  includeHandler))
    vertexShader = ToDispose(new VertexShader(device,
  bytecode));
// Compile pixel shaders
using (var bytecode = ShaderBytecode.CompileFromFile(@"Shaders\
Lights.hlsl",
  "PSAmbientLight", "ps_5_0", shaderFlags,
  EffectFlags.None, null, includeHandler))
    psAmbientLight = ToDispose(new PixelShader(device,
      bytecode));
... psDirectionLight
... psPointLight
```

17. Like the `GBuffer` class, we need to be able to bind, unbind, and clear the lighting render target. The following code snippet shows these methods:

```
public void Bind(DeviceContext1 context)
{
    context.OutputMerger.SetTargets(DSVReadonly, RTV);
}
public void Unbind(DeviceContext1 context)
{
    context.OutputMerger.ResetTargets();
}
public void Clear(DeviceContext1 context)
{
    context.ClearRenderTargetView(RTV, new Color(0,0,0,1));
}
```

18. To complete the `LightRenderer` class, we implement the abstract `DoRender` method. This begins by retrieving the device context and backing up the current context state so that we can restore it after rendering the lights.

19. We then assign the G-Buffer SRVs, set the Output Merger blend state, retrieve the camera parameters from the frustum, and then iterate over each of the lights.

```
// Retrieve device context
var context = this.DeviceManager.Direct3DContext;
// backup existing context state
int oldStencilRef = 0;
Color4 oldBlendFactor;
int oldSampleMaskRef;
using(var oldVertexLayout =
  context.InputAssembler.InputLayout)
using(var oldPixelShader = context.PixelShader.Get())
using (var oldVertexShader = context.VertexShader.Get())
using (var oldBlendState = context.OutputMerger
  .GetBlendState(out oldBlendFactor, out oldSampleMaskRef))
using (var oldDepthState = context.OutputMerger
  .GetDepthStencilState(out oldStencilRef))
using (var oldRSState = context.Rasterizer.State)
{
    // Assign shader resources
    context.PixelShader.SetShaderResources(0,
      gbuffer.SRVs.ToArray().Concat(new[] { gbuffer.DSSRV
      }).ToArray());
    // Assign the additive blend state
    context.OutputMerger.BlendState = blendStateAdd;
    // Retrieve camera parameters
    SharpDX.FrustumCameraParams cameraParams =
      Frustum.GetCameraParams();

    // For each configured light
    for (var i = 0; i < Lights.Count; i++)
    {
        ... see next step
    }
    // Reset pixel shader resources (all to null)
    context.PixelShader.SetShaderResources(0, new
      ShaderResourceView[gbuffer.SRVs.Count + 1]);

    // Restore context states
    context.PixelShader.Set(oldPixelShader);
    context.VertexShader.Set(oldVertexShader);
    context.InputAssembler.InputLayout = oldVertexLayout;
    context.OutputMerger.SetBlendState(oldBlendState,
      oldBlendFactor, oldSampleMaskRef);
```

```
    context.OutputMerger
      .SetDepthStencilState(oldDepthState, oldStencilRef);
    context.Rasterizer.State = oldRSState;
}
```

20. For each of the lights in the previous `for` loop, we need to first choose the correct shader based on the type of light, and update `perLightBuffer` with the current light's parameters. As our G-Buffer has been stored in view-space, we will transform the light parameters into the same space using the `PerObject.View` matrix before updating the constant buffer resource.

```
PerLight light = Lights[i];
PixelShader shader = null; // Assign shader
if (light.Type == LightType.Ambient)
    shader = psAmbientLight;
else if (light.Type == LightType.Directional)
    shader = psDirectionalLight;
else if (light.Type == LightType.Point)
    shader = psPointLight;

// Update the perLight constant buffer
// Calculate view space position and direction
Vector3 lightDir = Vector3.Normalize(Lights[i].Direction);
Vector4 viewSpaceDir = Vector3.Transform(lightDir,
  PerObject.View);
light.Direction = new Vector3(viewSpaceDir.X,
  viewSpaceDir.Y, viewSpaceDir.Z);
Vector4 viewSpacePos =
  Vector3.Transform(Lights[i].Position, PerObject.View);
light.Position = new Vector3(viewSpacePos.X,
  viewSpacePos.Y, viewSpacePos.Z);

context.UpdateSubresource(ref light, perLightBuffer);
context.PixelShader.SetConstantBuffer(4, perLightBuffer);
```

21. Now we check whether the light needs to be rendered full screen using the screen-aligned quad, or only the region defined by a light volume. In our implementation, directional and ambient lights will always be applied to the full G-Buffer (that is rendered fullscreen). For a point light, we only want to use the full G-Buffer if the bounding sphere is clipping the near- and far-clip plane of the frustum.

```
// Check if the light should be considered full screen
bool isFullScreen = light.Type == LightType.Directional ||
                    light.Type == LightType.Ambient;
```

```
if (isFullScreen || (cameraParams.ZNear > viewSpacePos.Z -
  light.Range && cameraParams.ZFar < viewSpacePos.Z + light.
Range))
{
    // Use SAQuad to process entire G-Buffer
    context.OutputMerger.DepthStencilState = depthDisabled;
    saQuad.ShaderResources = null;
    saQuad.Shader = shader; // Set appropriate light shader
    saQuad.Render();
}
else // Render volume (point light)
{
    ... see next step
}
```

22. In the case above, when the camera is not fully enclosed by the point light's volume, we need to scale and position the volume mesh for the light (for example, a sphere). Prior to rendering the mesh, we determine whether to cull front or back faces, and whether to perform a greater-than/lesser-than depth test.

```
// Set appropriate shader
context.PixelShader.Set(shader);
context.VertexShader.Set(vertexShader);
MeshRenderer volume = pointLightVolume;

// Prepare world matrix
Matrix world = Matrix.Identity;
world.ScaleVector = Vector3.One * light.Range;
world.TranslationVector = Lights[i].Position;
volume.World = world;
var transposed = PerObject; // Transpose PerObject matrices
transposed.World = volume.World;
transposed.WorldViewProjection = volume.World *
  PerObject.ViewProjection;
transposed.Transpose();
context.UpdateSubresource(ref transposed, PerObjectBuffer);

if (cameraParams.ZFar < viewSpacePos.Z + light.Range)
{
    // Cull the back face and only render where there is
    // something behind the front face.
    context.Rasterizer.State = rsCullBack;
    context.OutputMerger.DepthStencilState = depthLessThan;
}
else
```

```
    {
        // Cull front faces and only render where there is
        // something located in-front of the back face.
        context.Rasterizer.State = rsCullFront;
        context.OutputMerger.DepthStencilState =
          depthGreaterThan;
    }
    volume.Render();
```

23. This completes the `LightRenderer` class. The following code snippet shows how
    you might use this with the G-Buffer and render the result to screen:

```
// Initialize light renderer and lights
var lightRenderer = ToDispose(new LightRenderer(sphereRenderer,
  saQuad, gbuffer));
lightRenderer.Initialize(this);
// Define lights
lightRenderer.Lights.Add(new PerLight
{   Color = new Color4(0.2f, 0.2f, 0.2f, 1.0f),
    Type = LightType.Ambient
});
lightRenderer.Lights.Add(new PerLight
{   Color = Color.Red,
    Position = new Vector3(0, 8, 1),
    Range = 10,
    Type = LightType.Point
});
// Fill G-Buffer
...
gbuffer.Unbind(context);

// Lighting pass
context.PixelShader.SetConstantBuffer(0, perObjectBuffer);
// Prepare perObject for use in LightRenderer
perObject.ViewProjection = viewProjection;
...
perObject.InverseProjection =
  Matrix.Invert(projectionMatrix);
lightRenderer.PerObject = perObject;
lightRenderer.PerObjectBuffer = perObjectBuffer;

// Assign the Frustum (from projection matrix)
lightRenderer.Frustum = new
  BoundingFrustum(projectionMatrix);
```

```
// Clear the render target, bind, render, unbind
lightRenderer.Clear(context);
lightRenderer.Bind(context);
lightRenderer.Render(); // Render lights
lightRenderer.Unbind(context);
// Restore default render targets
context.OutputMerger.SetRenderTargets(this.DepthStencilView
  , this.RenderTargetView);
// Render the light buffer using SA-Quad's default shader
saQuad.Shader = null; // use default shader
saQuad.ShaderResources = new[] { lightRenderer.SRV };
saQuad.Render();
```

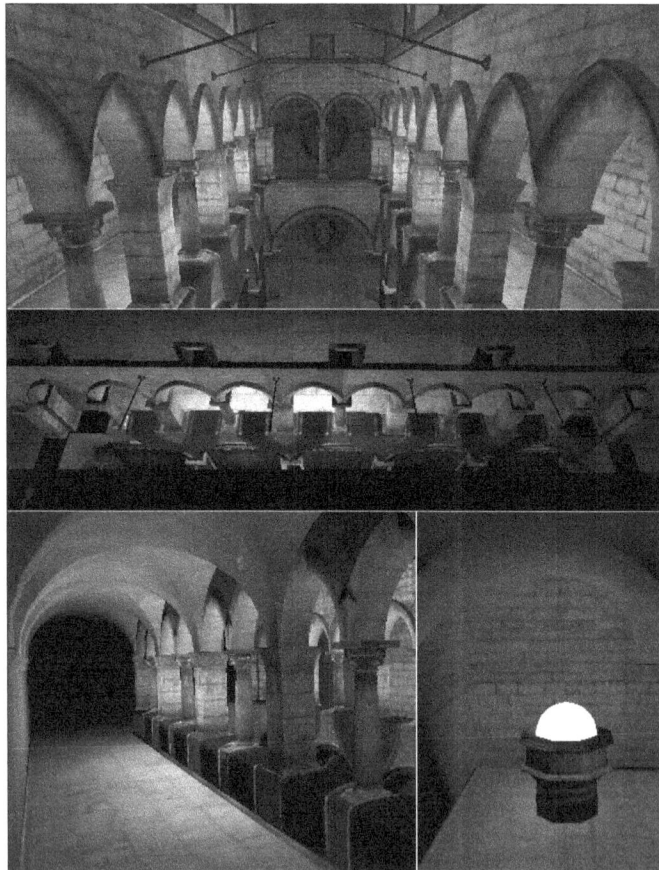

Final result of the lighting pass

The previous screenshot shows the resulting output with 14 point lights and a single ambient light.

How it works...

In this recipe, we have implemented a method for culling light volumes based on their depth in order to only render where the light is likely to have an impact upon the final rendering result. The following diagram shows four objects: A, B, C, and D, lit by three point lights: 1, 2, and 3:

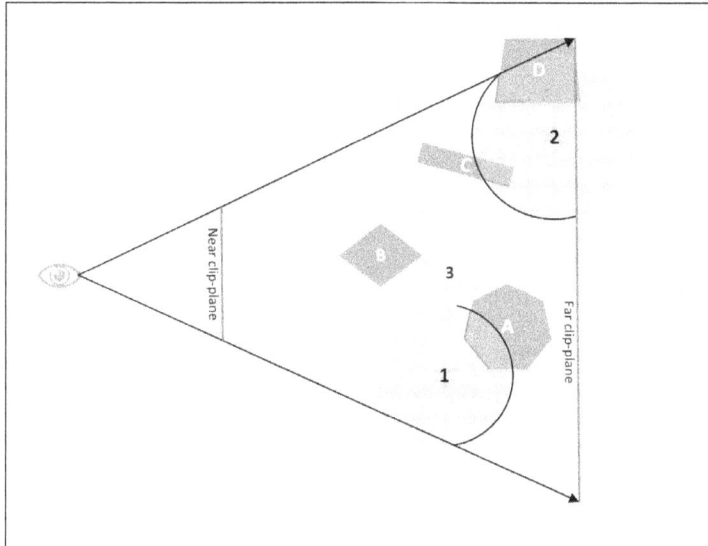

A diagram showing how light volumes are rendered. The outlined halves of light 1 and 2 represent the faces that are rendered, while the outlined portions of A, C, and D represent which pixels will be affected after the depth tests.

The area of each light's volume that will be rendered is determined as follows:

-   The first light is within the frustum near and far clip planes; therefore, we choose to cull the front faces and set the depth test so that the light volume fragments will only render if they have a depth greater than the contents of the depth buffer at that point, that is, render when there is something in front of the back faces of the light volume. The highlighted portion of object A shows the area of the G-Buffer that will have lighting applied for the first light.

-   The second light on the other hand partially lies beyond the far clip plane; therefore, we choose to cull the back faces and set the depth test so that the light volume fragments will only render if they have a depth lesser than the contents of the depth buffer at that point, that is, render when there is something behind the front faces of the light volume. The highlighted portions of objects C and D show the areas of the G-Buffer that will have lighting applied for this light.

-   The third light fully encloses the frustum; therefore, we use a fullscreen quad to process the entire buffer, applying lighting to all four objects. There is no depth test in this instance.

By using this approach, it is clear that the number of fragments that need to be processed by the pixel shader are greatly reduced for the first two lights. The last light, however, potentially wastes time processing pixels that have no content. This could be addressed by using the stencil buffer when rendering the geometry into the G-Buffer and enabling stencil testing within the subsequent lighting pass. By using the stencil buffer, we could exclude any portions of the screen that do not have anything rendered or that we do not want to participate in the lighting pass. A prime example is the skybox of outdoor scenes, where potentially a large portion of the screen does not require any lighting operations. As with render targets, the depth buffer cannot be bound for reading and writing at the same time. In order for us to use the depth buffer from the G-Buffer stage as both, an SRV to retrieve position information and for depth testing, we have created a read-only DSV using `DepthStencilViewFlags`.

```
dsvDesc.Flags = DepthStencilViewFlags.ReadOnlyDepth;
```

There's more...

There are of course many ways to optimize the rendering of lights for deferred rendering. One is to use the rasterizer stage's **scissor test**, allowing a region of the screen to be enabled to render while culling anything that would be rendered outside this region. Another approach for efficient lighting is **tiled deferred rendering**, where the screen is divided into imaginary tiles. Lights that impact a specific tile are grouped and processed together (also known as light binning).

See also

- Overview of a number of different deferred rendering techniques along with example code can be found in *Deferred Rendering for Current and Future Rendering Pipelines* by *Andrew Lauritzen*, Beyond Programmable Shading, SIGGRAPH 2010, July 2010 at `http://visual-computing.intel-research.net/art/publications/deferred_rendering/`
- Stencil buffer for deferred lights at `http://www.altdevblogaday.com/2011/08/08/stencil-buffer-optimisation-for-deferred-lights/`
- Light Indexed Deferred Rendering at `https://code.google.com/p/lightindexed-deferredrender/`
- Performance comparison of light indexed deferred rendering and tiled deferred rendering at `http://mynameismjp.wordpress.com/2012/03/31/light-indexed-deferred-rendering/`

Incorporating multisample anti-aliasing

One of the problems with classic deferred rendering is that to support the built-in hardware anti-aliasing, we must implement some extra shader code to correctly sample from the MSAA G-Buffer. More recent improvements in Direct3D have made this problem easy to solve by using the SV_SampleIndex and SV_Coverage pixel shader system-value semantics to run the shader for each sample and to determine which samples are covered by the current fragment.

Getting ready

It is necessary that all render targets are created with multisampling enabled. This includes the render targets of the G-Buffer, the depth buffer, and also the light accumulation buffer of the light renderer. Our implementations of the GBuffer and LightRenderer classes already support multisampling provided we pass in the correct sample description to the GBuffer constructor, for example, new SampleDescription(4, 0).

Our existing ScreenAlignedQuadRenderer must be modified to use the multisampling pixel shader found in the *There's more...* section of *Implementing a screen-aligned quad renderer*. A good way to organize this would be to check if the first ScreenAlignedQuadRenderer.ShaderResources SRV has a ShaderResourceView. Description.Dimension of SharpDX.Direct3D.ShaderResourceViewDimension. Texture2DMultisampled or not and choose the default pixel shader accordingly. This will allow us to continue to use the same class when MSAA is on or off.

Be sure to have the Direct3D debug layer active during development. This provides useful information to help address any incorrect configuration of resources.

How to do it...

We'll begin by updating our existing HLSL code to read the G-Buffer. We'll then update each of the LightRenderer pixel shaders.

1. First we need to use the multisampled textures of the G-Buffer by changing Texture2D to Texture2DMS, as shown in the following HLSL snippet.

    ```
    Texture2DMS<float4> Texture0 : register(t0);
    Texture2DMS<uint>   Texture1 : register(t1);
    Texture2DMS<float4> Texture2 : register(t2);
    Texture2DMS<float>  TextureDepth : register(t3);
    ```

    Unlike the **Texture2D** resource, the **Texture2DMS** resource requires a **<data_type>** to be specified, for example, **Texture2DMS<float4>**

2. Next, we update the signature of our `ExtractGBufferAttributes` function to use `Texture2DMS` resources and include one additional parameter to control which sample index will be retrieved as highlighted in the following code snippet:

```
void ExtractGBufferAttributes(in PixelIn pixel,
                             in Texture2DMS<float4> t0,
                             in Texture2DMS<uint> t1,
                             in Texture2DMS<float4> t2,
                             in Texture2DMS<float> t3,
                             in int sampleIndex,
                             out GBufferAttributes attrs)
{
    int3 screenPos = int3(pixel.Position.xy, 0);
    float depth = t3.Load(screenPos, sampleIndex);
    attrs.Diffuse = t0.Load(screenPos, sampleIndex).xyz;
    attrs.SpecularInt = t0.Load(screenPos, sampleIndex).w;
    attrs.Normal = UnpackNormal(t1.Load(screenPos, sampleIndex));
    attrs.Emissive = t2.Load(screenPos, sampleIndex).xyz;
    attrs.SpecularPower = t2.Load(screenPos, sampleIndex).w * 50;
...
}
```

3. Our updated pixel shaders will use a similar approach to the multisampling pixel shader of the screen-aligned quad; in addition, we will use the `SV_Coverage` pixel shader input semantic. Let's go ahead and make these changes to each of the `LightRenderer` pixel shaders. The following updated point light shader shows the highlighted changes:

```
float4 PSPointLight(in PixelIn pixel,
    uint coverage: SV_Coverage,
    uint sampleIndex: SV_SampleIndex) : SV_Target
{
    GBufferAttributes attrs;
    // Is sample covered
    if (coverage & (1 << sampleIndex))
    {
        ExtractGBufferAttributes(pixel,
            Texture0, Texture1,
            Texture2, TextureDepth,
            sampleIndex,
            attrs);
...
        return float4(LightContribution(attrs, V, L, H, D,
            attenuation), 1.0f);
    }
    discard;
    return 0;
}
```

This completes our HLSL changes. Before updating our render loop, be sure to compile the MSAA pixel shaders within `LightRenderer`. By placing the MSAA pixel shaders in a new file and using the existing `isMSAA` variable within `CreateDeviceDependentResources` to conditionally compile the MSAA and non-MSAA shaders, we can support both scenarios.

4. Within our `D3DApp` class we need to enable multisampling for the swap chain, as shown in the following code:

```
protected override SwapChainDescription1
CreateSwapChainDescription()
{   var description = base.CreateSwapChainDescription();
    description.SampleDescription =new SampleDescription(4,0);
    return description;
}
```

5. We can then put it all together in our `D3DApp.Run` method as shown in the following code sample:

```
GBuffer gbufferMS = ToDispose(new
  GBuffer(this.RenderTargetSize.Width,
    this.RenderTargetSize.Height,
    new SampleDescription(4, 0),
    Format.R8G8B8A8_UNorm,
    Format.R32_UInt,
    Format.R8G8B8A8_UNorm));
gbufferMS.Initialize(this);
...
var lightRendererMS = ToDispose(new LightRenderer(sphereRenderer,
saQuad, gbufferMS));
... add lights
lightRendererMS.Initialize(this);
...
// Fill G-Buffer
...
gbufferMS.Unbind();

// Lighting pass
...
lightRendererMS.Unbind();
context.OutputMerger.SetRenderTargets(this.DepthStencilView, this.
RenderTargetView);

saQuadMS.Shader = null; // use default shader
saQuadMS.ShaderResources = new[] { lightRendererMS.SRV };
saQuadMS.Render();
```

6. The following sequence of screenshots shows the comparison of the final render and G-Buffer contents between aliased and anti-aliased MSAA x4:

Comparison between aliased (top) and anti-aliased (bottom) from left: light pass, diffuse/albedo, normals, depth

How it works...

As discussed in the *Implementing a screen-aligned quad renderer* recipe, the `SV_SampleIndex` input system-value semantic causes a pixel shader to be run for each sample instead of for each pixel (for example, four times for 4xMSAA). This works great for a screen-aligned quad as, by definition, we know that when rendered it will fully cover all samples and, therefore, all samples are required. However, when rendering our light volumes or other smaller regions, we are potentially wasting time calculating the lighting for a sample that isn't even covered by the current fragment. This is where we can use the pixel shader `SV_Coverage` input semantic to determine if the current sample index is covered or not. Each bit of the coverage value indicates whether that sample is covered by the fragment, for example, a coverage value of **1** indicates that only the first sample is covered whereas a value of **3** indicates that both, the first and second samples are covered as shown in the following diagram:

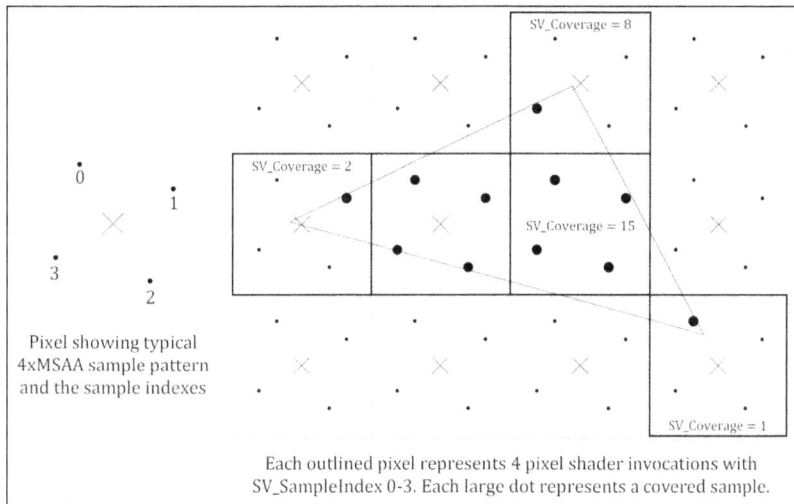

Relationship between MSAA rasterization, SV_Coverage and SV_SampleIndex

When we determine that the sample is covered, we execute the relevant operations; otherwise, we exclude the pixel shader result via a call to `discard`.

There's more...

An optimization might be to detect edge pixels and store them in a stencil. We can then perform an MSAA shading pass only for those pixels, while using another pass that only reads a single sample for all other pixels. Or alternatively, run a blur over those pixels.

See also

▶ HLSL semantics at `http://msdn.microsoft.com/en-us/library/windows/desktop/bb509647(v=vs.85).aspx`

▶ *Rasterization Rules* at `http://msdn.microsoft.com/en-us/library/windows/desktop/cc627092%28v=vs.85%29.aspx`

11
Integrating Direct3D with XAML and Windows 8.1

In this chapter, we will cover the following topics:

- ▶ Preparing the swap chain for a Windows Store app
- ▶ Rendering to a CoreWindow
- ▶ Rendering to a XAML SwapChainPanel
- ▶ Loading and compiling resources asynchronously

Introduction

In this chapter, we will look at how to integrate Direct3D rendering into a Windows Store app within Visual Studio 2013 using SharpDX and C#.

Extensible Application Markup Language (**XAML**) is an XML-based language created by Microsoft that is most commonly used for creating UI layouts for .NET Framework applications. XAML was originally used with the **Windows Presentation Foundation** (**WPF**) and Silverlight but has also been used for designing workflows within Windows **Workflow Foundation** (**WF**). Generally, a C# Windows Store app is built using XAML.

Preparing the swap chain for a Windows Store app

In this recipe, we will look at the code necessary to create a new class inheriting from the D3DApplicationBase class from *Chapter 2, Rendering with Direct3D*, that will prepare a swap chain description for use in a Windows Store app for Windows 8.1. We will also prepare a Windows Store compatible version of the Common library we have used throughout this book.

Getting ready

To target Windows 8.1, we need to use Visual Studio 2013.

Before commencing, we will need to have the SharpDX 11.2 WinRT binaries at hand. At the time of writing this book, this requires using the latest development package (2.5.1) found on the SharpDX webpage http://sharpdx.org/news/. For the remainder of the chapter, we will assume that these can be located upon navigating to .\External\Bin\ DirectX11_2-Signed-winrt under the solution location.

> There exists a SharpDX NuGet package; however, at the time of writing this book, the package has not yet been updated for Windows 8.1 and Direct3D 11.2.

How to do it...

We'll begin by creating a new class library and reusing a majority of the Common project used throughout the book so far, then we will create a new class D3DApplicationWinRT inheriting from D3DApplicationBase to be used as a starting point for our Windows Store app's render targets.

1. Within Visual Studio, create a new **Class Library (Windows Store apps)** called Common.WinRT.

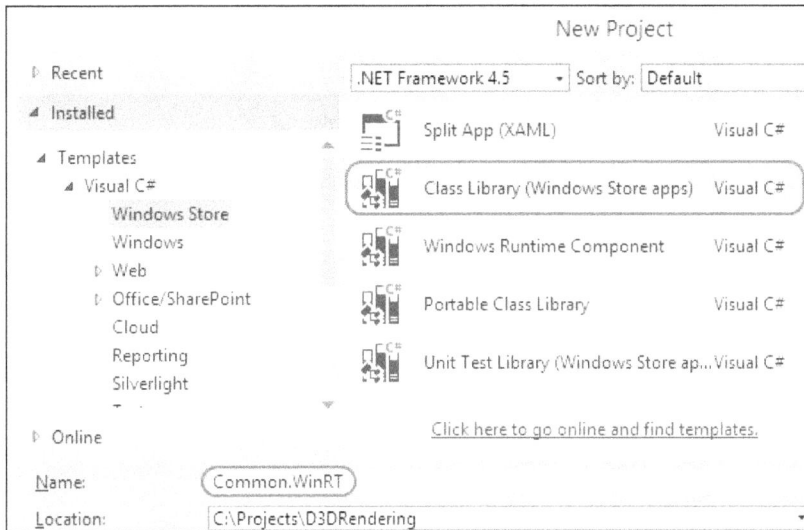

New Project dialog to create a class library project for Windows Store apps

2. Add references to the following SharpDX assemblies: `SharpDX.dll`, `SharpDX.D3DCompiler.dll`, `SharpDX.Direct2D1.dll`, `SharpDX.Direct3D11.dll`, and `SharpDX.DXGI` within `.\External\Bin\DirectX11_2-Signed-winrt`.

3. Right-click on the new project; navigate to **Add** | **Existing item...**; and select the following files from the existing `Common` project: `D3DApplicationBase.cs`, `DeviceManager.cs`, `Mesh.cs`, `RendererBase.cs`, and `HLSLFileIncludeHandlers.hlsl`, and optionally, `FpsRenderer.cs` and `TextRenderer.cs`.

4. Instead of duplicating the files, we can choose to **Add As Link** within the file selection dialog, as shown in the following screenshot:

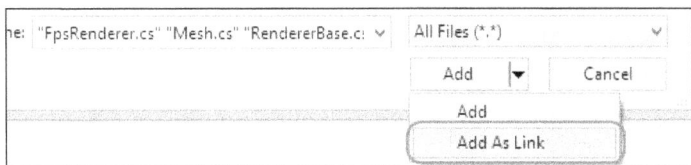

Files can be added as a link instead of a copy

5. Any platform-specific code can be wrapped with a check for the `NETFX_CORE` definition, as shown in the following snippet:

```
#if NETFX_CORE
    ...Windows Store app code
#else
    ...Windows Desktop code
#endif
```

6. Add a new C# abstract class called `D3DApplicationWinRT`.

```
// Implements support for swap chain description for
// Windows Store apps
public abstract class D3DApplicationWinRT
    : D3DApplicationBase
{
...
}
```

7. In order to reduce the chances of our app being terminated to reclaim system resources, we will use the new `SharpDX.DXGI.Device3.Trim` function whenever our app is suspended (native equivalent is `IDXGIDevice3::Trim`). The following code shows how this is done:

```
public D3DApplicationWinRT()
    : base()
{
    // Register application suspending event
    Windows.ApplicationModel.Core
        .CoreApplication.Suspending += OnSuspending;
}
// When suspending hint that resources may be reclaimed
private void OnSuspending(Object sender, Windows.ApplicationModel.
SuspendingEventArgs e)
{
    // Retrieve the DXGI Device3 interface from our
    // existing Direct3D device.
    using (SharpDX.DXGI.Device3 dxgiDevice = DeviceManager
.Direct3DDevice.QueryInterface<SharpDX.DXGI.Device3>())
    {
        dxgiDevice.Trim();
    }
}
```

8. The existing `D3DApplicationBase.CreateSwapChainDescription` function is not compatible with Windows Store apps. Therefore, we will override this and create a `SwapChainDescription1` instance that is compatible with Windows Store apps. The following code shows the changes necessary:

```
protected override SharpDX.DXGI.SwapChainDescription1
CreateSwapChainDescription()
{
    var desc = new SharpDX.DXGI.SwapChainDescription1()
    {
        Width = Width,
        Height = Height,
```

```
               Format = SharpDX.DXGI.Format.B8G8R8A8_UNorm,
               Stereo = false,
               SampleDescription.Count = 1,
               SampleDescription.Quality = 0,
               Usage = SharpDX.DXGI.Usage.BackBuffer |
                   SharpDX.DXGI.Usage.RenderTargetOutput,
               Scaling = SharpDX.DXGI.Scaling.Stretch,
               BufferCount = 2,
               SwapEffect = SharpDX.DXGI.SwapEffect.FlipSequential,
               Flags = SharpDX.DXGI.SwapChainFlags.None
           };
       return desc;
   }
```

9. We will not be implementing the Direct3D render loop within a `Run` method for our Windows Store apps—this is because we will use the existing composition events where appropriate. Therefore, we will create a new abstract method `Render` and provide a default empty implementation of `Run`.

```
public abstract void Render();

[Obsolete("Use the Render method for WinRT", true)]
public override void Run()
{ }
```

How it works...

As of Windows 8.1 and **DirectX Graphics Infrastructure** (**DXGI**) 1.3, all Direct3D devices created by our Windows Store apps should call `SharpDX.DXGI.Device3.Trim` when suspending to reduce the memory consumed by the app and graphics driver. This reduces the chance that our app will be terminated to reclaim resources while it is suspended—although our application should consider destroying other resources as well. When resuming, drivers that support trimming will recreate the resources as required.

We have used `Windows.ApplicationModel.Core.CoreApplication` rather than `Windows.UI.Xaml.Application` for the `Suspending` event, so that we can use the class for both an XAML-based Direct3D app as well as one that implements its own `Windows.ApplicationModel.Core.IFrameworkView` in order to render to `CoreWindow` directly.

Windows Store apps only support a **flip presentation model** and therefore require that the swap chain is created using a `SharpDX.DXGI.SwapEffect.FlipSequential` swap effect; this in turn requires between two and 16 buffers specified in the `SwapChainDescription1.BufferCount` property. When using a flip model, it is also necessary to specify the `SwapChainDescription1.SampleDescription` property with `Count=1` and `Quality=0`, as **multisample anti-aliasing** (**MSAA**) is not supported on the swap chain buffers themselves. A flip presentation model avoids unnecessarily copying the swap-chain buffer and increases the performance.

> By removing Windows 8.1 specific calls (such as the `SharpDX.DXGI.Device3.Trim` method), it is also possible to implement this recipe using Direct3D 11.1 for Windows Store apps that target Windows 8.

See also

▸ The *Rendering to a CoreWindow* and *Rendering to a SwapChainPanel* recipes show how to create swap chains for non-XAML and XAML apps respectively

▸ NuGet Package Manager can be downloaded from `http://visualstudiogallery.msdn.microsoft.com/4ec1526c-4a8c-4a84-b702-b21a8f5293ca`

▸ You can find the flip presentation model on MSDN at `http://msdn.microsoft.com/en-us/library/windows/desktop/hh706346(v=vs.85).aspx`

Rendering to a CoreWindow

The XAML view provider found in the Windows Store app graphics framework cannot be modified. Therefore, when we want to implement the application's graphics completely within DirectX/Direct3D without XAML interoperation, it is necessary to create a basic view provider that allows us to connect our DirectX graphics device resources to the windowing infrastructure of our Windows Store app.

In this recipe, we will implement a `CoreWindow` swap-chain target and look at how to hook Direct3D directly to the windowing infrastructure of a Windows Store app, which is exposed by the `CoreApplication`, `IFrameworkViewSource`, `IFrameworkView`, and `CoreWindow` .NET types.

This recipe continues from where we left off with the *Preparing the swap chain for Windows Store apps* recipe.

How to do it...

We will first update the `Common.WinRT` project to support the creation of a swap chain for a Windows Store app's `CoreWindow` instance and then implement a simple *Hello World* application.

1. Let's begin by creating a new abstract class within the Common.WinRT project, called `D3DAppCoreWindowTarget` and descending from the `D3DApplicationWinRT` class from our previous recipe. The default constructor accepts the `CoreWindow` instance and attaches a handler to its `SizeChanged` event.

   ```
   using Windows.UI.Core;
   using SharpDX;
   ```

```
using SharpDX.DXGI;
...
public abstract class D3DAppCoreWindowTarget
    : D3DApplicationWinRT
{
    // The CoreWindow this instance renders to
    private CoreWindow _window;
    public CoreWindow Window { get { return _window; } }

    public D3DAppCoreWindowTarget(CoreWindow window)
    {
        _window = window;
        Window.SizeChanged += (sender, args) =>
        {
            SizeChanged();
        };
    }
    ...
}
```

2. Within our new class, we will now override the CurrentBounds property and the CreateSwapChain function in order to return the correct size and create the swap chain for the associated CoreWindow.

```
// Retrieve current bounds of CoreWindow
public override SharpDX.Rectangle CurrentBounds
{   get
    {
        return new SharpDX.Rectangle( (int)_window.Bounds.X,
(int)_window.Bounds.Y, (int)_window.Bounds.Width, (int)_window.
Bounds.Height);
    }
}
// Create the swap chain
protected override SharpDX.DXGI.SwapChain1 CreateSwapChain(
    SharpDX.DXGI.Factory2 factory,
    SharpDX.Direct3D11.Device1 device,
    SharpDX.DXGI.SwapChainDescription1 desc)
{
    // Create the swap chain for the CoreWindow
    using (var coreWindow = new ComObject(_window))
        return new SwapChain1(factory, device, coreWindow,
            ref desc);
}
```

This completes the changes to our `Common.WinRT` project. Next, we will create a *Hello World* Direct3D Windows Store app rendering directly to the application's `CoreWindow` instance.

3. Visual Studio 2013 does not provide us with a suitable C# project template to create a non-XAML Windows Store app, so we will begin by creating a new C# Windows Store **Blank App (XAML)** project.

4. Add references to the SharpDX assemblies: `SharpDX.dll`, `SharpDX.Direct3D11.dll`, `SharpDX.D3DCompiler.dll`, and `SharpDX.DXGI.dll`. Also, add a reference to the `Common.WinRT` project.

5. Next, we remove the two XAML files from the project: `App.xaml` and `MainPage.xaml`.

6. We will replace the previous application entry point, `App.xaml`, with a new static class called `App`. This will house the main entry point for our application where we start our Windows Store app using a custom view provider, as shown in the following snippet:

```
using Windows.ApplicationModel.Core;
using Windows.Graphics.Display;
using Windows.UI.Core;
...
internal static class App
{
    [MTAThread]
    private static void Main()
    {
        var viewFactory = new D3DAppViewProviderFactory();
        CoreApplication.Run(viewFactory);
    }
    // The custom view provider factory
    class D3DAppViewProviderFactory : IFrameworkViewSource
    {
        public IFrameworkView CreateView()
        {
            return new D3DAppViewProvider();
        }
    }

    class D3DAppViewProvider
        : SharpDX.Component, IFrameworkView
    {
        ...
    }
}
```

7. The implementation of the `IFrameworkView` members of `D3DAppViewProvider` allows us to initialize an instance of a concrete descendent of the `D3DAppCoreWindowTarget` class within `SetWindow` and to implement the main application loop in the `Run` method.

```
Windows.UI.Core.CoreWindow window;
D3DApp d3dApp; // descends from D3DAppCoreWindowTarget
public void Initialize(CoreApplicationView applicationView)
{ }
public void Load(string entryPoint) { }
public void SetWindow(Windows.UI.Core.CoreWindow window)
{
    RemoveAndDispose(ref d3dApp);
    this.window = window;
    d3dApp = ToDispose(new D3DApp(window));
    d3dApp.Initialize();
}
public void Uninitialize() { }
public void Run()
{
    // Specify the cursor type as the standard arrow.
    window.PointerCursor = new CoreCursor(
        CoreCursorType.Arrow, 0);

    // Activate the application window, making it visible
    // and enabling it to receive events.
    window.Activate();

    // Set the DPI and handle changes
    d3dApp.DeviceManager.Dpi = Windows.Graphics.Display
      .DisplayInformation.GetForCurrentView().LogicalDpi;
    Windows.Graphics.Display.DisplayInformation
      .GetForCurrentView().DpiChanged += (sender, args) =>
    {
      d3dApp.DeviceManager.Dpi = Windows.Graphics.Display
        .DisplayInformation.GetForCurrentView().LogicalDpi;
    };

    // Enter the render loop. Note that Windows Store apps
    // should never exit here.
    while (true)
    {
        // Process events incoming to the window.
        window.Dispatcher.ProcessEvents(
            CoreProcessEventsOption.ProcessAllIfPresent);
```

```
        // Render frame
        d3dApp.Render();
    }
}
```

8. The D3DApp class follows the same structure from our previous recipes throughout the book. There are only a few minor differences as highlighted in the following code snippet:

```
class D3DApp: Common.D3DAppCoreWindowTarget
{
    public D3DApp(Windows.UI.Core.CoreWindow window)
        : base(window)
    { this.VSync=true; }

    // Private member fields
    ...

    protected override void CreateDeviceDependentResources(
        Common.DeviceManager deviceManager)
    {
        ... create all device resources
        ... and create renderer instances here
    }
    // Render frame
    public override void Render()
    {
        var context = this.DeviceManager.Direct3DContext;

        // OutputMerger targets must be set every frame
        context.OutputMerger.SetTargets(
          this.DepthStencilView, this.RenderTargetView);

        // Clear depthstencil and render target
        context.ClearDepthStencilView(
          this.DepthStencilView,
          SharpDX.Direct3D11.DepthStencilClearFlags.Depth |
          SharpDX.Direct3D11.DepthStencilClearFlags.Stencil
          , 1.0f, 0);
        context.ClearRenderTargetView(
          this.RenderTargetView, SharpDX.Color.LightBlue);

        ... setup context pipeline state
        ... perform rendering commands

        // Present the render target
        Present();
    }
}
```

9. The following screenshot shows an example of the output using `CubeRenderer` from the recipes in *Chapter 3*, *Rendering Meshes*, and overlaying the 2D text with the `TextRenderer` class:

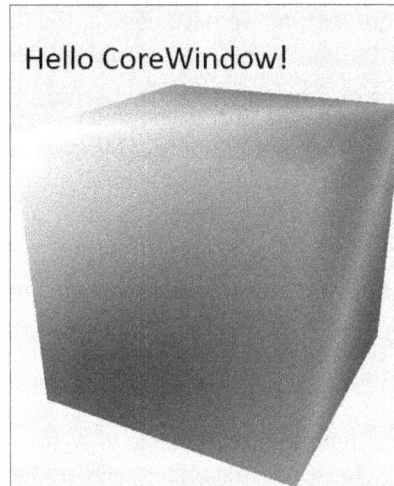

Output from the simple Hello World sample using the CoreWindow render target

How it works...

As mentioned, Visual Studio 2013 only provides templates for XAML-based Windows Store apps in C#. Therefore, we started with the C# **Blank App** (**XAML**) and then removed the XAML classes so that we could use our own view provider.

To create our own basic view provider, it is necessary for us to define a view provider factory and a view provider class: `D3DAppViewProviderFactory` and `D3DAppViewProvider`, respectively, in our sample. Within the static `Main` entry-point, we then create an instance of our view provider factory and tell the application singleton to run our factory using `CoreApplication.Run`. Our custom view provider implements the four methods of the `IFrameworkView` interface: `Initialize`, `SetWindow`, `Load`, and `Run`. Within `SetWindow`, we create a swap chain for the provided `CoreWindow` and initialize our `D3DAppCoreWindowTarget` concrete descendent class.

The `D3DAppCoreWindowTarget` class connects to the `SizeChanged` event of `CoreWindow` within the constructor, provides the size of `CoreWindow` through the `CurrentBounds` property, and finally creates a swap chain using the `SharpDX.DXGI.SwapChain1` constructor that accepts a `CoreWindow` instance. The equivalent in native code would be to use the `IDXGIFactory2.CreateSwapChainForCoreWindow` method.

```
// Create the swap chain for the CoreWindow
using (var coreWindow = new ComObject(_window))
    return new SwapChain1(factory, device, coreWindow, ref desc);
```

Within the `D3DAppViewProvider.Run` function, we initialize the **dots per inch** (**dpi**) for our device resources and enter our main application message loop, invoking the event dispatcher with a call to `CoreDispatcher.ProcessEvents`. After processing the events, we call the `D3DAppCoreWindowTarget.Render` method. The message loop here replaces the use of the `D3DApplicationBase.Run` method we have used in the rest of this book, necessitating a few structural changes to our `D3DAppCoreWindowTarget` descendants, such as creating renderer instances within the `CreateDeviceDependentResources` method. There is one critical difference when rendering a frame with a flip model swapchain—and therefore all Windows Store apps—it is that we must set the Output Merger render targets for every frame.

There's more...

Our C# DirectX Windows Store app implementation is very similar to how you would create a DirectX Windows Store app in C++. Visual Studio provides two C++ DirectX templates, **DirectX App** and **DirectX App (XAML)**. This recipe is a roughly equivalent C# version of the C++ DirectX App template.

The ability to compile HLSL at runtime was unavailable in Windows Store apps on Windows 8, and manually copying the DLL to the build directory only worked within development environments. However, Windows 8.1 now includes the latest version of `D3DCompiler` (47) with the OS and is available for compiling HLSL at runtime within our Windows Store apps. The downloadable source for this chapter includes the `HLSLCompiler` static class that provides a wrapper for compiling shaders from HLSL files within a Windows Store app; this includes a synchronous and asynchronous implementation. As the `D3DCompiler` binaries are part of the OS, there is no need to include a post-build event to copy the `d3dcompiler_*.dll` file to the build directory. This should still be done for desktop applications under Windows 8.1.

See also

▸ For more information about the setup of a custom view provider, and application and windows events, see *How to set up your DirectX Windows Store app to display a view* on `http://msdn.microsoft.com/en-us/library/windows/apps/hh465077.aspx`

▸ The *Loading and compiling resources asynchronously* recipe includes an implementation of compiling HLSL code from files asynchronously

Rendering to an XAML SwapChainPanel

In this recipe, we will render to an XAML `SwapChainPanel`. This panel allows us to efficiently render using Direct2D/Direct3D within an XAML Windows Store app. By integrating Direct3D into XAML we are able to use XAML to create flexible and dynamic UIs for our DirectX application. Or we can use the power of DirectX to implement advanced 2D or 3D rendering techniques within a wider XAML application.

A swap chain that participates within an XAML composition, such as the `SwapChainPanel` swap chain, is also known as a **composition swap chain**. The `SwapChainPanel` XAML element is new to Windows 8.1.

This recipe continues from where we left off with *Preparing the swap chain for Windows Store apps*.

How to do it...

As with the previous recipe, we will first update the `Common.WinRT` project to support the creation of a swap chain for the Windows Store app XAML `SwapChainPanel` element. We will then create a simple *Hello World* sample that demonstrates the integration of Direct3D into XAML.

1. Let's begin by creating a new abstract class called `D3DAppSwapChainPanelTarget` within the `Common.WinRT` project, descending from the `D3DApplicationWinRT` class.

```
public abstract class D3DAppSwapChainPanelTarget
    : D3DApplicationWinRT
{

    private SwapChainPanel panel;
    private ISwapChainPanelNative nativePanel;
    public SwapChainPanel SwapChainPanel {
        get { return panel; }
    }
    public D3DAppSwapChainPanelTarget(SwapChainPanel panel)
    {
        this.panel = panel;
        nativePanel = ToDispose(ComObject.As
            <SharpDX.DXGI.ISwapChainPanelNative>(panel));

        this.panel.CompositionScaleChanged += (s, args) =>
        {
            ScaleChanged();
        };
        this.panel.SizeChanged += (sender, args) =>
        {
            SizeChanged();
        };
    }
    ...
}
```

2. Next, we retrieve the current size of the `SwapChainPanel` element taking into consideration the scale composition (that is, zoom).

```
public override int Width
{   get
    {
        return (int)(panel.RenderSize.Width *
            panel.CompositionScaleX);
    }
}

public override int Height
{   get
    {
        return (int)(panel.RenderSize.Height *
            panel.CompositionScaleY);
    }
}

public override SharpDX.Rectangle CurrentBounds
{
    get
    {
        return new SharpDX.Rectangle(0, 0,
            (int)panel.RenderSize.Width,
            (int)panel.RenderSize.Height);
    }
}
```

3. Within Windows 8.1, a composition swap chain's visuals are exposed to touch scaling and translation scenarios via a touch UI. The following code snippet shows how we can apply this transformation:

```
protected void ScaleChanged()
{
    // Resize the SwapChain appropriately
    base.CreateSizeDependentResources(this);

    // Retrieve SwapChain2 reference and apply 2D scaling
    using (var swapChain2 = this.SwapChain.
QueryInterface<SwapChain2>())
    {
        // 2D affine transform matrix (inverse of scale)
        Matrix3x2 inverseScale = new Matrix3x2();
```

```
            inverseScale.M11 = 1.0f / panel.CompositionScaleX;
            inverseScale.M22 = 1.0f / panel.CompositionScaleY;
            swapChain2.MatrixTransform = inverseScale;

            // Update the DPI (affects Direct2D)
            DeviceManager.Dpi = 96.0f * panel.CompositionScaleX;
        }
    }
```

4. Next, we override the `CreateSwapChainDescription` method to apply settings specific to connecting a swap chain to the `SwapChainPanel` instance with the `IDXGISwapChainPanelNative` instance.

```
protected override SwapChainDescription1
  CreateSwapChainDescription()
{
    // Create description in base D3DApplicationWinRT
    var desc = base.CreateSwapChainDescription();
    // Update as SwapChainPanel requires Stretch scaling
    desc.Scaling = Scaling.Stretch;
    return desc;
}


protected override SharpDX.DXGI.SwapChain1
CreateSwapChain(SharpDX.DXGI.Factory2 factory, SharpDX.Direct3D11.
Device1 device, SharpDX.DXGI.SwapChainDescription1 desc)
{
    // Create the swap chain for XAML composition
    var swapChain = new SwapChain1(factory, device, ref desc);
    // Attach swap chain to SwapChainPanel
    nativePanel.SwapChain = swapChain;
    return swapChain;
}
```

5. This completes our changes to the `Common.WinRT` project. Now we will use the `D3DAppSwapChainPanelTarget` method within a Windows Store app.

6. Begin by creating a new C# **Blank App (XAML)** project and adding the SharpDX and the `Common.WinRT` references.

7. Add a new blank page to the project, and name it `D3DPanel.xaml`.

8. Open the new XAML file in the designer (*Shift + F7*), and change the `Page` tag to `SwapChainPanel`, as shown in the following screenshot:

```
<Page                                          <SwapChainPanel
    x:Class="Ch11_02HelloSwapChainPane             x:Class="Ch11_02HelloSwapChainPa
    xmlns="http://schemas.microsoft.co             xmlns="http://schemas.microsoft.
    xmlns:x="http://schemas.microsoft.             xmlns:x="http://schemas.microsof
    xmlns:local="using:Ch11_02HelloSwa             xmlns:local="using:Ch11_02HelloS
    xmlns:d="http://schemas.microsoft.             xmlns:d="http://schemas.microsof
    xmlns:mc="http://schemas.openxmlfo             xmlns:mc="http://schemas.openxml
    mc:Ignorable="d">                              mc:Ignorable="d">

    <Grid Background="{ThemeResource A              <Grid Background="{ThemeResource

    </Grid>                                        </Grid>
</Page>                                        </SwapChainPanel>
```

Changing the Page element to SwapChainPanel

9. Now, open the C# code for the XAML file (*F7*), and change the class we inherit to `SwapChainPanel` instead of `Page`.

```
public sealed partial class D3DPanel : SwapChainPanel
{
...
}
```

10. Within the default constructor, we will initialize a new instance of a `D3DApp` class (that inherits from the `D3DAppSwapChainPanelTarget` class), and create the rendering loop using the `Windows.UI.Xaml.Media.CompositionTarget.Rendering` event.

```
D3DApp d3dApp;
public D3DPanel()
{
    this.InitializeComponent();

    // Only use Direct3D if outside of the designer
    if (!Windows.ApplicationModel.DesignMode
        .DesignModeEnabled)
    {
        d3dApp = new D3DApp(this);
        d3dApp.Initialize();
        CompositionTarget.Rendering +=
            CompositionTarget_Rendering;
    }
}

void CompositionTarget_Rendering(object sender, object e)
{
    if (d3dApp != null)
        d3dApp.Render();
}
```

11. The D3DApp class itself is implemented in exactly the same way as we did for the *Rendering to a CoreWindow* recipe, with the exception that it descends from D3DAppSwapChainPanelTarget and the constructor looks like the following code snippet:

```
class D3DApp: Common.D3DAppSwapChainPanelTarget
{
    public D3DApp(Windows.UI.Xaml.Controls.SwapChainPanel
        panel) : base(panel)
    {
        this.VSync = true;
    }
...
}
```

How it works...

The default constructor accepts a SwapChainPanel instance, attaches a handler to its SizeChanged and CompositionScaleChanged events, and retrieves a reference to the ISwapChainPanelNative interface. The SwapChainPanel XAML control descends from Windows.UI.Xaml.Controls.Grid and therefore, supports layouts for child controls and can be added as a child to other controls. As can be seen from the following sequence of screenshots, the panel allows our Direct3D output to integrate with the XAML UI composition, including user inputs, transitions, and storyboards:

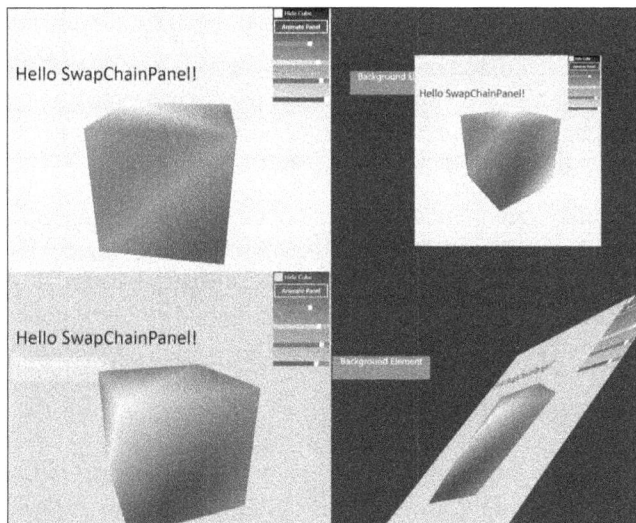

SwapChainPanel with spinning cube, Hello World text, and an XAML stack panel child control, top: zoomed in and zoomed out, bottom: transparency and XAML transformation applied through a storyboard.

Although the panel allows any number of immediate child controls as would a regular grid, the Microsoft guidelines indicate that no more than eight immediate child controls should be used. Another best practice is to avoid placing a control over the entire swap chain panel in order to prevent overdraws. Each child control of the swap chain panel can then contain any number of subsequent child controls depending on the element type; for example, the UI in the top right of each of the previous screenshots is contained within a `StackPanel` instance that is an immediate child of our `SwapChainPanel` implementation.

By retrieving the `ISwapChainPanelNative` interface from the `SwapChainPanel` instance, we have connected our new swap chain to the panel through the `ISwapChainPanelNative.SwapChain` property (natively this is done through the `ISwapChainPanelNative.SetSwapChain` method). The panel then takes care of associating the swap chain with the appropriate area on the screen.

The `Windows.UI.Xaml.Media.CompositionTarget` class is a static class that represents the display surface on which our application is being drawn. The `Rendering` event is fired for each frame, allowing us to integrate our Direct3D rendering with the XAML scene. For applications that require more control over the frame rate, a separate rendering loop thread can be implemented, provided there is appropriate synchronization in place to prevent threading issues when resizing/rescaling during the render loop.

As with the previous recipe, we must set the Output Merger render targets in each frame of our `D3DApp` class's `Render` method.

There's more...

When changing the size of a composition swap chain, it is possible to set the `SwapChain2.SourceSize` property provided, the new size is less than or equal to the original swap chain size. This identifies a portion of the swap chain to be used when presenting its contents to the display and is more efficient than using the `SwapChain.ResizeBuffers` function which forces the swap chain buffers to be physically resized.

There are a couple of other approaches to rendering Direct3D surfaces to XAML controls using brushes. We can use the `Windows.UI.Xaml.Media.Imaging.SurfaceImageSource` and `Windows.UI.Xaml.Media.Imaging.VirtualSurfaceImageSource` classes and their corresponding DXGI interfaces, `SharpDX.DXGI.ISurfaceImageSourceNative` and `SharpDX.DXGI.IVirtualSurfaceImageSourceNative` respectively. However, these are not suitable for real-time rendering—instead they can be useful for effects or rendering content that requires less frequent updates.

See also

> ▶ For more information on XAML and DirectX interoperation within Windows Store apps using `SurfaceImageSource`, see `http://msdn.microsoft.com/en-us/library/hh825871.aspx`

Loading and compiling resources asynchronously

Within Windows Store apps, it is desirable to keep your application as responsive as possible at all times. Instead of showing a static splash screen for the duration of compiling shaders and loading resources, in this recipe we will initialize our renderers and resources using the `async/await` keywords.

Getting ready

For this recipe, we will continue from where we left off in the previous recipe *Rendering to an XAML SwapChainPanel*.

How to do it...

We will first make changes to the `SwapChainPanel` C# class file and then update the `CreateDeviceDependentResources` implementation to support asynchronous resource creation. Lastly, we will take a look at some of the additional changes necessary within the code for loading meshes and textures.

1. Let's begin by opening the `D3DPanel.xaml.cs` file and registering an event handler for the `Loaded` event within the constructor.

   ```
   public D3DPanel()
   {
       this.InitializeComponent();
       this.Loaded += swapChainPanel_Loaded;
       CompositionTarget.Rendering +=
           CompositionTarget_Rendering;
   }

   private void swapChainPanel_Loaded(object sender,
     RoutedEventArgs e)
   {
   ...
   }
   ```

2. We will move the initialization of the `D3DApp` descendent of `D3DAppSwapChainPanelTarget` from the default constructor into the `Loaded` event handler.

   ```
   // Only use Direct3D if outside of the designer
   if (!Windows.ApplicationModel.DesignMode.DesignModeEnabled)
   {
   ```

```
    d3dApp = new D3DApp(this);
    d3dApp.Initialize();
}
```

3. Within the `D3DApp` class, we update the `CreateDeviceDependentResources` signature to include the `async` keyword as shown in the following snippet:

```
protected async override void
  CreateDeviceDependentResources(Common.DeviceManager
  deviceManager)
{
...
}
```

4. Now when we compile our shaders, load our meshes, or initialize our renderer instances, we can do something like the following code snippet:

```
// Compile shader, the event caller will continue executing
using (var bytecode = await HLSLCompiler.
CompileFromFileAsync(@"Shaders\VS.hlsl", "VSMain", "vs_5_0"))
{ ... }

// Load mesh
var meshes = await Mesh.LoadFromFileAsync("Character.cmo");

// Other CPU-bound work
await Task.Run(() =>
{
... (e.g. initialize renderers)
});
```

> Awaiting an asynchronous operation means that although our event handler runs on a background thread, the logic within it still runs in a synchronous manner. Where appropriate, we can also start multiple tasks to take advantage of parallel processing (for example, to initialize multiple renderers upon separate threads).

5. A full example of the `CompileFromFileAsync` function from the previous snippet is shown in the following code snippet:

```
public static async Task<ShaderBytecode>
  CompileFromFileAsync(string hlslFile, string entryPoint,
  string profile, ShaderMacro[] defines = null)
{
    if (!Path.IsPathRooted(hlslFile))
        hlslFile = Path.Combine(Windows.ApplicationModel
            .Package.Current.InstalledLocation.Path,
```

```
            hlslFile);
    CompilationResult result = null;
    // Compile the HLSL in a separate thread and await it
    await Task.Run(() =>
    {
        var shaderSource = SharpDX.IO.NativeFile
            .ReadAllText(hlslFile);
        // Compile the shader file
        ShaderFlags flags = ShaderFlags.None;
#if DEBUG
        flags |= ShaderFlags.Debug |
            ShaderFlags.SkipOptimization;
#endif
        var includeHandler = new HLSLFileIncludeHandler(
            Path.GetDirectoryName(hlslFile));
        result = ShaderBytecode.Compile(shaderSource,
            entryPoint, profile, flags,
            EffectFlags.None, defines, includeHandler,
            Path.GetFileName(hlslFile));

        if (!String.IsNullOrEmpty(result.Message))
            throw new CompilationException(
                result.ResultCode, result.Message);
    });
    return result;
}
```

6. To check when resources are ready, we use a new ResourcesReady flag as shown in following code snippet:

```
bool ResourcesReady = false;
protected async override void
  CreateDeviceDependentResources(Common.DeviceManager
  deviceManager)
{
    ResourcesReady = false;
...
    ResourcesReady = true;
}
public override void Render()
{
    if (!ResourcesReady)
        return;
    var context = this.DeviceManager.Direct3DContext;
...
}
```

7. By incorporating some XAML on the `MainPage.xaml` to show a loading screen or menu, we can keep our application responsive while the resources continue to load. The following screenshot shows a simple example running in the Windows Store app device simulator:

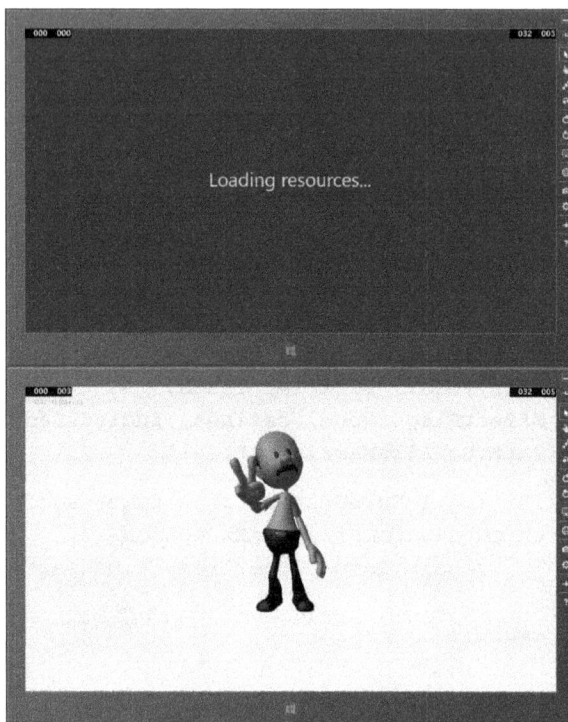

Running in simulator—top: showing loading message while compiling shaders and loading meshes.

How it works...

The `async` and `await` keywords are a language construct that leverages asynchronous support in the .NET Framework 4.5. By using the `async` modifier, you specify that a method, lambda expression, or anonymous method is asynchronous. The `await` operator on the other hand, is applied to a task in an asynchronous method (a method decorated with the `async` modifier) in order to suspend the execution of the method until the awaited task is completed.

In the previous recipe, where we were initializing the `D3DApp` instance within the constructor, the `CreateDeviceDependentResources` event handler ends up running synchronously regardless of the `async/await` commands used. By moving this initialization out of the constructor and into the `Loaded` event, we are then able to take advantage of an asynchronous implementation.

The `async` keyword works for us here because `CreateDeviceDependentResources` is an overridden event handler attached to the `DeviceManager` instance within the `D3DApplicationBase` class constructor as shown here: `DeviceManager.OnInitialize += CreateDeviceDependentResources;`

As the `CreateDeviceDependentResources` event handler will now continue running asynchronously while the `CompositionTarget.Rendering` event fires for each frame, we must set a flag to indicate when the resources are ready to be used and then check this flag within the `D3DApp.Render` function before attempting to render. With the main Direct3D application class implementing asynchronous resource creation, there is no need to use the `async/await` keywords within other renderers' `CreateDeviceDependentResources` functions. If we did this, it would be necessary to also check when those renderers' resources are ready before attempting to render a frame.

Loading a mesh at runtime uses the `await` keyword as well, because the `Common.Mesh.LoadFromFileAsync` function utilizes the `Windows.Storage.StorageFile` class for file I/O in Windows Store app. The `CompileFromFileAsync` method provides a wrapper around the Direct3D 11 `Compile` function, implementing the `async/await` keywords. The ability to compile shaders at runtime within Windows Store apps is new to Windows 8.1. For Windows Store apps under Windows 8.0, it was possible to do so within development environments and only if copying the library manually to the build directory.

There's more...

In the downloadable content for this book, available on the Packt website, the projects `Ch11_03CreatingResourcesAsync` and `Common.WinRT` also include changes necessary to load textures from a file. Windows Store apps do not support the `ShaderResourceView.FromFile` function and instead require you to provide your own **DirectDraw Surface** (**DDS**) file and image-loading routines.

The static class `Common.LoadTexture` includes the following functions:

- `LoadBitmap`: This loads a bitmap using **Windows Imaging Component** (**WIC**)
- `CreateTexture2DFromBitmap`: This creates a `Texture2D` resource from `SharpDX.WIC.BitmapSource`
- `SRVFromFile` and `LoadFromFile`: These either load a DDS file using a C# ported version of DDS code from Microsoft or load regular image formats using WIC. They return a `ShaderResourceView` method and/or a `SharpDX.Direct3D11. Resource (Texture1D/Texture2D/Texture3D)` function.

The only change to the updated `MeshRenderer` class in the completed project for this recipe is to call `LoadTexture.SRVFromFile` instead of `ShaderResourceView.FromFile`, which is no longer available with Windows Store apps.

See also

▸ Asynchronous programming with the `async` and `await` keywords at `http://msdn.microsoft.com/en-us/library/hh191443.aspx`

▸ For compiling mesh objects, see the *Loading a static mesh from a file* recipe in *Chapter 3, Rendering Meshes*

Further Reading

- MeshLab, developed at the Visual Computing Lab of ISTI - CNR.
- Blender, by Blender Foundation at `http://www.blender.org/`.
- *Compute Shader Filters*, *Alamia M.*, which can be found at `http://www.codinglabs.net/tutorial_compute_shaders_filters.aspx`.
- GPU PerfStudio 2, AMD.
- *DirectX 10 Tutorials*, *Anguelov B.*, which can be found at `http://takinginitiative.wordpress.com/directx10-tutorials/`.
- *Phong Tessellation* (*ACM SIGGRAPH Asia 2008 papers*), *Boubekeur T.* and *Alexa M.*
- *Fluid simulation: SIGGRAPH 2006 course notes* (*ACM SIGGRAPH 2006 Courses. Boston, Massachusetts*), *Bridson R., R. Fedkiw, M. Müller-Fischer*.
- *Exporting Animated Models From Blender To XNA*, *Brown J.*, which can be found at `http://blog.diabolicalgame.co.uk/2011/07/exporting-animated-models-from-blender.html`.
- *Nvidia-mesh-tools*, *Castaño I.* The NVIDIA mesh processing tools is a collection of tools and libraries, designed to be integrated in game tools and asset conditioning pipelines.
- *Screen-aligned Quads*, *Chapman J.*, which can be found at `http://www.john-chapman.net/content.php?id=6`.
- *SSAO Tutorial*, *Chapman J.*, which can be found at `http://john-chapman-graphics.blogspot.com.au/2013/01/ssao-tutorial.html`.
- *The elements of nature: interactive and realistic techniques* (*ACM SIGGRAPH 2004 Course Notes*), *Deusen O., D. S. Ebert, R. Fedkiw, F. K. Musgrave, P. Prusinkiewicz, D. Roble, J. Stam*, and *J. Tessendorf*.
- *Energy Conservation in Games*, *Driscoll R.*, which can be found at `http://www.rorydriscoll.com/2009/01/25/energy-conservation-in-games/`.

- *Vertex skinning*, Galanakis R., which can be found at `http://tech-artists.org/wiki/Vertex_Skinning`.

- *Introduction to the Direct3D 11 Graphics Pipeline* (nvision 08), Gee K.

- *Open Asset Import Library (Assimp)*, Gessler A., T. Schulze, K. Kulling, and D. Nadlinger.

- *General-Purpose Computation on Graphics Processing Units*, (GPGPU.org), which can be found at `http://gpgpu.org/`.

- *Deferred Shading*, Hargreaves S.

- *Automatic pre-tessellation culling*, Hasselgren J., J. Munkberg, and *T. Akenine-Moller*.

- *Dual-Paraboloid Reflections*, Hayward K., which can be found at `http://graphicsrunner.blogspot.com.au/2008/07/dual-paraboloid-reflections.html`.

- *View-independent environment maps*, and *Proceedings of the ACM SIGGRAPH/ EUROGRAPHICS workshop on Graphics hardware*, Heidrich W., and *H.P. Seidel*.

- *Specular BRDF Reference*, Karis B., which can be found at `http://graphicrants.blogspot.com.au/2013/08/specular-brdf-reference.html`.

- *Real-time creased approximate subdivision surfaces*, Kovacs D. J., Mitchell, S. Drone, and D. Zorin, and Proceedings of the 2009 symposium on Interactive 3D graphics and games.

- *Deferred Rendering for Current and Future Rendering Pipelines*, Lauritzen A., and *Beyond Programmable Shading* (SIGGRAPH 2010), which can be found at `http://visual-computing.intel-research.net/art/publications/deferred_rendering/`.

- *Computing Tangent Space Basis Vectors for an Arbitrary Mesh*, Lengyel E., which can be found at `http://www.terathon.com/code/tangent.html`.

- *Mathematics for 3D Game Programming and Computer Graphics*, Third Edition, Course Technology Press, Lengyel E.

- *Approximating Catmull-Clark subdivision surfaces with bicubic patches*, Loop C. and S. Schaefer.

- *Approximating subdivision surfaces with Gregory patches for hardware tessellation* (SIGGRAPH Asia 2009 papers), Loop C., S. Schaefer, T. Ni, and *I. Castaño*.

- *Introduction to 3D Game Programming with DirectX 11, Mercury Learning and Information*, Luna F.

- *A fast, small-radius GPU median filter*, McGuire M., and *ShaderX6: Advanced Rendering Techniques*, W. F. Engel, Course Technology.

- *Pipelines for Direct3D Version 11, Microsoft*, which can be found at `http://msdn.microsoft.com/en-us/library/windows/hardware/ff569022(v=vs.85).aspx`.

▶ *DirectX and XAML interop* (*Windows Store apps using C++ and DirectX*), Microsoft 2013, which can be found at `http://msdn.microsoft.com/en-us/library/windows/desktop/hh825871.aspx`.

▶ *Immediate and Deferred Rendering, Microsoft*, which can be found at `http://msdn.microsoft.com/en-us/library/windows/desktop/ff476892(v=vs.85).aspx`.

▶ *DirectXTex texture processing library*, S. *Hargreaves* and C. *Walbourn*, *Microsoft*, and *Codeplex: DirectXTex*, a shared source library for reading and writing DDS files.

▶ *Benchmarking C#/.Net Direct3D 11 APIs vs native C++, Mutel A.*, which can be found at `http://code4k.blogspot.com.au/2011/03/benchmarking-cnet-direct3d-11-apis-vs.html`.

▶ *Gpu gems 3, Nguyen H, Addison-Wesley Professional.*

▶ *Efficient substitutes for subdivision surfaces in feature-quality games* (*ACM SIGGRAPH ASIA 2010 Courses*), *Ni T.*

▶ *Efficient substitutes for subdivision surfaces* (*ACM SIGGRAPH 2009 Courses*), *Ni T., I. Castaño, R. Peters, J. Mitchell, P. Schneider*, and *V. Verma.*

▶ *Feature-adaptive GPU rendering of Catmull-Clark subdivision surfaces, Niessner M., C. Loop, M. Meyer*, and *T. Derose.*

▶ *Analysis and Implementation of Local Subdivision Algorithms in the GPU, Nunes G., R. Braga, A. Valdetaro, A. Raposo*, and *B. Feijo. Proceedings of the 2011 Brazilian Symposium on Games and Digital Entertainment, IEEE Computer Society.*

▶ *NVIDIA Graphics SDK 11 Direct3D.*

▶ *Practical implementation of dual paraboloid shadow maps, Osman B., M. Bukowski*, and *C. McEvoy*, and *Proceedings of the 2006 ACM SIGGRAPH symposium on Videogames.*

▶ *Reconstructing position from depth, Pettineo M.*, which can be found at `http://mynameismjp.wordpress.com/2009/03/10/reconstructing-position-from-depth/`.

▶ *Position from depth 3: Back in the habit, Pettineo M.*, which can be found at `http://mynameismjp.wordpress.com/2010/09/05/position-from-depth-3/`.

▶ *Average luminance calculation using a compute shader, Pettineo M.*, which can be found at `http://mynameismjp.wordpress.com/2011/08/10/average-luminance-compute-shader/`.

▶ *Compact Normal Storage for Small G-Buffers, Pranckevičius A.*, which can be found at `http://aras-p.info/texts/CompactNormalStorage.html`.

▶ *Gaussian blur with linear sampling, Rákos D.*, which can be found at `http://rastergrid.com/blog/2010/09/efficient-gaussian-blur-with-linear-sampling/`.

▸ *Real-time local displacement using dynamic GPU memory management, Schäfer H., B. Keinert,* and *M. Stamminger,* and *Proceedings of the 5th High-Performance Graphics Conference.*

▸ *Creating DirectX Interop Libraries for XAML Metro Style Apps Part 1: Direct2D, Skakun F.,* which can be found at `http://labs.vectorform.com/2012/05/creating-directx-interop-libraries-for-xaml-metro-style-apps-part-1-direct2d/`.

▸ *Ciclos Town - 10 Male Characters, Teixeira R.,* which can be found at. `Blendswap.com`.

▸ *Silk Gaming Library: Vertex skinning a mesh, Trullinger M.,* which can be found at `http://silk-ge.blogspot.com.au/2010/11/tutorial-vertex-skinning.html`.

▸ *Understanding Shader Model 5.0 with DirectX 11, Valdetaro A., G. Nunes, A. Raposo,* and *B. Feijó.*

▸ *High-quality shadows with improved paraboloid mapping, Vanek J., J. Navrátil, A. Herout,* and *P. Zemčík. Proceedings of the 7th international conference on Advances in Visual Computing (Volume Part I), Springer Verlag.*

▸ *Curved PN triangles, Vlachos A., J. Peters, C. Boyd,* and *J. L. Mitchell,* and *Proceedings of the 2001 symposium on Interactive 3D graphics.*

▸ *Spherical, Cubic, and Parabolic Environment Mappings,* The University of North Carolina, *Zimmons P.*

▸ *Dual Paraboloid Mapping In the Vertex Shader, Zink J,* which can be found at `http://members.gamedev.net/JasonZ/Paraboloid/DualParaboloidMappingInTheVertexShader.pdf`.

▸ *Practical Rendering and Computation with Direct3D 11, Zink J., M. Pettineo,* and *J. Hoxley, A. K. Peters, Ltd.*

Index

[PACKT] Thank you for buying
Direct3D Rendering Cookbook

About Packt Publishing

Packt, pronounced 'packed', published its first book "*Mastering phpMyAdmin for Effective MySQL Management*" in April 2004 and subsequently continued to specialize in publishing highly focused books on specific technologies and solutions.

Our books and publications share the experiences of your fellow IT professionals in adapting and customizing today's systems, applications, and frameworks. Our solution based books give you the knowledge and power to customize the software and technologies you're using to get the job done. Packt books are more specific and less general than the IT books you have seen in the past. Our unique business model allows us to bring you more focused information, giving you more of what you need to know, and less of what you don't.

Packt is a modern, yet unique publishing company, which focuses on producing quality, cutting-edge books for communities of developers, administrators, and newbies alike. For more information, please visit our website: www.packtpub.com.

Writing for Packt

We welcome all inquiries from people who are interested in authoring. Book proposals should be sent to author@packtpub.com. If your book idea is still at an early stage and you would like to discuss it first before writing a formal book proposal, contact us; one of our commissioning editors will get in touch with you.

We're not just looking for published authors; if you have strong technical skills but no writing experience, our experienced editors can help you develop a writing career, or simply get some additional reward for your expertise.

[PACKT]
PUBLISHING

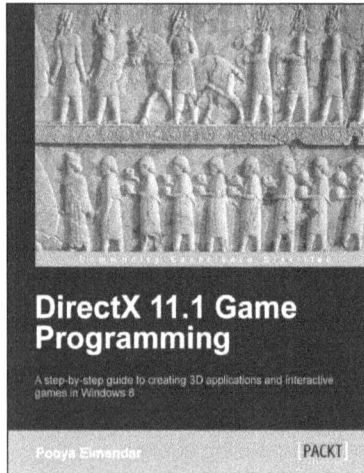

DirectX 11.1 Game Programming

ISBN: 978-1-84969-480-3   Paperback: 146 pages

A step-by-step guide to creating 3D applications and interactive games in Windows 8

1. Learn new features in Direct3D 11.1

2. Discover how to develop a multithreaded pipeline game engine

3. Understand shader model 5 and learn how to create an editor for the game

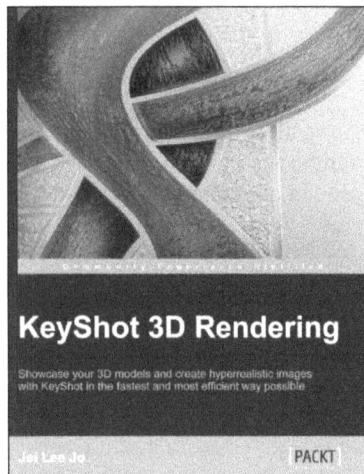

KeyShot 3D Rendering

ISBN: 978-1-84969-482-7   Paperback: 124 pages

Showcase your 3D models and create hyperrealistic images with KeyShot in the fastest and most efficient way possible

1. Create professional quality images from your 3D models in just a few steps

2. Thorough overview of how to work and navigate in KeyShot

3. A step-by-step guide that quickly gets you started with creating realistic images

Please check **www.PacktPub.com** for information on our titles

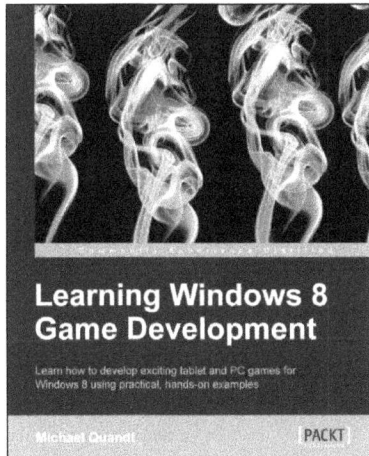

www.ingramcontent.com/pod-product-compliance
Lightning Source LLC
Chambersburg PA
CBHW080140220326
41598CB00032B/5121